Praise for *Fighting Westway*—

"*Fighting Westway* provides a deep and highly nuanced analysis of a landmark environmental battle that, though it took place two decades ago, remains highly relevant in today's fractious political economy."
—**Thomas O. McGarity, Joe R. and Teresa Lozano Long Endowed Chair in Administrative Law, University of Texas School of Law, author of** *Freedom to Harm: The Lasting Legacy of the Laissez Faire Revival*

"William W. Buzbee's absorbing history unearths the complex and fascinating events, personalities, and regulations that conspired to create one of New York's most public failures of city planning—and one of its most memorable triumphs of citizen activism. At the beginning of a new mayoral administration, this book is a timely reminder that urban advocacy is never out of fashion in the city that never sleeps."
—**Elizabeth L. Bradley, author of** *Knickerbocker*

"*Fighting Westway* is a very good book on a rich topic. William W. Buzbee has done impressive research and is well acquainted with environmental litigation in general and his main protagonists in particular."
—**Oliver A. Houck, Tulane University Law School, author of** *Taking Back Eden*

For Lisa, Tian, and Seana
and my parents,
John and Ellen Buzbee

FIGHTING WESTWAY

FIGHTING WESTWAY

*Environmental Law, Citizen Activism,
and the Regulatory War That Transformed
New York City*

WILLIAM W. BUZBEE

CORNELL UNIVERSITY PRESS   ITHACA AND LONDON

First published 2014 by Cornell University Press
First printing, Cornell Paperbacks, 2014

Printed in the United States of America

Library of Congress Cataloging-in-Publication Data

Buzbee, William W., 1960– author.
    Fighting Westway : environmental law, citizen activism, and the regulatory war
that transformed New York City / William W. Buzbee.
        pages cm
    Includes bibliographical references and index.
    ISBN 978-0-8014-5190-4 (cloth : alk. paper) —
    ISBN 978-0-8014-7944-1 (pbk. : alk. paper)
    1. Express highways—Law and legislation—New York (State)—New York—
History—20th century. 2. Westway (New York, N.Y.) 3. Express highways—
Environmental aspects—New York (State)—New York—History—20th century.
4. Green movement—New York (State)—New York—History—20th century.
5. New York (N.Y.)—Politics and government—1951– I. Title.
    KFX2071.B89   2014
    388.4'11097471—dc23   2013037423

Cornell University Press strives to use environmentally responsible suppliers
and materials to the fullest extent possible in the publishing of its books. Such
materials include vegetable-based, low-VOC inks and acid-free papers that are
recycled, totally chlorine-free, or partly composed of nonwood fibers. For further
information, visit our website at www.cornellpress.cornell.edu.

Cloth printing   10 9 8 7 6 5 4 3 2 1
Paperback printing   10 9 8 7 6 5 4 3 2 1

CONTENTS

FIGURES

ACRONYMS

APA   United States Administrative Procedure Act

CAA   Clean Air Act

CWA   Clean Water Act

EIS   Environmental Impact Statement

EPA   United States Environmental Protection Agency

FHWA   Federal Highway Administration

FWS   United States Fish and Wildlife Service

NEPA   National Environmental Policy Act

NMFS   National Marine Fisheries Service

ROD   Army Corps of Engineers Record of Decision

SEIS   Supplemental Environmental Impact Statement

WESTWAY CHRONOLOGY, 1971–1985

Years	Plan progress and state and local politics	Congressional actions influencing Westway	Clean Air Act battles	National Environmental Policy Act and linked Clean Water Act battles
1950s to 1969 1969	Elevated West Side (Miller) Highway deteriorates; pier usage for shipping dwindles.	Federal interstate highway segments funded at 90%, with costs paid to completion. National Environmental Policy Act (NEPA) enacted.		
1970		1970 Clean Air Act (CAA) amendments strengthen law.		
1971 November December	Wateredge Study issued by N.Y. State Urban Development Corp.; proposes demolition of Miller Highway, new highway eligible for federal interstate funding, development in Hudson River, new public access to river. Endorsed by Governor Rockefeller and Mayor Lindsay. New West Side Highway approved for federal interstate funding. West Side Highway Project created.			

Years	Plan progress and state and local politics	Congressional actions influencing Westway	Clean Air Act battles	National Environmental Policy Act and linked Clean Water Act battles
1972 October	Sydec and head Lowell Bridwell hired to manage West Side Highway Project.	Clean Water Act (CWA) enacted; includes protective Section 404 limitations on "dredging and filling."		
1973–74	Late 1973 collapse of part of West Side Highway. Project starts to be called Westway.	Representatives Studds, Abzug, and others succeed in enacting "interstate transfer" trade-in option; highway for mass transit trade possible.		
1974	Draft Environmental Impact Statement (EIS) issued; prepared by Sydec for federal agencies. "Modified outboard" option in Hudson River becomes New York favorite. Opposition grows; trade-in championed; air concerns raised. Adjacent community boards and gubernatorial candidate Hugh Carey oppose.	Abzug-led amendments to trade-in provision allow value increase with inflation, adjust referenced cost estimate, and allow trade for transit and replacement road mix (1974 to early 1976).	First court challenges filed by William Hoppen for Action for Rational Transit opposition coalition claiming Westway inconsistent with state CAA planning obligations.	Draft describes interpier waters as polluted and lacking in life. Federal natural resource agencies submit letters critical of Draft EIS.
1975	New Governor Carey switches to Westway support. Carey and Mayor Beame approve the modified outboard plan.			

Years	Plan progress and state and local politics	Congressional actions influencing Westway	Clean Air Act battles	National Environmental Policy Act and linked Clean Water Act battles
1976 December	President Ford endorses during campaign. Dept. of Transportation (DOT) Secretary William Coleman approves Westway.			
1977 January–February September October December	Final EIS issued. New Carter administration DOT head Brock Adams reassesses but approves Westway. Mayoral candidate Ed Koch calls Westway a "disaster" that will not be built.		Clean Air Campaign and other groups, represented by Al Butzel, contest "indirect source" air permit for Westway; U.S. Environmental Protection Agency (EPA) also opposes. Hearings officer recommends permit denial. Dept. of Environmental Conservation (DEC) commissioner Peter Berle agrees and denies permit; governor replaces Berle with new DEC head, Robert Flacke.	Final EIS responses to comments call interpier waters slated for Westway fill "devoid" of life and "biologically impoverished"; accompanying study calls waters a "biological wasteland." Data in appendices contradict these claims. More criticism of aquatic claims; project refuses to supplement EIS.
1978 April December	New Mayor Koch changes mind, supports Westway after Governor Carey pledges transit fare support. Board of Estimate votes in opposition to Westway.		Federal agencies clash over air permit; EPA still opposes, but Federal Highway Administration (FHWA) and DOT support Westway.	Further critical comments regarding aquatic impacts. Over project objections, N.Y. State agrees to EPA call for more fishery sampling.

Years	Plan progress and state and local politics	Congressional actions influencing Westway	Clean Air Act battles	National Environmental Policy Act and linked Clean Water Act battles
1979 October			N.Y. State counsel devises "briar patch" solution to air infirmities.	New sampling reveals many fish in planned Westway site.
1980 May August October November December	Carey reneges on transit commitment; Koch says reconsidering Westway support; seeks broad input. Deputy Mayor Robert Wagner recommends against Westway but also calls project acceptable.		Air permit recommended and issued. No appeal by opponents.	Sampling extended. Internal Army Corps of Engineers and FHWA and project concession about substantial fishery presence, but no Supplemental EIS prepared. Corps Division grants Section 404 permit. National Marine Fisheries Service (NMFS) objection pulls together fishery data and risks.
1981 May July September	President Reagan personally endorses Westway. Governor Carey and Mayor Koch sign new agreement on Westway finances; Koch renews Westway support. Reagan gives N.Y. $85 million check in photo-op event.			Federal natural resources agencies do not pursue all objections; EPA declines to veto project under Section 404(c). Butzel, representing Clean Air Campaign and other opponents, challenges Section 404 permit in court.

Years	Plan progress and state and local politics	Congressional actions influencing Westway	Clean Air Act battles	National Environmental Policy Act and linked Clean Water Act battles
1982 January–June April	State legislature passes bill limiting state obligation to pay for Westway costs; governor vetoes.			After two lengthy trials, two opinions by Judge Griesa reject adequacy of NEPA analysis and Section 404 permit grant.
1983 February April September October–November	Thomas Puccio report recommends against Westway.	Congressional rider proposed that claims to be for the "Protection of Striped Bass" but is actually intended to allow Westway despite risks; growing protests lead to rejection.		Second Circuit upholds Judge Griesa NEPA and CWA permit rejections. Corps decides on new two-winter striped bass study; Governor Cuomo objection leads corps leadership to shorten to four months.
1984 May June November	Corps issues new Draft Supplemental EIS (SEIS) on fishery risks. State Commission on Investigation issues report critical of Westway process. Final SEIS issued.	Congressional committee report criticizes Westway water permit process; hearings and documents reveal hidden concessions of fishery risks.		January-to-April testing again reveals substantial young striped bass use of Westway site. Draft SEIS states significant risks to young striped bass; site a "shelter" and "potentially vital." Draft criticized as understating risks. Final SEIS reverses conclusions about risks but without explanation.

Years	Plan progress and state and local politics	Congressional actions influencing Westway	Clean Air Act battles	National Environmental Policy Act and linked Clean Water Act battles
1985	State legislature again passes legislation limiting state obligation to pay for Westway cost overruns; governor vetoes.			FSEIS strongly criticized by opponents and federal natural resources agencies.
January 24		Congressional opposition to Westway grows.		Corps issues Record of Decision with intent to grant Section 404 permit. EPA declines to veto project under Section 404(c).
February 25				Corps issues Section 404 permit.
May 20				Third trial about Westway fishery impacts starts.
August 7		Efforts to rescue Westway with a trade-in extension fail.		Judge Griesa rules against Westway permit; issues permanent injunction.
September 11		House of Representatives votes 287 to 132 to cut off funding for Westway landfill.		Second Circuit issues mixed decision but upholds Judge Griesa's rejection of NEPA analysis and Section 404 permit; reverses permanent injunction.
September 11–30	Mayor Koch and governor at first press for Westway but surrender. DOT approves $1.75 billion trade-in; commits 60% to mass transit, rest to road and river-edge path.			
1986 and on	More of trade-in funding goes to mass transit than anticipated. Hudson River Park created for Lower West Side waters and piers. Conflicts over uses of piers and waters continue.	Trade-in dollars accelerated through efforts of Senator D'Amato.		

FIGHTING WESTWAY

INTRODUCTION

F
ROM 1971 TO 1985, battles raged over Westway, a 4.2-mile, multibillion-dollar highway, development, and park project proposed for placement in the Hudson River, in New York City. This project was, on a per-mile basis, the most expensive highway ever proposed. Federal interstate funding would have flowed into a financially struggling New York City. By utilizing new landfill in the Hudson, extending at times almost a thousand feet out, Westway would have destroyed dozens of piers and the waters between them. It also, however, would have created new land for development, made many adjacent properties skyrocket in value, and created space for a new river-edge park atop tunneled portions of the highway. In Mayor Ed Koch's words, the project could have been an "enormous economic lift to the city [since] 90 percent would be paid by the federal government, including all inflationary aspects, so the city was protected."[1] As one Army Corps of Engineers regulator who worked on Westway later reflected, "I think the original planners were clever enough" to ask, "'How can we get as much federal money as possible to redevelop this area?'"[2] It paid to think big.

Powerful business and civic leaders like David Rockefeller called it a transformative project supported by the "past three Presidents of the United States, the past four Governors of New York State and every mayor of New York City since John Lindsay."[3] The editorial boards of the *New York Times* and the *Daily News* and many business and labor leaders also backed Westway. So did New York's two United States senators.

Figure A.1. A 1952 aerial photograph looking north up the Hudson River, showing the piers that would have been demolished and replaced with fill for Westway. This perspective is much like the sketched "modified outboard" image showing Manhattan with Westway, in chapter 1, figure 1.4. (*Source: Museum of the City of New York photo archive.*)

Citizen opponents, their lawyers, and federal agency staff and scientists, however, fought a tenacious, multifront war against Westway. Project opponents questioned the certainty of federal dollars, arguing that funds of this magnitude would never keep flowing from Washington. Either New York City or State would end up footing much of Westway's bill, or, in the words of the leading citizen opponent, Marcy Benstock, the project would end up a partially constructed "landfill in the Hudson River oozing sewage sludge dredged from the [Hudson's] bottom," leaving "a transit system in ruins."[4] Opponents advocated that New York's leaders utilize a new Westway-linked legal option, trading Westway's billions of federal highway dollars for mass transit improvements and a modest replacement road.

Opponents and federal natural resource agency scientists and staff also highlighted environmental risks that Westway posed to air quality and water resources. Of particular importance, legally required analyses called the Hudson River waters and interpier areas slated for Westway "biologically impoverished" and a "wasteland." This official claim echoed much repeated political rhetoric. One Westway supporter characterized the Westway site as "a sewage settling tank" lacking any fish.[5] Even after fish surveys found unusually high numbers of young striped bass right where Westway was to be built, often more than in any other area in the vast Hudson River estuary, former mayor Koch offered to "build the [striped bass] a motel in Pough-keepsie where they c[ould] breed to heart's content."[6] Westway's supporters doubted that the fish were threatened and even questioned that Westway's opponents and federal natural resource agencies really cared about the fish. But striped bass at the time were struggling and plummeting in numbers along the Eastern Seaboard. Planned destruction of important aquatic habitat through Westway's massive filling triggered some of environmental law's strongest protections.

Despite its powerful supporters, by the end of September 1985, Westway stood defeated. On the same day that New York State and City officially surrendered their Westway hopes, New York State governor Mario Cuomo wrote a personal letter to opponent Benstock: "Marcy, Congratulations! I commend your commitment, your courage and your competence. I hope next time we will be on the same side."[7] Over twenty years later, former mayor Koch also credited Benstock with Westway's defeat. She was "the brains" of the opposition.[8]

Westway's defeat remains shocking to its champions, especially considering the power of its supporters. Westway's struggles and defeat are still today periodically mentioned as evidence of environmental laws run amok, or of America's loss of vision, or of the perils of citizen activism and power in legal arenas.[9] It is mentioned in connection with large urban projects, stadiums, engineering responses to climate change, the role of science in constraining legal and political choices, and highway versus mass transit battles. It is another piece of data in seemingly never-ending debates over the value of this nation's environmental laws and the administrative state. Commentators often attribute Westway's defeat to a bureaucratic snafu or a hostile single judge, building the case that its demise lacked justification or constituted a frustration of democratic priorities.

Through close examination of Westway's battles and fate, this book dispels numerous myths about Westway's history, stakes, and defeat. Westway's defeat was not some antidemocratic fluke but was consistent with the law's dictates and shaped by substantial coalitions pursuing diverse but overlapping goals in local, state, and federal venues. Citizens, a swelling number of opposition groups working at all levels of government, and opponents' lawyers—helped in crucial respects by allied federal natural resource agency staff and scientists, as well as several congressional actions—were able to fight and ultimately defeat Westway. This book provides a window into these strategic choices and their repercussions, drawing on extensive archival research into the efforts of these advocates and officials, including political advocacy, legal filings and transcripts, and interviews with many of the major Westway stakeholders.

New York City's intense politics, outsize personalities, media scrutiny, and leading urban role also give the Westway tale a substantial New York City component. Famed urbanist Jane Jacobs and "power broker" Robert Moses are part of the story, albeit more in cameo appearances than as protagonists. Westway's battles and fate were shaped by the political imperatives, priorities, and choices of New York City and State politicians, citizens, business leaders, and unions, as well as the support and opposition of dozens of not-for-profits and organizations, some created just to influence the Westway war. Westway's fate also changed New York City. Federal dollars and federal laws, however, played critically important roles in both enabling and hobbling Westway; it was by no means just a New York City project. Given the pervasive influence of federal laws and funding on urban politics, finances, and infrastructure, Westway's path illuminates broader questions about the capacity of cities to control their fates.[10]

The book also, however, uses the Westway war to illuminate how high-stakes regulatory wars are fought, especially in settings involving environmental laws and other risk regulation. Most Americans have a feel for civil-setting common-law cases and criminal courtroom battles. In contrast, few histories reveal actual strategizing and advocacy choices in public law battles with far higher stakes, whether over environmental risks, risky products, constraints on corporate wrongdoing, resource extraction and commercial use of public resources, government priorities, or urban setting megaprojects, like Westway, that raise environmental concerns. Instead, legal battles are most often presented through excerpts of judicial opinions or descriptions of who won. The worlds of legislation, Congress, and administrative agencies—the arenas of public law—are most often studied with a focus on endgame results, regulatory design, or doctrines shaping how the law should be interpreted. This book, in contrast, shows how partisans fought over Westway, thereby both explaining the project's fate and illuminating how lawyers and advocates in high-stakes regulatory battles strategically use legal artillery and political voice to achieve their goals.

Regulatory wars like that fought over Westway occur in the middle ground between politics and work under established laws. The realm of politics shapes priorities and choices, but the law also channels and constrains the political realms. Laws sometimes trump politics, and sometimes extraordinary political action can surmount usual legal constraints. Since the early 1970s, strengthened environmental and risk-regulation laws and a more transparent process have transformed contemporary high-stakes regulatory wars in the United States. Powerful political and private-sector support no longer guarantees anything. Many vulnerable environments are now protected, and citizens—including those subject to regulation, not-for-profit organizations, and those seeking protection of the laws—have been granted powerful participatory and litigation rights. You cannot understand Westway or other high-stakes regulatory wars if you ignore the law, especially differences among laws and how laws can be strategically wielded in light of underlying facts and science. As observed by scientist and former Westway regulator Dennis Suszkowski, "Westway [was a] dinosaur that almost survived in its age [but was] caught up in a new regulatory environment."[11]

But to acknowledge the power of legal changes protecting the environment and empowering citizens does not mean that Westway faced sure defeat. Partisans' choices and skills matter in regulatory wars. Westway's opponents and their lawyers engaged in a long, hard-fought war against the project, ultimately focusing on stronger legal and political contentions and strategies than did Westway's supporters. Citizen opponent Benstock and her NYC Clean Air Campaign, along with her many environmentalist and opposition allies, remained active in legal venues but never ceased opposition grassroots efforts in local, state, and federal venues. They countered political efforts to trump usual legal constraints and worked to build a substantial and effective political coalition opposing Westway. The opponents' highly effective lead counsel, especially Al Butzel and later Mitchell Bernard, also played a crucial role. On the other side, governmental legal irregularities and harmful judgment calls by Westway's supporters pervaded the battles. The federal trial judge who reviewed essential regulatory judgments about Westway, Thomas P. Griesa, was willing to listen, learn, and expect compliance with the law, regardless of the power of Westway's supporters.

Westway's fate did not, however, turn simply on gamesmanship or strategic imprudence. The opponents were especially benefited by scientific data and legal changes that gave them strong motivation, a record and basis for legal attacks, and opportunities for coalition building. Without empowered citizens and their lawyers who could and did raise environmental and fiscal concerns and participate in political, regulatory, and judicial venues, Westway would exist today. It had powerful supporters and massive resources on its side, but the opponents also benefited from a growing opposition coalition. Westway's war was characterized by competing democratic coalitions pursuing different priorities and visions. The law's priorities and protections, however, tipped the scales.

Some bemoan Westway's defeat and blame its opponents, the judge, or the law itself. Others celebrate its defeat. This book shows, however, that the Westway story is about much more than a mere war of attrition, death by delay, or minor administrative missteps. Westway pitted sophisticated adversaries with wildly disparate resources against each other in a war over a multibillion-dollar highway and development project, with substantial commercial and environmental interests at stake. Accusations and findings of dishonesty, political arm-twisting, and courtroom concessions and disasters add up to a fascinating and sometimes seamy tale. Portions of the Westway story have been told, but no one has yet told the story in a complete and accurate way. The focus here is on Westway's legal and regulatory battles, especially the endgame litigation and political work from roughly 1982 to 1985, but to tell those portions of the story requires that the stage be set.

1

THE WESTWAY PLAN

WESTWAY'S INCEPTION can be traced to two key events, one local and one federal. When, in the early 1970s, large chunks of the elevated West Side Highway (also known as the Miller Highway) started falling, including an infamous much-photographed 1973 collapse that deposited a truck on the surface road below, a transportation fix was inevitable. Planners and city officials quickly began to look at ways to link highway replacement with major development plans. The other key event happened years earlier.

The federal government in the post–New Deal era, especially during the presidency of Dwight Eisenhower, became centrally involved in funding construction of interstate highways.[1] At first these highway dollars were focused on linking cities to create a national interstate highway network, but eventually such funds could be used for interstate highways running through urban centers. The prospect of federal dollars that could underwrite substantial local patronage and fund urban improvements encouraged cities like New York to think big but at little local cost. So long as a transportation route was designated for construction and addition to the interstate system, federal-aid highway funds would be available.[2] The traditional terms of that federal funding were remarkably good, with 90 percent paid by the federal government, including cost escalations, and 10 percent by the state. As the West Side Highway aged and started to fall apart, a replacement funded by federal dollars held an obvious allure. Westway grew out of this confluence of genuine

Figure 1.1. The 1973 collapse of a segment of the West Side Highway under the weight of a truck was often mentioned by Westway advocates as evidence that a replacement highway was unavoidable. *(Source: 1974 Draft Environmental Impact Statement; United States Army Corps of Engineers; Federal Highway Administration; New York State Department of Transportation; photographer Ted Cowell.)*

transportation need and the promise of federal funding for a huge public works project in New York City. In the words of mayoral adviser and lawyer Edward Costikyan, no one "in his or her right mind" would suggest Manhattan needed a new six-lane highway. But Westway was a strategy allowing New York to take advantage of "federal largess." "The genius of Westway is that its planners were capable of seizing upon an existing Federal program, designed for other purposes, and using it to accomplish an essential municipal purpose: the reconstruction of Manhattan's Lower West Side waterway."[3]

Project planners no longer had to consider competing maritime uses of Manhattan's lower West Side piers. For well over a century, New York City was one of the world's most active ports, with schooner and later freight and passenger ships docking at dozens of piers along the West Side of Manhattan, as well as along the East River. After the elevated West Side Highway was built for use by cars, mostly during the 1930s, access to piers, nearby shops, warehouses, and entertainment was possible by passing under the elevated highway. By 1970, however, Manhattan's Lower West Side was no longer a bustling port, having lost much of that work to the large, flat spaces in nearby New Jersey, Brooklyn, and other parts of the country that were more suitable for new containerized shipping. Occasional passenger ships would still utilize a West Side pier, but the era when massive bows of ships would tower over adjacent streets had come to an end. Many of the dozens of piers jutting close to a thousand feet into the Hudson had fallen into disuse. Some were now twisted metal frames disappearing into the waters.

Planners hoped that a massive public works project like Westway would improve New York City's dire fiscal situation. In the late 1960s and early 1970s, the city was still mired in economic woes.[4] It was just starting to emerge from a sustained fiscal crisis that had left it teetering on the edge of bankruptcy, desperate for state or federal support.[5] The city's crime rate had skyrocketed. Unhappy municipal unions in sector after sector went on strike, with transit workers, teachers, and sanitation workers all taking their turn. The cascade of bad news led to a real estate downturn and the exodus of many workers and families to the surrounding suburbs. Times Square and adjacent midtown blocks were overrun with strip joints.[6] New York City residents had long depended on subways far more than cars, but subways were increasingly decrepit, dangerous, unreliable, and covered in graffiti.[7] Movies highlighted the city and especially its subways as filled with criminals on the prowl. As the economy slipped further, city services suffered, as did the city's balance sheet. After New York City sought federal help in 1975, the federal rebuff provoked one of the *New York Daily News*'s most famous deadlines: "Ford to

Figure 1.2. This photograph shows a southern perspective from Twenty-Third Street, with the elevated West Side Highway overhead to the left, the then-vacant Chelsea Piers to the right, and the World Trade Center Towers in the distance. The elevated highway was soon demolished, and the areas in the foreground would have been replaced with surface roads, five blocks of newly developable land, and a river-edge park and sunken highway to the right (west). (*Source: 1974 Draft Environmental Impact Statement; United States Army Corps of Engineers; Federal Highway Administration; New York State Department of Transportation.*)

City: Drop Dead."[8] Just two years later, during a blackout, looting devastated the city.[9] For good reason, city planners in the early 1970s desperately sought ways to bring money, jobs, vitality, and hope to the embattled city.

Building next to and even in the Hudson to create land and business opportunity was an opportunistic habit dating back to Manhattan's earliest days. Washington Irving's *History of New York* quotes an early Dutch resident as suggesting driving "piles into the bottom of the river, on which the town should be built," thus "rescu[ing] a considerable space of territory from those immense rivers."[10] More recently, when the World Trade Center was built between 1966 and 1973, the massive resulting excavation material was placed in adjacent Hudson River waters. The center's two massive towers fell during the attacks of September 11, 2001, but the adjacent river fill now sits under the Battery Park City development. Virtually none of Manhattan's shores remain the same as when the island first started being settled by Europeans.[11]

In Westway environmental impact documents, the Army Corps dated the earliest consideration of West Side Highway replacement to 1956. Serious work on it, however, really began around 1970, during the administration of Mayor John Lindsay. Ed Logue, the head of New York State's Urban Development Corporation, in late 1970 set up a special Wateredge Development Study to look at plans for the road and surrounding area.[12] Headed by Samuel Ratensky, a senior city planner in the city's Housing and Development Administration, the study group developed an array of plans. Ratensky had studied with Frank Lloyd Wright and, along with his assistants, sought to find means to meet transportation needs, foster development, and provide citizens greater access to the river.[13] Among Ratensky's aides was Craig Whitaker, then a mere twenty-nine. Whitaker had studied architecture at Yale and worked with the Peace Corps in the Philippines. He started his work on Westway with the perspective that many large-scale projects were "very destructive"; he was interested in avoiding such ravages.[14] Through circumstance and his own persistence, Whitaker ended up one of Westway's most experienced designers and advocates over the long planning process and battles. He remains fascinated by Westway and its fate. Ratensky, Whitaker, and the others worked through an array of planning options before they devised the basics of the plan that became Westway.[15]

In the early 1970s, state legislation allowed preliminary work on replacing the elevated West Side Highway but included requirements that planners consider environmental effects. Planning for a replacement accelerated after the photogenic 1973 road collapse and after surveys revealed widespread deterioration, much caused by salt use during winter months. The New York City transportation commissioner, Michael Lazar, stated that the "salami-ing of the highway has brought us to the point where we must come to grips with the fact that the West Side Highway, as it presently exists, does not exist."[16] A city policeman captured well New Yorkers' reactions to yet more news of West Side Highway decrepitude: "It's just the dirty old West Side Highway falling apart."[17]

Planners hence were thinking about much more than just replacement of a dilapidated elevated roadway. Whatever would replace the West Side Highway had the potential to transform the Lower West Side up to midtown, spur development, and provide citizen access to the Hudson. As the 1966 Tri-State Transportation Commission stated, "replacement" or "renewal" of the West Side Highway "coupled with new land uses provides an unparalleled opportunity for civic improvements."[18]

In May 1971, New York State, through the State Urban Development Corporation, issued its Wateredge Development Study. The study included recommendations that closely tracked elements and goals of the overall package that soon became known as Westway; it also involved many of the same planning personnel. The study explicitly called for fashioning a replacement road so it would be eligible for federal and state interstate highway dollars. Again and again, the study emphasized the benefit of "potential for major new development," especially if the space between the bulkhead and pierhead lines could be turned into "new land." It spoke of "the liberation of the waterfront for optimum major development." In addition to language focused on business development, the study also emphasized opportunities for "improving the environmental quality of upland areas along the Hudson River." It rejected use of filling as too expensive and instead mainly relied on a deck erected on vertical posts known as piles. Reluctance to use a filling strategy would soon disappear.

Once the city and state in November 1971 successfully added the planned Westway highway segment to the federal interstate highway system map and hence made the replacement highway eligible for 90 percent federal funding, with a 10 percent state match, an institutional vehicle to keep the project moving was essential. The West Side Highway Project, a city-state joint project, was created in December 1971 to move Westway's incipient plans to reality. Although Westway was a city-state government project ultimately funded mainly by federal highway dollars, this umbrella organization, the West Side Highway Project, was run by a private consultant, the former federal highway administrator under President Lyndon Johnson, Lowell K. Bridwell, and his company, Sydec. One of Westway's attorneys, Frederick "Fritz" Schwarz, describes Bridwell as a big man with a powerful mind and presence. Others characterized Bridwell as "brilliant, a genius."[19] He created a small working group for Westway decision making. Bridwell sought to avoid unwieldy regulatory structures and dispersed decision making, instead creating a "single-manager structure," with himself as the key manager.[20] He stayed in this role for eight years. Like hundreds of others across the private and public sectors, Bridwell devoted years of his life to Westway.

The somewhat uneasy quasi-private and quasi-public nature of the West Side Highway Project during the Bridwell-Sydec phase started Westway on a strong footing but also created vulnerabilities. In one respect, the project reflected a dramatically different mind-set from earlier large-scale New York City and regional developments, especially those involving Robert Moses. At several different points during the early 1970s, the project sponsored public hearings at which Westway proposals were discussed and responses, critical and favorable, voiced. This was not a secret project or one jammed down citizens' throats without opportunities for interested parties to speak. It was also apparent, however, that a priority for the project was to keep Westway moving. Bunny Gabel, an opponent of Westway who allowed her home to become the New York City office of the Friends of the Earth, recalls that opponents initially thought that they might win their arguments on the merits and were "pacified" by these "participatory exercises." Opponents soon discerned that little if anything they said made a difference. In her words, "[i]t took us too long to realize that public participation doesn't necessarily mean a share in the decision-making process."[21]

When concerns and opposition began to surface, the project's managers sought to elude controversy and proceed without delay. They worked hard to control information and at critical points later even bypassed federal agencies, including the critically important Army Corps, after the Army Corps and federal natural resource agencies started asking tough questions about fishery impacts. The project surely hoped to benefit from a strategic move favored by master builder Robert Moses, who again and again during his storied career would race to get construction moving as opposition mounted.[22] By moving the Westway project rapidly into the construction phase, perhaps no regulator or court would really dare to say no. Or so Westway's supporters hoped.

Officially, several alternative plans were on the table, but the basics of the preferred plan that became known as Westway were quickly apparent. Alternatives ranged from modest repair and replacement efforts to the "outboard" option that would include the landfill, buried highway, and park plan. With some minor alterations that mainly involving engineering changes that allowed the fill portion to be narrowed, a "modified outboard" plan became the leading Westway proposal.[23] Critics of Westway never thought the claimed alternatives were really on the table for consideration. The transit advocate Theodore Kheel stated that alternatives were "set up simply as straw choices and meant to be knocked down."[24] Remarkably, although much around Westway changed and the project was buffeted by challenges again and again, other than a few modest revisions, Westway's advocates stuck with this modified outboard proposal from its initial selection in 1974.[25]

ALTHOUGH THE SO-CALLED modified outboard plan that became known as Westway had been slightly scaled back from the original outboard plan, the project remained huge in every respect. It would have projected from the existing shoreline out into the Hudson as much as 970 feet, with an average of 600 feet. Piers, shoals, and flowing river would have been replaced with new fill that displaced a bit over 210 acres of Hudson River bottom. It would have created a total of 227 acres of existing or newly created land, with 169 acres created by the new landfill. That fill would have required 8.4 million cubic yards of sand fill and 1.1 million cubic yards of stone fill, while over 3 million cubic yards of structurally unsuitable material at the site would have had to be moved. EPA estimated that the fill would involve moving 9.7 million cubic yards of dredge material from the lower bay of New York Harbor for use as clean Westway fill.[26]

A new, six-lane, interstate highway link would go under about half of this new landfill, providing greater citizen access to the river above tunneled portions of the highway. West Street (also called Twelfth Avenue) would include four lanes for most of its length but six lanes at its south and north ends. At periodic intervals, interchanges projecting into adjacent neighborhoods would link Westway to the city's streets. Such interchanges would necessitate alterations to streets and relocation of businesses, including north of Battery Park City and around the Gansevoort-Meat Packing District at Fourteenth and Fifteenth Streets. By Twenty-Ninth Street, the highway would emerge to the level of a new platform on pilings, and at Thirty-Fifth Street it would start to rise to join by Forty-Second Street with the still-existing elevated highway that stretched up Manhattan's mid to upper West Side.

Earlier tentative proposals to extend the project up along the Upper West Side, potentially affecting Riverside Park, included plans to bury the adjacent highway and extend park space into the Hudson and up to the George Washington Bridge.[27] Although booklet descriptions of this extension included only park space, Upper West Side residents were concerned about destruction or impairment of Riverside Park, new development, and truck traffic using the highway.[28] After John McNally, Mary Ann Rothman, and other opponents formed groups such as the Coalition against the West Side Expressway and Save Riverside Park, their vociferous opposition spurred a state legislative change precluding such an extension along the Upper West Side.[29]

Westway-related changes in the plan that survived basically ended at Forty-Second Street. All decision documents included a new ninety-three-acre park that would sit above the tunneled highway for the middle portion of the Westway project.[30] Nothing in any of Westway planning or decision documents, however, committed the city or state to a particular park design. It was really a plan that included later, unspecified plans for that acreage. The Westway highway segment itself would have been 4.2 miles long, with 2.6 miles of park and paths for biking or walking extending the length of the project.

Through this massive landfilling in the river, combined with removal of former road surfaces and demolition of the elevated West Side Highway, Westway would create almost one hundred new acres of developable land.[31] This land would be state-owned, and at some point was likely to be given, sold, or leased for private development. Later city negotiations with the state gave the city control over this new developable land, but with state representatives maintaining a consultative role.[32] This was less land for development than the Wateredge Study had sought but still a huge swath of valuable and desirable real estate. Vagueness about what exactly would be built on this newly cleared and created land denied opponents a firm target for criticism. An early leaflet discussing the Westway plan alluded generally to residential and commercial uses and likely scale of such new buildings, but details or legally binding commitments were missing. Artist renderings showed low-scale new building and pedestrians moving freely between new local surface streets and a river-edge park. No one ever knew specifics about whether new buildings would block light or views or who would build or manage the buildings.[33] No binding commitments were made regarding the nature or scale of such development. And without such details about ownership and development plans, even supposed tax-generation benefits of new development were speculative.

THIS DESIGN was well fashioned to accommodate political realities and seize funding opportunities. Westway appeared to be a textbook example of what Harvard urban policy and government professors Altshuler and Luberoff call "Do No Harm Planning," in which "even projects of the sort that had traditionally been most disruptive, such as new expressways and airports, should be sited, designed, and mitigated so as to leave no victims in their wake." Robert Wagner Jr., deputy mayor for policy, noted that Westway's design limited "relocation and disruption during construction."[34] Westway "managed to avoid nearly all existing homes, parks, and major business structures" while also creating huge opportunities for patronage, employment, and creation of a park.[35] This presented what surely looked like a win-win situation for the city, its citizens, and its business and labor interests.[36] Short- and long-term jobs would be created, some adjacent real estate would leap in value, almost a hundred acres of new real estate space would be created for government disposition, an unsightly highway would be buried for much of its length, and citizens would have a new river-edge park to enjoy. And, at least initially, none of this would be paid for by the cash-strapped city.

Planners claimed that such a replacement project would "act as a catalyst for the orderly redevelopment of Manhattan's lower West Side."[37] Actually, since much of the developable resulting land would have been claimed either from the Hudson's waters or from land that had never been developed, the project was more about "development" than "redevelopment." In the shorter term, but likely over at least a decade of Westway building, construction of Westway alone was claimed to promise over thirty-six thousand man-hours of work during this period of devastatingly slow real estate and construction activity. Private ripple benefits, especially in the form of real estate values that would escalate with the creation of an adjacent park, could also have been huge. However, the project's disruptions, displacements, and westward expansions also would have imposed major costs on many adjacent businesses,

Figure 1.3. This schematic provides north-facing cross-sections of Westway, showing the magnitude of its filling of the Hudson River west of the World Trade Centers, at Bank Street, and at West Twentieth Street. *(Source: 1977 Final Environmental Impact Statement; United States Army Corps of Engineers; Federal Highway Administration; New York State Department of Transportation.)*

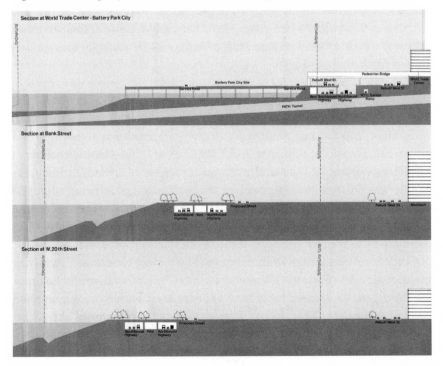

residents, property owners, and likely the city in the form of infrastructure costs and service expenses[38]

That Westway was in substantial part a prodevelopment scheme was not a hidden agenda but an overt selling point for the project. Opponents disputed the job benefits claims and worried about diverted city and state resources, but for construction companies, unions, and real estate developers, Westway undoubtedly promised huge benefits. The new acreage available for development and massive engineering and construction work foretold a boon for businesses, banks, and law firms involved with Manhattan real estate and infrastructure construction.

This initial conception was estimated to cost between and $1 and $2 billion, with 90 percent paid for by federal dollars once it was added to the interstate system.[39] Soon the project's official estimate solidified at slightly over $2 billion. Even at these quite conservative cost estimates, supporters, detractors, and reporters all agreed with one basic reality about Westway: it would be the most expensive highway ever built in the United States. Its actual costs would likely have reached in the $4–7 billion range but could have soared far higher[40] Looking back and comparing Westway and other large-scale megaprojects such as Boston's "Big Dig," which involved only two miles of tunnel and escalated in cost from an estimated $4 billion to approximately $15 billion,[41] a prominent Westway advocate (speaking not for attribution) estimated that Westway would have cost in the tens of billions of dollars, perhaps as much as $30 billion when completed. Others, like Craig Whitaker, think Westway's plan avoided engineering complexities that would have caused such skyrocketing costs.[42]

Whatever its exact final costs, once this highway segment was added to the federal interstate highway system map, as it quickly was in 1971, New York City planners achieved the key goal of federal 90 percent funding until completion. This funding tradition virtually guaranteed cost overruns. If two billion became four, would New York City lose? Absolutely not, according to project supporters. That federal munificence drove Westway. In the words of Harvard Business School professor Regina Herzlinger, writing while the Westway battles were still under way, the "only question answered" during the planning process "was simply '[w]hich alternative will bring the most money to New York City?'"[43] The "pressure of free Federal dollars is inexorable, their virtually limitless nature irresistible."[44] Later New York City mayor Ed Koch similarly explained Westway as driven by its federal and state funding. New York City would never have built Westway with its own money—it was too expensive.[45] Years later, Governor Mario Cuomo argued that Westway "allows New York to recapture almost $2 billion in federal gasoline taxes and highway user fees that New Yorkers have been paying to Washington

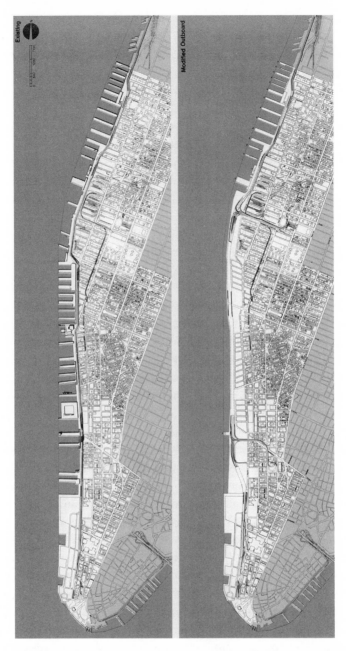

Figure 1.4. Existing: This overhead map perspective shows Manhattan's shore, piers, and roads as they existed when Westway's planners settled upon the project's modified outboard plan. Aquatic habitat between those piers that would have been replaced with fill became central to Westway's battles. *(Source: 1977 Final Environmental Impact Statement; United States Army Corps of Engineers; Federal Highway Administration; New York State Department of Transportation.)* Modified: This overhead map perspective shows the Westway modified outboard plan. With modest changes to some road interchanges, this remained the plan for Westway until the project's defeat. A river-edge park would have been above the middle tunneled portion of the project, with developable land in the open quadrants to the right, as well as newly configured surface roads. *(Source: 1977 Final Environmental Impact Statement; United States Army Corps of Engineers; Federal Highway Administration; New York State Department of Transportation.)*

year after year."[46] These claims of endless federal funding, however, were questionable.

At a certain point, as occurred with Boston's Big Dig overruns, excess can attract attention and criticism, and Congress or the Federal Highway Administration (FHWA) might intervene to address waste. These were risks, but federal payment of cost escalations exceeding initial estimates was not prohibited but the norm. With jobs and economic growth eternal city priorities, and surely political patronage and favoritism motivators as well, federal and state funding of interstate highway projects was pitched by supporters as akin to a blank check for the benefit of the city and the thousands of Westway workers. And to further sweeten the deal, the fiscally strapped city would also be paid $100 million for rights of way and removal of a problematic, high-polluting incinerator.

Even at its inception, city officials anticipated questions about city priorities. Why such a huge investment on a highway project in a city far more dependent on subways and buses? Westway opponents estimated that more than 78 percent of Manhattanites did not own cars; fewer than half of New York City's residents owned cars. Even when subways were at their nadir due to crime and reliability concerns—a period that was at its worst during the Westway battles—about 3.5 million riders used mass transit every day.[47] Despite working for a mayor, John Lindsay, who consistently championed Westway, city transportation commissioner Constantine Sidamon-Eristoff in 1971 spoke bluntly in support of Westway but also acknowledged New York's more significant transit needs: to get the "90–10 Federal funds it's got to be part of the interstate highway system." Sidamon-Eristoff added, however, that if "I had a billion dollars at my disposal, I'd spend it on mass transit, not highways, but the money for this program is earmarked for highways only, and this may be the last chance we have to get it for the city."[48]

Opponents repeatedly questioned the "blank check" nature of federal funding for Westway, and with reason. Interstate highway funding dollars were dwindling, leading opponents to doubt that Westway's high and likely rising price tag would ultimately be underwritten by the federal government and state. Internal city memoranda and later city-state negotiations revealed that New York City officials, too, worried about loss of federal support.[49] Publicly, however, federal underwriting of all costs, including overruns, remained a selling point for Westway's champions. Later, threatened escalations in cost helped tip the scale against Westway in Congress and in votes by the state legislature.

Infamous New York power broker and master builder Robert Moses was, by 1974, of lesser influence over New York's future, but he remained a powerful force. Whether because of jealousy over a huge project that he could not claim as his own or because he wanted to comment on the merits, Moses offered an unsparing critique of Westway in a 1974 pamphlet that was not solicited by anyone.[50] He argued for less complicated plans, culminating his critical assessment with language leaving no question about his views. He saw the leading plans as "too expensive and time-consuming." Anticipating eventual federal legislative responses to Westway, he asked, "Can you picture Western and California Congressmen standing mute while the United States Department of Transportation approves the spending of such monstrous sums to build a four-mile expressway section on the Hudson representing all the Federal aid in a Rocky Mountain state for decades?"[51]

The leaflet also revealed that Moses was a master of colorful hyperbole:

> To sum up: how do sane West Side argufiers hope to capture a big federal highway handout for a four mile West Side Highway certainly finally costing a billion and a half. . . . I am for public works and for government aid within reason but my imagination is staggered by the demand of a ninety or even fifty percent handout at Washington for a race-track highway on the West Side of Manhattan.
>
> How much longer can such a shindig go on? Five years? Ten years? This is not orderly consideration. It is a mob dividing up stage money, an Anvil Chorus, a byword, a hissing and a yapping, a spectacle of bamboozlement. If this is the road to progress, I am the retired Gaekwar of Baroda. No responsible West Siders in my acquaintance will much longer countenance such brouhaha.[52]

Despite the sharp criticism by Moses (and the encyclopedia searching it requires) and more muted criticism of others, plans continued apace. But his comments about illogic, excess, delay, and mounting opposition proved remarkably prescient.

This modified outboard plan that became known as Westway provided so many benefits for local interests that proponents originally did not expect stiff local opposition. As anticipated, real estate interests, banks, and most unions became strong advocates for Westway's construction. Their numbers were tiny compared with the millions of citizens who daily rely on New York City's mass transit, but their monetary interests in Westway were huge and political clout considerable. Early obstacles seemed to be swept away. Highway air pollution impacts were a concern but were initially dismissed by Westway planners. Softer impacts, such as water quality and fisheries, were barely noted by planners. Even opponents initially gave fishery issues little attention. Despite the massive filling that Westway would entail, the only persistent early critical comments and questions about aquatic impacts were in comment letters submitted to the Army Corps of Engineers by the federal natural resource and environmental agencies, specifically, the United States Fish and Wildlife Service (FWS), the National Marine Fisheries Service (NMFS), and the Environmental Protection Agency (EPA). Later, those comments became crucial, but initially they prompted little attention or concern.

As hoped, in Westway's earliest public meetings, the reception was mostly favorable. The Urban Development Corporation and city leaders worked hard to develop a wide base of support at the federal, city, and community levels. The *New York Times* reported in 1971 that the earliest Westway-related plan was presented "without fanfare, at some 40 or 50 meetings with a cross-section of concerned officials and citizens. It is said to have been well received so far." The director of program development for the Urban Development Corporation and Samuel Ratensky reported to the *Times* that "[t]hus far, particularly since the character of its over-water construction would not cause human dislocation, the project has met with general approval."[53]

2

HIGHWAYS, SUBWAYS, AND
THE SEEDS OF DISSENT

ARLY OPTIMISM about general approval of Westway quickly
proved baseless. New York City's fiscal crisis weighed in favor of
accepting any federal handouts, especially if the city could count on a
blank check for all costs to completion, but part and parcel of that crisis and a
degraded quality of city life were mass transit woes. Crime, graffiti, and poor
track and subway car conditions had turned New York City's once renowned
subway system into a source of anxiety and frustration. Billions of dollars
were needed to begin to rectify these problems. An expensive highway project like Westway stood in marked contrast to neglected mass transit. It was
certainly indisputable that New York City citizens cared about and relied on
subways far more than on highways. Suburban commuters were the dominant users of metro-area highway links. Supporting new highway construction seemed like a case of misplaced city priorities.

Initially, however, federal highway dollars were available only for interstate highway projects, so arguments about spending priorities bordered on
the irrelevant. The old West Side Highway was crumbling, and a replacement
was needed. And if federal and state dollars would foot the bill and inject some
vitality into New York City's economy, so much the better. From the city's perspective, Westway initially involved no denial of any alternative uses. No other
federal funds were readily available to revitalize New York City's struggling
real estate industry and help with the city's fiscal woes. State and city leaders
therefore did not see alternative investments in mass transit as an option.

The divorce between Westway highway spending and mass transit needs was short-lived. Federal legislative amendments championed between 1972 and 1976 by Massachusetts representatives and Bella Abzug, a U.S. congresswoman from New York City, quickly changed Westway's political and fiscal calculus. Through these amendments, Westway dollars suddenly had two competing uses: highways or mass transit, or even a mix of both. These federal legislative changes, made in part as a result of Westway opposition, virtually ensured that Westway would face persistent opposition.

HOW URBAN LEGISLATORS defeated the powerful highway lobby and recast this long-standing interstate highway funding formula is one of the remarkable parts of the Westway battles. This statutory change depended on cross-city alliances, especially effective cooperative and tag-team efforts of New York and Massachusetts legislators, and even support from Republican presidents. New York City was not alone in planning for a major highway project when many citizens and local politicians preferred redirecting highway funds to other uses. Massachusetts, in particular, found itself with money for a politically unpalatable highway. With the growing environmental movement, increased urbanization, and many of America's cities struggling fiscally and with urban decay and crime, a growing coalition of politicians saw "busting" the federal highway trust fund as necessary.[1] Interstate highway funding under the Highway Trust Fund had been almost beyond attack since its creation in 1956, but that support was waning.[2] Forces favoring highways remained politically dominant, but over time a mass transit coalition was emerging to challenge the exclusive highway focus. Congresswoman Abzug, supported by then congressman Ed Koch, joined these efforts to change federal transportation law both so it was less skewed in favor of highways and so it would provide a means for redirecting dedicated highway dollars.

Transit advocates had experienced some minor successes prior to the efforts to enact the "interstate transfer," or "trade-in," provision that proved critical to Westway battles. The Federal-Aid Highway Act of 1970 opened up the Highway Trust Fund to pay for construction of preferential bus lanes and corridor parking areas supporting mass transportation. These provisions, however, were relatively minor in scope and did not allow any funds if the expense was greater than the construction costs for a conventional highway.[3] The legislative debate over whether to "bust" the Highway Trust Fund was delayed until 1972. In the meantime, mass transit supporters sharpened their attacks, criticizing federal spending as grossly imbalanced. For every federal dollar spent on mass transit, thirty were spent on highways.[4] President Richard Nixon spoke in favor of greater support for mass transit.[5] Given growing public

Figure 2.1. This sketched image, looking north, shows the westward extension of Westway out into the Hudson River. The white space to the left (west) of the World Trade Center Towers became the site of Battery Park City. The empty white spaces farther up the Hudson were new land slated for real estate development. A linear park would have run along the edge of the Hudson above the tunneled portion of the highway. *(Source: 1977 Final Environmental Impact Statement; United States Army Corps of Engineers; Federal Highway Administration; New York State Department of Transportation.)*

environmental concerns, especially over traffic congestion, urban pollution levels, suburban sprawl, and a looming energy crisis with escalating gasoline prices and shortages, mass transit proponents went on the offensive.

New York City's Bella Abzug proved crucial to the battles for mass transit, as well in articulating arguments against Westway. Famous for her large, floppy hats, her political toughness and smarts, and also her position as a prominent liberal member of Congress during the early women's rights moment, Abzug was a strong voice for America's cities.[6] She also had a pragmatic streak that proved critical to the legislative changes that transformed the Westway battles. She declared in 1972 that "[m]ass transit has been a poor step-child when it comes to federal help. . . . We must stop looking upon the highway trust fund as a sacred cow and start being realistic as to our transportation needs."[7] Other legislators, such as Representative Charles Vanik of Cleveland, joined her and argued that the "highway trust fund has become an 'untouchable' that we worship without reason. Those who benefit from highway contracts with the Federal Government have successfully protected it from any mass transit 'funding intrusion.' Our cities are quickly becoming 'seas of concrete.' "[8] Representative (and later mayor) Ed Koch argued at the time that new highways "simply attract more cars." Mass transit support was the answer for America's "central cities."[9]

Despite some bipartisan congressional support for greater mass transit funding, the 1972 session ended without major change. Nevertheless, most insiders knew that some compromise was inevitable. Federal highway funds were running short. Tom Lewis's popular history of the interstate highway system explains that "[b]oth sides knew that the days of a dedicated trust fund were numbered. . . . Faced with the prospect of no funds at all, the highway interests would have to compromise."[10]

Nineteen seventy-three and 1974 proved to be the critical years when the federal highway interests lost ground to urban and mass transit advocates. The comprehensive Federal-Aid Highway Act of 1973 (1973 Act) was the product of a protracted political battle.[11] Support for mass transit was strong and increasing, but the highway lobby had so far stood its ground. The breakthrough compromise was to propose drawing mass transit funding from the general Treasury rather than from the Highway Trust Fund itself.[12] Such a solution was necessary because rural members of Congress feared that the fund would otherwise be depleted by costly mass transit projects.

Most critical to changing Westway's battle lines, the 1973 legislation under debate and as ultimately passed included an interstate transfer provision. The first interstate transfer proposal was made in committee by Gerry E. Studds (D-MA), following testimony by Massachusetts governor Francis Sargent.[13] Cities choosing not to build an approved segment of the interstate highway system would be able to exercise a new trade-in right, applying the money authorized for such construction to mass transit programs. Governor Sargent and his legislative allies were reluctant to surrender approximately $700 million in federal interstate highway dollars initially committed for the Boston-area Southwest Expressway. Threatened disruptions had provoked vocal protest from area residents. Massachusetts no longer wanted to pursue that project.[14] And, like New York, the Boston metropolitan area had a mass transit system desperately in need of funding. To retain those hundreds of millions of federal dollars, Sargent and Studds supported a new federally sanctioned means to trade those dollars in for mass transit expenditures. For older cities dependent on mass transit, and even younger growing cities developing mass transit systems, such an option could provide valuable flexibility.

The Studds amendment permitted trust funds earmarked for a segment of the interstate system to be used for certain mass transit needs upon a determination that the segment would not be built. This amendment initially failed. But a proposed committee bill would have allowed states to request general Treasury funds for mass transit in amounts equal to the unused portions of trust fund monies from withdrawn interstate construction segments.[15]

In a crucial difference, however, trade-in dollars would not be subject to unlimited escalation at federal and state expense; they would be limited to the cost of the withdrawn route as reflected in the 1972 Interstate Cost Estimate for an approved interstate highway project. Trade-in dollars were thus capped at the estimated cost of a replaced interstate highway segment. Despite these limitations, under this bill, states and localities would have substantially more autonomy to set their own transportation priorities than existed under prior rigid federal rules. Highways and mass transit under such a bill, if it were enacted into law, could eventually compete for the same dollars. But by freezing the trade-in value during a period of inflation, as well as eliminating the open federal financial spigot that continued to fund highway construction cost escalations, the trade-in provision provided limited appeal for cash-strapped cities. House and Senate committees battled over a variety of trade-in permutations.

Mass transit advocates brought their fight to the House floor. Their coalition now included the Nixon administration, governors, big-city mayors, urban members of Congress, several labor unions, and an environmental group known as the Highway Action Coalition that had been on the front lines of the trust fund battle.[16] Despite an aggressive mobilization in favor of the trade-in option, it lost on a 190–215 vote and was not added to the bill.[17] The vote was split along urban-rural lines. Transit advocates blamed a wave of election-year campaign contributions by highway interests for the defeat.[18]

The House-Senate conference had to reconcile bills that differed in funding mass transit either from the Highway Trust Fund or from general Treasury funds. After a lengthy legislative deadlock, a compromise was reached that maintained the trust fund's highways-only approach in fiscal 1974 and then phased in mass transit uses during fiscal 1975–76.

Most significant for the Westway battles, conferees revived the House interstate transfer provision, provided that replacement funds came from general revenues rather than from the trust fund, as Studds and Abzug had wanted.[19] The final bill passed the Senate 91–5 and passed the House 382–34.[20] President Nixon signed the bill into law, hailing how the law would provide state and local governments "flexibility . . . to set their own transportation priorities . . . rather than locking them into further highway expenditures which can sometimes make such problems even worse."[21] While the protransit coalition fell short of winning its ideal legislation, since general revenue-based trades would require legislative appropriations, the result was still a tremendous victory for mass transit relative to the inflexible policies of the trust fund from 1956 to 1973.[22]

In light of this legislation, Westway's interstate highway dollars could now be traded for mass transit. But only New York's leaders could seek this redirecting of Westway's billions. And the capped trade-in amount, at least initially, made its value uncertain during a time of high inflation. Nevertheless, these federal legislative amendments would quickly change Westway politics.

THE LOCAL NEW YORK CITY politics and motivations regarding these and subsequent linked federal legislative changes were complicated. During these legislative maneuverings, Abzug worked closely with her staff and New York City government liaison, Peter J. Kiernan. Kiernan was for many years a leading New York State and City appointed politician. He served as chief counsel to state Democrats and as a special counsel to Governor Cuomo in connection with 1980s Westway park-planning efforts, and he worked actively on the New York City convention center project. In 1973 and 1974, early in Kiernan's political career, New York City's deputy mayor, Jim Cavanagh, asked Kiernan to work in Washington with Representative Abzug, focusing on New York City mass transit and public works issues.

Abzug's reputation as a tireless worker and brilliant tactician led Kiernan to fear a period of "indentured servitude."[23] But off to Washington he went, often commuting with Abzug from New York City to Washington and even picking her up at 6:30 in the morning. Despite Abzug's long working hours and demanding expectations for others, Kiernan and Abzug quickly developed a good working relationship. He viewed her as a "brilliant lawyer and brilliant parliamentarian." Kiernan recalls that many others in Congress treated her as a pariah, but she had developed some close working relationships, including that with Gerry Studds, who shared her passion for mass transit.

Kiernan first assisted with efforts to have the Westway segment designated part of the federal interstate highway system. He personally thought the Westway project was a "brilliant, brilliant" idea. To take 90 percent in federal dollars, "without limitation," and use those dollars to correct a mistake in transportation planning, foster development, build a park, and provide citizen access to the river, could create great value for the city. Kiernan anticipated that financially struggling New York City would see tremendous and direct fiscal benefits. During its decade or so of construction, thousands of workers and businesses would have been enriched. He and his New York City leadership clients preferred Westway to the trade-in idea, but if Westway's fate became uncertain, at least some flexibility in the use of Westway dollars could benefit the city.

Looking back during a recent interview, Kiernan recalled Abzug as "virulently anti-Westway." Her West Side Manhattan constituency opposed Westway.

She, like other Manhattan members of the House of Representatives at that time, including later governor Hugh Carey and later mayor Ed Koch, mirrored her constituents' concerns about its threatened disruptions and highway focus. Most state legislators also opposed the project.

Once the trade-in option became law, however, an enduring Westway battle line was drawn. The initial addition of the option did not go unnoticed. New York City mass transit advocate Theodore Kheel, in August of 1973, saw the linkage and advocated trading Westway funds for rail transit.[24] Kheel's comments about Westway and the trade-in were sufficiently important to prompt a *New York Times* article. Other opponents took note and started to change their Westway arguments to use this new legal and fiscal reality for a city that had always been overwhelmingly dependent on its mass transit system. Westway became a prime example of the choice between highways and mass transit. Lowell Bridwell called the Westway controversy a "war against highways and automobiles."[25] This newly legitimated choice between highways and mass transit did implicate several major political divides. Would the choice between Westway and subways be a good government act or be driven by patronage and moneyed interests? Opponents argued that New York should prioritize investment in mass transit systems crucial to the city's economy and focus on less wealthy workers without access to cars and limousines. Westway supporters, however, were concerned with retaining what one real estate developer called "'the professional decisionmakers" who "don't take mass transit'" but controlled business location decisions critical to New York's economic vitality.[26] If they faced highway misery, they might abandon Manhattan. And downtown's struggling real estate, especially the Wall Street area, also linked its revival to reduced traffic.[27] The Westway opposition's most visible leader, Marcy Benstock with the Clean Air Campaign, sharpened her criticisms and goals. She was dismissive of the Westway plan and its park, championing instead that New York use the trade-in option for Westway. She described Westway in one of her many incisive sound bites: "It's a Trojan horse. Sure, it's got every amenity under the sun. But you don't make a massive highway acceptable by plopping a flower pot on top."[28]

At a later hearing on Westway design choices, Abzug distilled her key talking points in opposition to Westway. She passionately criticized it as a "fraud–a fraud on the people of this City, a fraud on the unemployed construction workers who have been promised jobs, and a fraud on those businessmen who see it as a necessary step in the economic renascence of New York."[29] She particularly challenged claims that it would be a jobs generator. Instead, she said it would disrupt area businesses and would generate few jobs for lots of money. Much of the Wetway money would go to out-of-state businesses. Other more modest plans for the West Side Highway area, she claimed, would over the long term generate more jobs and revenues. Abzug saw in the interstate transfer trade-in option a means to respond to Massachusetts's needs and perhaps also turn Westway's highway dollars into a savior of New York City's struggling and degraded subways. Kiernan sensed that Abzug sought "a silver bullet to kill Westway."

Westway opponents and mass transit advocates saw several remaining problems with federal law. The first was the fixed amount that would be received with a trade-in. A trade-in would never provide the blank-check "cost to completion" treatment historically afforded highways. But it suffered from a second monetary infirmity. During a period of high inflation and other increasing project costs, a trade-in without cost adjustment would quickly end up paying just a fraction of a traded-in highway's true costs. And with streams of money motivating the political calculus of any city or state considering a trade-in, monetarily disfavoring the trade-in option due to a rigid monetary cap could threaten its prospects. Furthermore, the requirement that a trade-in be used just for mass transit created another disincentive to pursue the trade-in option. It also limited the possibility for building coalitions with less urban jurisdictions in support of a cost-adjusted trade-in. Even if a grand highway like Westway were not to be built, some new road would be needed. In addition, as the bill was initially drafted, mass transit projects built with trade-in dollars received 80 percent federal funding rather than the 90 percent provided for highways, although changes a few years later brought that percentage up to 85 percent.[30] Finally, overall federal funding remained skewed to highways, with too little funding for mass transit. For Abzug and her mass transit allies, fixing all these problems was crucial to their larger agenda.

In 1974, Congress passed and President Gerald Ford signed the National Mass Transportation Assistance Act of 1974, which, for the first time, provided operating subsidies for urban mass transit systems.[31] (Ford had just assumed the presidency following President Nixon's resignation.) Although the bill did not deal with the interstate transfer provision, it was a major victory in its own right for large cities, and New York in particular.[32] Abzug was at the forefront of the coalition pushing for mass transit subsidies.[33] Securing the funds required a difficult fight given fears that new spending would be inflationary and the looming threats of a veto.[34]

In the Federal-Aid Highway Amendments of 1974, Abzug had a critical success in changing the 1973 interstate transfer provision. Her amendment changed the calculation to measure the value of the trade-in "as of the date of withdrawal" rather than as of 1972.[35] In 1975, Congress faced increasing pressure to further open the Highway Trust Fund to nonhighway interests.[36] Even President Ford, who hailed from the car manufacturing state of Michigan and had, not surprisingly, long been a highway advocate, changed his views. Ford introduced a bill that would have "virtually dismantled" the fund by limiting its use to financing completion and maintenance of the interstate highway systems.[37] That did not succeed.

Additional 1975 amendments to the interstate transfer provision, however, were substantial and met with success. The House and Senate bills included provisions, sponsored by Abzug and Senator Ted Kennedy, respectively, increasing the flexibility of the interstate transfer provision, thereby increasing the breadth of political support.[38] First, the amendment relaxed the interstate transfer provision by allowing localities to use interstate transfer funds for mass transit and arterial-highway purposes.[39] The 1975 proposal would enable New York to reject Westway but also use some of the federal funding to refurbish the existing West Side Highway or surface roadway, rather than being limited to mass transit alternatives. Second, the amendment declared that construction costs would now be measured at the time of approval of the substitute project or the date of enactment of the bill, whichever was *later*, rather than at the "date of withdrawal" as in the 1974 amendments.

Other states' legislators began to link Westway and these funding changes, attacking Westway for excess, much as Robert Moses had predicted. The trade-in provision and the latest cost-adjustment benchmark provision were attacked as a pork-barrel scheme designed to boost Westway trade-in funds. Ohio Republican William H. Harsha argued that Abzug's cost estimate provision "would allow a state to fatten up the turkey for the kill . . . redesigning an interstate highway project for the sole purpose of increasing the cost, then withdrawing the segment and walking away with an artificially escalated federal share."[40] New Hampshire Republican James Cleveland similarly criticized Abzug's provision as the "Abzug Shuffle" because it rewarded New York for the cost overruns of a project that would be abandoned should the trade-in option be exercised.[41]

Despite Abzug's opposition to Westway, her efforts were not applauded by the project's opponents. Benstock and others did not share Abzug's enthusiasm for this newfound trade-in flexibility. Gabel recalls opponents targeting her with criticism, including two protests involving chants and signs outside her office, press criticism, and strongly critical letters to her office. They wanted *all* Westway money to go to mass transit improvements. The risk that Westway trade-in dollars would be siphoned off for road changes was too high. Abzug responded to criticism with memos, letters, and comments of her own. Westway's critics seemed unaware that her focus was on compromise to garner a necessary winning legislation coalition. Without victory on the cost-adjustment amendments, a Westway trade-in could be worth hundreds of millions of dollars less.

Despite controversy and criticism from both highway and mass transit advocates, as well as the unexpectedly harsh criticism from Abzug's local Westway opposition allies, the Senate and House passed these amended bills by overwhelming votes in December of 1975. Once the legislation was signed by President Ford on May 5, projects like Westway were threatened by a far more favorable trade-in option. A city benefiting from a trade-in would both receive much more money and retain flexibility in use of those funds. The final bill became known as the Federal-Aid Highway Act of 1976.[42]

Abzug understood the significance of these latest amendments to Westway and New York City's subways. Federal Westway dollars now had two potential end uses: Westway in all its "modified outboard" glory or cost-adjusted funds that could be used for modest road repairs and investment in mass transit improvements. Federal largesse was not met with mere open arms but with coalitions competing for its best use. She urged Governor Carey and Mayor Abe Beame to take advantage of these new provisions and trade the Westway interstate segment for mass transit funds.[43] These midstream changes in federal highway funding options proved to be among the most critical legal developments for Westway.

Kiernan recalls John Zucotti, then chairman of the New York City Planning Commission, saying to Kiernan about the trade-in amendments, "You just killed Westway."[44] While other concerns over air and water impacts engaged regulators and the courts for the coming decade, a consistent motivation for most Westway opponents was to secure Westway funds for mass transit improvements. Federal law legitimated a new choice of transit over highways. The trade-in option, plus the modern generation of environmental laws with their enhanced citizen participation and litigation rights, critically changed the Westway war.

3

THE ART OF REGULATORY WAR

THE WESTWAY BATTLES added up to a hard-fought fourteen-year-long regulatory war. In the mid-1970s it was just getting under way. Regulatory wars like Westway differ from wars involving soldiers, weapons, and physical destruction, but they nonetheless involve a recognizable form of war, with distinctive adversaries, legal resources akin to artillery, strategies, and sources of power. Regulatory wars occur in the middle ground between the realm of politics and judicial legal venues. In the political realm, power reigns supreme, and democratically accountable institutions generate laws. In judicial legal venues, statutes, regulations, and perhaps case law precedents constrain legal actors and limit the range of outcomes. In regulatory wars, the government is always a player, with citizens, not-for-profits, and business interests competing to influence a political choice that is itself shaped and constrained by the law. As with all wars, the particular path and outcome of a regulatory war is hard to predict.

In any war, resources and skills are critical. Those resources include obvious attributes, especially money, expertise, knowledge, power, and strength. Surprise and sound strategies can also secure victory. In Sun Tzu's classic ancient text *The Art of War,* he emphasizes the importance of strategic assessment and foresight, especially attention to the opponents' attributes and options: "An excellent general should understand how to analyze and assess the terrain . . . the manpower and material resources of both his side and the enemy."[1] The art in fighting a regulatory war, however, is not just in careful assessment and resources but in adept manipulation of varied options. As Sun Tzu notes, music, colors, and tastes are limited in number, but "their variations and blending" produce beauty. Similarly, military formations are limited in number, but "their variations and combinations will give rise to an infinite series of maneuvers." Success requires adjustment to dynamic change: "[T]he way to win victory in a battle is decided by altering the tactics according to [the] enemy's changing situation. Accordingly, the way to fight never remains constant, [much as] water never flows in the same way."[2]

Similarly, in any legal battle, learning and adjustment are essential for success. In the Westway battles, legal and regulatory changes, as well as crucial brilliant and imprudent legal and political choices, sent the project on an uncertain and difficult course. Where a regulatory war involves many actors with different motivations, resources, weaknesses, and strengths–and most high-stakes wars do involve diverse, clashing actors—the exact course of a conflict is nearly impossible to predict. Nevertheless, the basic elements and terrains of regulatory war, and how it differs from the purely legal or political, can be identified and illuminated.

Perhaps the quintessential image of the law and legal battle is linked to the work of opposing lawyers in court, arguing before a judge. Legal thrillers focus on this role. Law schools focus intensely on how judges reason, with court decisions typically the focal point of analysis. The image of two legal sides arguing before a judge is central. Typically the law presents the key rules and constrains the modes of legal combat. Lawyers seek to make their client's facts look better than the other side's in light of the law, and judges interpret and apply the law. Surprises and unsettled legal questions often arise and require intellectual dexterity and judgment, but the institutional setting is predictable. Judges also shape the law's content in interpreting the law, whether the law under interpretation is the product of many other judges' earlier common-law reasoning developed case to case or the product of politics. Through briefs and court arguments, lawyers seek to shape judges' views of the law so they can emerge victorious. Lawyers and judges create new twists in the law's development. In the courtroom setting, issues and judicial relief are limited and focused.

Seemingly far from this quintessential legal focus on judicial settings stands the realm of politics. Politics is also a battleground. It is dominated by elected officials, political operators, and lobbyists, as well as the electorate and citizens who both vote and give voice to their preferences. The political realm involves debate over political priorities and policymaking through legislation and executive action. When action is carried out by the executive branch, that typically refers not to the president but to administrative agencies (sometimes in the form of departments) that implement and enforce goals and programs created by statutes. But the president does head the executive branch and occasionally gets involved in high-stakes decisions ostensibly delegated to agencies. Federal agency officials are not directly accountable to the electorate, but agency leaders are presidentially appointed, often subject to legislative confirmation. Elections, campaigns, and popularity are central motivators for political actors subject to electoral accountability.

In a democracy, the realm of politics offers great power to change society's very ground rules. Civil and criminal laws guide and constrain agency officials, judges, and lawyers, but new and changed laws periodically emerge from the political crucible. In the political realm, virtually any issue and goal can be in play. Rather than a focused and limited venue for disagreement as exists in the courts, the political realm is institutionally complex, the numbers of actors potentially vast, and trade-offs of unrelated goals common.

These distinct images of law and politics may make for good pedagogy and entertainment but miss the vast area where law and politics overlap. It is in the realm of overlap that regulatory wars are fought. These wars require unusually sophisticated strategic mastery. With large numbers of actors and institutions, adjustment to dynamic change is essential.

This leads us to two questions. What exactly is regulatory war? And what makes Westway a good example of such regulatory wars?

IN A REGULATORY WAR, a major proposal or issue involving a government entity will be under review or in a state of flux. Numerous legal and political institutions will play roles. Both the political and legal realms are engaged. Neither the political nor the legal world controls outcomes, yet both influence what will happen. In a regulatory war, the narrow and focused realm of judicial combat may be part of the picture, but the institutional matrix is more complex. Regulatory wars also, however, tend to arise in an environment where existing laws and regulations constrain both the legal and the political.

In contrast to military wars, where strength plays the critical role, regulatory wars are framed by law. The law itself is a critical resource, taking sides in most legal battles by preferring certain policy outcomes.[3] Laws, however, vary in their goals, strengths, and power. In the realm of environmental law—especially since new legislation strengthened those laws by the early 1970s—water and air quality, fish, endangered species, and safe drinking water, among many other goals, were now national priorities protected by law. They remain so today. Powerful interests, whether governmental or private, may see those laws as a hindrance but be bound by them nonetheless. The same is true in other areas of regulation; if workplaces, products, or pharmaceuticals need to provide a specified degree of safety, that mandate becomes nonnegotiable.

In essence, the law takes most regulatory wars outside the realm of mere political or private power; political leaders or powerful private actors cannot just get their way. As Peter Kiernan observed about Westway's travails, not all politicians understood the import of these legal changes: "authoritarian modes of governance had collapsed."[4] The law grants entitlements, protecting people or resources that may otherwise lack clout. The law also sets up procedural hurdles and requirements that both open up the process and constrain how partisans can seek to accomplish their goals. Regulatory wars framed by law thus virtually always involve far more numerous stakeholders than one typically finds in judicial venues. Yet compared with the political realm, the law usually narrows the number of stakeholders with substantial influence.

In a democracy, at least in the United States, the realm of politics creates most of the laws that form the basic ground rules for regulatory wars. Congress, aided by the president (unless a law is enacted by overcoming a presidential veto), passes federal statutes that are the laws framing regulatory wars. State and local laws are the products of those governments' own similar legislative process. Statutes articulate broad goals, criteria, and means to accomplish those goals. They typically empower and constrain administrative agencies that take the next crucial step, putting flesh on the bare-bones law in most statutes. Agencies also are the initial interpreters and enforcers of most statutory law.

In the Westway case, several sorts of statutory laws were at play. Highway and transportation statutes created the financing vehicle for the originally proposed Westway; without federal highway dollars, Westway would never have even been under consideration. The new statutory trade-in option created a major impetus for the Westway opposition. Federal law thus enabled New York City to afford Westway but also now motivated its opponents.

Federal and state environmental laws were also critical to the course of Westway's battles. The first wave of major federal legislation protecting the environment had just been passed in the early 1970s. The key laws implicated by Westway were the National Environmental Policy Act (NEPA)[5] (the federal environmental impact statement law), the Clean Air Act (CAA),[6] and the Clean Water Act (CWA).[7] NEPA requires disclosure and analysis of a proposal's effects, carried out through a multistage participatory process that can result in a large analytical document called an Environmental Impact Statement, or EIS. New information, proposal changes, or analytical inadequacies can also trigger a similar "supplemental" EIS process. The EIS includes both a "draft" stage and a "final" stage. As a result of Supreme Court decisions that quickly weakened NEPA, NEPA does not guarantee environmentally benign results but does require full and forthright analysis of environmental risks and choices. It also often results in discovery of impacts that trigger other laws' protections. Most major road projects, for example, will trigger both NEPA analysis and the Air Act's protections. The CAA contains strategies to reduce air pollution, usually through requirements that do not bar anything but that instead require planning to achieve reduced levels of pollution. Thus, even a proposal that might otherwise cause prohibited air degradation can usually be permitted if offset by other pollution reductions. Similarly, NEPA EIS analysis of a water-based project like Westway elicits information and analysis that will also influence actions under the Water Act.

Most of the Clean Water Act also acts as a "right to pollute" law that limits pollution but does not preclude it. However, one provision of the Water Act, the dredge-and-fill limitations set by Section 404, does more than just limit levels of pollution. Section 404 erects several independent and potentially unyielding obstacles to discharge of fill in America's waters. Most important for Westway were three separate permit hurdles. If a proposed project involving discharge of dredged or fill material into federally protected waters does not need to be in those waters (that is, is not water dependent), or that fill would cause significant degradation of aquatic resource, especially harm to important fishery breeding grounds and habitat, or an action's impacts are uncertain, Section 404 and its implementing regulations (confusingly called "guidelines" under this law) basically prohibit a Section 404 permit. Thus, the key federal environmental laws implicated by Westway required analysis and minimization of harms and in one instance posed a potential roadblock to a project like Westway.

This combination of NEPA's analytical and disclosure provisions and other laws' substantive protections remains part of contemporary regulatory battles over the environment, risk, development, and economic growth. Current and future battles over oil drilling, pipelines, timbering, new manufacturing facilities, climate change regulation, and real estate development inevitably will trigger this legal combination. Any building at the land-water edge raises Section 404 issues, a situation that led to three major Supreme Court cases between 1985 and 2006 involving that section and the reach of federal power.[8] The Westway war involved a few common but powerful pieces of legal artillery.

Administrative agencies implementing and enforcing laws typically do so with an additional layer of law in the form of regulations that take broad statutory language and create more detailed and operational rules. Regulations are subordinate in authority to statutes passed by Congress, but once they are enacted (or "promulgated," in legal parlance) and overcome any initial challenges to their legality, they are law that is binding on private actors, regulators themselves, and judges.[9] Only if later changed through a similar regulatory process do regulations cease to be authoritative. Many of Section

404's long-standing protections are drawn both from statutory language and from long-standing implementing regulations that add detail and criteria for assessing when fill should be prohibited.

Similarly, a body of law built up from decades and sometimes centuries of judicial decisions creates precedents that frame how regulatory wars are fought. This body of law is often characterized as "administrative law" in that it involves bodies of doctrine that are presumptively applicable to the many hundreds of agencies and thousands of different regulatory tasks. Much of administrative law doctrine interprets or puts flesh on the somewhat bare-bones language of a law passed at the tail end of the New Deal, the Administrative Procedure Act, known by most lawyers as the APA.[10] The APA serves to create presumptive modes of regulatory action and rights to judicial review but can still be supplanted by later or more subject-specific laws. Administrative law doctrine typically adds an additional layer of law that influences how battles are fought under more substantive and issue-specific statutes like the Clean Air and Water Acts.

Because administrative law doctrine is derived from a hybrid of long-standing lines of case law and the sixty-five-year old APA, administrative law tends to develop in incremental form. Radical changes are unlikely. As arose repeatedly in the Westway war and is discussed more below, a key tenet in administrative law is the idea that judges should show deference to politically accountable agency choices.[11] A court's deferential posture does not mean an agency will win but instead signifies that agencies are given a space in which they can exercise their expert and often science-laden judgment, influenced by more politically accountable discretion.[12] But agencies are also constrained. Laws are not subject to piecemeal dismantling or case-by-case renegotiation. Agencies must make choices in light of underlying facts, data, and legal criteria. This call for deference is thus often met with calls by regulatory stakeholders for courts to police and make real the political commitments set forth in statutes and regulations. These paired and countervailing calls—for deference and for enforcement of the rule of law—are ubiquitous features of regulatory wars.

In rare circumstances, a narrow issue or project moving through the complex stages of a regulatory war in battles constrained by the law will receive direct political attention. Congress, again aided by a president who signs legislation to make it law, can trump all ordinarily applicable laws and regulations and resolve a specific controversy. Legislators, typically at the behest of powerful constituents, will occasionally insert narrowly focused, dispute-specific legislation within massive appropriations bills. Such appropriations riders, if signed into law, are a conclusive political trump.[13] Legislation in the form of appropriations riders has at times resolved high-stakes environmental controversies to allow otherwise prohibited environmental destruction. Most famously, or perhaps infamously, a rider ended the snail darter battles litigated in *Tennessee Valley Authority (TVA) v. Hill*.[14] When the Supreme Court protected the snail darter under the Endangered Species Act's provisions, it stopped a dam and lake project under construction. Although a statutorily created committee of top federal officials found that the challenged Tellico dam flunked cost-benefit analysis, Congress passed an appropriations rider that authorized building of the dam despite the law's usual prohibitions.[15] During the 1990s, timbering projects blocked by courts enforcing environmental laws were similarly rescued by appropriations riders.[16] As described below, at a few critical points Westway's stakeholders similarly sought to secure defeat or victory through a legislative fix. However, Congress seldom focuses with such narrowness and clarity. Instead, it generally leaves major pieces of legislation intact and only periodically amends major laws when many interests are clamoring for change. As a result, regulatory wars will ordinarily be multifront and multiyear battles that are shaped by law.

A regulatory war thus has several key characteristics that render it different from the purely political and solely legal. If law and politics are at opposite ends of a continuum, regulatory wars occur in the middle of the range. A regulatory war involves an issue or proposal that is moving through the political and regulatory process, virtually always involving administrative agencies charged with ensuring that congressionally enacted laws are an implemented and enforced reality. These agencies—in the Westway battles chiefly highway agencies, environmental and natural resource agencies, and the Army Corps of Engineers—have great power in their circumscribed areas of authority.

State agencies play similar roles under state laws that often track federal law's subject areas. In addition, state agencies sometimes assume "delegated" roles under federal law, essentially standing in the shoes of federal regulators and taking over initial implementation and enforcement roles, subject to varying degrees of federal oversight.[17] State actors also act under their own separate state laws that can share subject turf with federal law or provide wholly different or additional regulatory requirements. Each agency has a subject turf, and statutes limit each agency's domain.

SOME REGULATORY WARS are fought over products such as tobacco, with consumer protection and health-oriented agencies making key decisions. Others may involve economy-changing forays into new areas of regulation such as car safety, workplace toxics, prohibition of discrimination, constraints on emissions of greenhouse gases contributing to climate change, oil drilling, securities industry conflicts of interest, and protection of union activity in the workplace. Sometimes they involve vast sums of money, such as long-standing litigation seeking to recover billions of dollars for Native Americans whose proceeds from use of their land were mishandled.[18] Other regulatory wars involve large-scale projects, like Westway, that involve numerous agencies and enormous sums of money and will change the physical environment on a vast scale and trigger the procedures and protections of several laws. In all these regulatory war settings, how private and public actors seek to achieve their goals is constrained and guided by statutes, regulations, and agency policies, as well as by the interpretations of those laws and regulations by courts. Statutes and regulations shaping regulatory wars usually are not designed for any one battle or single threat. They constitute a broader statement of national or state goals and means to accomplish those ends.

Many regulatory wars arise out of tensions between public or private goals pursued years after enactment of different priorities and requirements that have become durable features of the law.[19] Individual, groups, and even government officials may hope to avoid a problematic regulatory requirement, but they will seldom have the clout to change the law, whether it is set forth in a statute or in regulations. And if they do seek to change or bypass the law, a question is whether the law's broader goals and protections will be lost if, piece by piece, the initial political bargain is undone. Many environmental laws are in essence an agreement of mutual forbearance; everyone benefits if the environment is protected through a collective agreement, even though many interests will later hope that they can be granted an exception. Laws effectively empower some interests by making their goals preferred under the law.[20] Many statutes set political priorities and create protections but then require an additional participatory regulatory process that allows for more finely tuned assessment and sometimes flexibility.

Where the law sets rigid requirements and roadblocks, however, the regulatory war can be all about overcoming those key barriers or, for opponents, about driving the project into an unmoving legal obstacle.[21] Truly unmovable legal obstacles, however, are rare. And even in those rare instances, politics offers a safety valve if the underlying statute can itself be changed or subjected to a project-specific exemption.

Eventually, when the stakes are high, skirmishing before agency regulators ends up in court. As Alexis de Tocqueville observed over 150 years ago, "There is hardly a political question in the United States which does not sooner or later turn into a judicial one."[22] That observation remains true today. Courts are far from the only important legal institution, but they remain an essential element in regulatory wars, primarily in policing the actions of the key legal actors, administrative agency officials. When a regulatory challenge lands in court, a judge's authority is limited, but agencies and those who participated before agencies and then a reviewing court are also constrained. Expert agencies are expected to apply statutory law and their own regulations with procedural propriety and honesty. They must explain their actions in a way that is reasonable or, in the oft-stated legal term of art, must not be "arbitrary and capricious."[23]

If agencies comply with the law and provide adequate explanation for their choices, they stand in a greatly favored position before reviewing courts. Judges cannot substitute their own views of policy or resolve inherently political battles. They are expected to show deference to regulators' judgments. A posture of deference means that reasonable regulatory, factual, and political judgments of agencies and legislators are presumptively worthy of judicial respect. For Westway's supporters, again and again their most powerful play was to emphasize the need for judicial deference to political judgments.

But typically only government actors or victors before agencies (for example, the recipient of a disputed environmental permit) will play the deference card. Lawyers and their opposition clients who lost in the realm of politics or before an agency will seek victory in the courts by trying to weaken or eliminate judicial deference. For many decades, however, prevailing law has limited opportunities for judicial scrutiny of political and regulatory choices due to risks of judicial overreaching. Judicial deference decidedly tips the scale in favor of the government. This deference variable means that victory before an agency is often the most important stage in a regulatory war. A loss before the agency usually presages a loss before a later reviewing court. Judicial doctrines requiring deference mean that even strong "roadblock" laws may, in application, be less protective than the law's terms indicate.

Despite this judicial deference to agencies, agencies are constrained in two critically important ways. First, they cannot reinvent their basic mission and legal constraints on their actions.[24] Second, the basis and rationale for an agency action is not subject to ongoing adjustment.[25] An agency has to explain itself and later, before a court, has to work with that original, contemporaneous explanation.[26] An agency cannot strategically keep adjusting in light of opponents' attacks. Agencies hence have to make a sound and well-justified choice the first time around. Litigants challenging the government will try to persuade courts to adopt a more active and probing posture where they can show factual findings followed inadequate process, "a strong showing of bad faith or improper behavior," or other indicators of irregularity.[27]

In the United States, two additional sources of uncertainty and complexity arise in regulatory wars. Both are distinctive and unusual traits in American law. First, although the federal government is headed by only one executive, in the form of the president, executive agencies with different subject turfs can engage in direct disagreement.[28] Federal agencies can be at war with each other over the very same proposal, even where the proposal is itself federal or federally funded and even if the president has made clear his preference regarding that proposal. Each agency, as well as the president, has to "take care" that the laws are "faithfully executed."[29] Because most laws hand particular tasks and goals to specified agencies, they must faithfully serve in their legally mandated institutional roles. Structures and procedures often exist to resolve such differences, but by the time an internal executive branch debate is resolved, a substantial written record of contrary views will often exist. That record may influence later judicial challenges. Agencies answering to the same executive branch leadership and sometimes even within the same department can even oppose each other in court. During the Westway war, several federal agencies were repeatedly at loggerheads, publicly opposing each other in regulatory and judicial settings. Scientists within federal natural resource agencies provided key comments in opposition to actions of the Army Corps, also an agency of the federal government.

Similarly, state agencies and officials retain their own separate areas of legal authority. They usually can decide against a project or proposal under state law even if the action has surmounted federal hurdles. This may initially seem odd under a constitutional system that declares federal law "supreme," but it is the logical and almost inevitable structure in hundreds of laws.[30] If a polluter or source of environmental harm or risk can meet federal standards, that does not mean a city or state must, for example, authorize a new project or allow increased pollution. To preserve these fundamental state and local choices, most federal laws allow state and local governments to provide their citizens or the environment with greater protections than under federal law.[31] State and local governments are the main regulators of land uses. However, if a proposal or project violates federal law, state law cannot trump that federal law. States themselves are often combatants in battles involving federal actions in federal courts. Rather than involving "the government," in the sense of a single, key governmental actor, regulatory wars often involve numerous clashing federal and state agencies and officials.

The second additional source of uncertainty and complexity in regulatory wars arises from modern law's substantial legal empowerment of citizens, combined with laws and court doctrine allowing citizens to battle directly against powerful private and public interests. Many regulatory wars involve a government choice and private business interests seeing potential profit if they can secure a favorable regulatory action. But unlike traditional court actions, where two opponents battle it out, regulatory wars often also involve citizens and other entities, including not-for-profit organizations, which are not championing economic interests and may also strongly oppose the government.

Part of this development of broad participatory rights arose out of 1930s and 1940s business discomfort with the growing power of agencies and the modern administrative state.[32] To check government overreaching, the APA authorized aggrieved citizens to challenge agency illegality in court. Citizens' substantial roles in regulatory wars also followed almost inevitably from 1950s and especially 1960s civil rights victories and Vietnam War protests. Citizens had come to appreciate the power of their individual and collective voices. The Watergate debacle, involving illegality, venality, dishonesty, and cover-ups at the highest levels of government, confirmed citizen skepticism and the substantial possibility that government leaders would, under pressure, lie. Similar disclosures of government manipulation of information about the Vietnam War further heightened citizen distrust. At the more local level, New Yorkers had experienced both the benefits and the disruptions of hundreds of massive neighborhood-changing projects built under the vision and power of Robert Moses.[33] Citizen opposition in all possible venues was a near certainty, especially against a massive and disruptive project like Westway that was funded by dollars that could be traded in for mass transit.

During the Westway battles and still today, statutory changes gave increasingly active citizens both new motivations and new artillery. Some of that newfound strength derived from participation and litigation rights. Most statutes require regulatory transparency and numerous opportunities for citizen oversight and participation. The key NEPA statute's Environmental Impact Statement process, for example, requires public disclosure and opportunities for comment, and it requires agencies to respond to comments and criticisms when explaining their actions. However, in Westway's case, as in many others, citizen oversight and input under NEPA occurred well after its plans were virtually final and certain. As former Westway Federal Highway Administration lawyer Edward Kussy observes, litigation over major projects is in part the result of frustration citizens feel about their ability actually to influence a project.[34] NEPA thus by no means guarantees citizens a voice at a stage when a project might be reconsidered or redesigned, but at least it gives them a point at which they can offer input or voice protest.

Similarly, both the long-standing 1946 APA and environmental laws' "citizen suit" provisions—now a standard element in environmental laws enacted after the early 1970s—grant citizens rights to challenge statutory and regulatory violations in court.[35] By the time Westway gained steam, citizens were not just relegated to speeches and picketing but could influence the regulatory process and go to court to challenge private or government illegality. Government failures to acknowledge significant citizen objections and comments could themselves result in judicial rejection.[36] And often citizens and business interests are part of polycentric, multiactor battles that involve both attacks on the government and efforts to buttress the defenses of embattled regulators.[37] These citizen participation and litigation rights started to be wielded around the time Westway's battles started. These participatory rights, coupled with substantive amendments strengthening the nation's environmental laws, gave citizens and not-for-profit groups newfound power. In addition, the newly enacted highway trade-in provision gave mass transit and clean air advocates new motivation and a least a fighting chance after years of dominance of the highway-building lobby.

In addition, in any regulatory war, incentives for citizen action are often strengthened by fee-shifting provisions.[38] A well-grounded challenge may result in the plaintiff challenger's attorney's fees and costs being underwritten by the federal government or a private law violator due to statutory fee-shifting provisions. The promise of a potential award of fees creates modest incentives for attorneys to take on cases for clients lacking resources, even where the lawsuit would be against the federal government. Citizens are unlikely to win and hence seldom will receive an award of fees and costs, but such representations at least do not inevitably result in poverty for the lawyers or their clients. Westway's opposition was funded by individuals' efforts, not-for-profit fund-raising, and, after court victories, court awards of attorney's fees and costs.[39] A fund-raiser on the Hudson River sloop *Clearwater* included folk singer and activist Pete Seeger and famed environmentalist David Brower.[40] Opposition lawyers were not paid anything close to their usual market rates, but through these fund-raising efforts, they received some compensation as they proceeded.

Citizen participation and litigation rights and fee incentives are critical to understanding regulatory wars in the United States. Even if all major politicians and agency actors are in agreement, a dissenting citizen or group can challenge that decision and consensus in court. Short-lived political coalitions may favor a particular regulatory outcome, but more durable legal requirements in underlying laws may remain and be enforced by citizens. A particular project, like Westway, may have substantial support among currently elected politicians at some or all levels of government and may create localized or short-term benefits. Existing laws and regulations, however, may reflect much more enduring and shared goals that run counter to short-term or local political incentives. Long-term and short-term perspectives will often clash in regulatory wars. Internal agency debates over Westway, as well as citizen participation and litigation rights, proved critical to the path of the Westway war.

Regulatory wars thus involve competing interests applying and using the law. Political judgments by legislatures and presidents provide general priorities and occasionally set rigid requirements. Promulgated regulations and case-specific judgments by agencies guide the battles. Well-established administrative law doctrine further shapes how stakeholders will frame their contentions. Statutes and agency regulations and traditions also collectively create the process that channels such disputes. Where public priorities and political choices are at stake, and the particular issue or battle has implications for thousands or millions of people and similarly high financial stakes, investments in the regulatory war will skyrocket.

Thus, between these new procedural rights, substantive protections, and incentives for stakeholder participation, Westway faced a newly challenging regulatory environment. Former Army Corps regulator Dennis Suszkowski correctly observed that the project was born at the end of an earlier era of huge megaprojects and other environment-changing actions that proceeded with little public scrutiny or judicial review.[41] The truly bad and illegal could be questioned, but grand, large-scale proposals also were at risk. These legal changes empowered citizens to stand against seemingly overwhelming private and public power.

But citizen activists' roles are not universally lauded. One of the United States attorneys fighting for Westway, Marc Rosenbaum, saw a downside to citizens' ability to participate and oppose actions championed by the government. In his view and experience, most citizens are apathetic. Only the highly committed end up participating in a regulatory war and using the law to further their preferred ends. Activists thus can "usurp the voice of the community,"[42] in his view. But the real question is what community's views and priorities? Activists seldom can succeed unless they can find in the law a lever that gives them power. When they do, then that legal lever can allow small groups of activists to achieve results that may run counter to the current interests of a local majority or the preferences of powerful public or private actors. And, undoubtedly, at times powerful interests will jam through regulatory approvals for projects for private gain that do little for local populations. Power and strategic advantage will be seized, regardless of partisans' goals, but the law can constrain such power grabs.

Westway supporters also griped that citizen opposition had become seemingly reflexive, stemming from distrust of authority even when a government project was a good idea. In architecture critic Ada Louise Huxtable's words, New Yorkers had too often been "lied to and coopted," making many of them "partisan, protective, and paranoid."[43] Westway planners, such as Craig Whitaker, saw Westway as a magnificent project that was the very opposite of destructive projects imposed upon citizens and neighborhoods during the period when Robert Moses reigned.[44] For example, the Lower Manhattan Expressway, often referred to as Lomex, had in the late 1960s been proposed to address crosstown downtown traffic ills with an expressway across Soho.[45]

It had threatened to displace many residents and businesses and indisputably would have created serious air pollution problems. It also threatened to fragment neighborhoods. As a result of these problems and an effective opposition that included the renowned urban scholar Jane Jacobs and a broad coalition, the expressway was defeated.[46] The law, however, did not play the crucial role in the defeat of Lomex; grassroots opposition and politics did. In the Westway war, both its planners and citizen opponents saw themselves as inheritors of the Lomex mantle. Westway's planners saw themselves not as descendants of Robert Moses but as motivated by environmental goals and a desire to improve the city with a park and river access. Richard Kahan, counsel to Westway project, said that "[e]verybody on th[e Westway] team hated highways."[47] Similarly, the Army Corps, which had long overseen huge construction projects on land and in America's waters, had by the early 1970s started to integrate environmental protection into its mission.[48]

But many of Westway's critics saw lessons in citizens' victory against the road and focused on how Westway shared attributes with Lomex. Westway too was a huge road project; perhaps it too could be killed if citizens stood their ground. Distrust ran deep at the time. Westway was different, but active citizens were skeptical. The growing environmental movement had become yet another area of activism and protest. In the Westway war, later revelations of inaccurate, selective, and arguably dishonest claims added fuel to the fires of those inclined to distrust.

BECAUSE MULTIPLE FEDERAL, state, and local laws do not dictate any regulatory sequence, a major strategic call in any high-stakes regulatory action is how and where to fight key regulatory battles. Invariably, all stakeholders, both private and governmental, will strategically look for their most favorable venues.[49] Every favorable judgment will be used in later venues to gain momentum and claim legitimacy. Later decision makers will be told that there is no need for scrutiny. And when the fight eventually lands in court, victories secured before key regulatory agencies or political officials will be trumpeted to argue that the judge should show deference and keep out of the political realm. Victors before agencies will argue that courts should not displace the agency's more expert and politically accountable judgments.

An important asymmetry exists in such a sequence of approvals. A regulatory warrior who needs approvals in numerous venues has no choice but to deal with every legal hurdle. Resources will need to be expended on each stage of review, although an uncontested proceeding will obviously demand less time and money. Regulatory opponents, in contrast, do not need to fight at every stage. Instead, they can save their fire for the critical approvals or the issues of greatest concern, especially approvals involving laws or regulations that give opponents a decent chance of success. If a particular stage of review is make-or-break for a project, then that stage will become a focus for attacks. And each sign of regulatory irregularity can be used to chip away at the protections offered by judicial deference to agency judgments.

Regulators and their lawyers defending a government action will always seek to limit judicial scrutiny. Few settings terrify government lawyers more than seeing senior government regulators in court, on the stand, seeking to explain a decision that was not well explained or perhaps not even understood the first time around. First, most regulatory acts are actually collective, bureaucratic exercises that no one person can personally explain.[50] Second, the art of cross-examination combined with the challenges of remembering difficult past judgment calls or even seemingly minor decisions can reduce many witnesses to a state of nervous exhaustion. Lawyers are trained to probe and reveal errors and inconsistencies; trained or natural witnesses are a rarity. With heightened judicial scrutiny, the sometimes seamy or at least messy world of political motivations and deals can founder before a reviewing judge. Judges should know intellectually that the openness and propriety of the judicial process are often not found in the political world.[51] Nevertheless, they can be shocked by the raw power, poorly justified political choices, and opportunistic political dealings that drive many legislative and regulatory actions. That judicial shock can help challengers seeking to overcome deference arguments.

Politics, regulatory actions, and judicial proceedings hence each offer different sorts of accountability and reliability. Politicians are often electorally accountable but can act with little science or data to back up their actions; they may be responding to passing, short-term political priorities or benefits. Agencies making regulatory decisions, such as the Army Corps issuing Section 404 dredge-and-fill permits, are a step removed from electoral accountability. They must, however, act through an open, transparent process and in a manner consistent with mandates and criteria set in laws and regulations. Agencies have to explain their choices, show that their decisions are supported by science or data before them, and establish that they are acting rationally, or at least not in an arbitrary and capricious manner. Those regulatory choices are also subject to judicial oversight, while political choices at the legislative level are seldom subject to review for their wisdom or basis. All federal judges reviewing disputed regulatory actions are immune from electoral pressures due to their appointment with life tenure, but they must conform to the edicts of statutes, regulations, and past case law. They have some latitude to develop case law when presented with new or unsettled questions, but their law-creating power is limited. By reviewing private and government action to ensure it is well justified, judges both enforce earlier legislative and regulatory choices and provide a check on arbitrary or illegal action. They often mediate between old legislative priorities that remain in the law and later private or government actions that strain at the leash of the law. And unless a judge serves on the United States Supreme Court, appellate judicial review constrains judicial overreaching.

In addition, regardless of the stated legal framework, reviewing judges' predilections, skepticism, or confidence will shape how they look at a case.[52] Battles over judicial confirmation reflect just this reality; judges, not just the law, influence judicial outcomes. Where the reviewing judge gets the rare benefit of a trial reviewing a questionable agency action, then the trial judge's control of the courtroom, ability to ask questions, and broad "equitable" powers to fashion relief and even put a complete halt to a major government action further shift the controversy away from a deferential posture. As former assistant United States attorney Marc Rosenbaum reflected in recalling his work on Westway, federal district court judges wield tremendous power. Once a trial judge issues an order, you need two appellate judges to reverse the judge, and if the appeal is to the Supreme Court, five justices. "If they don't, then the president must carry out" the district court judge's edicts.[53] Hence, a single judge sitting in review of high-stakes regulatory actions can potentially bring all to a halt. Trials revisiting regulatory actions, however, are rare. Usually agency actions rise or fall on the basis of their own record and explanation at the time of the decision.

REGULATORY WAR thus involves many actors and political and judicial institutions. Any complicated and uncertain sequence creates opportunities to evade scrutiny or shine a bright light on one tiny project element or wear down the opposition. When an issue is large and shared by many actors—as, for example, is the case with efforts to protect fisheries or deal with a ubiquitous challenge like global carbon emissions contributing to climate change—splintered regulatory turfs may mean that no one political actor or agency will see the whole picture or feel an issue is its responsibility. Each agency with potential responsibility will look at the underlying issue through a different lens, with different statutory missions. Similarly, citizens or groups concerned about a degraded environment, discrimination, or some other social ill may not be sure where they should seek a curative response. A "regulatory commons" can exist, where no entity has primary regulatory responsibility, but regulatory turf is shared in tentative and uncertain ways.[54] Regulatory inattention and failures to protect important resources can result. And if a proposal or project is huge and involves many people and entities that need to move together to bring a project to completion, the presence of many diverse actors can confound efforts to protect a resource or to complete that project or regulatory initiative. The plight of many fisheries is a prime example; splintered regulatory roles have contributed to the decimation of many commercial fish species.[55]

Where a project or regulatory proposal triggers environmental concerns, as almost any large urban land use project will do, science data and predictions create additional uncertainties and grounds for battle. With a large city-changing project like Westway, where thousands of design and spending choices were up for grabs, politics will shape what is proposed for building, and dozens of regulatory hurdles will need to be surmounted. Underlying scientific realities, in contrast to many other elements of regulatory wars, can pose an obstacle that neither power nor legal prowess can overcome.

Many sorts of regulatory wars exist, but perhaps none involve more opportunities for strategic moves and countermoves than large-scale, urban, land-use-changing megaprojects like Westway that threaten the environment.[56] Because such projects involve major changes in land use, they must surmount local regulatory reviews if they are to succeed at all. Because state and federal dollars make possible many such large highway, park, and redevelopment projects, state and federal financial approvals and monitoring are inevitable. If a project threatens the environment, environmental laws will be triggered. Changed land uses, especially on a large scale, will hence virtually always incite some opposition. Someone will be moved, their home or business threatened, air or water quality affected, or a cherished city attribute impaired. Divisions among affected citizens and politicians will create an uncertain political terrain. If government dollars are footing the bill, often justified concerns with patronage, pork-barrel projects, and waste will be voiced. Or those dollars could be spent on different priorities, creating competing interests, much as Westway presented the choice of spending federal dollars on a highway, development, and park project or on mass transit. Opponents will thus always seek to enlist political opponents or even seek to kill a project through the political trump of a legislative prohibition or funding cutoff. Someone will eventually move the battle into the courts.

Leadership continuity and power can also be powerful determinants in regulatory wars, but these factors can favor either supporters or opponents of a regulatory action. Large projects like Westway are sure to have many individuals devoting years of their lives to see their work come to fruition. They will be full-time supporters and paid for their time. Many lawyers, lobbyists, and public relations personnel will see their task as simply to move projects or other regulatory goals through the legal and political maze. Lowell Bridwell sought to act as such a facilitator for Westway. However, as a regulatory action, goal or project becomes more complex and time-consuming, continuity of workers may be lost. Political leadership may change. And if a project or task is huge, the reality of many institutions and actors may mean that no one is really in control. As reflected in upcoming chapters in the Westway tale, a large project can become a lumbering giant without any supporter making overall strategic choices.

Although opponents of a project or regulatory action will typically lack resources and have few, if any, full-time professionals working in an opposition role, they can actually be advantaged by their small numbers. As happened in the Westway battles with the effective work of Marcy Benstock and the lead opposition attorneys Al Butzel and Mitchell Bernard, a few strategically smart and highly knowledgeable citizens and lawyers may, over time, have a finger on the pulse and vulnerabilities of a project or regulatory challenge. They may have an advantage, or at least a source of strength, due to the continuity of their efforts and the deep knowledge sometimes lacking in project supporters. And effective citizen leadership and attorney skills can make a huge difference.

As with military wars, a critical element in regulatory wars is strategic use of disparate resources. The tobacco industry for decades used its huge resources to fight off regulation and defeat injury suits in court.[57] The automobile industry fought seatbelt and airbag regulation in what the Supreme Court characterized as the regulatory equivalent of war.[58] Financial institutions have similarly fought regulatory constraints for years, benefiting from decades of lax oversight. Pharmaceutical companies and other producers of occasionally dangerous products fight against tort injury lawsuits in individual states, in Congress, before agencies, and in the courts. By securing legislation capping damages, they have sought to reduce the profitability of such suits and have even sought decisions that federal legislation or regulation preempts all other legal projections. In Professor Tom McGarity's phrase, for the past twenty years a "preemption war" has been under way.[59] With billions of dollars at stake after the Exxon Valdez spill, Exxon funded scholarship and science studies and battled in numerous courts to limit its liability.[60]

Complexity and drawn-out regulatory reviews thus often favor wealthy interests in regulatory wars, at least where the battle is to avoid regulation or avoid admissions of liability. Opponents of change and new regulation will strategically use their power and wealth to wear down the opposition and fragment if not scare politicians and regulators. Opponents of regulation often succeed, but from time to time new regulatory statutes or bodies of regulation with real power still emerge. They often follow a public crisis or heightened citizen concern.

DELAY CAN be used by proponents and opponents of a government action but generally will favor the opposition. However, since government actions can impose regulatory burdens or authorize an activity, delay can be a strategic goal of industry, citizens, or not-for-profits. Some degree of delay is an inevitable effect of increased opportunities for public participation and legal challenge, as well as multiplying analytical obligations that are part of the new post-1970s era of an enlarged administrative state and strengthened environmental and risk-regulation laws.

Delay can benefit either side in a megaproject regulatory setting like the war over Westway. A project supporter can wear down and keep the opposition confused by drawing the process out or perhaps moving the project simultaneously through several regulatory reviews. Supporters can benefit from a mix of speed, delay, and snowing of opponents and regulators with voluminous supportive materials. Multithousand-page regulatory analyses, impact statements, and technical appendixes are common. Seldom can opponents keep up or match the engineering, scientific, and legal resources of project supporters. The same holds true in many high-stakes environmental and risk-regulation choices with a substantial science component. Consultants and industry and government lawyers can usually outpaper and outlast opponents. In the Westway war, massive analytical compilations were part of the supporters' efforts to make Westway unstoppable.

Still, delay and complexity can also be opponents' great allies. If opponents can stay in the game—and that is a major "if"—they can sometimes threaten a project's private or public funding. With delay, new electoral cycles can lead to new political coalitions and leadership; a project's support can dwindle or disappear altogether. New laws can create opportunities for attack. In addition, the time associated with environmental analysis, especially under laws like NEPA, can give time for opposition to gain momentum. Impact statements can reveal problems that engender political opposition. EIS data and analysis also can trigger other laws' more substantive requirements. Commenting on Westway while its fate remained uncertain, urban analyst and then Ford Foundation official Louis Winnick said that "[t]ime is always on the side of the opponents."[61] Longtime EPA Region II attorney Walter Mugdan, who worked on Westway early and late in its battles, emphasizes how delay can serve an equalizing function: "With big projects with so much momentum, delay is crucial. It can give time for others to look into [environmental] impacts, buy time, and . . . [allow] other legal and science" concerns to "take root."[62] Speaking about Westway to a prominent business group founded by banker David Rockefeller, Governor Mario Cuomo reflected on his work as a lawyer in Queens who fought to stop projects for clients. "If you know the right techniques, you can stop anything."[63] He added, "Is it a good result? No. Is it a good system? Yes."[64]

Senator Moynihan, an ardent supporter of Westway, was especially critical of this newfound power of citizens to block projects. He bemoaned how critics can delay and sometimes kill grand governmental actions. Starting in the 1970s, in his view, "civic reputation began to be acquired by people who prevented things from happening. . . . [M]any things get stopped now for no reason."[65] Current New York senator Charles Schumer shares that view, commenting after defeat of a proposed West Side sports stadium, "A culture of inertia has set in. . . . Criticism predominates over construction. . . . It doesn't matter how small a constituency or flawed an argument the critic possesses."[66]

When President Reagan, ten years into the Westway battles, presented an essential $85 million check in support of Westway's construction, he blended concern with delay with criticism of regulation. He stated that "people tell me that the name Westway has become a code word for a bureaucracy strangling in its own regulations." He hoped that Westway would be "a reality" and "create parkland and new areas for commerce and industry . . . [and] save millions by easing the flow of people and goods. But most important, . . . create jobs." Reagan saw the Westway delays as a threat to the project; as it turns out, he overestimated the momentum his support would create.

Opponents of Westway saw delay as one of their allies, and many groups and individuals remained project opponents, but few opponents other than Marcy Benstock, Bunny Gabel, and John Mylod and opposition lawyers Butzel and Bernard stayed in the game and acted strategically as Westway rolled on. They were assisted by an early and stalwart opponent in Congressman Ted Weiss. Michael Gerrard, a Westway opponent and activist both as a citizen and later as a lawyer, says Weiss and other opponents saw the benefits of delay but focused more on what potential actors and laws could really stop the project. "Representative Ted Weiss convened strategy sessions of leading Westway opponents in his district office every couple of months."[67] Gerrard "kept a running tally of all of the legal handles and their status" and reviewed them with others. "We discussed how to make the most of each one. We were acutely aware that we needed to win on only one front."[68] Brian Ketcham, an expert on transportation and air pollution who was associated with Citizens for Clean Air, saw delay in itself as the opposition's greatest ally.[69] "Everybody knows how these things work. . . . [Y]ou comb through the environmental impact statement and try to find flaws. You delay and delay and pretty soon the whole project disappears." Ketcham went so far as to say that "if I were the only person on earth who was opposed to the Westway, I could have stopped it all by myself."[70]

Westway's convoluted path reveals nuances in the art of regulatory war but casts doubt on excessive claims that mere delay and citizen opposition predestined the project for the graveyard. Most laws wielded in the Westway war set priorities but also provided safety valves and room for adjustment. Westway kept chugging on, overcoming barrier after barrier, for many years. In regulatory wars like this, political momentum and power will often carry the day, but occasionally particular laws' requirements and even prohibitions will prove far more powerful. Laws seldom dictate political choices, but they set the boundaries for those choices. The law makes particular interests paramount and privileged. Delay was part of the Westway battles, but more in the sense mentioned by Walter Mugdan, allowing issues to "take root." Mistakes, environmental realities, an enduring clash over highways versus mass transit, and strong legal mandates in one law proved far more critical to Westway. Westway's fate was ultimately determined by the project's merits and effects, as shaped by the resources wielded in regulatory wars. Laws and linked federal dollars motivated and enabled New York to pursue Westway, provided the mass transit trade-in as motivation, and protected air and water resources. Those laws also gave citizen opponents a voice in legal and political venues and their lawyers the power to influence regulatory decisions and, when necessary, check illegality in court.

4

THE ROAD WARRIORS AND
THE NEW ENVIRONMENT

POLITICAL ECONOMIC THEORY predicts that concentrated interests with high financial stakes in a disputed matter will tend to outcompete more dispersed interests lacking strong financial personal incentives.[1] This will likely often be the case, but at least in the Westway battles, monetary interests and the existence of a person or entity with comprehensive knowledge did not go together. The construction companies, unions, agency officials, lawyers, banks, and real estate interests that supported Westway had monetary interests at stake that were both individually large and in the aggregate even larger. Opponents had nowhere near supporters' monetary resources. They also generally lacked significant individual monetary stakes in Westway or alternatives to Westway. Since Westway was championed not just by private interests, but city, state and federal officials, it had almost unlimited resources at its disposal. And when Westway battles turned to the courts, government and private-sector attorneys, paid for by taxpayers, defended the project. Resources available for the war were skewed against project opponents.

However, the post-1970s world of environmental law and the open, transparent setting of administrative law transformed the regulatory process applicable to a project like Westway. Protective environmental goals were national policy. These fundamental changes live on today. But protective laws and an open regulatory process do not ensure that the law's written aspirations will be an enforced reality. Regulatory wars always occur in the middle ground

Figure 4.1. In 1977, Westway's opponents held a fund-raising cruise on the Hudson River sloop *Clearwater*. From left to right, Mary Ann Rothman, Sandra Church, Marcy Benstock (in glasses), Dan Gabel, and Bunny Gabel (leaning forward). The man with the silver hair facing the camera is David Brower, founder of the Friends of the Earth and past executive director of the Sierra Club. The bearded man two to the right of Brower is Tom Stokes. The others are unidentified. *(Source: Courtesy of Bunny Gabel; photographer unknown.)*

between the legal and political; when political preferences regarding a pending action are strong and private stakes huge, capitulation within the halls of government may follow. Citizens, often assisted by lawyers, can nonetheless participate, give voice to their views, challenge unfounded claims, and battle before agencies and in the courts. The skills and endurance of citizen participants and their lawyers can determine a disputed regulatory action's fate.[2]

Westway's opponents were many but were often coordinated and arguably led by a citizen activist, Marcy Benstock. Slight, with blackish hair typically worn in bangs, Benstock is not a physically imposing presence. Her matter-of-fact, Great Lakes-accented voice is also hardly one to rally the masses. Her tenacity, intelligence, and deep knowledge of Westway and politics, however, made her a powerhouse opponent. She does not suffer fools or foolish questions gladly. But during the Westway battles, and still today, she is a font of knowledge others have long forgotten. In many respects, Benstock was a near poster child for America's newly empowered and skeptical citizens, albeit in a highly educated and unusually driven frame.

Educated at Harvard, with a later master's degree in economics from the New School for Social Research, Benstock had by the 1970s become an astute political actor. She formed an organization in New York City called the NYC Clean Air Campaign. Under that umbrella, she had earlier worked to shut down high-polluting residential incinerators on New York City's Upper West Side. She had also worked on books with water activist David Zwick, describing the operations of America's newly strengthened environmental laws. Through those efforts, she developed a sense of how to move citizens, governments, and the legal system. She describes herself as akin to a "jailhouse lawyer."[3] Assisted at several stages in the protracted Westway battles by highly effective counsel, she proved to be a formidable adversary. She had citizen and organizational allies, chief among them Robert Boyle of the Hudson River Fishermen's Association, John Mylod of the Hudson River Sloop Clearwater, Inc., and Bunny Gabel of the Friends of the Earth. But Benstock (acting through the Clean Air Campaign) was the citizen with the energy and knowledge to maintain a constant oppositional presence.

In order to underscore that she was not a one-person opposition but part of a broader coalition that mounted a sustained battle against Westway, Benstock points to numerous leaflets, hearings, and statements where many dozens of groups and far more individuals shared her opposition to Westway. Most local legislators opposed the project.[4] Indeed, even candidates Koch and Carey ran for mayor and governor, respectively, as strident opponents of Westway; if that was an unpopular stance, it was an unusual election position to take. As discussed further below, objections of federal agency scientists and staff played a crucial role, as did growing political opposition at all levels of government. Benstock was not a lone gadfly. She remains insistent that she was not the leader of the opposition or the chief strategist, although others, including her allied Westway opponents, identify her by name and characterize her as a savvy strategist or the opposition's leader. In ways quite consistent with written records and others' reflections, Benstock characterizes herself as a "hard worker" and, most important, the "one person who knew everything that was happening." She was the "repository of all information." Indeed, given the increasing number of citizens and agency officials who were part of Westway's opposition, and hundreds if not thousands working in support of Westway, she admits that she "didn't know much of what was happening." No one could. Nevertheless, more than any other person, she "knew everything about everything" and worked to "pick[] up the slack if something was not getting done in any of the arenas by someone else."

Decades after the Westway battles ended, Benstock is the opponent most frequently recalled by Westway's major players. Former mayor Koch, who after being elected mayor became a Westway supporter, ruefully laughed when discussing Benstock's effective work, stating that "she was the brains of the outfit." "They were very smart . . . [to defeat Westway] they had to have beaten the unions in Congress. But to their great credit. I mean I admire their competence. They beat the unions and the banks and the advocates for Westway."[5] *Village Voice* columnist Jack Newfield similarly credited Benstock as the most significant opponent: "[T]here have been many heroes and heroines in the . . . resistance to Westway. . . . But only Marcy Benstock . . . fought Westway, to the exclusion of anything else."[6] When Newfield wrote, that opposition had lasted eight years, but in the end Benstock devoted almost fourteen years to the defeat of Westway. Even today, she works on related battles, among them seeking to stop or minimize commercial development in or over the Hudson in connection with Hudson River Park.

Benstock's motivation? Certainly not money, which was never abundant for her or her not-for-profit NYC Clean Air Campaign. Still today she works out of a small office that after the 9/11 terrorist World Trade Center attacks has moved several times. Benstock identified her love of subways and New York's mass transit as a key motivation: "I treasured the subways more than the theater or the beaches or the parks, or the nice restaurants. I loved looking at the faces each day in the subway cars."[7] She is also a true believer in this nation's environmental laws and open-government principles, a belief somewhat incongruously combined with a strongly skeptical, almost conspiratorial view of what wealthy private interests and government actors will do to achieve their goals. She questions whether the closed West Side Highway collapse under the weight of a cement truck was an accident; she believes it was a "stunt" to hasten support for Westway.[8] Of a key Westway actor and witness, Benstock stated, "I was furious at [his] contempt for democracy."[9] Others say that Westway became "her life" and that "her capacity for righteous anger is what makes her so uncompromising and relentless."[10] An editorial Benstock wrote captures well her skepticism juxtaposed with great faith in the power of people and the law. "The greatest enemy of the environment, of cities that are decent places for all of us to live, of democracy itself right now seems to me to be the great cynicism and despair that many people have about the world at large. I'm not saying that there aren't good reasons for that despair—only that things can be changed in unexpected ways when people go out and try."[11]

Benstock's influence, however, never waned, in large part due to her consistency in providing accurate information to anyone who would listen, as well as her ability to motivate her allies and later her lawyers in litigation. Her main citizen opponent allies, John Mylod and Bunny Gabel, readily point to Benstock as the key opposition leader.[12] *New York Times* editor and columnist John Oakes relied on her in writing three powerful anti-Westway columns and stated that "no one I know has ever gotten any mistaken information from Marcy. . . . I have never met a better supplier of facts in my life than Marcy."[13] *New York Times* Pulitzer Prize–winning reporter and later op-ed columnist Sydney Schanberg was aware of her work and views, but her fervor left him nervous.[14] Nevertheless, his hard-hitting columns blasting Westway and covering later court battles ended up consistent with arguments and information Benstock shared widely. Through many hundreds of leaflets regarding Westway, innumerable advocacy and strategy meetings, and hundreds of filings made by her attorneys, Benstock framed the Westway battles.

As the battles dragged on, letters and op-eds in New York City metropolitan area newspapers, as well as regulatory filings and missives to politicians and regulators, evidenced a proliferation of pro- and anti-Westway groups. Business for Mass Transit, Action for Rational Transit, Citizens for Clean Air, the Clean Air Campaign, the West Side Ad Hoc Committee against the Interstate, along with environmental groups like the Sierra Club and transit supporters like the Permanent Citizens Advisory Committee to the Metropolitan Transit Authority, opposed Westway in numerous venues. Action for Rational Transit itself included over fifty organizations among its members.[15] Position papers opposing Westway identified over a hundred groups that opposed the project, or at least favored a trade-in over Westway. Project supporters, fearful of lacking a similar voice, also created advocacy groups. David Rockefeller announced the creation of the New York City Partnership to speak on "such issues as rent control and the development of the Westway." Other corporate and not-for-profit leaders were named as participants.[16] New York Citizens for Balanced Transportation—a pro-Westway group headed by W. H. "Tex" James, the former publisher of the *Daily News*, and directed by Carolyn R. Meinhardt—remained a persistent pro-Westway voice at all levels of government, as well as in the newspapers. The Business/ Labor Working Group, another Rockefeller-linked entity, called Westway its "'number one priority'" for "'revitalization'" and a "'rallying point for private commitment and investment.'"[17] Members and leadership of unions and assorted construction associations regularly spoke in Westway's support at public hearings.

However, perhaps crucial to Westway's fate, no single person on the pro-Westway side served that cause in a single-minded, dedicated manner. During the early years, Lowell Bridwell sought to be that person, but his turf was limited. Other state and federal actors, and certainly citizen opponents and judges, all were outside his control. In Westway's later years, no one person on the supporters' side looked at the overall picture with the authority to make long-term strategic calls. In contrast, opponents had in Marcy Benstock one person who provided continuity, knowledge, commitment, the ability to "translate" complex materials, and a sound strategic sense.[18]

Moreover, Benstock and her opposition allies were represented before agencies and in courts by a small number of highly effective lawyers. While the opposition's lead lawyer shifted late in the battles, the lawyers were all from a single law firm and had worked together before that transition.[19] On the government side, similarly brilliant but more trial-savvy lawyers worked hard to keep Westway on track, but the firms and lawyers representing the United States and New York State shifted at several points.

Among the opposition lawyers who assisted Benstock and other Westway opponents was Harvard College and Law School graduate Albert Butzel, who as a young lawyer had worked with Lloyd Garrison and environmentalist clients to defeat the Storm King power station in the Hudson highlands. That major infrastructure project led to one of the first federal environmental litigations.[20] The resulting *Scenic Hudson* case is viewed by many as one of the watershed cases changing the path of environmental law, legitimating and enforcing requirements that energy projects consider environmental harms. Furthermore, in that battle and in subsequent Hudson River battles over power plant cooling and fishery impacts, Butzel and environmentalist allies documented the Hudson's fish populations and threats they faced. When Westway later turned to fishery impacts, Butzel was already familiar with the issue and Hudson fishery experts.

Benstock also worked with Michael Gerrard, a young law student and later lawyer and eventually professor. She worked with Gerrard in an array of meetings and forums where Westway was the subject of discussion. His work particularly focused on energy usage and much-referenced studies challenging claims that Westway, and highway projects in general, would provide greater employment and other economic benefits than would investment in mass transit.[21] He later worked for the city and eventually became a partner at the environmental law boutique Butzel & Cass, later renamed Berle, Kass & Case. He subsequently moved to Arnold & Porter and became a prominent environmental lawyer and prolific environmental law scholar. Gerrard now teaches at Columbia University Law School.

To avoid a conflict due to Peter Berle's work as New York State's top environmental official with the Department of Environmental Conservation, an offshoot firm, Butzel & Kass, handled the Westway litigation. Butzel led the litigation efforts through 1984, when two younger firm lawyers took over. The lead lawyer by 1984 was Mitchell Bernard, a Princeton and New York University Law School graduate. He is now the director of litigation at one of America's preeminent public interest environmental groups, the Natural Resources Defense Council (NRDC). He had left the firm to pursue his interest in the theater and by 1984 had returned to work in the firm's space, but just on Westway. He was joined just before the 1985 trial by Jean McCarroll, a graduate of Radcliffe College (now known as Harvard) and NYU Law School, as well as a former teacher and striped bass fishing enthusiast who viewed herself as "instinctively an environmentalist."[22] She subsequently worked as an environmental and land use lawyer at Carter Ledyard in New York City. They had little trial experience in 1985 but proved their mettle and creativity in Westway's ultimate legal battles.

Benstock offered high praise for the opposition's lawyers but also viewed them with some resentment: "Those lawyers, perhaps all lawyers, always think they did everything when in fact they had no interest in finding out or building on what other people were doing, especially people who weren't wealthy or powerful."[23] The citizen and organizational opponents of Westway did far more work, in her view. And since between 1971 and February 1975, opponent Gabel counted 519 Westway-related meetings of "interested groups," plus innumerable rallies, petition drives, and fund-raising efforts, citizen opposition efforts probably did dwarf the hours of legal advocates.[24]

Citizen activists and opponents like Benstock may have had mixed feeling about their lawyers, but project opponents and their lawyers were empowered by the changing world of environmental, transportation, and administrative law.[25] In the words of Westway opponent and Hudson River Clearwater head, John Mylod, "without the ability to go to court, we would have lost."[26] By the mid-1970s, these changing bodies of law created several difficult legal challenges that Westway's supporters had to overcome. They had to accomplish thousands of tasks, including securing interstate highway designation and obtaining funding, engaging architects, engineers, and planners, all the while maintaining momentum and political support. Opponents, in contrast, could maintain a far narrower focus. They could search for points of weakness or key regulatory hurdles and concentrate their efforts. This does not mean that such areas of focused attention could not and did not reveal genuine problems. Instead, the law provided focal points for opponents' attacks. The focal points in a regulatory war are dependent on the issues or problems raised by an action or project.

It is important not to overstate the role of the litigating opponents and their lawyers. They can keep a project embattled. Sometimes they can defeat the government or stop a harmful private proposal. However, any regulatory war can be decisively resolved by political action that terminates or guarantees an action or project. Furthermore, environmental and risk regulation tends to turn on questions dependent on science and expertise; the actions of expert staff and scientists within agencies can make a critical difference in a regulatory war.

Benstock, Butzel, and Bernard were far from the only dissenters regarding Westway. Despite broad federal, state, and local executive branch leadership that supported the project—namely, mayors, governors, and presidents—many other government actors opposed it. Several federal environmental and natural resource agencies were allied with the citizen environmentalists. Although federal agency leadership later wavered, agency scientists and staff repeatedly voiced their opposition to the Westway project. Their consistent refrains about air pollution increases, water impacts, and fishery harms became increasingly important as the Westway battles progressed. New York State's Department of Environmental Conservation also had to decide whether to issue an essential air pollution permit and also retained authority over water resources. It too at times was aligned with the opposition.

Assorted votes over the years indicated that most New York metro-area local, state, and federal elected legislators opposed the project. A 1980 memorandum to President Jimmy Carter mentioned the support of unions, David Rockefeller, business groups, and the United States Department of Transportation but bluntly conceded that Westway was opposed by "all Manhattan elected officials," along with environmental groups and federal environmental agencies.[27] Polls of city residents indicated more overall opposition than support, especially with the trade-in option on the table.[28] The City Club of New York supported the trade-in option over Westway, as did the community boards representing adjacent areas.[29] Numerically, public hearing opponents dwarfed project supporters.[30] An extended skirmish in city politics concerned whether the Board of Estimate or the mayor controlled the decision whether to proceed with Westway. The Board of Estimate was a body that at the time included representation of most of New York City's leadership, including the heads of the five boroughs. The board voted in opposition to Westway, but a court later concluded that Westway decision-making leadership resided with the mayor.[31] Similarly, several years into the Westway war, as well as in the endgame battles, the state legislature twice passed legislation that refused to commit state funds to pay for Westway costs if for any reason federal support fell short; that legislation, however, was vetoed both times by the then governor.[32] Other opponents included Representatives Ted Weiss and Elizabeth Holtzman, as well as City Council President Carol Bellamy and State Attorney

General (and later senate candidate) Robert Abrams, as well as many other officials and hundreds of citizens who submitted statements to regulators in opposition to Westway. In fact, once the trade-in alternative was on the table, no electoral, legislative, or regulatory vote, tally of commentators, or poll ever indicated that Westway had a supportive majority. Later developments revealed federal legislative opposition as well.

Among the opposition legislators during the late 1970s was Ed Koch. When still a congressman successfully running for mayor, Koch did not mince words in opposing Westway: Westway was an "economic" and "environmental disaster" that would "not be built."[33] Part of his district included Greenwich Village; many of those constituents had opposed the project. Similarly, before he was elected governor, congressman and gubernatorial candidate Hugh Carey called the project "ill conceived" and a threat to "air quality." He argued that cities had to cease being "swayed by the siren song of highway trust moneys."[34] Carey characterized Westway as a "planning and ecological disaster."[35] When having to appeal to the broadest popular electorates at the city and state level, both Koch and Carey saw strong opposition to Westway as the sound campaign stance.

But once in leadership roles, they flip-flopped and became Westway champions. Koch, who served as mayor from 1977 to 1989, presided over the city during most of Westway's critical battles. He conceded that this was a project driven by federal and state dollars. Without federal dollars, the city "couldn't afford it."[36] In their belated Westway support, they joined past executive branch leaders, including past New York governors and mayors, three presidents of the United States, and New York's two United States senators.[37]

Mayor Koch's reversal from ardent and vocal Westway opponent to supporter was essential for Westway to be built. If New York City's leadership did not want Westway, it had no future; federal highway funds are not forced on unwilling states and cities. But Koch did become a Westway champion, a shift driven by his different constituencies, institutional roles, and consideration of powerful private-sector constituents' priorities. A substantial part of the constituency he had served as a congressman resided just east of Westway's planned site. Many residents feared years of construction disruption and massive changes to their neighborhood. Representative Koch opposed Westway on grounds that residents in the Village continued to assert for many years. As a mayoral candidate he maintained that view.

But once elected mayor, Koch was confronted with executive responsibility for all of New York City. He had to focus not just on his Greenwich Village congressional constituents but on millions of other city residents. In Koch's words, he "had only one goal and that was to help the city. If I didn't get reelected, fuck it. I'll always make a living. But I want[ed] to be a great mayor which could be done by saving this city. Whatever it took, I was in."[38] That goal of "saving the city," however, did not necessarily mean he should support Westway. Competing uses for Westway dollars remained a legal option, but that did not make those other uses equally attractive politically. Like all municipal leaders, he faced a near imperative to foster economic vitality, growth in jobs, and ever-increasing tax revenues to finance growth and provide key municipal services.[39] And because New York City was just emerging from a fiscal crisis and real estate downturn when Koch became mayor, he and his administration focused on ways to foster growth and provide tangible signs of city growth and vitality. Private and government investments were critical to New York City's fiscal health. But Koch's own explanation also reveals a focus on particular constituents' desires.

Koch recalled that New York's governor, the banks, most unions, and business leaders like David Rockefeller "importuned" him as a new mayor to reconsider his Westway opposition, and he did just that.[40] Supporters and opponents prepared clashing analyses about net benefits of Westway or the trade-in. Perhaps the most detailed critique was an internal analysis by a Tri-State Regional Planning Commission staffer. This commission was, at the time, the designated official transportation planning agency for the New York metropolitan area. That staffer, George Haikalis, concluded that Westway offered "minuscule" benefits. Other "cut-rate facelifts" would yield more park and provide mass transit improvements to the "noisy, dirty, and unnecessarily grisly subway system."[41] A few months later, however, the Tri-State Commission produced a report favoring Westway but with analysis that was ridiculed by Westway opponents and found mystifying by the comptroller general of the United States.[42] Koch also had to consider that Governor Carey was now unyielding in wanting Westway. Koch, like any New York City mayor, regularly had to seek favorable treatment, or at least cooperation, from the governor and state. Koch's own internal study also questioned whether New York City would really see trade-in dollars if it abandoned Westway. Koch therefore shifted his focus to extracting state-level commitments to hold city mass transit fares steady for four years. If Carey would agree, Koch would join in supporting Westway.[43] Carey agreed, although he soon reneged.

To explain his embrace of Westway and his reversal of views, Koch focused on the nature of New York's economy and a major source of its wealth:

> Some cities have gold mines, other cities have car plants, other cities have steel mills. New York City's main contribution in term of generating jobs is development. Development is very important to New York City. It is an industry for us. So while I am not for irresponsible development and I am not for uncontrolled development, I am for development.[44]

For Koch, Westway's real estate development and construction benefits trumped allegedly uncertain trade-in dollars and the modest political embarrassment of his highly visible reversal to become a Westway supporter.

Koch continued to vacillate at times, especially after Governor Carey imposed a subway fare hike on New York City, breaking his earlier commitment. Mayor Koch publicly declared that his prior commitment was under reconsideration. He mailed a questionnaire to dozens of influential city leaders to elicit their views on Westway. This was in part a strategic move to extract new state support, but dozens of responses followed, revealing both Westway support and, along with many other indicators, substantial opposition among the city's business, civic, and governmental leadership.

After the mayor's office received responses, Deputy Mayor Robert F. Wagner Jr. provided Koch with a lengthy, frank, and fair-minded appraisal of Westway versus the trade-in option. Wagner's memorandum, like the many responses to Koch's solicitation, confirmed that opposition to Westway was by no means a marginal position. That memorandum conceded risks that Westway would not truly be a free gift for New York City, and it called acceptance of the trade-in for mass transit "preferable" and a "fairly clear" choice since "the city's survival depends on the survival of its mass transit system."[45] It also, however, cataloged benefits of Westway and called Westway and the trade-in option "acceptable" alternatives, with both offering benefits.[46] Westway was better as "a development strategy." It acknowledged that the trade-in option had thus far been a reliable option for other jurisdictions, but it still viewed the trade-in as less certain than highway dollars. Notably, this frank memorandum's slight preference for the trade-in option was written before subsequent revelations of air and water impact concerns; with only New York City's interests in the balance, and on the basis of extensive responsive letters and memoranda, the city's deputy mayor saw the trade-in as the better alternative. Koch sent the memorandum to Carey, stating that he too leaned in favor of the trade-in option.

But after this period of wavering, on July 30, 1981, Mayor Koch and Governor Carey signed a new written state-city agreement about Westway. That agreement's terms shifted many of the cost risks of Westway to the state and increased the city's control of resulting development; whether it would have been enforceable or resulted in state payments to the city after any future breach of commitments was far from clear.[47] Koch ultimately remained a Westway champion. Neither he nor other New York City mayors felt they could refuse Westway's construction and the thousands of jobs it would create, the creation of almost a hundred acres of land for government disposition and likely new real estate development, and eventually enhanced values for land adjacent to a new park. The 90 percent highway funding by the federal government, always touted as paid to completion even if there were cost increases, and 10 percent by the state remained the crucial factors. Despite the new Koch-Carey agreement, critics never stopped questioning whether Koch and other leaders were adequately considering infrastructure and maintenance costs and the risk that an excessively costly highway project might lead to a federal funding cutoff, perhaps in midconstruction. But by 1981, many of those risks were now assumed by the state.

The Westway project had ample federal dollars and united supportive government leadership, at least in the executive branches. Federal dollars would create a bonanza of benefits for the city and private firms and companies that would profit from Westway's financing, legal work, and construction. But competing mass transit uses for those dollars, air pollution impacts at the edge of planning and measurement capacity, and unexpected fishery impacts, combined with newly empowered citizens who maintained their steadfast opposition, quickly derailed Westway's momentum. Regulatory, judicial, and ultimately legislative hurdles awaited.

5

SEARCHING FOR WESTWAY'S ACHILLES' HEEL: AIR POLLUTION?

F ROM THE TIME of their preliminary designs in the early 1970s, Westway's planners were fearful of bureaucratic foot-dragging and inertia. They hoped to avoid a lengthy regulatory war. Although they shunned the heavy-handed strategies and road-dominated focus of Robert Moses, they also sought to streamline and coordinate their actions and reviews. Early commentators actually praised Westway project director Bridwell's openness to public input and his "commitment to community participation and interaction."[1] But as the opposition's motivations and concerns crystallized, most of the 1970s hearings only served to highlight Westway's fundamental dividing lines—support or opposition, highway, development, and park versus mass transit. A *New Yorker* essay captured the fractious nature of these hearings. At a "state hearing room in Two World Trade Center, all hell is breaking loose. Environmentalists insulting construction workers. Construction workers heckling public officials. Three hearing officers . . . huddle in bewilderment . . . as a speaker, ignored by everybody but the official reporter, drones on."[2]

New York City's serpentine land-approval process allowed for local review of Westway. Although community board hearings were at times heated and opposition forces clearly persistent, early on Westway was dealt no major blows. A massive 1975 report was issued jointly by community boards 2, 7, and 9, which were known collectively as Combo and represented the neighborhoods adjacent to Westway's planned footprint. Combo's chairman

Figure 5.1. The Westway opponents' lead lawyer for a decade was Al Butzel. Prior to his work in opposition to Westway, he assisted efforts to defeat the Con Edison Storm King project. In this image he is speaking at a 1982 conference discussing the Storm King battles. *(Source: Courtesy of Albert K. Butzel; photographer unknown.)*

was Robert Kagan, father of Supreme Court Justice Elena Kagan. Combo, Kagan, and their consultants stated their objections to Westway and called for scaled-back transportation improvements. They quoted author Robert Caro's observation that the highway projects of Robert Moses did not alleviate congestion but would attract "more automobiles onto them, thus forcing the building of more highways—which would generate more traffic and become congested in their turn, in an inexorably widening gyre."[3] They predicted the same for Westway and reported many flaws in Westway's initial 1974 Draft EIS.

A never-ending venue for argument was in the realm of politics and public opinion. Supporters and opponents clashed again and again over the basic merits of Westway. Would it be New York's greatest new park since Riverside Park? Or was it a disguised highway motivated solely by patronage and potential profit? The highway versus mass transit trade-in choice was always part of the equation. Month after month, and ultimately over several years, questions about the reliability of federal monetary support were raised by both project supporters and opponents. Supporters called highway funds a sure thing but questioned whether trade-in dollars would actually materialize. They stated concerns with a Congress that might balk at a massive trade-in for New York City and therefore refuse to make the necessary appropriations. Opponents, in contrast, kept track of the many successful trade-ins but highlighted dwindling interstate highway funds. When the Federal Highway Administration deducted $327 million of Westway funding, with most of that deduction attributed to project land slated for private development, opponents seized upon similar future risks as Westway's costs rose.[4] They also highlighted costs to build and maintain new infrastructure that would be associated with Westway's highway, park, and new developable land.

Opponents tested Westway and its supporters to discover whether the project might have a fatal legal vulnerability, an Achilles' heel. One opponent early on called for someone to find Westway's "own little snail darter," referring to the fish that, for a time, stopped the midriver dam in *TVA v. Hill*.[5] No one on either side was initially sure if such a fatal weakness existed, but the regulatory, litigation, political, and legislative battlegrounds ended up akin to a lengthy war in which weaknesses were revealed and exploited, remedial fixes made, and counterattacks rolled out over roughly a decade.

BOTH SUPPORTERS and opponents turned their initial focus to Westway's air impacts. The air pollution links were the most obvious project risks. First, any new highway will change traffic patterns and resulting pollution. Because New York City already suffered from serious air pollution problems, no one could ignore Westway's potential effects. Second, with the trade-in choice of highway or mass transit now explicitly recognized in federal law, advocates could in proceedings for air permits compare the more benign effects of mass transit expenditures and investment in Westway's highway. Third, New York State and City had under the recently enacted Clean Air Act committed to a federally required and approved plan, referred to as a State Implementation Plan (SIP), designed to bring New York into compliance with federal National Ambient Air Quality Standards. These standards, referred to as NAAQS, were then and remain now nationally set minimum levels of air cleanliness. NAAQS are set for a handful of the most ubiquitous sorts of air pollutants emitted by numerous sources. They basically set the level of air quality to which all Americans are entitled. Areas with more degraded air—called nonattainment areas—are subject to more stringent requirements. In states' implementation plans, state air regions come up with strategies to maintain or reduce levels of pollution. What nonattaining areas cannot do, however, is grant a permit for a source or project that will cause a worsening of air quality unless equal or greater pollution reductions are secured.

An early air pollution attack was filed in 1974 by attorney William Hoppen on behalf of Action for Rational Transit and the Council of Commuter Organizations, along with numerous other groups. This early challenge focused on claimed inadequacies in the SIP and on EPA's scrutiny of New York's SIP. The groups sought a judicial order compelling greater consideration of the trade-in option or greater support for mass transit. This first attack was an early version of what subsequently in the 1990s came to be known as an environmental justice (or racism) argument, looking at the distributional impacts of Westway if built. This attack sat dormant for several years after a few hearings but ultimately was dismissed on several grounds. Because air-permitting deliberations had not yet occurred before state and federal agencies, the time for judicial challenge had not arrived. The claim was not yet ripe, and another legal actor—the state Department of Environmental Conservation, or DEC— had jurisdiction to make this initial determination under the Clean Air Act's delegated program structures.[6]

Butzel and his clients opposing Westway focused instead on the Westway air permit application, participating as opponents in hearings before the New York State DEC. The Clean Air Act utilizes a form of "cooperative federalism" that seeks to enlist states in carrying out federal tasks. Under the Clean Air Act, states are presumptively "delegated" responsibility for preparing their air quality regions' SIPs. The federal government can perform this planning role if states do not fulfill their planning or enforcement duties. However, given the many local trade-offs in deciding how to reduce pollution, New York and other states then and still today have jealously fought to keep those decisions for themselves. And EPA, which would have to step in if a state did not do its work, has always been reluctant to do implementation planning for a state. Not only can states retain their planning role, but they can also even more broadly take over other federal Clean Air Act programs and tasks. Hence, New York's DEC was performing a role that was required by federal and state law. These state hearings were similar in form to a trial, with witnesses, lawyers, introduced documents, and an administrative law judge controlling the hearing and making the initial posthearing decision.

Whatever DEC decided would not, however, be the final word. Under the Clean Air Act, EPA retains both a participant role and a sort of appellate reviewing role. It can either participate in and comment on state permitting proceedings or, more commonly, review and reject a permit that a state chooses to grant. And both state and federal regulatory decisions can eventually wind their way into state or federal courts.

Air permit applications can and have been denied, but since one source of air pollution can generally be balanced with decreases by other polluters, the Clean Air Act seldom results in an outright permit denial. The Act is thus an unlikely project killer. It generally is a "right to pollute" statute, controlling but not prohibiting pollution. Either the polluter seeking a permit or the local jurisdiction can secure necessary offsetting pollution. But if a state is not meeting federal ambient standards, then the challenges for a new source of pollution become tougher. New York City was at the time struggling with failures to attain several federal ambient air standards. If Westway would unavoidably increase air pollution, it might face a permit denial. Without such a permit, it could not be built.

Given the huge stakes, Westway's and the city's and state's leadership closely watched these proceedings. They paid millions of dollars for attorneys' and consultants' fees to protect the project. Robert Abrams, by this time New York State's attorney general, had earlier in his political career explicitly opposed Westway, so he viewed himself as facing a legal conflict of interest and hence unable to represent the state. He therefore stuck with the decision of the previous state attorney general, Louis Lefkowitz, to have the state and project represented by a private law firm. One of New York's preeminent law firms, Cravath Swaine & Moore, represented them in the air proceedings.

Fritz Schwarz was the lead attorney from Cravath, assisted at times by Richard Hirsch, Catherine Raymond, and even on some filings by later famed litigator David Boies.[7] Schwarz, a descendant of the founder of the famous toy store FAO Schwarz, had just returned from a stint in the federal government as the chief counsel of the U. S. Senate Church Committee, investigating alleged abuses and illegality by U. S. intelligence agencies. Throughout Schwarz's career, he juggled public- and private-sector work, maintaining a sterling reputation for integrity and dignity. He later served as board chair of the Natural Resources Defense Council and as New York City's "Corporation Counsel," the top lawyer for New York City, from 1982 to 1986. His steady hand and willingness to guide his own client proved critical in the lengthy air battles. City, state, and federal political leaders also kept up their advocacy and, when necessary, sought to change regulatory personnel to improve Westway's prospects.

As Benstock, Al Butzel, and their opposition allies litigated in the air permit proceeding during 1977 and 1978, attorneys from EPA, especially Walter Mugdan, often sat at the opposition's counsel table and joined challenges to the lawfulness of a Westway air permit.[8] Under New York City's SIP, the city had to adopt enforceable strategies to protect air quality. Among the measures in the SIP at the time was an "indirect source permit" program. New York State would have to determine that permitting Westway would not exacerbate the city's air pollution woes. Westway was considered an indirect source of air pollution because it could attract new cars and pollution to the area, thereby potentially contributing to city nonattainment of federal ambient air quality standards.

This challenge largely turned on whether easier transportation flows on Westway's larger highway would bring an increased number of cars and pollution into New York City and the areas around Westway or just move existing traffic more easily and thereby reduce pollution. A related issue was whether various traffic choke points and points of exit from the Westway tunnel would cause violations of federal clean air standards, especially for carbon monoxide. Carbon monoxide creates severe localized risks. Project proponents conceded it would bring many thousands of new cars onto the highway itself. They claimed, however, that with improved traffic flow, ventilation systems, and the tunnel construction, the project would either be air-quality neutral or improve the air. In addition, Westway supporters argued that limited access to Westway would prevent pollution increases.

The opponents and their lawyers, relying on both their own investigations and the strong analysis of traffic and air impacts by Dan Gutman (who eventually served as a consultant to EPA), claimed that the project would induce traffic, increasing the numbers of cars in the city and increasing use of Manhattan parking lots. Butzel, his wife, Benstock, and Gabel themselves walked Manhattan's streets, tallying available parking spaces to show errors in the project's data and air pollution claims.[9] They argued that drivers and pollution would shift to Westway, causing localized air deterioration. Gutman showed flaws in the data relied upon by Westway's supporters. Air pollution expert Brian Ketcham also assisted opponents during the hearings. If opponents were correct in these assertions, Westway could add to city congestion and degrade the air, especially along the Lower West Side.

ASSISTANCE FOR WESTWAY'S challengers came first from two unexpected sources, one from a top federal regulator, the other from a permit proceeding concession. As the permit application was pending before the state, the regional director of EPA, Eckhardt Beck, stated that he disapproved of Westway.[10] In that view, he was aligned with the views his attorneys were advocating in the ongoing permit proceeding and that were reflected in most EPA staff analyses. And though he was not at that moment deciding on a permit, Beck would soon have an official, timely role to play since EPA oversees state SIP planning and compliance. His statement was thus only an indicator of his sentiments, but, given EPA's critical upcoming roles, it appeared to presage future EPA challenges to any state permit grant.

Beck's unrequested and unrequired statement left state and local officials livid. Governor Carey, in particular, sought Beck's removal and in one of Westway's memorable insults, called him a "lunkhead." Beck, getting into the spirit of the exchange, retorted that he would "rather be a lunkhead than a convict." He explained that no matter the strong feelings over Westway, he had to stand ready to be "sure that all the environmental laws and regulations are fully met," and that its "sponsors . . . [must] show that the project will not harm a crucial aquatic resource, the Hudson, and will not prevent New York City from achieving the clean-air standards needed to protect public health. They have not yet done so."[11] Despite Carey's calls for Beck's removal, EPA's top administrator, Douglas Costle, initially said he would not interfere with the regional administrator's judgments. Environmental opponents of Westway seized on this unexpected opportunity, manufacturing green buttons sporting the words "Lunkheads for New York."

The second unexpected assistance came from the state itself. During the air permit proceedings before the appointed administrative law judges, the state conceded that it had the burden to establish that Westway could be built and New York City could still fulfill its obligations to improve the air. This was not necessarily wrong, but it also was not a clearly established legal issue. Butzel viewed this as creating a critical and serendipitous advantage for the opponents.[12] This meant that the onus was on the state to deal with technical and scientific uncertainties to establish its right to a permit. Uncertainty thus became the opponents' ally, rather than giving the project and state latitude for judgment that challengers would have to overcome.

The DEC's staff had made a preliminary determination that Westway's permit should be granted, but because of the substantial public interest and controversy over Westway, the DEC commissioner, Peter Berle, determined that a public hearing was necessary. Westway's air permit proceedings ultimately ended up before three different administrative hearing officers, all appointed by New York's DEC, who would have to sort through the many contested factual claims and counterclaims about Westway's air impacts. Dozens of days of hearings and thousands of pages of exhibits and transcripts explored issues over several years, often at the limits of science and human prediction.

The first administrative law judge appointed to resolve air permit questions was Columbia law professor (and later dean) Albert J. Rosenthal. With the consent of the parties and to avoid later duplicative hearings, two sorts of hearings were held. General hearings open to the public and presided over by other hearing officers were held during April and May of 1977. These hearings allowed comment on any aspects of Westway. Rosenthal himself presided over "panel" hearings focused on more technical and legal questions of air impacts and requirements of state and federal law for an indirect source like Westway. These hearings included both questions and issues identified in advance and what Rosenthal characterized later as "arguments and rebuttals [that] flowed back and forth among panels of opponents, proponents, and members of the DEC staff."[13]

These hearings were finished by June, but then a decision had to further await an authoritative DEC interpretation of what materials were relevant to this permit decision. In one of the well-established quirks of regulatory law, even though the state and project sought the permit and were in fact litigants before the administrative law judge, the judge's role was institutionally viewed as within the DEC's regulatory hierarchy. The permit application decision was ultimately one for the state agency. Although Rosenthal had been appointed as an administrative law judge to resolve relevant disputed questions of law and fact, authoritative DEC interpretations of underlying laws and regulations were binding on Rosenthal.

The DEC, by a letter from Region 2 attorney Jack Lipkin, advised Rosenthal in July about how to measure the world with and without Westway, or what was called the "no-build alternative." This issue was a critical one. It determined what was the baseline or status quo air situation, which in turn influenced assessment of degradation that could be caused by Westway. The DEC also addressed the thornier question of how to consider the trade-in option in assessing air impacts and permit alternatives. Lipkin's letter tiptoed carefully. The trade-in was not to be considered in assessing the impacts of the no-build alternative. The DEC did not, however, preclude consideration of the trade-in option, stating that "the Department does not object to a consideration of the air quality impacts of the Interstate Transfer, insofar as such impacts are ascertainable." In other words, consideration of the trade-in option was not required by federal or state law, but the state permitted Rosenthal to consider it. Rosenthal thus ended up assessing the relative impacts of Westway (the so-called modified outboard plan), the no-build alternative, and a modest replacement plan referred to as the "modified arterial." And the trade-in option's impacts were also factored into the analysis. Rosenthal was clear, however, that his task was not to assess the "desirability of the project" overall or to assess anything other than air impacts and compliance with legal requirements.

Had the state and project, collectively referred to as the "applicant" by Rosenthal, carried their conceded burden to establish that Westway would not degrade air quality, as needed for their indirect source air permit? Rosenthal's answer was no. This setback stunned Westway's supporters. Rosenthal acknowledged that permit proceedings are predictive and hence necessarily conjectural, but he repeatedly found that the permit applicant had offered "ingenious" calculations that "lack[ed] credibility." Statistical analyses and causal tracing of road uses and impacts were not persuasive. He cited studies showing the "tendency of traffic to fill up underutilized roads" and commented that the vastly more expensive Westway plan surely was expected to produce something more substantial "than a mere cost saving of at most five to ten minutes per trip."

More problematic for the applicant, Rosenthal caught tensions between arguments about Westway's growth-inducing benefits and claims of its benign air effects. He cited as especially problematic Westway advocates' promise that Westway would act as a "catalyst" for new "esthetic [and] commercial revival of the lower West Side," while the applicant's air permit calculations predicted only trivial differences between the alternative road plans under consideration. He looked for consistency but found it wanting. Either planners should assume and calculate Westway would do little or should factor in catalyzed growth. "The notion than an extra billion dollars would have so little consequence seems inherently incredible," he stated.

Halfway into his opinion, Rosenthal turned to the interstate transfer trade-in option. He conceded that the impacts of redirection of hundreds of millions of dollars to mass transit were hard to predict with certainty. Nevertheless, he stated that "it seems fairly clear that in the absence of such funding the transit system will continue to worsen." The Westway applicants' technical reports under review, however, "reflected no effects whatever" from a possible exercise of the trade-in option. They argued that without Westway, there would be no trade-in. Rosenthal, however, said that he had to assess the application "as of the present time," and by 1977 a trade-in option was legally and politically a definite option. He said that if traffic constraints and transit improvement were both pursued, they could yield "dramatically more impressive results than either in isolation." Exact predictions were impossible, but he found the permit application and underlying data fatally flawed. Instead of struggling with such calculations, the applicant had, in Rosenthal's words, come to the "conclusion that since the effects of Interstate Transfer cannot be precisely quantified they must be treated as zero." Uncertainty was one thing, but ignoring complexity and trade-in benefits would not do.

He identified two other flaws in the application. In its earlier-prepared Clean Air Act SIP, New York had committed to traffic control and transit improvements. New York had stated that "[e]very priority must therefore be given to modernizing and upgrading the existing facility" and to reversing the "decline in transit ridership." However, the state as Westway applicant was asking, "in effect, that the premises of the State Implementation Plan previously issued by this Department are to be treated as invalid." In effect, New York State had in legal documents taken dramatically different positions, calling transit improvements critical in the SIP but in Westway advocacy barely noting transit improvements that could be financed by traded-in Westway dollars. The applicant had not justified such inconsistency or explained why transit was no longer a priority. Finally, he addressed other air impacts, especially

carbon monoxide pollution. There too, he found the applicant had not established that new violations would not occur, especially at "access streets, exit
ramps, or ventilator towers." The applicant had failed to carry its burden of
proof for both carbon monoxide and other pollutants.

Because Rosenthal was acting as a hearing officer for the state DEC, not
EPA, he was not bound by EPA's views in opposition to the permit, but they
were "entitled to great respect" and legitimately viewed as "persuasive." Deference to EPA views did not mean Rosenthal had to agree with them. Still,
showing deference to EPA meant allowing the agency's views to be given special weight. With deference to an expert agency, the scale can and usually
does tip, as EPA's opposition views appeared to do here.

Summing up, Rosenthal concluded that the applicant had not carried its
burden, that EPA's views supported that view, and that it was "more probable
than not" that a trade-in alternative (which would have included building of
the more modest modified arterial) would improve or arrest deterioration of
the New York City mass transit system. The trade-in hence would result in
fewer vehicle miles traveled than under the Westway plan. A contrary conclusion would also contradict the state's legally binding and federally approved
SIP. He therefore recommended denial of the air permit.

FURY OVER THIS DECISION was immediate and public. Bridwell characterized the ruling as having "many errors" and predicted a reversal by Commissioner Berle. The *New York Times* in an editorial criticized Rosenthal's
manipulation of uncertainty: "Since no one can draw firm conclusions about
traffic and pollution, all that is ultimately proved is that the city's figures can
be knocked into a cocked hat–along with everyone else's. That seems hardly
enough to justify justify killing Westway, which is meant to offer a great deal
more than just a road—with the right safeguards."[14]

While public and political disagreements over Westway swirled, especially during the mayoral campaign, the DEC reviewed the Rosenthal recommendation. Governor Carey, who hierarchically stood over the clashing state
Department of Transportation (which sought the air permit) and the DEC
(which had so far denied it), publicly questioned the need for yet more studies
of Westway impacts. Carey was criticized for seeming to push for an outcome
while regulators had to carry out their legal roles. He later stated through
intermediaries that he was not trying to "'coach' the Commissioner," who
he knew had to review the report under binding state and federal law.[15]
Unlike the *New York Times* editorial page, Carey understood that the Westway battles were not just about political choices but about political choices
that had to surmount legal hurdles under federal law. But by getting involved

and expressing his views, he undoubtedly increased pressure on Berle, who served at Carey's pleasure. Berle was also, however, known as a true environmentalist and was a past law partner of the lead Westway opposition lawyer, Al Butzel. How Berle would decide was anyone's guess.

In December, to the consternation of federal, state, and city leadership, as well as Bridwell and project personnel and other Westway supporters, Commissioner Berle upheld Rosenthal's recommended denial of the state permit. He too found that New York State's Department of Transportation, the permit applicant, had come up short, failing to carry its legal burden.

Much as a child will strategically choose a parent to elicit the desired answer, or litigants will seek court locales where judges or juries are believed to be sympathetic, political and regulatory stakeholders can venue shop. And where that decision maker is a political appointee, his or her outright removal is possible. As Governor Carey and EPA regional administrator Beck clashed, federal leadership serving under President Jimmy Carter in Washington intervened. The secretary of the Department of Transportation, Brock Adams, wrote EPA administrator Costle, criticizing Beck as trying to override "a cabinet level decision . . . of which the President was fully informed."[16] "It seems to me that moving from agency to agency compounds the complaint of Federal delay and red tape." He also wrote to the chair of the federal Council on Environmental Quality, or CEQ. The CEQ is a smaller but powerful environmental council housed within the White House. It serves in many important roles, chief among them resolving environmental clashes among agencies and overseeing how agencies should comply with NEPA.

In his missive to the then CEQ chair, Charles (Chuck) Warren, Adams noted the broad leadership support for Westway over two administrations, pointing out that both he and his predecessor at the Transportation Department, William T. Coleman Jr., had signed off on Westway. He closed, "If Westway is not to be built, we should have reached this decision as a unified Federal position nearly two years ago. If it is to be approved, then we should not have some regional director in New York saying that his judgment overrides that of other Federal agencies and the Governor."[17]

Adams thus viewed Westway approvals as fundamentally a political choice, unconstrained by the edicts of environmental laws. In this, his views were legally wrong but consistent with a persistent strain of argument that often appears in high-stakes environmental battles, especially where economic and environmental interests clash. If Westway was the result of executive branch leaders' choices at all levels, should ordinary legal hurdles stand in the way? Adams thought not, a viewed shared vocally by other Westway supporters. Others vehemently responded to Adams. State and federal legislators wrote to President Carter, calling for him to allow agency officials to follow the law.[18] They also voiced their opposition to Westway. Fourteen members of the city council did the same, challenging Adams's assertion that opposition was "narrowly based."[19] Under the law, these critics were right: Westway could escape this sequence of difficult regulatory hurdles only if some overarching Westway-specific federal, state, and city laws were enacted. Such exemptions were extraordinarily unlikely. In a regulatory war like that fought over Westway, law shapes choices in the political domain.

But even without such project-specific exemptions, substitution of new sympathetic decision makers could make a decisive difference. *New York Times* op-ed writer John Oakes criticized political leaders who sought removal of officials who had had "the guts to blow the whistle on Westway."[20] In Oakes's view, Carey had reconsidered his Westway opposition after he was elected governor and after "Carey's principal financial and political backers (including some of the biggest real estate developers and construction unions around) helped convince him that New York's multi-billion-dollar transit needs must take second place to a super-extravagant superhighway." Federal leaders responded to Carey in a joint letter, denying that there had been federal delays and stating that all awaited New York's air permit decision.

In this setting of political hardball and with billions in potential benefits and patronage at stake, both federal and state leaders acted. If the law was a hindrance, at least new decision makers might utilize their discretionary latitude to grant Westway project applications. Beck was reassigned to Washington in what was characterized as a promotion and replaced by Chuck Warren as the regional administrator. Berle was forced to resign and he too was replaced with an official hoped to be more friendly to Westway, Robert Flacke.

But the Westway project still had to respond to the DEC rejection, even if ultimately more sympathetic decision makers stood ready to act. New York went back to the drawing board, running new analyses and seeking to address logical gaps found fatal by Rosenthal and Berle. During this phase, Bridwell, his staff, and elected superiors pushed hard for a rapid resolution. Their attorney, Fritz Schwarz, played a critical sort of legal role that is often inadequately appreciated. He did not just acquiesce in his clients' wishes or initial commands, nor did he ramp up the litigation team for battle. Instead, he resisted his clients' entreaties, including direct calls by Governor Carey seeking rapid action.[21] Schwarz shifted into a counseling role, explaining how pushing hard for short-term success could lead to longer-term problems and even to Westway's defeat. He refused to proceed until uncertainties had been better resolved. He offered to resign his counsel role if his clients disagreed. The project and Governor Carey backed off, acquiescing to Schwarz's more deliberate strategy.

Following Schwarz's advice, the project slowed things down, checking their work more carefully and seeking hearing delays when data errors surfaced. State transportation commissioner Hennessy conceded that problems needed to be addressed: "It would affect the credibility of our presentation if it came up during the hearing."[22] Federal judge Griesa, who saw Schwarz's work in later phases of Westway, noted in a recent interview how Schwarz did well by challenging his own clients. In Griesa's words, Schwarz served in an important role when he "raised them up."[23] As Griesa's several later opinions revealed, he did not observe such forthrightness in all of Westway's advocates. Schwarz's approach proved wise, although blunt political actions changing Westway's decision makers surely also helped Westway's prospects.

At this point, after a second hearing officer, Columbia Law School professor Curtis Berger, had resigned, a third hearing officer, former appellate judge John Marsh, had taken over. During this second round of early 1979 hearings, the Westway applicant was essentially allowed another bite at the regulatory apple. This was not unusual but the regulatory norm. Regulatory or judicial rejection of a regulatory application seldom is the death knell for an applicant; applicants can seek to address factual or legal infirmities. Under Schwarz's guidance, the project's analysis and planning became stronger.

This time Westway met with success. The permit application included additional data as well as modest project revisions to address carbon monoxide concerns. The earlier hearings had established that at tunnel entrance and exit points carbon monoxide could concentrate and cause violations of federal law. The new project changes amounted to little more than restricting citizen access to polluted areas through plantings near Westway tunnels. The solution—called the "briar patch" strategy by Westway's litigators at the time—succeeded in getting Westway's air pollution exposure risks below problematic levels.[24]

Opponents kept up their arguments, but they had lost this round. They could no longer convincingly point to errors and inconsistencies. Most important, they could not point to discrete violations of environmental legal requirements. Hearing officer Marsh recommended that the state grant the permit.

One other concurrent air skirmish was also resolved in Westway's favor. Although the federal Department of Transportation supported Westway, and Vice President Walter Mondale in a speech indicated White House support, EPA's regional office identified a legal infirmity. New regional administrator Chuck Warren publicly questioned whether New York could turn down desperately needed Westway trade-in dollars for mass transit and still comply with new requirements derived from 1977 amendments to the Clean Air Act. New York City, under this new amendment, had to meet "Basic Transportation Needs" as "expeditiously as is practicable" under its State Implementation

Plan.[25] Warren had quickly proved himself no more manageable regarding Westway than was his predecessor, Eckardt Beck. If New York's SIP was inadequate, then the main Clean Air Act sanction was a freeze on federal highway funds. And, as every New York official knew, federal highway funds were slated to pay for 90 percent of Westway. These questions, raised on the eve of the presidential election, provoked vocal objections from Governor Carey and threats by Senator Moynihan and representatives in the House to modify the law to take away such EPA authority.

The Carter White House intervened following pro-Westway communications from David Rockefeller, although memoranda to President Carter advised him not to get involved directly, lest his actions be "perceived as an effort to compromise EPA's statutory independence."[26] Instead, the heads of DOT and EPA in Washington worked out their transportation planning roles in a new "formula" that "'cut[] the legs out from under E.P.A. in New York,'" as one official stated.[27] But when Warren and the EPA Region 2 office persisted in raising this concern, the White House intervened again, with staff expressing hope for favorable decisions in support of Westway. If that was not possible, "a final decision on this matter should be postponed until after November," thus appearing to call for political delay on Westway until after election day.[28] Another memorandum to White House chief domestic policy adviser Stu Eisenstat reviewed the conflict and recommended that White House staff leadership tell Warren that "the Administration wants conditional approval of the SIP and expedited review of the Westway environmental problems." The memorandum said this situation was "significantly damaging the President among important groups in New York State." A scribbled note, apparently initially by Eisenstat, said that the situation had "heavy political overtones."[29] An October visit to New York City by Republican presidential opponent Ronald Reagan, which included explicit statements of support for Westway while he was surrounded by workers in hard hats, surely added to Carter White House electoral concerns.

Later that month, on October 31, 1980, the new state environmental commissioner, Robert Flacke, granted the Westway air permit. Butzel decided not to appeal the permit up the judicial ladder. The underlying law and regulations were unchanged, but design modifications to address air violations, acceptance of delay where necessary to address infirmities, and personnel changes did the trick.

Tentative objections by EPA's regional office regarding the air permit and "basic transportation needs" also had been quelled. Neither the region nor the EPA administrator took any action adverse to Westway. Westway's proponents had won this round over Westway's air impacts. But time had passed, and the opposition's focus was sharpening.

6

WESTWAY'S FILL AND AMERICA'S PROTECTED WATERS

D URING 1978 TO 1980, while the Clean Air Act challenge was under way, Westway partisans scrutinized other regulatory requirements, especially those related to water impacts. The main two requirements were imposed by the analytical mandates of the National Environmental Policy Act and the Clean Water Act's provisions broadly prohibiting discharge of fill in waters of the United States, including the Hudson River.

The Army Corps of Engineers and the Federal Highway Administration, the agency that was the crucial conduit for federal highway funding, had to comply with NEPA and analyze impacts associated with Westway. The Corps was legally responsible for water-related impacts, while highway-related analysis was the obligation of the FHWA. They both proceeded largely to adopt a privately prepared EIS, written and published in its initial draft in 1974 and finalized in 1977 under the project's supervision. While the Corps's link to the project was the forthcoming Section 404 permit application needed for Westway's huge filling operation in the Hudson, its Environmental Impact Statement under NEPA had to look at the full array of direct and indirect effects of the project, alternatives and their impacts, and resulting cumulative harms.[1]

Opponents were unified in their opposition to Westway but differed in their motivations. The preference for mass transit over a highway was a broadly shared view, and air pollution concerns were identified by almost all opponents. A few opponents, however, had a near exclusive focus on protecting the Hudson River. Hudson-focused opposition groups included the Hudson River Sloop Clearwater, founded by Pete Seeger and headed by John Mylod, and the Hudson River Fishermen's Association, headed by Robert Boyle. Marcy Benstock's many press releases and sustained advocacy had a persistent transit orientation—she called the trade-in advocacy a "rallying cry"— but she bridles at the accusation that the fish did not matter to her or her group.[2] She remained active throughout the water battles and quickly developed great facility with Section 404's protective requirements and prohibitions.[3] Even without revelation of substantial fishery threats, river advocates like Boyle and Mylod would have opposed Westway's aquatic habitat destruction; they also agreed that mass transit should be favored over highways. But they questioned claims that Westway's aquatic impacts on the Hudson would be benign. What started as intuitive doubts soon became well-grounded skepticism and environmental concern.

Westway's supporters, in contrast, repeatedly questioned whether Westway really could matter, especially to water resources like Hudson River fisheries. They doubted that human activity could imperil nature's seemingly limitless bounty and capacity for resilience. The nation's newly strengthened environmental laws had followed crisis events such as major oil spills, burning and grossly polluted rivers, and air pollution that made many of the nation's cities smoggy and soot-laden. These well-publicized realities did not shake Westway supporters' dismissal of environmental concerns as a makeweight issue. Whether the proposed Westway interpier areas were a dead zone or teeming with life, surely a few hundred acres off of Manhattan could not really matter. Incremental harms to the environment seemed invisible, or at least seemed dwarfed by more obvious, immediate, localized benefits. Similar dismissals of environmental risks remain ubiquitous, whether over climate change, permits for offshore oil drilling, clearing of one more forest, or lopping off of another mountaintop to mine coal. Legislators, regulators, and courts remain embroiled in clashes over whether there really is need to protect wetlands from pollution and filling for small or large developments. Few people thought that killing of ubiquitous passenger pigeons could ever make a dent in their numbers, let alone lead to their extinction. And protection of natural habitat that is of uncertain value, especially in an urban environment, may seem irrational. In Westway's case, could a polluted river's edge next to Manhattan's skyscraper canyons and pavement really be worthy of protection, especially when measured against a multibillion-dollar project? Proponents of Westway thought not. Regardless of partisans' motivations and views, federal law required close analysis of Westway's fishery impacts, especially harms to striped bass. These laws and linked impacts soon became the focus of regulatory and judicial controversy.

THE PARTICULARS OF NEPA and the CWA became central to Westway's future. The language of NEPA, which was enacted in 1970, reflects strong environmental aspirations: it opens by "recognizing the profound impact of man's activity on the interrelations of all components of the natural environment," stating that it is the "continuing responsibility of the federal government to use all practicable means" so to "create and maintain conditions under which man and nature can exist in productive harmony."[4] Its key operative provisions "authorize[] and direct[] that, to the fullest extent possible," all laws and regulations shall be interpreted to further such environmental goals." It specifies one of the key means to such goals, namely, preparation of environmental analyses and impact statements, as well as consultation between agencies reviewing or proposing a project and expert federal environmental and natural resource agencies.[5] Regulations flesh out these requirements. One of those important regulations required that if a decision had to be made in a setting of scientific uncertainty, a deciding agency had to undertake "worst case" analysis.[6] NEPA's ringing, aspirational language is like a Magna Carta requiring federal actors to protect the environment.

But NEPA's broad language was not matched by detailed mandates to translate those aspirations into concrete actions. That shortcoming was amplified in many Supreme Court decisions that since its earliest days narrowed NEPA's reach. By the time Westway's water battles were raging, NEPA required nothing more than full and forthright public disclosure of the proposal, alternatives to the proposal, effects of the proposal and its alternatives, cumulative impacts of the project and other sources of environmental harm, and discussion of mitigation measures that could be adopted. In cases involving other environmental disputes under NEPA, the Court had made abundantly clear that while NEPA has substantive goals of protecting the environment, its means to that end are purely procedural.[7] Under NEPA, with full and forthright analysis, a project could proceed even if it would cause avoidable but not illegal environmental destruction.

In contrast to NEPA, which was now an informational and procedural hurdle, the Clean Water Act had a substantive kick that could block projects. The statute, which was amended into its modern, greatly strengthened form in 1972 and again in 1977, has an explicit goal of protecting the "chemical, physical, and biological integrity of the Nation's waters."[8] Many contemporary Section 404 battles involve environments in the regulatory gray area between water and land. Not Westway. No one debated that Westway was subject to federal protection under the Clean Water Act. It would require dredging and filling on a massive scale in the Hudson River, a protected "water of the United States," for 4.2 miles, extending at times close to a thousand feet into the river. Manhattan's Lower West Side shorefront of operational and crumbling piers would be replaced with sand, concrete, a highway, tunnel, pilings, and a park.

In contrast to judicial interpretations that had been shrinking NEPA since 1970, Section 404's regulations, as amended in 1980, matched the section's protective presumptions. No filling in waters is allowed unless the underlying project is "water-dependent," meaning that no upland alternative could fulfill a project's essential goals.[9] Even if a project is water-dependent and hence gets past Section 404's first roadblock, it cannot be built if it will cause "significant degradation" to important aquatic habitat.[10] Prohibited degradation includes harms to "aquatic ecosystem diversity, productivity, and stability," and includes "loss of fish and wildlife habitat." Only if such harms can be undone or counteracted by "mitigation" efforts can an initially harmful project subject to Section 404 proceed. And, in an important additional protective presumption, a Section 404 permit must be denied if a fill permit applicant cannot address uncertainties about impacts and give the Army Corps grounds to make a "reasonable judgment" that no prohibited harms will occur.[11] With only small exceptions, the contours of these protections have remained constant now for decades, regardless of the party controlling the White House. As concluded in a later internal Army Corps memorandum prepared as advice for Westway deliberations, these various regulatory requirements created a "guilty until innocent" philosophy, requiring the discharger to establish that no unacceptable adverse impacts would occur.[12]

NEPA thus served as a vehicle to get information out into the open and required analysis tailored to address Section 404's protections, but on its own it mandated nothing in the way of outcomes. In contrast, significantly harmful water impacts, projects that did not have to be in the water, and uncertain impacts all could trigger the Water Act's powerful antifill mandates and protective presumptions of Section 404. The law tilted all presumptions against a massive filling project like Westway. Westway was in the midst of a battle that involved more than mere disclosure and procedural mandates. It faced a major substantive hurdle. However, as usual, application of these substantive and protective mandates in a permit setting by a reviewing agency are subject to deference by a later reviewing court.

The Army Corps of Engineers was the point player for these Section 404 requirements, required to seek comments from other expert agencies and the public and then decide whether to grant or deny the permit. The Fish and Wildlife Service and National Marine Fisheries Service had to assess the importance of estuarine fishery resources and comment on the risks posed by Westway. Regulations mandated that the action agencies had to give "great weight" to their expert views, although later in Westway's battles that language was slightly weakened. If the Corps and these natural resource agencies clashed, they could "elevate" interagency disagreements over a regulatory action within the executive branch. The Council on Environmental Quality, within the White House, would resolve any such clashes.

The Environmental Protection Agency was not the permitting agency under Section 404, but it also had commenting authority. Under Section 404(c), however, EPA also has an unusual and rarely exercised power: if it believes a project permitted by the Army Corps would cause significant environmental harm to aquatic resources, it has the power to reject the conclusions of that otherwise coequal agency. Under this statutorily granted power, after opportunity for citizen notice and comment regarding the veto option, EPA can "prohibit" such fill if it "will have an unacceptable adverse effect on municipal water supplies, shellfish beds and fishery areas (including spawning and breeding areas), wildlife or recreational areas." Thus EPA was not just in a reactive role but could undertake its own regulatory review and prevent "unacceptable" harm to important aquatic resources.

Westway's players thus were battling over far more than just a few lines of the Clean Water Act or a simple yes or no on a permit. Several layers of law as well as different agencies and actors were involved. Their different cultures and areas of focus meant each would look at Westway and its massive river filling through a different political, scientific, and legal lens. Each was a decision maker subject to advocacy by supporters and opponents of Westway.

Underlying scientific reality limited the options of Westway's supporters, but Bridwell and allied city and state leaders had three basic options. Under the first option, Westway's proponents could admit that the project did not need to be in the river or that as planned it would cause significant degradation to important habitat. Either concession, however, would have doomed Westway in its modified outboard form. A concession of Section 404 legal barriers would create two alternative strategic paths. Under one, the trade-in option could then be utilized, funding a more modest upland road and mass transit improvements. A second path would claim project water dependence and even acknowledge the importance of the area and project risks but then develop mitigation strategies that would undo enough of the harms so a permit could be granted. Large-scale mitigation efforts undoing harms of the fill would be a long shot, however; it would be difficult to replicate the ecological functions of the little-understood Manhattan edge of the Hudson. Still, mitigation of fill harms is another way to avoid the roadblock created by Section 404.

If the supporters did not want to surrender Westway despite a concession of significant fishery impacts that could not be mitigated or due to the arguable existence of an upland alternative, the second option to avoid Westway's

demise would be a congressional rescue. This might occur through an appropriations rider or a freestanding law that trumped otherwise applicable laws
and authorized the project. Westway was sufficiently debatable on the merits to make such a specific enactment unlikely. Still, there was a precedent.
Placement of World Trade Center excavation fill in the Hudson, which created land on which Battery Park City now sits, circumvented otherwise legal
restrictions due to federal legislative changes that declared that site no longer
a protected navigable water.[13] The Trade Center and Battery Park fill, however, also benefited from planning and initiation of site work that preceded
Section 404's current strong protections. Despite that important difference,
perhaps Westway could gain a similar congressional exemption.

A third option was to concede nothing. The responsible agencies and
project would first declare the project water-dependent. They then would
need to assess the science and regulatory requirements. If they could credibly
claim that Westway was benign or the threatened river habitat unimportant,
Westway could overcome Section 404's regulatory hurdles.

These were not, however, three equally tenable options. Depending on
what water surveys and analysis revealed, fishery impacts could pose a genuine challenge. The Clean Water Act's Section 404, with its antifill presumptions and protective prohibitions, had the potential to be the critical legal
barrier to Westway.

7

THE PUBLIC FISH STORY

WESTWAY'S CHAMPIONS decided to go for it all. They repeatedly claimed in key public documents that Westway's mix of highway, park, and redevelopment goals required it to be in the river. They also asserted that it posed no risk to Hudson River aquatic habitat, mainly because the habitat was a "biological wasteland."

The 1974 Draft EIS was the first essential public environmental document about Westway that touched on fishery impacts. The Draft started the multistep process of disclosure and analysis required by NEPA. A draft is not some unimportant or unofficial document; it is the responsible agency's official data and analysis about an action's impacts. The fact that an agency issues a draft rather than a "finding of no significant impact" means that the agency acknowledges at least the likelihood or probability of environmental harms that may be significant. Other agencies and the public can review and comment on that draft. After that comment phase, the agency reassesses its analysis, responds to comments, and prepares the final EIS. Again, at that point, comments can be filed. Unless changed yet again, that final EIS forms the critical basis for the agency's decision whether to proceed with a project under the Army Corps's "public interest" review. This component of the Corps's review predates the enactment of NEPA and the 1972 Clean Water Act amendments. In its modern form, public interest review involves assessment of whether a project subject to the Corps's oversight is, assessed in light of overall impacts and in light of NEPA goals and Section 404 protections, in the public interest. In the case of Westway, the impact statement and public interest review would also tie into the decision whether to grant the Section 404 dredge-and-fill permit. The Section 404 review process would formally begin after the issuance of the Final EIS, but the EIS documentation would itself be crucial in providing underlying facts and analysis relevant to most of both the NEPA and Section 404 requirements.

The position of the Army Corps and the project, as set forth in the public EIS documents, was stated without equivocation: there would be no fishery harms. If anything, the aquatic environment would benefit. The Draft EIS had been privately prepared for the project by Sydec, the company whose principal, Lowell Bridwell, was at that point managing the Westway project. Regardless of the actual author, legally these views were imputed to the Army Corps and the Federal Highway Administration.

The 1974 Draft EIS discussion of fishery impacts was direct and short.[1] Westway would cause no adverse impacts. The area was too polluted and degraded. The text's conclusions were accompanied by pictures of garbage-laden, oily water sitting stagnant between piers that would be replaced by Westway. The Westway area was subject to rapid and "violent" environmental changes that made it a difficult environment except for "rather unique resident organisms which can tolerate rapid and severe fluctuations in salinity."

Figure 7.1. This photograph of polluted Hudson interpier waters was accompanied by 1977 descriptions of the area's polluted state and claims that the area was biologically impoverished and a wasteland that was devoid of life. Actual data and subsequent challenges revealed the falsity of this description. *(Source: 1977 Final Environmental Impact Statement; United States Army Corps of Engineers; Federal Highway Administration; New York State Department of Transportation.)*

The inshore and interpier area thus "consists of a relatively few species of fish and invertebrates, and a large microbiological population associated with decomposition of organic wastes." An accompanying schematic showed no reference to fish other than tomcods. The water quality discussion emphasized the garbage, oils, and fecal matter that periodically "rise[] to the surface in a 'boil,' and spread[] out over the surface of the basins." As for recreational enjoyment of the Hudson, the Draft stated that "[m]ere contact with the water would be hazardous for a person, [and] swallowing some of it would cause serious medical consequences."

EPA and the federal natural resource agencies criticized the Draft as lacking an adequate basis: it was "deficient such that an opinion as to the project's impact . . . cannot be rendered." The U.S. Department of Commerce similarly commented that the impact on marine resources "is not thoroughly explored and we are unable to provide additional input" without more information regarding "potential impact on aquatic resources." A comment letter from James T. B. Tripp of the Environmental Defense Fund reviewed the Clean Water Act's new protective mandates and called for permit denial.[2] As Westway planning and air battles continued, the phase between the Draft and Final EIS stretched out.

The Final EIS emerged in 1977. The earlier questions and comments about fishery impacts elicited even stronger denials in the book-length comments and responses on the Draft EIS, issued along with the 1977 Final EIS. In response to critical questions and comments from New York State's Department of Environmental Conservation, the project (for the federal agencies) stated the following: "The interpier areas appear to be almost devoid of macro-organisms and we therefore consider the fill of the interpier basins will cause a minimum loss of marine productivity for other than micro-organisms." The inshore area was characterized as "biologically impoverished" and as having "little impact on the overall Hudson River estuary productivity and even less on the New York Bight and other oceanic components or marine ecosystems." Basically, as described by the Final EIS, Westway landfill in the Hudson could not matter because biologically the proposed Westway site was a virtual dead zone. These conclusions were said to be based on field monitoring, consultations with many experts "who have studied the river," and an extensive literature search.

An accompanying technical report was both more equivocal in places and similarly strong in others in denying fishery impacts. In language that the EIS itself did not acknowledge, the technical report conceded that surveys found some fish in the interpier areas, with larger numbers in the northern reaches of what would be the Westway landfill. It also stated that in the interpier areas "the full cycle of biological food chain exists." Despite these concessions, it, too, concluded by characterizing the Westway interpier areas as a "biological wasteland."[3]

The decision to proceed with Westway and give little weight to fish impacts in the key public 1974 and 1977 EIS documents was quite consistent with common views of the Hudson at that time. No one wanted to fall into the Hudson during the 1970s and early 1980s. It was heavily polluted, especially after heavy rains that at times overwhelmed New York City's sewage systems and resulted in untreated effluent and street waste discharging directly into the river. All along the Hudson, towns and cities added their own pollution, and the sediments in the area had long been contaminated with metals and other pollutants from the city's heyday as an industrial center. North of the city, well upriver, sediments were severely contaminated with highly toxic PCBs, now attributed primarily to a General Electric facility in Hudson Falls. Shipping itself was not benign, and pollution from ships' fueling and maintenance had further left polluted sediments in the area that could be stirred up with tidal movements, storms, or dredging and filling. Opponents' claims that Westway would dredge up toxic sludge were not far-fetched. And apart from lower-income residents who sometimes fished for their own dining tables, city residents almost never thought of the Hudson as a habitat yielding fish of importance. Due to pollution concerns, some types of fishing were in fact banned.

Federal natural resource scientists, especially those at agencies like the Fish and Wildlife Service, the National Marine Fisheries Service, and EPA, viewed the Hudson through a completely different lens. The river was a critical estuary for a wide array of aquatic resources. Prior to Westway-related studies, little was known about the Westway interpier areas in comparison with other portions of the estuary or the larger eastern seaboard fishery of which the Hudson was a part. Despite that lack of precise knowledge, these scientists knew that the Hudson remained an important, functioning estuary. The issue of Hudson River fisheries had been given a substantial airing several years earlier in the famous Storm King and power plant fishery impact battles, both of which had involved attorney Butzel.[4] Those conflicts had confirmed that, despite its polluted state, at least farther north, the Hudson was still a vital fishery.

Although EPA regional administrator Beck voiced his concerns with Westway's fishery impacts before his strategic reassignment to Washington, the issue had been lurking well before then. In the public Westway documents, however, especially the Draft and Final EIS, Westway's importance to aquatic habitat and fish was denied. The habitat was "biologically impoverished," "devoid" of fish, and a "wasteland," and its destruction was of no consequence. Slowly a far different reality emerged. Some 1977 and 1978

criticisms and comments were made public in political venues or in comments on the Final EIS or in opposition to the proposed Section 404 permit
for Westway. A great deal more, which is recounted below, however, remained
unrevealed to the public until federal court trials and subsequent state and
federal investigations several years later.[5] This period was filled with strategic
moves that proved critical to Westway's future.

STRENGTHENED FINAL EIS DENIALS of fishery impacts triggered even
stronger critical comments from the federal natural resource agencies. Certitude about the supposed lack of impacts was characterized as unfounded. A
fundamental division grew between the federal natural resources agencies—
EPA, FWS, and NMFS—on one side, and the Army Corps and Federal Highway Administration on the other. Subsequent investigations revealed an almost
willful failure of the FHWA and Army Corps to look at fishery impacts. During
this phase, the Highway Administration proved to be more a Westway advocate than neutral follower of the law. Its own senior ecologist, Charles DesJar-
dins, was never consulted prior to release of the 1974 Draft Impact Statement.
He later "had problems" with it and raised questions, but none of his superiors
asked for a formal review.

In response to the Final EIS, EPA publicly reiterated its concerns, submit-
ting an official letter of objection to transportation secretary Adams. EPA
called for more investigation before "irreversible and irretrievable" resource
commitments were made at the Westway site. Only four days letter, Adams
said no: there was "no reason to change the decision" of federal leadership to
support the project. All three of the federal natural resource agencies then
submitted public letters calling for the Army Corps to deny the Section 404
landfill permit. These agencies stated that Westway flunked two of Section
404 requirements—it did not need to be in the water, and due to impact
uncertainties that an applicant needed to overcome, the permit could not be
approved.

Instead of responding itself to the agencies' 1977 objections—objections
that under binding regulations had to be given "great weight" by the Army
Corps—the Corps forwarded the objections to the Westway project's managers for comment. By doing this, the Army Corps, the agency charged with
protecting America's waters and assessing impacts of proposed fill, instead
farmed out its key NEPA roles to the applicant whose proposed actions had
to be scrutinized. In mid-May of 1978, it received the project's response,
coordinated for the state by Bridwell and Sydec. The project reiterated its
views that Westway posed no risks to Hudson River fishery resources. The
response went on to malign EPA's objections, stating that "review of the EPA

submission indicates that it is fundamentally biased and prejudged [*sic*], and that [EPA's comments] contain[] sufficient inaccuracies, misinterpretations and misrepresentations to render the Regional Administrator's conclusions meaningless." These were not the Army Corps's words but were written for the Corps. They hardly reflected the giving of "great weight" to the views of expert natural resource agencies.

Nevertheless, in late May, the Corps forwarded the project's response without comment or change to the three federal natural resource agencies, prompting another round of official criticisms and persistent agency objections. NMFS disputed the claim that the Westway area was "typical" estuary habitat, stating that the Final Impact Statement's own technical report acknowledged that the "full cycle of [the] biological food chain" exists in the Westway interpier area. Far from being typical, the area should be viewed as "somewhat unique" and "a useful and supportive portion of the lower Hudson ecosystem." And EPA's August 1978 letter was even more pointed, criticizing the project for just choosing to "restate its existing data in a more emphatic manner rather than to perform the necessary additional research." EPA also referenced additional Hudson River fishery studies undertaken between the Draft and Final EIS that suggested that the "interpier areas" could "provide a relatively protected area for fish seeking forage and shelter." EPA reiterated its view that the project could not be built in "conformance with the Section 404(b) guidelines" that created strongly protective presumptions and mandates against fill. Regional administrator Beck still recommended permit denial. Environmentalists echoed these concerns, with the Environmental Defense Fund similarly characterizing the fishery assessment as inaccurate and out of date and the Final EIS in need of supplementation.

The Army Corps and Federal Highway Administration continued to stick to their view that the existing analysis was adequate, the project area of no aquatic significance, and the project deserving of a permit. In a critical step, however, a high-level meeting was held at the Army Corps's New York office in December of 1978 to discuss the persistent natural resource agencies' objections. Senior officials of the regional office of EPA, the FHWA, and the Army Corps attended, as did New York State's commissioner of the Department of Transportation, William Hennessy.

Hennessy criticized EPA for its perceived opposition to Westway, but EPA's criticisms were heard. Hennessy broke ranks and declined just to stonewall EPA and the other federal natural resource agencies. He agreed to undertake more fishery studies. The reasons for Hennessy's agreement remain murky. He may have realized that data were needed to refute concerns about fishery impacts, or perhaps he thought more study was needed to come up with mitigation strategies to allow a Section 404 permit despite aquatic harms. He later testified that EPA threatened to oppose other state DOT projects unless the studies were done, but EPA representatives denied any such pressure. Regardless of the actual motives, the state agreed to fund a study to gather additional fishery data.

THIS LATE 1978 AGREEMENT to undertake more fisheries investigation created confusion and a legally unsettled period. Because little information actually supported the EIS claims about Westway's lack of aquatic risks, any new surveys could provide crucial missing information. The reliability of that data, however, depended on the rigor and duration of the new studies. Longer and more rigorous investigation would reveal more, but Westway's champions worried about delay.

The project's staff scrambled to start testing but also sought to limit its scope. Ecologists and natural resource experts favored at least a year's study, but the project sought to limit the study to six months.[6] The earlier water quality report had identified the winter as potentially when the site would be of greatest importance as shelter, but deliberations stretched into the winter without testing getting under way. The FHWA even considered skipping any winter testing under a theory that "little activity takes place then," despite the inconsistency with its own earlier EIS documentation and contrary expert views. EPA and the other agencies objected to missing the winter months. Bridwell in turn accused them of engaging in "counterproductive stalling tactics." This time, despite its concerns that any inadequate fishery study would lead to challenges in court, EPA backed down, accepting a study that was planned to cover only the eight months of April through November. The FWS persisted in its view that the project was not water-dependent and thus should not be permitted, and it also argued that winter sampling was needed. Despite these views, the Lawler, Matusky and Skelly engineering firm (known as LMS) was tapped for the fishery sampling and analysis.

Despite general, though not unanimous, agreement on undertaking a new fishery study, the Army Corps's district engineer, Colonel Clark Benn, repeatedly advocated going ahead and granting the permit. He persisted in this view even while the LMS study was under way. Army Corps staff disagreed with Benn's view, joining earlier criticisms of the Final EIS as having "little useful information on the biotic community." The new fish studies continued without any permit decision.

The LMS study's early results did not provide the reassurance desired by Westway's champions. Early sampling found fish in the Westway interpier area, contradicting the EIS claims that the area was biologically impoverished and a wasteland. New York State's Department of Transportation agreed to extend the testing through the winter in light of the preliminary results. The project held data back from the Army Corps due to concerns that the data would become publicly available under the federal Freedom of Information Act. But in May of 1980, after the sampling was finished and data existed regarding the critical winter months, the project provided the Corps with a "progress report." That report, however, covered only April to November, omitting data from the winter months.

Even those preliminary, partial data and the progress report clearly contradicted the impact statement claims. The Corps's own scientist, Robert Pierce, concluded that this partial report revealed that the interpier area was actually "a viable estuarine environment with diversity and abundance trends as expected for this type of salinity regime." The Corps's planning division chief concluded the data could justify a permit denial but recommended waiting for the full study results. EPA more emphatically pointed out contradictions between the EIS and the preliminary results. Those early results already revealed that the area was utilized by many Hudson River fish species, in part as a "fish spawning and nursery area."

The project, State Department of Transportation, and Federal Highway Administration were not blind to the import of these results. Project planners and the Highway Administration had received word from the Army Corps that a permit grant would be "more defensible and greatly strengthened" if project planners developed mitigation plans to offset anticipated harms. They started exploring mitigation strategies that, if viable, would allow a permit grant by counteracting harms associated with Westway construction. If the water impacts could not be mitigated, the CWA basically mandated a Section 404 permit denial. Even in the face of these problems, however, project manager Bridwell told planners to think about mitigation strategies but with "no basic change" to the Westway design.

THIS LAST ROUND of communications and deliberations about the new fish study data was still unrevealed to the public. Despite all the interagency conflict and discussion, as well as the new data, the only public official statements about Westway's fishery impacts continued to be the EIS language about the area's being biologically impoverished and the accompanying report calling it a wasteland. Internally, however, the troubling data's significance was understood.

Internal August 20, 1980, meeting notes kept by Highway Administration ecologists and water engineers characterized the studies as already establishing that the proposed Westway site "provides habitat as an overwintering nursery area for several fish species," including "striped bass . . . rather extensively." Building Westway as planned could lead to "potential loss" that could "be significant in terms of direct population losses" and cause "adverse effects on the level of future stocks . . . for the lower Hudson area."

Only in September 1980 were the full LMS results summarized and shared in a meeting with the Army Corps and federal natural resource agencies. The presentation included new mitigation options. The natural resource agencies again voiced their opposition, this time supported by the new data, but the point person at LMS, C. Braxton Dew, questioned the significance of any threatened harms. The August conclusions summarized in Highway Administration memos appear not to have been shared at this meeting.

A major strategic question remained for the project, state, and Army Corps: should the EIS be supplemented in light of this new information? Supplementing it would cause delay but would avoid judicial rejection under case precedents requiring courts to vacate and remand agency actions if an agency "sweeps" troubling facts under the rug. The private law firm advising the Department of Transportation, the Beveridge & Diamond firm, supplied a privileged communication containing the legally questionable conclusion that no supplementation was needed. In early October, the Highway Administration took the same position in a communication to the Army Corps, stating concerns with "cost and delay" that would "significantly delay the benefit to the future highway users and to the city of New York." Although EIS analysis is supposed to inform decision makers, the Highway Administration appeared to see Westway's construction as a foregone conclusion.

Concerns with costs, delays, and genuine regulatory hurdles further shaped Army Corps deliberations over Westway and the fish impact problem. Now that fishery impacts appeared likely, the Army Corps was forced to define the fundamental nature of the Westway project and perhaps even reconsider elements of its basic design. If it was a water-dependent project, then it might surmount the first of Section 404's several hurdles. If it was really a highway project with some other tangential benefits that did not require its placement in the water, then the legal presumptions against filling with unnecessary water impacts were likely insurmountable. But serious fishery harms posed a new and potentially devastating hurdle that had not earlier been anticipated. Was this important fishery habitat threatened with "significant degradation"? Even if the answer was only a "maybe," Section 404 regulations required a permit denial.

So the Corps in late 1980 began to explicitly define Westway in a way requiring it to be in the water. In response to objection letters, the Corps asserted that "Westway is not just a highway, but an integral corridor plan that must also provide for the urban renewal of the West Side of Manhattan." Defining Westway as a highway and urban renewal project meant that alternatives meeting that mix of goals were few, if any.

In November, the Army Corps simply terminated the debate. Without the benefit of any new supplemental EIS (known as an SEIS) analysis of now irrefutable striped bass impacts, and without correction of the official but undoubtedly erroneous EIS fishery claims, the Army Corps stated its intent to grant Westway's key Section 404 permit. In a letter explaining that choice to the federal natural resource agencies, the Corps division engineer, Major General Bennett L. Lewis, stuck by the view that the Westway "area is neither critical for the fish . . . nor is it unique." Lewis concluded that the project permit was "in the public interest," "subject to revised plans incorporating on-site mitigation measures." Lewis also partially justified his decision to grant the permit by defining Westway as more than just a highway project: it "was specifically designed to stimulate the economic revitalization of the West Side of Manhattan, as well as to provide for the efficient movement of people and goods." Lewis's statement triggered a statutory period for objections by other federal agencies but appeared to be a prelude to an official Army Corps grant of the Section 404 permit.

This permit grant was legally vulnerable within the executive branch and in the courts. The fishery impacts still existed and had not been explained, and no actual mitigation plan yet existed. In addition, the Final EIS presented little information on alternatives that met the more complex profile of Westway now being used by the Army Corps to justify a permit grant. If it was a highway and redevelopment project, what sorts of alternatives were there and what would be their impacts? The EIS did not provide that information.

Anticipating elevation objections that would soon reach the desk of Corps leadership, in early December of 1980, Edward L. Rogers, the deputy assistant secretary of the army for civil works, reviewed Lewis's permit decision.[7] Rogers would be advising the army assistant secretary if the permit decision were elevated. He found the discussion of alternatives "most summary" and the decision to approve a project based on nonexistent mitigation plans irregular. The normal practice was to "work out mitigation as part of the permit-granting process, not after-the-fact." Rogers feared that this already delayed project would experience further delays in light of these irregularities.

Rogers correctly anticipated the lines of attack by the natural resource agencies. In their letters starting the process of elevating their objections up the Army Corps and executive branch hierarchy, the agencies argued that there were less harmful alternatives, especially an inboard alternative that would not involve fill and destruction of aquatic habitat. The mitigation plans were also found lacking.

A crucial development arrived in the form of a December 29, 1980, memorandum accompanying the public NMFS letter starting the elevation process within the Corps. This NMFS memorandum delved deeply into the

new fish population information Lewis had ignored. It educated all readers about fishery harms that had previously received little public attention.
NMFS pointed out that new October-to-May surveys had revealed "major
concentrations of young striped bass in the interpier areas." The substantial concentration was important because of "a marked decline" in striped
bass population "throughout its Atlantic Coast range." The letter continued
with detailed information about the substantial economic value of striped
bass-related activity, estimated at approximately $100 million a year. NMFS
pointed out that Congress had even passed a specific new law to identify
the roots of the striped bass population decline. NMFS viewed the interpier
area as providing shelter, food, and habitat for juvenile striped bass "overwintering" that was "essential for their survival" and also "critical" due to
losses of other habitat. NMFS scientists questioned whether any other habitat
existed that could similarly shelter these fish. Too much earlier habitat loss
had occurred, and the new riprap edge of Westway would not provide similar protection. NMFS's bottom line about Westway's impacts was strongly
stated: "[T]he survival of the entire Hudson River population and its substantial contribution to the Atlantic coast fisheries would be jeopardized."

Congressman Ted Weiss, the New York City representative from the
Twentieth District and longtime Westway opponent, on December 30, 1980,
wrote a letter directly to Joseph Bratton, the chief of engineers for the Corps.
The letter argued against Westway on the merits, stated a preference for a
mass transit trade-in, and emphasized Clean Water Act protections. It was
not just his letter, however. Making palpable for Bratton that New Yorkers
were not uniformly for Westway, even if its mayor and governor were, the
letter was signed by twenty-two other opponents of Westway elected to office,
many in leadership positions representing city constituencies. It included
city council president Carol Bellamy, Manhattan borough president Andrew
Stein, future mayor David Dinkins, and many others.

Within the Corps, a zoologist and ecologist for the chief of engineers, Dr.
John R. Hall III, wrote a February 4, 1981, memorandum that, like the NMFS
letter, saw great risk in Westway.[8] He called the habitat "significan[t]," mentioned the Hudson River striped bass's growing importance, and observed
that "few shoreline areas" in the area offer "similar physiographic relief which
have proven distributions of striped bass." He also said that mitigation "will
not" effectively compensate for the loss of the interpier areas. Records are
unclear regarding who within the Corps reviewed Hall's analysis.

On February 18, 1981, despite detailed objections within the Corps, from
the federal natural resource agencies, and from city politicians, the first-level
elevation-process decision maker, Major General E. R. Heiberg III, went
along with Lewis's earlier permit grant. He too emphasized Westway as a

"total package" and was untroubled that the "mitigation will be developed." He assumed that it and other "fisheries enhancement measures" would counteract the aquatic harms.

The time for the next round of elevation objections to an Army Corps permit grant had arrived. But an unexpected silence instead followed. Despite their enduring and vehement objections all the way through the process, at least during the Carter administration, the federal natural resource agencies did not continue to push their objections up the executive branch elevation ladder. Reasons for this sudden loss of fortitude were never stated. It was, however, during the early 1981 transition from the Carter to the Ronald Reagan administration, and such transitions often leave agencies in a state of flux. In addition, President Reagan had campaigned with an explicit goal of reducing regulatory burdens and was widely expected to be weaker on protection of the environment than President Carter. Whatever the reason, the anticipated next level of objection elevations did not occur.

However, one major federal Westway hurdle remained. EPA still had authority to veto the Army Corp's Section 404 permit grant under Section 404(c)'s unusual legal veto provision. EPA could veto the permit-granting judgment of another federal agency, the Army Corps, if, after notice and comment opportunities, EPA found that harms to aquatic habitat would be unacceptable. Such a veto had at that point never been exercised, recalls EPA's regional administrator at the time, Chuck Warren.[9] Warren was a holdover from the Carter administration. His concerns about Westway's air impacts had earlier provoked a flurry of Carter White House communications immediately before the election. Now Warren had before him the crucial water permit. He had thought it unlikely that senior EPA leadership would support such a veto during the waning days of the Carter administration, and he viewed White House or central EPA support as even less likely with the new administration. Nevertheless, as the regional administrator, Warren and his staff had to make that initial call, subject to oversight and possible reversal by EPA's administrator in Washington.

Memoranda were prepared for Warren that leaned both toward and against issuing a veto. At the end of March 1981, he officially declined to exercise his veto authority. He did so in an unusual way. Warren hand-endorsed a staff memo that discussed EPA options, stating that "I believe that 404(c) should be invoked on the merits of the project. However, I recognize[] that the attitude of the new Administration makes it impossible to comport [with] the law in this regard." Warren's assertion that a contrary decision was "impossible" was legally questionable, since any regulatory act rises or falls on the basis of both the law and the underlying facts; mere political leanings do not inevitably trump legal obligations and factual realities. If he had

Figure 7.2. On September 7, 1981, President Ronald Reagan presented New York leaders with an $85 million check for Westway construction, declaring that the project's approval (subsequently declared illegal) was a "victory over the inertia of bureaucracy." From left to right, Secretary of Labor Raymond Donovan (partially obscured), Governor Mario Cuomo, Mayor Ed Koch, President Ronald Reagan, Senator Daniel Patrick Moynihan (behind the others), construction worker Basil Powell, and Senator Alfonse D'Amato. *(Source: Ronald Reagan Presidential Library.)*

issued a veto, it might have been upheld within EPA and perhaps the courts if well founded under relevant facts and law. However, EPA's veto authority is phrased in terms of a permissive use of power—it "is authorized"—rather than containing language of mandate such as "shall." Due to this nuance of language, a challenge to an EPA action declining to veto a permit was difficult if not impossible to win in court. And since Warren had also ascertained that more senior EPA regulators would not back him if he issued a veto ruling, any regional veto decisions likely would have been overruled within EPA by Warren's superiors. Warren therefore declined the veto option but included his contradictory note of explanation for, in his words, "whatever good it might do."[10]

With that decision, federal agency hurdles to Westway suddenly vanished. A federal official stated, "It's all over. The last Federal obstacle to Westway has fallen."[11] The Army Corps officially issued the permit on March 11, 1981. Westway could proceed.

THREE DAYS AFTER the permit had cleared these regulatory hurdles, President Ronald Reagan met with New York City mayor Ed Koch near the planned Westway site. He praised the agency decisions and the promise of Westway progress. Reagan noted that "many of the federal financial and regulatory roadblocks" had been removed and that now the venue for action was before "state and local officials here in New York." Reagan noted that "there are differences among the various parties, but those differences are best resolved by the level of government closest to the people." He concluded that "Westway has the green light, and it's up to New York to drive through." Several months later, he presented Koch with the seemingly mandatory over-sized photo-op check, a check for $85 million to pay for land acquisitions essential for Westway to proceed.

But the Westway trade-offs and battles were far from over. It was during this period that, after Governor Carey authorized an increase in subway fares, Mayor Koch flirted with abandoning Westway in favor of the trade-in. But after several months of highly public vacillation, he decided to support Westway in light of the new city-state Westway agreement.

Marcy Benstock continued her opposition efforts, promising to continue pursuing the opponents' agenda "with budget cutters in Washington and in the Legislature in Albany."[12] She secured several supportive votes by both, as well as New York City legislative body votes against Westway, but they were either vetoed or lacked the legal power to stop the project.[13] Congressional battles and advocacy before federal agencies continued, but decisive public actions did not occur until months later. For those concerned with risks to the Hudson and fisheries, the Army Corps Section 404 permit grant did not end battles over water impacts. Citizens can object in court to unjustified regulatory decisions.

8

ENTER THE INDEPENDENT FEDERAL JUDICIARY AND THE POWER OF LAW

T HE PROCESS of regulatory politics and decision making is not insulated but porous. Information can flow freely and informally, and
government officials do not control outcomes; citizens have participatory and litigation rights, and courts end up reviewing most major regulatory
actions. While the more formal written regulatory position taking had occurred
regarding Westway aquatic impacts, far more informal communications continued among government regulators and between regulators and citizens. The
internal federal battles had gone on for several years, with Benstock and other
opponents of Westway monitoring the process as best they could.

Opponents' focus on fishery impacts increased during early 1981 due to
communications between EPA's Chuck Warren (at the time serving as the
regional administrator) and Al Butzel, who was still serving as the attorney
for Benstock's group and several other groups opposing Westway. Warren
recalls predicting that air objections would not prevail but also suggesting
to Butzel that Section 404 provided stronger grounds for judicial relief.[1] Butzel agrees, recalling that Warren drew Butzel's attention to the detailed late
1980 NMFS elevation objection letter and attachment memorandum.[2] That
memorandum explained why Westway was so risky and the fishery impacts
so significant. Butzel, Benstock and their allies soon sought and obtained
copies of other objections and talked with officials and scientists about the
fishery impacts. Slowly information came out about the internal government
and Westway project debates over striped bass risks.

Warren's tip led Butzel and a young lawyer at his firm, Michael Gerrard, to seek the expert views of Ian Fletcher, a fisheries biologist with extensive experience with Hudson River fisheries. Fletcher had worked on earlier Storm King and Hudson River power plant fish studies and had provided expert assistance to both environmentalists and the federal government. The Westway opponents provided Fletcher with the underlying data about fishery populations in the Westway interpier and other areas of the Hudson. This was the information gathered in connection with the EIS and subsequent to it at the behest of the State Department of Transportation after the federal natural resource agencies' persistent objections.

Fletcher studied the information for two hours before reappearing in Gerrard's office. He declared, "Jesus Christ, Mike, this place is crawling with fish."[3] Fletcher had deciphered the actual data, some going back to the early 1970s. He found that it established a high abundance of fish, especially striped bass, right in the so-called interpier areas where Westway was proposed for placement. Fletcher flatly disagreed with the Army Corps's still unequivocal public statements that denied fishery threats. Around the same time, a young director of the Hudson River Fishermen's Association, Peter Silverstein, also questioned the Westway impact statement's claims about fishery impacts, communicating those doubts to Bob Boyle—a *Sports Illustrated* writer, environmentalist, and later chairman of the Hudson Riverkeeper (as well as a moving force behind creation of river-keeper organizations)—and then to Al Butzel.[4] Butzel and Gerrard wrote a letter to the Army Corps criticizing the fishery claims, shortly before the Army Corps permit review process was finished. Their letter met with no greater success than did the NMFS detailed critique.

Throughout this 1981 period, Benstock kept working in political arenas, especially seeking to refute claims about Westway's benefits. She and other opponents also continued to argue to Mayor Koch and state legislators that Westway would be too expensive for the state and city and that mass transit would suffer without Westway trade-in dollars. Debate over these questions continued but with no resolution or change in the city and state choice to pursue Westway.

UNLIKE THE SHIFTING and uncertain world of politics, the courts demand clear, discrete allegations that can be tested in the judicial crucible. In May of 1981, Westway opponents packaged their various objections into a complaint and related motion papers that they filed in the United States District Court for the Southern District of New York. Action for Rational Transit (ART), an umbrella organization including many of the individuals and entities opposing Westway, focused on air and funding issues and was represented by William Hoppen. The Sierra Club, Benstock's group (the NYC Clean Air Campaign), the Hudson River Fishermen's Association, the Hudson River Sloop Clearwater, Inc., and several other named plaintiffs filed their own complaint naming the state Department of Transportation, the project and the Army Corps of Engineers as defendants. They were represented by Al Butzel as lead counsel and several more junior lawyers.

The norm in any judicial appeal from an agency action is to have that action adjudged based only on the agency's record and explanation at the time of the action. Such appeals thus tend to be mostly written critiques, where the only question is the adequacy of the agency's explanation. That adequacy is assessed against the record before the agency. In such a setting, all the odds ordinarily favor an agency, especially if it has actually gone through a full NEPA EIS process. Unlike many agencies that then and in subsequent years would try to dodge the work, delays, and costs of a full NEPA EIS by issuing a Finding of No Significant Impact, there was a full Westway EIS. The question was whether it was adequate and accurate. Westway's vulnerabilities largely hinged on the Army Corps's refusal to supplement or correct the EIS aquatic impact claims.

Under a case that was critically important then and remains so today, the *Citizens to Preserve Overton Park v. Volpe* case decided by the Supreme Court in 1971, there was one exception to the norm of record-based review.[5] If an agency's "factfinding procedures are inadequate" and the "administrative record" does not explain the agency's decision, then this well-established Supreme Court's precedent allows a district court judge to go beyond the original agency decision and record "to require some explanation." And if the decision cannot be understood from the agency's explanation and any findings, then "the court may require" that "administrative official[s] who participated in the decision . . . give testimony explaining their action." Despite the presumptions against such intrusive review, it can occur in order to ensure that there is "effective judicial review." At this point, both Clean Water Act- and NEPA-related challenges were ripe for review by the courts. Tensions between the EIS claims of no impacts, the natural resource agency objections, and the actual fishery data were stark, creating potent grounds for a judicial challenge.

All these regulatory actions and disagreements went before United States District Court judge Thomas Griesa. In early Westway hearings and decisions, Griesa showed little sympathy for the objecting plaintiff opponents and gave them no victories. Similarly, two years earlier, federal judge Richard Owen had dismissed as premature a challenge by Butzel and his clients claiming EIS inadequacy. Griesa was a former partner at a major corporate white-shoe firm, Davis, Polk and Wardwell, and an appointee of President Nixon. As noted by Fritz Schwarz, Westway attorney for New York State, Griesa was smart and fair but had a temper that could be triggered if he sensed misconduct by lawyers or the government.[6] One of the lawyers for the United States on Westway, Nicholas Gimbel, saw Judge Griesa as a moralist, an "ascetic by personal habit." Trying to describe Griesa but also get a laugh at a Westway retrospective, Gimbel said there were "overtones of Torquemada," the infamous Spanish grand inquisitor, in Griesa.[7] Gimbel was likely alluding to Griesa's renown as a judge who would often engage in his own intense direct questioning of witnesses. In this and other cases, he expected lawyers to temper their partisan zeal with respect for judicial integrity. He was known for immersion in the details and law related to his cases. A later key Army Corps decision maker stated of Griesa, "that sunuvabitch did his homework—he had to."[8] Perhaps his renowned inquisitive streak and law-and-order leanings would benefit the challengers, but no one knew. Nothing in his background indicated that he was an ardent environmentalist or antidevelopment.

At this point, the two different sets of Westway opponents pursued different strategies and relief in court. Although final state and mayoral choices about Westway had not yet occurred, steps were under way for roughly $100 million in expenditures to acquire properties needed for the project to proceed. Hoppen and his clients sought an injunction against this major step

Figure 8.1. United States District Court Judge Thomas P. Griesa, who presided over three lengthy Westway trials and numerous related hearings in his Southern District of New York courtroom, issued three decisions rejecting Army Corps of Engineers approvals of Westway. *(Source: Courtesy of the Chambers of Judge Thomas P. Griesa; photographer unknown.)*

in the Westway process. Judge Griesa was not persuaded. In a short opinion issued in July of 1981, he found that ART had failed to establish irreparable injury and had failed to show that the balance of hardships tipped in the plaintiffs' favor, as required under prevailing law.[9] The judge revealed reluctance to interfere with city and state choices and thought later relief would suffice if ART prevailed on the merits. Westway's champions won this round. Stopping a project of this magnitude was not easy.

In contrast to ART's claims, the fishery objections were timely and appeared far stronger. The law itself was stronger in NEPA's requirements of full, forthright, and honest disclosure. Even more potent, the Clean Water Act's protective presumptions against fill in waters of the United States were well tailored to favor the plaintiffs. The Westway opponents also had powerful allies in the federal natural resource agencies, allies who had provided a substantial written set of objections now in the agency record; under binding regulations, their comments had to be given "great weight" by the Army Corps and Highway Administration. The agencies had disappointed in not pursuing their objections up the executive branch ladder and in the fact that EPA had not even started a veto process, but their staff and scientist objections remained part of the regulatory record.

The Benstock-Butzel judicial attack now focused on these undisclosed fishery impacts. Their goal was to put before Judge Griesa the DEIS and FEIS and underlying documentation, as well as environmental consultants' data, memoranda, and the highly critical natural resource agencies' views. They sought to paint a convincing picture of willful inaccuracy in the FEIS and an illegal Section 404 permit grant based on the claim that the Westway area was a biological wasteland. Opponents did not have to grapple with the adequacy of nuanced analysis; the Army Corps had simply denied that fish used the area, had provided no analysis, and had ignored contrary data.

The strategic question was how to make a persuasive case before Judge Griesa. The plaintiffs had to overcome substantive presumptions of regularity favoring the defendant agencies and the procedural norm of deferential judicial review of the agency's explanation and record. The plaintiffs chose to go with an aggressive strategy. Shortly after they filed their complaint focused primarily on fishery impacts, they sent notices that they intended to take depositions of key government actors working on the Westway project. The defendants responded in kind, sending inquiries to the plaintiffs to explain the basis for their claims. The state and federal defendants also sought a knockout blow, filings motions to dismiss the plaintiffs' case.

In late September of 1981, plaintiffs filed an important but somewhat unusual motion, at least in this setting. They moved for summary judgment, despite the usual practice of deference to agencies and despite areas of remaining dispute. Usually, if there are disputed, material facts, a court will deny summary judgment motions. Perhaps, however, the judge would agree, as a matter of law based on those uncontroverted facts, that defendants had violated the law by not admitting in their EIS and Section 404 decision the reality of striped bass use and potential Westway impacts. So despite long odds, attorney Butzel thought the plaintiffs would win this motion. The motion contained lengthy affidavits of Butzel and Gerrard that laid out the fishery impact story, linking the story's key facts to attached documents.

Even if the motion were denied, it would educate Judge Griesa about the opponents' case theory. That education might help in any trial hearing. If Griesa allowed a trial with witnesses and arguments, he would be sitting "in equity." Instead of hearing a case "at law" about monetary damages, he, not a jury, would be deciding on the facts. He would have great discretion in overseeing such a hearing and in fashioning injunctive relief telling defendants what to do. Hence, whether granted or denied, the motion might help the opponents. The defendants, as was expected, filed their opposition to the opponents' motion and filed their own motions for summary judgment. In their view, the government's actions easily surmounted the threshold needed to justify the court's upholding of their actions. In the meantime, depositions of key witnesses proceeded apace.

Nicholas Gimbel and Stuart Bernstein were the assistant United States attorneys working for the federal agencies at the time of 1982 trials, with Gimbel in the lead role. They also had to run major decisions by their superiors in the high-powered United States Attorney Office for the Southern District of New York. Gimbel argued for deference, but he and his office and litigation team at this point made a hugely important strategic call. They did not oppose plaintiffs' call for a trial with witnesses, rather than doing battle just through briefs based on the underlying record. By this point the United States government lawyers had reviewed the key underlying EIS documents, objections, and exchanges among the federal agencies and Westway project. On the record alone, the federal agencies and the Westway actions were legally vulnerable. Plaintiffs hoped to use witnesses to blast apart the government's arguments, while the government hoped witnesses would buttress a paper record that, viewed by itself, was likely fatally weak. With supplementary explanation and judicial deference, perhaps its lawyers could surmount the hurdles posed by a trial and overcome problematic regulatory actions.

In December of 1981, Judge Griesa agreed that a hearing with witnesses was necessary. Implicit in his decision to hold a trial was that he needed additional explanation to understand and decide on the motions and ultimately decide whether to uphold the government actions. Since plaintiffs wanted a trial and defendants had decided that they too accepted the need for a trial, the rare circumstance of a trial to illuminate a regulatory action got under way. The fact of the trial would not itself be a source of later challenge on appeal, although arguments calling for deference to regulatory judgments would predictably remain a near constant.

THE PARTIES FILED pretrial memoranda, laying out their theories and anticipated evidence. The government memoranda emphasized deference and political judgments. The opponents emphasized the law's requirement of full and adequate disclosure, the strong presumptions and prohibitions against harmful fill in rivers like the Hudson, and the considerable evidence that the defendants had ignored the troublesome facts about fishery impacts. Court precedents called for rejection of government EIS claims upon a finding that agencies had "swept" problematic data "under the rug."[10]

A ten-day trial was held in Judge Griesa's courtroom, beginning in late January of 1982. Most of the trial involved testimony by the government officials whose names appeared on the key EIS documents and Westway project personnel, but the plaintiffs' most important witness was fishery scientist Ian Fletcher. Fletcher was an oceanographer at the University of Washington. He had also worked on striped bass studies in connection with the earlier Storm King litigation. Outside of federal natural resource agency scientists who had concluded that Westway posed significant risks to fish, Fletcher was the expert who helped opponents figure out, on the basis of various fishery studies and data, that the Westway interpier area was "crawling with fish."

Fletcher was a crucial witness for Butzel and the plaintiffs to explain the falsity of the EIS claims that the Westway site was devoid of life and a biological wasteland. He did that and more. He "told the [opponents'] story and educated the judge," in Butzel's recollection.[11] In the era before computer-assisted graphics, Fletcher and opponents' attorneys prepared several exhibits that used bar graphs to reveal actual fish capture data in the Westway areas in comparison with other areas in the Hudson River estuary. Those graphs provided an overwhelming counterweight to the EIS statements. Exhibit after exhibit focused on early 1980 capture data. A wasteland devoid of life? Not quite. In January, five Westway site areas were tested, capturing 610 young striped bass in one site alone and 668 in total. Across the river, one New Jersey site resulted in the capture of 168 bass. Of nine other sampled areas, the next most populous sampling site captured only 24 bass. Many striped bass (as well as other fish) were right where none were supposed to be, and most sampling found more striped bass in the proposed Westway site than anywhere else. No place along the east side of the Hudson came close. Subsequent months' testing continued to find a substantial and often the greatest number of striped bass where Westway would be built. Few were found when the Hudson was sampled deep midriver. Striped bass appeared to favor the river-land edge, and the Westway interpier sites were by far the areas most "crawling" with the young fish. But the government's official documents claimed the area was biologically impoverished and a wasteland.

Fletcher made another revelation that proved critical to undercut the government's credibility. Through Butzel's questions and Fletcher's answers, the plaintiffs revealed a misleading manipulation of the data. Although raw data showed that the Westway interpier areas were populated with many young striped bass, with few found anywhere else in near the same concentration, the defendants' fishery report itself averaged transects across the river. Someone working in support of the Westway project had basically used averaging of high and low capture areas. This averaging created a misleading impression that few fish were in the Westway area. The defendants' case never really recovered. Witnesses from federal natural resource agencies reiterated their objections to Westway. Through this testimony, federal agency witnesses provided crucial support for the similar conclusions of plaintiffs' fishery expert, Fletcher.

Figure 8.2. This exhibit, created for use by Westway opponents' fishery expert Ian Fletcher during a 1982 trial before Judge Thomas P. Griesa, put into stark form the inaccuracy of the claims that the Westway interpier waters were devoid of life. (*Source: National archives case materials from the Westway challenges.*)

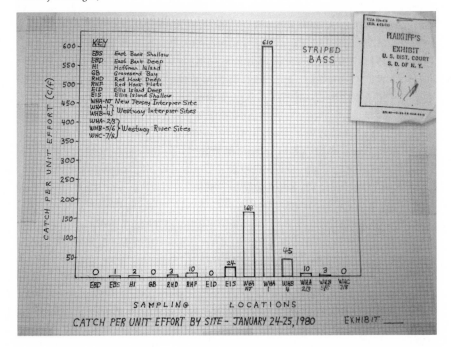

Put on the defensive by the plaintiffs' clean but powerful case, which in turn was based mostly on the defendants' own data and documents, the defendants relied on Westway project and federal agency witnesses to try to rehabilitate their case and EIS conclusions. Questioning by plaintiffs' counsel, however, punched major holes in their testimony. True to his reputation, Judge Griesa asked many questions of his own, expressing astonishment both at the small number of pro-Westway witnesses presented to explain their choices and at their failure to shed light on the disputed actions.

Just two months later, on March 31, 1982, Judge Griesa ruled.[12] All of ART's claims were dismissed. Most of the Butzel Sierra Club case opponents' claims were also dismissed, but that was not a surprise. Counting issues before the court, the defendants won on nine out of ten issues. Perhaps of greatest disappointment to the plaintiffs, the judge found the EIS discussion of project alternatives adequate.

However, on the striped bass issue that dominated the ten days of trial, Judge Griesa handed the plaintiffs a decisive victory. For the Westway project and federal defendants, the gap between EIS claims and the contrary scientific reality was simply too great to surmount. Plaintiffs had not just convinced the court that the Westway proponents had done an inadequate job. Griesa's March 1982 opinion revealed a judge who was stunned by complete failures to abide by the law and be honest with data.

Judge Griesa's opinion laid out what Section 404 of the Clean Water Act and its underlying regulations required. He emphasized that the federal government's own regulations mandated avoidance of "significant disruption" of "biological integrity of the aquatic ecosystem," especially mandating avoidance of disruption of fish spawning and nursery areas. Under binding regulations, natural resource agency views had to be given great weight. He also quoted the NEPA statutory and regulatory language emphasizing the need for full and forthright disclosure and analysis of environmental impacts. He acknowledged at length the limited latitude he had under deference principles to second-guess federal agency judgments.

Closely tracking the Fisheries Service December 1980 objection memorandum, supplemented with information gleaned at trial, Judge Griesa discussed for several pages the importance of the striped bass fishery. The trial also had educated him regarding the particular striped bass using the Westway area. Most of the bass found there were in their first two years of life, referred to as "young-of-the-year" and "yearling" fish. Fletcher's testimony and exhibits framed Griesa's factual conclusions, although he also reviewed and drew extensively on the actual data and conclusions in surveys and conclusion about the Westway site generated by the defendants' own consultants. "[T]here was a concentration" of young-of-the-year striped bass in the proposed Westway landfill area and "the concentrations . . . in these Westway and New Jersey [interpier] areas were immensely greater than in any of the other 25 locations sampled, running from the Lower Bay, south of Verrazano Bridge, as far north as Haverstraw Bay," thirty-five miles north of New York City. He stated that studies indicated that striped bass were "overwintering" in the Westway site. The bottom line was clear: the Westway site "serves as an overwintering refuge for juvenile striped bass." It was a "productive habitat" for fish, not a "biological wasteland."

Most of the rest of the opinion showed how the data flatly contradicted the EIS claims. When citizens and federal resource agencies critically commented on these claims both during the regulatory process and at trial, defendants never responded. Judge Griesa expressed puzzlement that the federal defendants did not present at trial Army Corps decision makers to explain their seemingly unjustified conclusions. The defendants relied heavily on one witness, a junior scientist named Linda Monte. She could not and did not explain away the data contradictions or alleviate Griesa's concerns. He found that "there is precious little material in the record" to explain the Corps's conclusions undercut by the actual fishery data and EIS objections.

Judge Griesa's opinion used occasional language of intentional wrongdoing by the defendants and their consultants, alluding to "manipulat[ion]" of data in a "misleading fashion," but it mainly described legal neglect. He looked askance at the Westway project's repeated refusal to provide new 1979–80 fishery data to the Army Corps out of concern about public revelation of the information. And when the data were summarized and shared, it "was done in a manner which masked the full significance of the information." The Corps remained passive, showing "no recognition of the duty . . . to make an independent evaluation of the fisheries question" and even ignoring its own biologist's conclusions about the project site.

Judge Griesa stated that "the actions of" the Army Corps "can only be explained as resulting from an almost fixed predetermination to grant the Westway landfill permit." Griesa also quoted the NMFS elevation objection memorandum at length. He focused on NMFS language that "we consider this area to be habitat essential for their survival," and "critical since suitable alternative habitats have been eliminated by development and pollution."

Summing up, Judge Griesa stated that the agencies had simply not done their legally required job. The Army Corps behavior revealed a "total failure" to comply with its legal obligations. And the question under NEPA was ultimately not whether the Westway site was critical to striped bass. Instead, honest disclosure of the truth was required, and "the fact that the proposed landfill would destroy a productive estuarine habitat for fish, including striped bass, is sufficient" to require disclosure under NEPA. The Corps "had no right to swallow up these issues, in the privacy of its bosom. It was required to make fair and open disclosure not only of the available facts, but of the responsible scientific views as to the risks involved." Because this was not done, NEPA's requirements were violated. For similar reasons, the Clean Water Act Section 404 dredge-and-fill permit lacked a "legally sufficient basis."[13]

Judge Griesa issued an injunction "setting aside the Corps of Engineers [Section 404 dredge-and-fill] permit" and remanding the issue to the agency to decide, in compliance with the law, if a permit could be issued. He left for a future date a hearing on additional terms of the injunction. The court's ruling was a resounding and project-threatening victory for the plaintiffs.

Judge Griesa was, at this point, more puzzled than angry. However, only the Army Corps had been the named federal defendant in this first trial. Plaintiffs now added the Federal Highway Administration to their complaint and sought to have any injunction cover it as well. Even though the same EIS had been relied upon by the Corps and the FHWA, and the judge had made apparent in no uncertain terms that the EIS was legally inadequate and the water permits therefore illegally issued, the FHWA made a strange request. It wanted its own trial. This was a strategically odd demand and a fateful and harmful decision for Westway. Griesa agreed to hold another trial, this time with the FHWA as the defendant.

WITH THE ADDITIONAL INFORMATION revealed at the first trial and a victory already in hand, the opponents were even more ready to reveal shortcomings in the Westway decision making. At a personal level, however, they did not relish another lengthy courtroom battle, especially given that the Butzel & Kass firm was compensated for Westway work at well below its usual market rate.[14] It was not even clear that the plaintiffs could gain anything more with another victory. It was also unclear what the FHWA thought it could gain or win, since the EIS and water permits had already been judicially rejected. And since most agencies fight to avoid trials, instead preferring to defend their decision and regulatory record, the FHWA request was doubly puzzling.

Outside the trial setting, the defendants from the first trial battled over the scope of injunctive relief and assessed how to proceed on remand. They also prepared papers for appeal to the United States Court of Appeals for the Second Circuit.

In the meantime, from mid- to late April of 1982, the FHWA had its days in court. As one of the defendants' lawyers subsequently commented, it was with that second trial that Westway's supporters really "lost the judge."

Through the trial, mysteries concerning the roots of misleading EIS and fish study language were solved but in ways deeply embarrassing to the defendants and their lawyers. Judge Griesa's puzzlement with legal shortcomings after the first trial became, by the close of the second trial, quite explicit anger over perceived dishonesty and manipulation of facts. Judges must be disinterested, but over the course of a lengthy battle they will come to know the lawyers and parties and build up confidence or, in the case of Westway, skepticism.

As was perhaps inevitable, the second Westway trial ended up illuminating and magnifying the egregious failures to disclose potentially significant aquatic impacts. After four days of trial and an additional posttrial hearing concerning potential perjury concerns, he issued a second opinion on June 30, 1982.[15] In an opinion that tracked much of his first posttrial ruling, Judge Griesa dismissed most of the plaintiffs' claims, retaining the fishery impact claims influencing the NEPA EIS documents and the Section 404 permit.

Judge Griesa did not back off of any of his earlier determinations. Instead, he added considerable detail that made the FHWA and project look particularly bad. He described conduct he viewed as reprehensible. He used findings of willful wrongdoing to justify extraordinary, unusual relief that would intrude into the defendant agencies' conduct and process when they reexamined the EIS and permit decisions. Regarding the 1977 EIS claims of no fishery impacts, Griesa stated that the initial error was the falsely certain claim of no life and hence no impacts. It was subsequent conduct that, he explained, shifted the misbehavior from unfounded false certitude to bad faith.

Much of his opinion focused on the response of the Corps, the FHWA, and project officials to the 1979 and 1980 fishery studies and resulting report by LMS. As clarified at the second trial, their story was that the LMS data were not problematic because, in the words of an FHWA witness, Graham Bailey, quoted by the judge, "'the fish had elsewhere to go.'" The defendants' story was that the LMS data created a mere "'data discrepancy'" that did not in itself reveal any problematic environmental impacts. Witnesses even claimed that the LMS report "led to the same conclusions as had been stated in the EIS—that the landfill would have little impact on the overall productivity of the Hudson estuary." The defendants relied heavily at trial on testimony of Bailey, Bridwell (the Westway project's director), and one of his main staffers, Joan Walter. In response, Judge Griesa let the defendants have it. "In connection with the three principal defense witnesses—Bailey, Bridwell and Walter—it is apparent that they have not disclosed the facts in a full and candid fashion." He found that their testimony was "characterized not only by a striking lack of plausibility on critical points, but also by a remarkable amount of inconsistency, evasion, and asserted loss of memory on matters where memory would be expected." And his opinion proceeded to be only more scathing as he explained the basis for his conclusions.

As with his first major posttrial opinion, Judge Griesa devoted considerable analysis to how the project and FHWA had withheld, selectively shared, and then manipulated new fishery data that the Army Corps awaited for its permit and EIS deliberations. These actions were not "taken in good faith" but were "designed to avoid public disclosure of a major environmental impact." The second trial also revealed details of the August 20, 1980, meeting that included LMS, the project, and the FHWA but notably excluded the Army Corps and any federal natural resource agencies.[16] Meeting participants admitted that Westway would pose a significant threat to fish populations, as revealed in two contemporaneous memoranda summarizing the meeting's discussions. The meeting discussion included the project's telling the FHWA that the Westway landfill could "'cause significant loss of fish population and subsequent adverse effects on the level of future stocks of the species in question in the lower Hudson area.'" One memorandum stated that the Westway site "'provides habitat as an overwintering nursing area . . . rather extensively . . . . The project fill would remove roughly 1/2'" of this habitat. The same memorandum continued by describing the meeting's conclusions: "It was felt that the potential loss could be significant in terms of direct population losses and subsequent adverse effects on the level of" fish in the area. The other memorandum conceded the discrepancy between the EIS and actual LMS data: "fish have been found in this area in much greater numbers than original studies indicated."

At trial, however, project witnesses Bridwell and Walter denied the memoranda's accuracy about many of Westway's claimed adverse effects on Hudson River stock of fish, testimony the judge found "entirely unconvincing." "The LMS data destroyed" the EIS theory. "It showed that the interpier area was a far more desirable habitat for fish than the main channel."

The manipulative averaging of data again led to judicial criticism, but the "seriousness of the misrepresentation has become even clearer in the second hearing." Now that Judge Griesa knew about the content of the August 1980 meeting, he was particularly incensed by the LMS report conclusion that for "the striped bass population, *the project area appears to represent one of many available habitats*" (emphasis added). This statement was actually contradicted by the survey numbers, and the FHWA and project knew the contrary reality, as reflected in the August meeting memoranda.

Much of the witnesses' evasion, as well as Judge Griesa's opinion, related to an October 9, 1980, letter by which the FHWA "formally advised the Corps of Engineers of the FHWA's view that a Supplemental Environmental

Impact Statement was not required in connection with the landfill permit application." But by the time of this letter, the FHWA was aware of the LMS report, the meeting acknowledging the troublesome import of the data, and also a letter from Butzel's firm that summarized the key new fishery data and explained why it made a supplemental EIS necessary. Nevertheless, the FHWA's letter to the Corps contained the following passage: "The more recent data, although to some degree providing better quantification . . . [and] information . . . *does not change the basic conclusion, that is, fish use the area*: the Project will have some impact on benthos, fish and other aquatic life; and therefore may have some long-term impact on the possibility of returning the 234 acres area to a more viable habitat" (emphasis added). The judge did not mince words: "This statement, and indeed the entire description relating to fisheries, was simply fraudulent." After all, the EIS and underlying materials had actually claimed that the Westway site was devoid of life and biologically impoverished; this new claim that "the basic conclusion" all along had been that "fish use the area" lacked any "conceivable justification."

While the exact author of the language was never determined, shortly after the trial but before Judge Griesa had issued his opinion, one of the state's lawyers, Gary Baise of the law firm Beveridge & Diamond, uncovered additional information. Baise went to the court and sought an opportunity to share and explain what he had found. He was concerned "as an officer of the court" about correcting an error he had in part furthered through his witnesses' testimony. As he explained in a posttrial hearing, he knew that disclosure would be revealing privileged attorney-client information, but he felt ethically obliged to do so. His clients did not want him to disclose but also did not prohibit this return to the court. Baise had found a sixteen-page memorandum from his firm to project director Bridwell. That memo contained the problematic "fish use the area" language. It appeared that the language either originated with Beveridge & Diamond or had been inserted in a memorandum by the firm in the course of providing advice. Judge Griesa found that witnesses Bridwell and Walter "knew of the obvious falsity of the letter and bear a responsibility for drafting or failing to correct it." He also could see "no justification whatever for Beveridge & Diamond setting forth a statement of facts which was so divorced from the truth."

Judge Griesa closed his opinion by concluding that "the FHWA and the Project did not act on a reasonable basis or in good faith." They did not reveal the new information not because it "was insignificant" but "because the information revealed a highly significant environmental impact which they wished to avoid disclosing." Their activities were "wholly improper" in influencing the Army Corps and in later "colluding" with the Corps in justifying the lack of a supplemental EIS. They acted in "willful derogation of the requirements of the law." Past approvals and actions were therefore "null and void." He issued a "final injunction" "since [the plaintiffs] have prevailed at trial on their claim against the FHWA."

IN SUBSEQUENT HEARINGS over the next few months, the overall issue of injunctive relief was argued and resolved. Judge Griesa did not mean to halt the Westway project but to hold physical progress in abeyance pending defendants' compliance with the law. He also, however, enjoined some of the federal monetary transfers that would fund Westway work. Because of the many improprieties, he took several unusually intrusive steps that would modify the political and regulatory process upon the government's reassessment of Westway. He appointed a special master, Lewis Kaplan, to oversee agency and project actions on remand. He also ordered the defendants to keep records of their meetings and deliberations. In addition, his ruling on injunctive relief ordered the defendants to reexamine and update all of their EIS, not just the fishery and aquatic impact sections. That, too, was unusual, since agencies on remand usually just need to address infirmities that courts have earlier found.

Despite their defeats in court based on egregious misrepresentations and failures to disclose risks as required by the law, the defendants sought a reversal in the Court of Appeals for the Second Circuit. They hoped that deference to agency judgments might allow them to prevail. That argument, however, was a long shot given the substantial trial evidence of impropriety, legal neglect, and abundant data contradicting public disclosures required by law. They had a better shot at overturning Judge Griesa's extraordinary injunctive relief. Both the intrusive special master appointment and the heightened record-keeping mandates were highly unusual. Judicial relief telling agencies procedurally how to do their work was in great tension with the Supreme Court's recent decision in the *Vermont Yankee* case.[17] In *Vermont Yankee,* the Supreme Court had come close to prohibiting judicial second-guessing of agency procedural choices. Courts could ordinarily assess only whether an agency action had an adequate substantive basis. But *Vermont Yankee* did not involve previous findings of serious agency improprieties, so how the Second Circuit would rule was hard to predict.

The Court of Appeals for the Second Circuit consolidated the ART and Sierra Club cases and initially planned to address the legal violations ruling and injunctive relief orders all together, but it subsequently broke the merits opinion and injunctive relief rulings apart. In December 1982, the court issued its first appellate ruling on the injunction against FHWA's paying for land acquired for Westway.[18] It did not question the underlying legal violations found by Judge Griesa but thought he overreached with his injunction. Westway was no longer at a standstill. Griesa's rulings had in a major way been rebuffed.

In late February 1983, the Second Circuit issued its other Westway opinion, this one on the question of the legal violations found by Judge Griesa and other extraordinary injunctive relief he had ordered.[19] This ruling was unanimous and a major loss for Westway and its champions. The Second Circuit opinion, authored by Judge Amalya Kearse, joined by Judges Thomas Meskill and James Oakes, closely tracked Griesa's review of the law and the facts. The Second Circuit upheld, with strong language, the trial court's conclusions but rejected some of Griesa's extraordinary relief. On the merits, the court agreed with Griesa's "thorough opinion." The appellate court's detailed recounting of the facts was characterized as involving facts "as to which we see no substantial dispute." The court agreed that the defendants had, in violation of NEPA's requirements, "swept under the rug" troublesome environmental impacts. Although a trial court has limited authority to review the factual conclusions of agencies under NEPA, Judge Griesa's opinions were "consonant with the proper scope of its review and the proper view of the obligations imposed on the FHWA and the Corps." Judge Griesa's findings of lack of good faith and false statements were also found "amply supported by the record." The court also agreed that "the record discloses that at every level of review the Corps simply ignored the views of sister agencies that were, by law, to be accorded 'great weight.'"

The appellate judges affirmed that the defendants had to prepare a supplemental EIS that addressed these shortcomings and also reassess the Section 404 permit decision. The court also agreed that the Corps could not farm the EIS work out to the state and project, although the FHWA did have such authority under special transportation-related statutory provisions. The court also upheld Judge Griesa's order that the defendants keep special written records in light of the "surprising dearth of evidence" explaining the initial agency decisions, the "faulty memories," and the "helter-skelter record-keeping practices." Four federal judges had now found the defendants worthy of rebuke.

Thus, on the key NEPA and Section 404 issues, the Court of Appeals upheld Judge Griesa's rulings and handed the plaintiffs a resounding victory. Two trials and now extensive appellate argument had resulted in three federal court opinions highly critical of the Westway process. All called into question whether Westway, if fully and honestly analyzed, could ever surmount legal hurdles, especially under Section 404. Three appellate judges agreed with Judge Griesa's conclusions regarding the law violations. No one dissented.

The opponents' victory was not complete, however. First, the court knocked out a Rivers and Harbors Act Section 10 claim on the basis of a Supreme Court opinion indicating citizens could not sue to enforce that law. The Second Circuit also rejected Judge Griesa's mandate that the defendants revisit the entire EIS; on remand the government defendants merely had to focus on language that had been found legally inadequate. Further supplementation remained a choice "committed to agency discretion" and hence was unreviewable by the courts. Finally, although the Second Circuit had nary a word of praise for the defendants, it questioned Griesa's emphatic "bad faith" findings leading to his appointment of a special master. The opinion stated that although the record "reflects distressing derelictions by the federal agencies, including a certain amount of bad faith by the FHWA, we believe the picture as to those agencies is not quite so unsavory as the . . . findings depict it." They saw Sydec, the Westway project manager run by Bridwell, as the main malefactor, not the FHWA. The appellate court closed with harsh criticism of the federal agency defendants: their conduct "may to a great extent be attributable to a willingness on the part of the agencies to sit back and allow others to do work entrusted to them, without bestirring themselves to develop accurate data."

THE FIRST MAJOR ROUNDS of the Westway war fought in federal court had resulted in a major victory for Westway's opponents. The question now was what the defendant agencies would do. And how would the many federal, state, and local politicians assessing Westway react? Politicians could short-circuit the Westway battles at any time by passing Westway-specific legislation. In addition, the window to trade in federal interstate highway funds was not unlimited. A change in federal law had moved the trade-in deadline to September 30, 1985; the law also called for completion of federal spending on interstate highway segments by September 30, 1990. These two deadlines put a squeeze on Westway's supporters to make quick progress and put the legal hurdles behind them.

9

REEXAMINING THE 1971–1982 DEBACLES

THE SCATHINGLY CRITICAL JUDICIAL rulings triggered hand-wringing and calls for federal and state investigations. Was Judge Griesa justified in his conclusions, or was he a trial judge who had misused his authority? A frequent claim was that he had rejected Westway due merely to what then New York governor Hugh Carey liked to call a procedural irregularity. Had the judge used his largely unreviewable power to control the courtroom and find facts to further some previously hidden anti-Westway animus? The Westway project was motivated by political benefits but had now caused a political black eye. Supporters hoped new investigations would find error or point out means for Westway to proceed. Opponents saw investigations as an opportunity to further highlight all that was wrong with the project.

Federal and state investigations quickly got under way. Unconstrained by the formalities of federal court trial procedure and benefited by dozens of interviews, hearings, and reviews of voluminous documents, investigators had an opportunity to paint an even richer picture of the Westway battles up to 1982. In addition, these political investigations could look at the ultimate question that Judge Griesa really had no jurisdiction to examine: did the Westway project make sense?

IN JULY OF 1982, shortly after Judge Griesa's second posttrial ruling, candidate for governor and then lieutenant governor Mario Cuomo asked a prominent lawyer and past corruption investigator, Thomas P. Puccio, to look into the Westway missteps. Puccio had been the chief of the Organized Crime Unit Strike Force of the United States Attorney's Office for the Eastern District of New York. He had also done special investigation and prosecutorial work in connection with the ABSCAM political corruption sting operation resulting in multiple convictions of members of Congress. As lieutenant governor and later as New York's governor, the eloquent Cuomo was a steadfast and powerful supporter of Westway. Still, the irregularities illuminated by the opponents, the federal natural resource agencies, and four federal judges were embarrassing for New York State and the subject of much press criticism. Puccio accepted Cuomo's assignment and started work on his investigation in July of 1982.

Opposition attorney Butzel wrote a thorough memorandum to Puccio that—unlike court-linked advocacy that tends to allow only constrained, focused argument—allowed him to make the overall case against Westway.[1] This memorandum wove law and more political considerations together. His politically oriented criticisms echoed many of the arguments that opponent and client Benstock and other opponents had now been making for about eight years in many dozens of public hearings, press releases, interviews, and editorials and in hundreds of meetings with city, state, and federal regulators and politicians. Butzel distilled them into a powerful package. He emphasized the strong grounds for the courts' water permit rejections but only as the third reason for rejecting Westway. He instead stressed the benefits of the trade-in over Westway, pointing out transit needs, the track record of successful trade-ins, and how trade-in funds could be used to achieve many of Westway's claimed benefits. He also questioned Westway's redevelopment rationale, pointing out that Lower West Side revitalization was well under way, even with the "overhang" and "specter" of Westway construction disturbances and the barrier that new development could create between existing real estate and the Hudson. Affordable housing was already at risk. As a project to spur development, Westway was an "anachronism." Butzel conceded that Westway appeared to "gleam with gold" and could provide some benefits; it was not all "black or white." But it was not truly "free of charge." Park and infrastructure costs would be borne by the city or state, and risks remained that Westway funding would be cut off if its costs soared. The project's immense costs would likely impair New York's future efforts to gain federal support for other capital projects. Westway might "well be more of a burden than a boon." Puccio's subsequent report revealed just how effective Butzel had been in this political advocacy.

Puccio issued his report on April 25, 1983.[2] Although he had been appointed by pro-Westway Mario Cuomo (who had just become the governor of New

York State), Puccio's report was no rubber stamp of the state's actions. Far from endorsing Westway or finding judicial overreaching, Puccio criticized the state's Westway actions and directly questioned the wisdom of the project: "[I]t has now become a luxury that New York probably cannot afford." Despite a bit of hedging, he recommended that the state trade Westway dollars in for mass transit and a simpler replacement road. He also called for "an investigation by an appropriate state or federal agency" of irregular regulatory behavior in order to "restore public confidence in the integrity of the approval process." In less guarded comments provided to *New York Times* columnist Sydney Schanberg, Puccio was more blunt: Westway, in his view, was a "real estate boondoggle. People commit perjury because big money is at stake. There are heavy interests involved here."[3]

Puccio's report examined Westway's basic merits, especially in light of New York City's changed circumstances. His logic and even several language choices echoed Butzel's arguments. Puccio, like judges who receive an effective brief, adopted language, facts, and arguments he found persuasive. He too commented that neighborhoods abutting the Westway site were already revitalizing and increasing in value. Like Butzel, Puccio characterized Westway as a "spect[er]" for neighbors that would "cut them off from the Hudson." If the real estate market heated up even more as a result of Westway, affordable rental properties might disappear. In Puccio's view (and again using language in Butzel's advocacy), Westway had become "an anachronism."

In contrast to the natural and incremental real estate rebound under way even without Westway, Puccio noted that New York's mass transit remained in financial straits yet was critical to the city's health. A trade-in was now an attractive legal option with a track record of granted requests. And a trade-in would produce improvements quickly and virtually immediately start generating jobs in numbers "equal to or even greater than could Westway." Even though unions probably viewed Westway as "gleam[ing] with gold" (also a Butzel phrase), the trade-in would also offer huge employment benefits, perhaps to a more diverse population than would the Westway project. Puccio also focused on the vaguest element of the Westway plans, the 110 acres of new land set aside for real estate development. He pointed out that even if federal dollars paid for much of the landfill and highway costs, infrastructure costs for the new development would be borne by the state and city. But Puccio was not sure whether federal dollars would keep pouring in for Westway if its costs kept rising. Even without scrutinizing regulatory irregularities and fishery risks, Westway was of questionable worth.

His report's bottom line yet again echoed Butzel's memorandum: "Westway may well be more of a burden than a boon."

Governor Cuomo and Mayor Koch, as well as New York's senators Moynihan and D'Amato, nevertheless stuck to their view that Westway was worth building, as did the *New York Times* in yet more supportive editorials. But the *Village Voice* and the *New York Times* op-ed columnist Sydney Schanberg emphasized Puccio's report in their anti-Westway columns, as did opponents in their political advocacy.

ADDITIONAL STATE and federal investigations commenced. A special State Commission of Investigation undertook a major state-level investigation, with interview and document review powers utilized extensively. Its report, issued about a year later, in June of 1984, was entitled "The Westway Environmental Approval Process: The Dilution of State Authority." Much of the report tracked and reviewed Judge Griesa's opinions, but the commission reexamined those conclusions. Its "broader inquiry" resulted in even stronger condemnation of the defendants' actions and the regulatory process than found in Griesa's rulings or the Second Circuit's opinions. Its inquiry "substantially augmented the support found in the record for nearly all of Judge Griesa's findings."

This report attributed Westway's rocky path in part to the farming out of key governmental roles to private consultants and law firms. This privatization of government functions was tantamount to a "total surrender of responsibility" and caused many of Westway's problems. The near abdication of state roles led to a state "loss of control over Westway." Similarly the judicial "debacle" was in part the result of an "atmosphere of confrontation and distrust" between, on one hand, the state transportation department and the Federal Highway Administration and, on the other hand, the federal natural resource agencies.

On the key issue of fishery impact claims and cover-ups, the state commission reexamined the primary materials and Judge Griesa's conclusions. It too found that the defendants' documents, including the 1979–80 fishery study by LMS, created a "misleading impression of available equivalent habitats" for striped bass. In interviews with the commission, LMS fishery scientist C. Braxton Dew stood by his report but conceded that some key claims were "only a theory" or "only offered as a hypothesis." On the key issue of the claim that fish had "other places to go" if Westway destroyed the interpier areas, the commission reported that Dew acknowledged that the bulk of the support "was not to be found in the LMS report itself." Dew even told the commission that the Westway project's initial fishery analysis underlying the Draft and Final EIS was "the most shoddy biological work" he had ever seen.

The commission was scathing in its criticism of Westway project director Bridwell's testimony before Judge Griesa. Like Griesa, the commission focused on the false and misleading claim that new fishery data did not "change the basic conclusion, that is, fish use the area." In reality, as Judge Griesa had concluded, the new data flatly contradicted EIS language that the Westway area was devoid of life and a biological wasteland. That language had also led to the belated and awkward revelation by Beveridge & Diamond attorney Baise that his firm had put such language in one of its memoranda. During a trial colloquy, Griesa had lambasted the defendants regarding the "fish use the area" claim: he stated that he had "sentenced people to prison for securities fraud where the conduct was less blatant than the drafting" of this misleading characterization of the LMS data.

The commission stated that before Judge Griesa, Bridwell's trial testimony was not disastrous or obviously false. Nothing was "so incredible" as to "demonstrate a lack of truthfulness." In response to pointed questions from Griesa, Bridwell had stood by the document as "true, to the best of my knowledge." Basically, for someone to conclude he had testified falsely would "require almost an admission from him to cast doubt upon his veracity."

But the commission concluded that, "[s]urprisingly, Bridwell made such admissions" when testifying in connection with his new job as head of Maryland's transportation department. He had admitted that the LMS fishery study was shaped by lawyers to "improv[e] it" to be sure it was a "defensible document." It was his "assumption" that LMS would assist (as characterized by the commission) "by presenting their findings as favorably as possible to Westway." In Maryland, he conceded he had not testified accurately in Judge Griesa's court. Was "fish use the area" truly accurate and complete? No. "I readily concede that that was not as full and proper a statement as it should have been." Was there a justification for giving false and misleading testimony? He thought the truth "'would have been an absolute bomb in terms of the State's case." He thought it necessary "[g]iven the disposition of this judge, the atmosphere of this suit, the atmosphere in the courtroom." If he had more "fully explain[ed]," "then I would have shot down our side of the case." He stated that there was "a difference of opinion and judgment about how forthcoming and candid I should have been."

That lawyers and consultants will try to spin data to their client's advantage is no surprise. Misrepresentation is something far different, and Bridwell in his Westway trial appearance had crossed the line. The New York commission did not see Bridwell's misleading Westway trial testimony as a forgivable lapse of judgment or matter of opinion. Bridwell was "wrong. The obligation to answer truthfully questions asked at trial is not a duty subject to interpretation or waivable in the presence of a 'hostile' judge." The Maryland panel had concluded that Bridwell "'did not testify with complete forthrightness' or in a 'full and candid manner.'" The New York commission said that these conclusions were "charitable."

The commission also reviewed allegations that New York State's transportation commissioner, William Hennessy, had threatened to withhold state work from engineering consultant Brian T. Ketcham and his firm, Konheim and Ketcham, if he remained a vocal and active Westway opponent. The paper record was a bit inconclusive regarding Hennessy's motive, but the commission found that the overall effect and message were clear: "[F]uture opposition to Westway would come only at the risk of foregoing government employment."

The commission stated that the reliance on private actors to fulfill government roles resulted in quasi-governmental actions and documents that were little more than "briefs of an advocate." Government agencies favoring Westway "perceived their role to be an advocate of a particular goal and a steamroller of opposition, rather than a public agency subject to law." Private and public champions of Westway had consistently assumed a "party line" on the key fishery impact issue that "must have presented to the court the appearance of a conspiracy," leading to Judge Griesa's "evident animus" toward defense witnesses. The commission was "inclined to view certain of the acts found suspicious by Judge Griesa to be as much the result of derelictions of responsibility as of intentional bad faith." Former EPA administrator Beck told the commission that "he had never seen such a blatant attempt to 'railroad' through a program, regardless of statutory obligation, as he witnessed" with Westway. The commission stated that "[a]ttempts to manipulate or delay release of the LMS information served no purpose save to spawn the litigation in which the Project is now entangled."

The commission concluded that just as prosecutors in criminal law settings have to temper a desire for victory to be sure that they do not "neglect justice, so State agencies must not pursue their agendas with a single-mindedness untempered by responsibility." Blame rested on state officials, not on the judge, citizens, or natural resource officials raising objections.

A FEDERAL INVESTIGATION was undertaken by a congressional subcommittee headed by New York City congressman Ted Weiss. Weiss remained a vocal opponent of Westway and had long participated in strategy sessions in support of opposition efforts. Earlier, in a one-on-one phone call and even in a subsequent sit-down meeting directly with then President Carter, Weiss had explained, without success, why he thought the president should abandon the project.[4] But now Ronald Reagan was president. Weiss obviously could not control his congressional colleagues' actions and questions, and the report his committee would issue had to grapple with the facts as revealed in underlying documents and old and new testimony. His Intergovernmental Relations and Human Resources Subcommittee of the Committee on Government Operations held extensive hearings over four days and obtained voluminous documents detailing Westway's history. It also received and disclosed internal federal executive branch communications that likely would have remained undisclosable internal "deliberative" documents if sought by private parties.[5]

The report was issued on November 1, 1984. Entitled "The Westway Project: A Study of Failure in Federal/State Relations," it too raised major questions about Westway but focused most on the actions of the federal agencies. Like the state report, it emphatically affirmed judicial conclusions that Westway had been pushed through the regulatory process in violation of the law and despite troubling facts that had been downplayed or misrepresented.

The report especially emphasized the prevalence in all federal agencies of concerns about significant aquatic habitat harms, especially to striped bass. The committee uncovered internal memoranda and comments within the FHWA and Army Corps that were similarly concerned about significant aquatic harms.[6] These internal critics thought that existing data were inadequate to conclude that there were no risks. This federal investigation also revealed for the first time the internal meetings at which fishery harms were frankly discussed, even by or in the company of agencies that were publicly insisting on the "no harm" story. The Corps and FHWA appeared most concerned with regulatory delay, gave heavy weight to Westway project benefits, and gave inappropriate deference to conclusions of the State Department of Transportation about these benefits. These views were really just the views of the "applicant-in-fact."

Six of the committee's thirty-eight members filed a brief dissenting statement that stressed the prominent political leaders who supported Westway, leading to their argument that Westway disputes should be resolved expeditiously. They also thought Weiss's committee had overreached its turf in its investigation and report. They did not, however, question the majority's factual conclusions.

THREE LENGTHY INVESTIGATIONS and resulting reports had all concluded that Westway's woes were not the result of a misguided trial judge, three hoodwinked federal appellate judges, or a few citizen objectors. Westway was in trouble because of the law's protections, scientific data revealing project risks, and government and government agents' missteps, misbehavior, and failures to abide by the law. These investigations all found substantial problematic scientific and regulatory barriers to Westway. No opinion or report questioned what many scientists had concluded about Westway's fishery risks: many, perhaps most, Hudson River young striped bass used the interpier areas where Westway was slated to be built. And despite barely examining fishery risks and being an appointee of pro-Westway governor Mario Cuomo, even Thomas Puccio concluded that Westway made no sense. Nevertheless, in light of the Second Circuit's ruling and ongoing support of the mayor and governor, Westway remained a possibility.

10

WESTWAY'S SECOND CHANCE

WHILE POLITICAL INVESTIGATIONS into the earlier Westway debacles proceeded, the Westway battles returned to political and agency settings. Westway's proponents had won the air
permit battles, but little else was resolved. The trade-in option remained a
source of public and press debate. Supporters and opponents continued to
dispute whether Westway was publicly beneficial, a boondoggle, or driven
by the private benefits it would generate. But the judicial rejections of essential regulatory analysis and approvals had made clear that Westway's Section
404 permit and striped bass risks were a make-or-break issue for the project.
The Second Circuit Court of Appeals had affirmed several of Judge Griesa's
key judgments but had also rejected some of his unusually final or intrusive
relief. The defendants had to revisit their EIS and Clean Water Act Section
404 decision, but no court had told them what to say or do. Consistent with
common administrative law practice, this was a remand process where the
government could correct its missteps. Agencies merely had to follow statutory and regulatory requirements, obey upheld judicial edicts (including
heightened record-keeping obligations), and work honestly with what new
analysis revealed. Nevertheless, fearing loss of momentum or possible regulatory defeat, recently elected governor Mario Cuomo and other Westway
champions tried to short-circuit the regulatory process through two different
strategic end runs. These two actions resulted in a short-term advantage but
quickly put Westway into further jeopardy.

THE FIRST and most powerful end-run gambit was through a federal legislative subterfuge reportedly instigated by Governor Cuomo. During the late 1970s and early 1980s, plummeting striped bass populations and fishery catches along the Eastern Seaboard prompted an array of political responses. Despite the rarity of legislation that truly restricts commercial and recreational fishing (as well as any other resource extraction), an alarmed Congress considered several protective laws focused on striped bass, ultimately enacting laws funding studies of the fish and, a few years later, imposing fish-catch quotas and even limited moratoria on striped bass fishing.[1]

In late October of 1983, Friends of the Earth staff working on Capitol Hill heard of yet another apparently benign piece of striped bass legislation, a short attachment to a mammoth spending bill.[2] It was a classic "appropriations rider," where within a large spending bill a focused substantive amendment proposed to make a small piecemeal change in the law or specifically dictate a regulatory outcome. In addition, as is the norm with such riders, it was not subject to public hearings or overt claims of sponsorship by legislators. This amendment's title, "An Amendment for Protection of Striped Bass," gave no hint of a threat to the striped bass, nor did its text even mention Westway.[3] But its congressional champions, New York senators Patrick Moynihan and Alphonse D'Amato and New York congressmen Bill Green and Joe Addabbo, were reported to be behind the proposed amendment.[4] Newspapers reported that Governor Cuomo had asked the state's federal legislators to push for passage of the appropriations rider and that it had been drafted by the private law firm now representing New York State in the Westway litigation, Kaye, Scholer, Fierman, Hays and Handler.[5]

The bill did not mention Westway in so many words, but through descriptions of the projects it would apply to—defined in terms of when projects were added to the Interstate Highway System and subject to a Section 404 permit application—it was actually applicable only to Westway. And although its title and a one-page supportive memorandum distributed on the Hill characterized it as "for protection of striped bass," it actually had a near-opposite effect. Most important, it would have circumvented judicial and regulatory delays faced by Westway and substituted a legislative resolution. Westway regulatory reviews and approvals would no longer follow assessment of data and science on fishery impacts. The rider's language was convoluted and indirect, but it provided for government spending on Westway-related work if, after consultation with federal natural resource agencies, the Army Corps required 1.2 acres of "replacement habitat" for each acre of destroyed Westway interpier areas. In one provision it claimed it did not exempt the project from analysis for environmental impacts under NEPA. In its very next provision, however, it somewhat incoherently said that "pending final action" by the Army Corps, and "without further preparation or revision" of NEPA EIS documents, the secretary of transportation could fund and the Army Corps could review and issue permits for replacement habitat, demolition and removal work, construction of "tunnel protection" structures, and construction of thirty-nine acres of "prototype fill."

The appropriations rider bill thus did not explicitly state that all of Westway could be built, but its language would allow the project to proceed, with funding, despite the litigation and ordinary legal hurdles. If enacted, it would largely result in destruction of the Westway area via demolition, tunnel work, and prototype fill. By substituting its own replacement habitat design for the project-blocking power of Section 404, this rider bill would override Section 404's science-based decision making and eliminate, for Westway, the strong presumption of protection of significant fishery habitat. Congress would have trumped science-based analysis. No more fish studies would be needed, and despite new federal laws protecting striped bass, Westway could be built regardless of its fishery risks. Its net effect was to leave some room for NEPA analysis but eliminate Section 404 and its binding interpretive regulations as a substantive barrier to Westway. Judicial and even natural resource agency oversight and other potential environmental hurdles would largely be gone.

The *New York Times*, in one of its many pro-Westway opinion pieces, lauded this proposed legal change, stating that the "measure would build [the striped bass] a new fish town right now" and wisely short-circuit the delays associated with two years of fish study.[6] The *Times* editorial oddly characterized the rider as mandating that if the fish did not adapt to the new "fish town," then after "observing the reaction," a choice could be made between "road and fish." This was literally true, since the rider did not mandate the construction of Westway, but the *Times* piece created an erroneous impression: nothing in the rider called for new analysis or balancing of fishery harms and highway benefits. The rider would simply circumvent the law's usual environmental protections. The *Village Voice,* whose columnists and reporters consistently criticized Westway, called it a "cynical strategy" that "violate[d] every principle of open government" and would "undermin[e]" the law.[7] Prominent banker and chair of the New York City Partnership, David Rockefeller, traveled to Washington to meet with Reagan White House chief of staff James Baker and EPA administrator William Ruckelshaus and urge their support for Westway and the amendment.

After discerning that the rider's effects were contrary to its benign-sounding title, Marcy Benstock, along with John Mylod of the Hudson River Clearwater organization, raced to Washington to fight against its enactment.[8] They, environmental allies, and other Westway opponents fanned out to meet with legislators from both houses and both parties. They hit paydirt in the

Senate when Senator Robert Stafford, a Republican from Vermont, opposed the piecemeal undercutting of the environmental laws. Stafford made his views clear to D'Amato and Moynihan. In keeping with typical senatorial courtesies, Stafford's firm opposition killed the amendment in the Senate, at least for the moment.[9] In the House, however, Representatives Green and Addabbo pushed hard, adding in the ambiguous NEPA-protecting language, perhaps hoping to mollify Stafford if the House passed the rider and the bill returned to the Senate. They otherwise kept the rest of the proposed rider. Congressman Ted Weiss fought the amendment in key committees. Liberal Massachusetts Republican representative Sylvio Conte took on Green and Addabbo. "I know we have all laughed about big projects of this sort being held up by snail darters or furbish lousewarts, or in this case by striped bass," Conte observed. But he argued that where a court had found "bad faith" and "withhold[ing] of evidence," then "this sort of behavior should not be rewarded" by such a rider amendment.[10]

Friends of the Earth also wrote Appropriations Committee members in opposition to the rider, joined by senior members of many of America's pre-eminent environmental groups such as the Natural Resources Defense Council and the Sierra Club, but also Benstock's far smaller NY City Clean Air Campaign. They focused on how such a rider would "do remarkable damage to federal environmental law and the integrity of federal court decisions."[11]

By this time, the rider was no longer a piece of stealth legislation but the subject of fierce public debate. After letters, op-eds, and additional news coverage criticized the proposed exemption for Westway, the Reagan administration itself weighed in. Through officials at the Federal Department of Transportation, the administration stated that "[w]e don't think it is appropriate to support such amendments."[12] In a further blow that worried Westway supporters, the federal Department of Transportation during this period also declared its plan to withhold a portion of anticipated Westway funds due to fiscal and legal concerns. The federal government stated it still supported Westway, but the Department of Transportation awaited a "tangible sign" of favorable resolution of the battles before it would fully fund Westway activities.[13]

Prominent New York voices joined the opposition to the striped bass rider. Despite Governor Cuomo's contrary position, independently elected New York State attorney general Robert Abrams, a Westway opponent, similarly criticized the proposal. In his view, exemptions for single projects "would create an unjust and ill-advised precedent that will open the door to further exemptions and threaten the viability of our environmental laws."[14] New York Times op-ed columnist John B. Oakes published a scathing anti-Westway essay, characterizing the proposed rider as sought "in typical pork-barrel fashion when no one might be looking." He viewed the whole effort to push the "notorious and malodorous" Westway through as about more than just Westway: "It goes, as it has so many times before, to the integrity of government."[15]

With the spotlight of scrutiny now shining on the bill, firm legislative opposition and no support from President Reagan, the rider was defeated. A battle-ending legislative rescue of Westway had come up short.

THE CONGRESSIONAL APPROPRIATIONS rider strategy backed by Governor Cuomo had failed. Earlier in the fall, however, Cuomo had also sought to reverse an Army Corps ruling that threatened Westway with two winters of delay for additional study of striped bass impacts. Efforts to short-circuit the regulatory process and smooth the path for Westway thus continued.

That decision to undertake two winters of striped bass study had been made by the new district engineer for the Army Corps New York district office, Colonel Fletcher "Bud" Griffis. Griffis had assumed the district engineer position after yet another Westway-linked irregularity. The Department of Justice learned that Griffis's predecessor, Colonel Walter Smith, had been discussing future employment with Parson, Brinckeroff and Quade, the prime engineering contractor working on the Westway project for the state Department of Transportation. The Parson firm had already earned millions on Westway and stood to earn vastly greater amounts in the coming years if it were built. Smith's exploration of "revolving door" employment, where he would surrender his regulator role and work for the private sector, created a clear risk of conflict of interest on a project that had already suffered from government missteps. The Army Corps did not delay. Smith was removed from his position and Griffis was appointed in his stead as the new district engineer.

Griffis was thrust into a difficult, high-visibility Westway role. However, he arrived with extensive experience that prepared him well.[16] A West Point graduate who also held a doctorate in civil engineering, Griffis had earlier been a commander in Germany, overseeing air base construction. Soon after the early 1970s enactment of new restrictions on ocean dumping of garbage and the Clean Water Act, with its new anti-dredging and filling presumptions, Griffis managed research into dredging's effects. By the early 1980s, he was considering retirement, but, after brief work as a deputy division engineer, he accepted the March 1983 invitation to replace Smith. Griffis was now both the point person for the fisheries portion of the court-ordered SEIS and also the initial, key decision maker on the Section 404 dredge-and-fill permit.

Griffis first had to reassess Colonel Smith's last major Westway action. Shortly before his removal, Smith had decided against further fishery studies despite contrary advice from a panel of fishery experts. Those experts had concluded that at least two winters of striped bass study were needed to gauge Westway risks. Smith instead decided that with existing data and by using "worst-case" assumptions, the Westway process could comply with the law and continue without the two-winter delay. The Corps vacated that action due to Smith's employment discussions with the Parson firm. Now the same choice was before Griffis.

Griffis was not cloistered away from the press and politics. He and his office received regular inquiries from the offices of Senators D'Amato and Moynihan, and even sometimes the senators themselves.[17] Westway remained front-page news. At the time Griffis assumed his new role, the federal and state investigations into earlier Westway irregularities were ongoing. He conceded his difficult position: "I really worry about making the wrong decision. But if it were easy, it would already be made."[18] He conceded "it is lonely in the middle."[19]

Fishery impacts remained a crucial issue for Westway, in fact the most substantial stumbling block in the remanded NEPA and Clean Water Act Section 404 reviews. Data initially ignored in EIS documents but aired in the earlier trials had established that substantial striped bass populations in fact used the Westway interpier areas. No one could again claim they were a biological wasteland. An additional study of striped bass use of the Westway area during 1982 and 1983, undertaken at Smith's request to investigate mitigation options, had provided yet more data revealing young striped bass usage of the Westway interpier area. Some sampling found greater numbers along the New Jersey shore opposite Westway, but similar habitat on both sides of the river again had the highest numbers of yearling and young-of-the-year striped bass, suggesting yet again that for some reason the Westway interpier habitat was important to young striped bass found there. Figuring out through additional study more about Westway's relative importance, or at least relative levels of usage, was crucial. Substantial delay, however, could in itself doom Westway, due to either simple loss of momentum or failure to meet the September 1985 trade-in deadline. Griffis did not want to kill the project merely by delaying it. On the other hand, he was cognizant of the many criticisms of past Army Corps Westway failures.

Leading up to his own decision to require two winters of study, Griffis sought the advice of a new specially convened panel of fishery experts. It included experts aligned with Westway, supporters and opponents, fishery experts from federal and state agencies, and several nominally independent experts. Among the unaffiliated experts was William Dovel, a fishery scientist who had done extensive work on the Hudson and later, during the 1985 Westway trial, would become a critically important witness for the government.

In 1983, he was both sought out by the Army Corps and suggested by the Westway opponent plaintiffs.[20] These experts, as well as several of the lawyers on both sides of the Westway battles, met in Ossining, New York, in late July 1983. Griffis recalls that some scientists initially sought such lengthy reviews that Westway would die well before completion of fishery research. No matter how much some scientists wanted twenty years of study, as he half-jokingly recalls, that was not an option.[21] After extensive deliberations, the expert panel recommended two winters of study. Only two participants thought less or no study could legally and scientifically suffice. Griffis's Army Corps staff still favored no additional studies and use of worst-case analysis, a recommendation he initially favored.

After starting to draft a letter explaining a choice to undertake only one winter's study, however, Griffis had second thoughts. In his view, because past sampling data revealed occasionally high numbers of young striped bass in the Westway interpier areas, analysis based on required worst-case assumptions would "result in a denial of the permit."[22] Such a choice "didn't seem fair to anybody" after so much work had been done on Westway. He was reluctant to set himself up for a permit denial based on "arbitrary" or "artificial" assumptions that might be avoidable with additional data and analysis.[23]

Griffis's concerns were rooted in binding Army Corps worst-case-scenario regulations. Those NEPA regulations required worst-case EIS assumptions if data were inadequate or beyond the capabilities of science. Similarly, Section 404 required permit denial if the project was not water-dependent or if it posed significant fishery risks. The Clean Water Act also required permit denial if there were data gaps precluding applicant proof that prohibited harms would not occur. Worst-case analysis might end up unavoidable, but if new data were less erratic or showed less fish usage, they might allow less-dire assumptions about fishery impacts. To give Westway a chance, Griffis decided on a nineteen-month, two-winter study of fishery impacts. He disclosed his decision to those involved with the project and also sent a letter directly to Governor Cuomo.

This courtesy letter provoked the second Cuomo strategic effort to sidestep judicial and regulatory hurdles to Westway. The legislative rider bill had eventually failed; Cuomo and Westway's supporters saw the two winters of striped bass study as another threatening setback. Cuomo's effort to reverse that decision proved to be one of the most significant strategic errors during the Westway campaign. Although earlier embarrassing missteps by the Army Corps, FHWA, and New York State had hobbled and delayed Westway, the state and Corps again cut corners. Governor Cuomo sought to circumvent the usual sequence for Army Corps decision making. Instead of asking Griffis to reconsider or appealing the next step up the Army Corps hierarchy in accordance with Corps regulations, Cuomo wrote directly to the national civilian head of the Corps, William Gianelli. The Army Corps agreed to immediately review and potentially overrule the Griffis decision.

The Army Corp's central office in Washington convened yet another panel of fisheries experts to revisit this action. This panel, however, lacked any Hudson River experts, and the only overlapping expert from the Griffis Ossining session was one of the only two opponents of a two-winter study. Westway opponents and even Colonel Griffis himself viewed the panel as biased.[24] He described it as a "stacked deck" that included a scientist who had stated you couldn't "kill a striped bass with a hammer." It also lacked any environmentalists.[25] The central office invited Griffis and his district chief of regulatory affairs, Dennis Suszkowski, to explain their choice to Corps leadership and the new fishery panel. Suszkowski was another highly qualified and educated Corps official, with both a master's in marine environmental science and a doctorate in estuarine sedimentology.[26]

Griffis offered a careful explanation of the rationale for the additional winter's study, explaining how he anticipated it would eliminate the need for worst-case analysis.[27] Suskowski agreed that with more study, more reasoned scientific judgments could be made.[28] Memorandum and communications to and within the Reagan White House reveal that New York's senators, Governor Cuomo, and Mayor Koch expressed concern with regulatory delay, prompting direct communications among top White House staff, agency, and department leaders about Westway.[29] The Army Corps central office on December 16, 1983, shortened that new review to a mere four months. Given the date and necessary planning time, even that one winter of study would be partly missed.

With this decision, once again politics prevailed over facts, technocratic inquiry, and expertise, as well as more precautionary approaches to comply with the laws' protective assumptions. This might have seemed like the victory sought by Governor Cuomo, but resulting data would now inevitably be more limited; the odds of worst-case assumptions killing Westway went up substantially. Governor Cuomo perhaps also failed to anticipate how the judiciary would later respond to the abridged data collection, particularly when it was the result of interfering with the Army Corps's own experts' advice. In Griffis's retrospective view, there was "no way to win at that point."[30]

The opponents' lawyer, Al Butzel, immediately alerted Judge Griesa about this action. Griesa held a conference and sought explanatory briefing. Smith's earlier refusal to undertake additional fish sampling had also provoked the plaintiffs to request a contempt-of-court trial. Now they added the new Corps's decision to their litany of grievances. Griesa initially agreed to hold such a trial, leading to the parties' submission of contempt-of-court briefs and even an unsuccessful effort by New York to get a court of appeals "mandamus" order telling the judge not to hold a trial. The parties briefly commenced a trial on factual disputes underlying that motion, but the opponents ultimately backed down. Without surrendering possible renewal of such a motion, they agreed to await the new sampling results, the new Corps supplemental EIS, and the actual permit decisions.

As feared, early winter sampling was missed due to planning delays. Extensive new sampling by a private contractor, the New Jersey Marine Sciences Consortium, got under way in January and continued through April 1984. This sampling sought data to illuminate the critically important issue of relative abundance of striped bass in the Westway-affected areas compared with other portions of the Hudson and surrounding waters. On the basis of usage data, was Westway's site really more important than other surrounding areas in the Hudson River and nearby waters? They sought to use uniform sampling methods and collect a larger data set. They then would adjust for the amount of effort and areas sampled to paint a picture of the Westway site's importance compared with that of surrounding waters. The consortium also eventually undertook some tagging of striped bass in affected areas, hoping to determine whether bass remained in the area or where they moved. This study as ultimately approved did not, however, include sampling designed to determine striped bass habitat dependence or fish movement patterns, as the Corps's specially convened experts had earlier recommended.

The data collected through this 1984 fishery sampling proved challenging and vulnerable to varying interpretations. The raw numbers confirmed that the Westway interpier sites still contained many striped bass, but the numbers varied during different testing intervals. In a few other areas, especially across the river in somewhat similar habitat on the New Jersey shore, similar and sometimes higher striped bass numbers were found. At a few other testing intervals, substantial numbers of striped bass were also found upriver, near the Tappan Zee Bridge and Yonkers. Again, few young striped bass were found in the middle of the river. But at some time intervals, especially December and April, parts of the Westway site still showed highest or near highest numbers of striped bass. Right as the testing came to an end, in April, Westway-site striped bass numbers skyrocketed to their peak. Whether this was the start of a longer period of heavy Westway usage or a temporary blip could not be determined, given the study's termination by the Army Corps leadership. Few tagged fish were ever caught again. The question was what this revealed once numbers were adjusted to account for the intensity of sampling efforts.

Within the Corps, the Westway process caused great awkwardness and voluminous work. Due to Judge Griesa's record-keeping order that had been upheld by the court of appeals, Corps personnel not working on Westway avoided project work and those who were involved. In Suszkowski's recollection, "there was scuttlebutt that if anybody talked to any of us, they were going to become part of the record. So all of us working on Westway were persona non grata for a couple of years. People would look at us and turn away." The record-keeping mandate "put a damper" on "the kind of dialogue that we should have been having on a project of that magnitude."[31] Griffis remained active, as did Corps biologist Len Houston in drafting a new Draft SEIS and Dennis Suszkowski as the resident regulatory process expert. Griffis relied principally on Suszkowski to assist with the actual Westway permit decisions once the new SEIS process came to completion. Other than occasional contact with Corps and government Westway lawyers, Griffis, Houston, and Suszkowski were isolated and benefited from little informal give-and-take. Griesa had hoped to ensure that deliberations were recorded, but in the regulators' view, his required record keeping backfired by chilling regulators' deliberative exchanges.

Private fishery scientist William Dovel, however, was in regular communication with Houston, both by telephone and in person. Dovel also worked with the New Jersey Marine Consortium on sampling and tagging efforts on the river. He was not an employee of the Corps, although for parts of the Westway endgame he was a contractor for the Corps. Later, the source of his funding and goals became a major litigation question. At this point, however, he was one of the few people who would informally communicate with Houston about his EIS work.

Houston shared an initial version of the Draft SEIS with the Corps Westway team around May 1984. Griffis and Suszkowski reviewed the initial Draft for a day or two. Suszkowski, the resident expert on the Section 404 permit process, was "horrified with the loose way the language was being used." It was "all over the place," unclear, and words like "'significant' . . . were being thrown around" that would "cause problems . . . on the regulatory side."[32] Houston wanted time to edit and polish the Draft before it became public.[33] Suszkowski was reviewing with attorneys the substantial work needed on the initial Draft when, a day or two after Houston had shared the Draft, Griffis arrived and said, "'I think it's great. Let's put it out today. Let's get this thing going.'" When Suszkowski and others suggested editing it first, Griffis disagreed. Suszkowski recalls that Griffis responded, "'I think it's fine. It's only a draft. . . . Let's put it out.'" Griffis was the boss. The Draft was quickly printed and made public.

This was another remarkable and imprudent decision that almost unavoidably threatened trouble for Westway, regardless of the Draft's content. On a project of Westway's scale, it was inevitable that partisans would spend thousands of hours poring over the Draft. It was a permanent part of the regulatory record. Misleading claims on fishery issues had already delayed Westway by years. Whatever subsequently changed from this new Draft to the Final SEIS would need to be explained and would be part of whatever judicial review awaited Westway. Despite Westway's high stakes, prominent supporters and opponents, and previous judicial rejections and political criticisms, the Draft SEIS went out in a form that Suszkowski and Houston thought preliminary. The judgment call was for Griffis to make.

THE MAY 1984 Draft SEIS covered a number of other subjects, but the Westway striped bass analysis was everyone's focus. The Draft was a marked contrast to the 1977 EIS descriptions of the Westway site as a biological wasteland. Consistent with political reassessments of the earlier Westway battles, the Draft refuted any argument that the earlier fishery claims had been sound. In passage after passage, it acknowledged substantial striped bass usage of the Westway areas and resulting significant risks. A simple "nothing is there" conclusion was now an impossibility. The Draft's analysis grappled with the tougher question: just how important was the Westway site, especially for young striped bass found in substantial numbers in the area? In dozens of passages, the Draft concluded that the site was very important. These conclusions strongly supported the views of Westway's opponents and the natural resource agencies. The opponents' lawyers thought that the Draft signaled that they had won the Westway war.[34]

The Corps's Suszkowski similarly thought the project was destined for a permit denial, basing that view on the Draft language regarding the project's effects and also on occasional revealing comments by district engineer Griffis. The main reason Suszkowski did not wage more of a battle against the Draft's premature release, and why he thought Griffis allowed its release, was that they all thought the project was headed for a permit denial. Suszkowski thought that Griffis's view was roughly that since the Corps "was going to deny this thing somewhere down the line, what difference did putting out this crappy Draft really mean in the overall scheme of things."[35]

Griffis's own press release, which accompanied the Draft's release, seemed to indicate that he too thought the project was headed for denial unless effective mitigation measures could address dredge-and-fill harms. Griffis stated that the New York and New Jersey sides of the Hudson proximate to the Westway site were "extremely important to the life cycle of the striped bass" and the Westway site "an important habitat used by juvenile striped bass." The project might have "important long-term repercussions on this fishery resource."[36] He referred to New York State efforts to "mitigate long-term impacts on the resource." This reference to mitigation seemed to presume that Westway would cause significant harms, since mitigation would be legally required under Section 404 of the Clean Water Act only if necessary to avoid otherwise impermissible significant harms.

The Corps, counsel for the Corps, and other Westway supporters later sought to downplay the Draft's language predicting striped bass harms. But the Draft, using varied language, predicted substantial harms. In 151 pages of text, data tables, maps, and graphs, passage after passage in the Draft spoke of the Westway site's importance, cumulative impacts of other projects, and loss of protected habitat in the area and how "loss [of the project site] would be a significant adverse impact to the Hudson River stock of this species."[37] Applying worst-case analysis, and assuming, based on data collected, that one-third of both of the juvenile year striped bass populations (young of the year and yearling) used the Westway area, the Draft stated that "should all these fish perish from the loss of this habitat there would be a substantial adverse impact on the Hudson Fishery, with significant long-term declines."[38] The Draft also explained why it thought some worst-case assumptions were unlikely but under legally required worst-case assumptions generally assumed that 20 percent of juvenile striped bass would be affected.[39] The Corps did not think Westway was a "unique habitat," but "it does represent a substantial portion of a consistent and, on occasion, heavily used habitat."[40] During April, when catches were especially high, 20–33 percent of juveniles could be present in the Westway area. The catastrophic worst-case scenario estimated a 33 percent striped bass loss.[41]

With repeated reference to the theories of William Dovel, the Draft then developed a new explanation for the area's importance. These changing theories, and Dovel's role, would later became a focal point of Westway battles. Under this new theory, the Westway area and the few similar protected areas where the Hudson opened up to the much larger New York Harbor (usually referred to as the Upper Bay) were used as a "jumping off point," "a staging area," and "a shelter from which young striped bass undertake their first exposure to a more marine environment." The "piers serve both year classes as a point of respite from the energy demands of the faster current in the channel."[42] In particularly strong language, the Draft stated that the "Westway portion of the area . . . is an important part of a highly utilized and potentially vital winter refuge."[43] This new theory differed from earlier conclusions of opponents, federal fishery experts, and Judge Griesa that striped bass overwintered in the Westway interpier area.

That varying levels of striped bass were caught during different testing intervals was not a rationale for dropping the 20 percent estimate of affected bass, stated the Draft. After all, Westway would "impact subsequent groups that reach it later." In essence, cumulative or additive harms to different groups of striped bass at different times meant all would be affected. To drop percentages due to some periods of low catches would "underestimate[] that impact."[44] The loss of surrounding habitat over the years made the Westway site more important: "Essentially no natural shoreline remains outside the channel to serve as a shelter except the piers." Fish could "expire during this prolonged exposure." If Westway displaced the large protected interpier area, "finding sufficient shelter for fish after removing such a large part of that shelter would be a formidable task."[45] Under the worst-case analysis, "one-third of the final riverine habitat" would be destroyed, an "area large enough to seriously doubt whether all or most of the fish [a]ffected by its loss could be sustained elsewhere." This passage stated that "it is both an important habitat and a very significant adverse impact to the fishery," that would cause "severe repercussions to the stock of striped bass and most likely result in a major decline in stock size, th[]ough not its total demise." Again, however, the Draft pulled back from saying this was likely, calling it "very improbable in terms of magnitude of fish [a]ffected as well as the repercussions to the Hudson stock."[46] When discussing a "more likely interpretation," the Draft "would still project potential long-term repercussions to the stock but of a substantially reduced order of magnitude."

In critically important passages for all Westway partisans, the Draft summed up regarding striped bass impacts: "It would thus be imprudent to consider any such habitat loss as projected by the Westway landfill to be minimal, insignificant, or sustainable at current population levels. Some measurable long-term reduction in the overall stock along with a reduced recovery would be a reasonable expectation."[47] Again, these impacts were viewed not as probable but as worst-case predictions. The final two pages in the Draft, labeled "Conclusions," contained yet more key language seemingly linked to Section 404's general prohibition on filling that would cause significant degradation of fishery resources: the Westway site's "loss would be a significant adverse impact to the Hudson River stock of this species." It would not be "a critical blow" but would cause "long-term repercussions" and "depressed population levels." Considering other changes to river habitat causing cumulative impacts, the Draft predicted "more permanent long-term reduction in the Hudson productivity." Up to "one third of the striped bass juvenile population" would be affected under worst-case analysis.[48] Any additional new developments along the New Jersey shore would cause the "overall impact" to "increase." The possibility of mitigation was mentioned, but the Draft acknowledged "formidable obstacles" to designing and implementing an effective strategy.

The Draft's shift from data review to probable impacts and then to worst-case analysis was not a shift from the relevant to the far-fetched. Instead, protective worst-case assumptions under NEPA and similar antifill presumptions in the face of uncertainty under Section 404 were legally required. Given Governor Cuomo's end run and the Corps's resulting shortening of the sampling period, such assumptions were legally unavoidable and the impacts that the Corps had to consider.

This Draft SEIS was a dramatic turnaround from the earlier biological wasteland claims that had blown up in court. The Draft appeared to spell the death knell for Westway. It might have been prepared under a purely information-generating statute, NEPA, but the underlying action was subject to Section 404's substantive barriers. Section 404 prohibited filling in America's waters that would cause significant harms, especially to important fishery habitat. And where impact uncertainties required worst-case analysis under NEPA, Section 404 regulations required permit denial if because of data gaps an applicant could not establish lack of prohibited dredge-and-fill harms. In numerous passages, the Draft's language was heavily tilted toward a future permit denial. It was hard to see how any other outcome was legally possible.

NOW THE COMMENT phase arrived. Despite the Draft's language predicting risks and harms, the federal natural resource agencies and Westway opponents still criticized it as understating risks and characterizing Westway in unduly favorable language.[49] A few supporters thought the Draft too negative about striped bass harms. Westway partisans of all stripes spoke at Army Corps hearings soliciting comments on the Draft SEIS and the merits of Westway. Opponents outnumbered supporters four to one at the hearings. They characterized Westway as a "mirage," a "hoax," an "albatross," and a "bloated white elephant." Supporters continued with their familiar refrain that Westway was an opportunity to show our "political system has the capacity to make great decisions for our people." Numerous union workers advocated concern for people and jobs over concern for striped bass, even if fish do "go back to the time of the Lord."[50]

In particularly pointed criticism, the NMFS rejected Dovel's explicitly credited theory as lacking foundation; striped bass might use the Westway shelter as a "staging area," but it might also be their "final destination." Mitigating harms was, in NMFS's view, too speculative to be given any weight. NMFS argued that since two years of juvenile striped bass heavily used the Westway area, destruction of the site would cause harms to each class twice. The Department of the Interior similarly argued that the Draft underplayed harms and asserted that the Corps could not rely on Dovel's untested but favorable theory when operating under the constraints of worst-case regulations. The 20 percent impact assumption was characterized as "absurd" since actual data indicated use of Westway areas by "at least one third of both year classes."

EPA's July 16, 1984, comment letter noted that the Draft's language gave EPA "no choice" but to oppose a Section 404 permit. The claim that the Westway habitat was not unique was similarly rejected by EPA as without foundation and contrary to testing data. The fish-movement hypothesis was at most "an interesting theory" that lacked foundation. In addition, EPA commented, fish populations could adjust logarithmically rather than arithmetically. In other words, fish population harms can result in "rapid decline[s]," not just subtractions in numbers. EPA also thought the 20 percent impact was too low, stating that at least 33 percent would be more appropriate. All the natural resource agencies provided data about the huge commercial value of striped bass and the resulting monetary magnitude of risks posed by Westway. Once again, the federal natural resource agencies were uniformly critical of the Army Corps's EIS analysis. Even with the Draft's cataloguing of striped bass risks and harms, all thought it underplayed the risks.

EPA's leadership reiterated this conclusion a few weeks later in a letter from EPA administrator Ruckelshaus to Westway supporter David Rockefeller. In an earlier July 27 letter to Ruckelshaus, Rockefeller bemoaned Westway's delays and highlighted reasons he favored the project.[51] He said Westway would "retrieve a magnificent river frontage" and create parkland; the project involved far more than just a highway. Rockefeller blamed delays on "detractors," especially "the active and personal opposition of lower level bureaucrats in the federal agencies." Westway had for too long been "snarled in bureaucracy and legal delays." Rockefeller had asked Ruckelshaus to look again at alleged threats to the many young striped bass found in the planned Westway site. Those risks could be mitigated, he argued. His letter was not sent in a vacuum but followed meetings and conversations of Rockefeller and other Westway proponents with sitting United States senators and other top officials in the Reagan administration.

Ruckelshaus responded by firmly stating that because the Draft showed that the Westway landfill would have a "'significant adverse impact' on the striped bass population," Section 404 regulations would "forbid any permit." Applicable regulations did not (and still do not) allow permitting of projects that would cause "'significant degradation'" of waters or cause a "'significantly adverse impact' on fishery habitat and ecosystem productivity." In EPA's view, Westway could not be built. In contrast to the earlier EIS and permit battles, where EPA and the Army Corps were at loggerheads, EPA's view this time was based on the Army Corps's own language and analysis. Ruckelshaus did not rule out the possibility of a curative mitigation strategy.

He agreed that ongoing uncertainty about the project was unfortunate but otherwise stood by his staff's and the Army Corps's critical assessment of Westway harms.

Jersey City and several New Jersey politicians submitted comments opposing the project. They stated concerns that if Westway were built, New Jersey shorefront habitat would become critical and no longer available for development. The state might even become the site of required mitigation measures. These comments presaged an imminent legislative attack on Westway by New Jersey legislators.

On behalf of the Westway opponent litigants, Al Butzel and his legal team filed ninety pages of critical comments. Butzel was particularly incisive in questioning whether the Corps's analysis was in fact worst-case. The Draft relied on an unproven hypothesis about fish behavior, it assumed a 20 percent impact when the aggregate actual use of the Westway site over the sampling period exceeded that percentage, and April testing in itself found a much higher percentage use. Given the lack of any established effective mitigation measures, such measures could not be given any weight.

While no new striped bass data were collected during this period, the Corps's consultants had continued analyzing the sampling results. Martin Marietta completed a new statistical analysis in late July and put it in written form in August of 1984 for consideration by the Corps. This analysis concluded that as much as 44 percent of Hudson River young-of-the-year striped bass at times used the proposed Westway site. This was not a worst-case prediction but Martin Marietta's best statistical analysis of actual highest usage, drawn primarily from April sampling.[52] This analysis clashed with the Corps's use of lower percentages in the Draft under supposed worst-case frameworks. However, because this analysis arrived before the Final SEIS and permit decision, the Corps could still adjust its analysis.

With the Draft out and comments filed, the Corps had to turn the Draft into a Final SEIS. Judicial precedents also required the Army Corps to review the voluminous comments and criticisms and provide written responses. This was a massive undertaking relegated to the main EIS drafter, Len Houston. The FSEIS would be a separate document from the Corps's actual permit decision under Section 404 but would provide substantial information for that action.

Benstock and other opponents continued to press for a trade-in during this period, but no decisive political action resulted. Supporters and opponents waited for the Corps's next steps on the critical Final SEIS, another opportunity for comments, and a decision on the Clean Water Act Section 404 dredge-and-fill permit.

A BOMBSHELL LANDED six months later, in November 1984, when the Army Corps released its Final SEIS. Despite the absence of any new intervening data collection and the submission of uniformly critical expert natural resource agency arguments that the Draft underplayed risks, the Final's bottom-line conclusions were radically changed, and almost all in ways minimizing Westway harms. Corps chief of regulatory affairs Suszkowski "absolutely" knew that it was going to cause trouble, but the SEIS drafting fell principally to Houston, with revisions by Griffis.[53] Concessions of significant striped bass harms were gone. Final SEIS documents invariably change from Drafts but seldom substantially. If they do change, that change needs to be explained. Thus it was remarkable that the Final's text nowhere conceded that its key bottom-line conclusions had changed. Nor did its responses to comments about the Draft indicate any concession of a substantial change. Apart from conceding a shift away from the Corps's own earlier "staging area" theory to a theory positing striped bass migratory or transient behavior, the Corps claimed that changes reflected only linguistic clarifications and corrections. The Army Corps appeared to have learned little from its earlier judicial and political scoldings.

For supporters of Westway, these reversals meant that it might be built after all. For opponents, these particular language changes downplaying risks, yet without new data or explanation, were an unjustified outrage. If Westway received its Section 404 permit, these changes would inevitably be the focus of scrutiny before the courts.

Despite the lack of acknowledgment that the Final contained substantive changes, the Draft-to-Final changes were many. Of greatest importance, the basic conclusion was reversed. Where the Draft characterized the Westway site as a "potentially vital winter refuge," the Final stated only that the pier areas "have importance in helping conserve energy" for fish.[54] While the Draft predicted a "significant adverse impact" to striped bass and that it would be "imprudent to consider" Westway habitat loss as "minimal, insignificant, or sustainable at current populations," these passages were simply deleted in the Final. The Draft predicted Westway would "very likely cause a measurable degradation in future stocks," but the new Final language was softened to anticipate that the project would "very likely cause at least a perceptible decline in future stocks."[55]

In a particularly odd change, although the Final now predicted an increased 33 percent worst-case scenario striped bass loss, it somehow also minimized anticipated harms. In the Draft, a 33 percent loss was described as resulting in "a very likely significant or complete loss of all displaced fish," a "serious erosion of the species' ability to survive future impacts," and a "very significant impact" to the striped bass stock.[56] In the Final, however, a 33 percent impact was now stated as "*not* likely to significantly affect the overall stock."[57] Now the "magnitude of the depressed population [was] likely to be relatively small" and "not a critical or even minor threat to its well being."[58] These were not language tweaks but fundamentally changed conclusions. And these dramatically different assessments of whether risks were "significant" likely signaled a changed fate for Westway, given Section 404's near absolute prohibition on significant degradation of America's waters.

The Draft's most direct and dire predictions for striped bass risks had been in assessing Westway's cumulative impacts with other river changes. These predictions were simply gone in the Final. Instead, some "strain" was anticipated that would make striped bass populations "more susceptible" to future events.[59] Similarly, the Draft had admitted that the loss of Westway's sheltered areas could cause harms due to the lack of other available habitat. Landfilling the Westway site was viewed as a "substantial problem" and "[f]inding sufficient shelter for fish after removing such a large part of that shelter would be a formidable task."[60] No new data arrived during the interim between the Draft and Final, but the Final now offered a dramatically different theory. It dropped the sheltering and staging area language in the Draft and concession of risks due to cumulatively lost habitat. It instead championed a new theory that minimized risks. Striped bass use of the Westway interpier areas was "apparently random," and hence it was reasonable to assume that fish displaced could "utilize any of the remaining habitat across the channel, and possibly even some of the bottom left after the landfill."[61] That sampling produced almost no fish in the middle of the Hudson that might confirm cross-river migration was basically ignored in this passage.

On a related point, the Draft had rejected the idea that displaced fish moving downriver would reverse course and move north, up the river or into the upper harbor.[62] In contrast, the Final SEIS now hypothesized that displaced fish might "use areas above" the Westway site.[63] Whereas the Draft saw displaced populations using the site at different points in time as distinct populations that would experience additive losses, the Final now posited that the "same group of fish are using the same area" at different times and the same fish "can't be killed twice."[64] Tagged fish recapture had been minimal, almost nonexistent, thus providing no apparent support for claims of either sustained striped bass use or movement into other areas, but the theory and conclusion were reversed nonetheless.

On the one conceded analytical shift, replacing the "staging" and "sheltering" theory with the new "migratory" and "transient" use theory, the Final credited discussions and theories posited by William Dovel. Dovel had also been credited with the earlier "staging area" theory posited in the Draft. Dovel was the private scientist who had worked on Westway for the consulting company

Malcolm Pirnie, had done past work for environmental groups supported by the Rockefeller family, and also occasionally served as a consultant to the Corps. Later he would become a linchpin of the government's trial defense of its regulatory actions. The Final SEIS alluded to a supportive report shared by Dovel with the Corps. Dovel "formalized his initial ideas" in a report for Malcolm Pirnie, but "a final form was received in July" and had been "developed and expanded on since." The shift to the "migratory movement" theory was adopted after "discussing the concept with Dovel."[65]

The Final added one passage conceding threats to striped bass, but those threats were from future unnamed projects. If other future changes to the Hudson and New York Harbor destroyed habitat made more important due to the building of Westway, then a loss of closer to 100 percent of striped bass could result. But Westway was not itself the source of harm, and the Final did not see it and earlier changes as creating anywhere near such dire risks. However, for other jurisdictions eyeing potential waterfront development, especially New Jersey, this one passage served as a warning. Westway's development could preclude later Hudson River projects. The Final discussed mitigation options but ultimately found them "too uncertain" to influence overall impact statement analysis. But because harms and risks were now minimized, mitigation would likely not be needed to overcome any Section 404 substantive hurdles. These radical changes from the Draft-to-Final SEIS created a new major battleground, especially given their lack of accompanying explanation.

Since the government insisted in underlying regulatory materials and later upon judicial review that conclusions had not been changed, no one involved in this document at the time offered an explanation for analytical changes.[66] But the changes were stark. What could explain them? As came out in subsequent legal skirmishing, and is clearer now in reviewing contemporaneous governmental documents and in talking with regulators, the pressures on Corps regulators were extreme. The record-keeping mandate from the courts backfired by chilling deliberations within the Corps. It left Houston isolated and highly dependent on Dovel. Dovel remained willing to talk and regularly did so, likely adding to his influence. David Rockefeller and other top business and civic leaders were privately and in the press maintaining a stream of pro-Westway rhetoric. And, as was subsequently revealed, Rockefeller-linked interests were funding Dovel's striped bass report. That funding kept Dovel's study alive and yet again affirmed the power of Westway's supporters. (Later, that funding undercut the reliability of Dovel and his report due to the risk of pro-Westway bias.)

New York's political leaders similarly kept up the lobbying barrage, also entreating the White House to remain supportive of Westway. Those communications, and close monitoring of press coverage about Westway, were distributed among top White House staff and to department and agency heads.[67] President Reagan was more than willing to court labor's support, and Department of Labor head, Raymond Donovan, supported Westway, as did several of New York's powerful unions. Colonel Griffis then and now insists that he made the best call he could, given the data he had and under the law as he understood it. But within the executive branch and within the Corps, all but the federal natural resource agencies were applying pressure to approve Westway. A Final SEIS that looked like the Draft would have signaled the near-certain death of Westway. Massive pressure was on the Corps to avoid such a conclusion.

WHATEVER THE EXPLANATION for these changes, the Final SEIS was still far from the final step for Westway. District engineer Griffis had to work with the Final SEIS, consider any additional comments, and issue his own separate Record of Decision and Section 404(b)(1) Evaluation on Westway. For that decision, he would have to apply the substantive protections of the Clean Water Act and its implementing regulations to decide whether Westway could legally receive a permit. The Final SEIS conclusions hinted at the likely outcome but did not dictate a result.

The substantive decision facing Griffis and the Army Corps under Section 404 of the Clean Water Act was severalfold. Egregious earlier legal violations caught in the 1982 trials had made it easy to prove that the Corps had violated both NEPA and Section 404. Now that even the state and Corps admitted the presence of many striped bass in the Westway area, the law's regulatory hurdles had to be applied to a more complex conceded reality. These Section 404 regulatory guidelines, which were binding on the Corps, remained the same as during the earlier Corps 1981 Westway decisions that had been rejected in court. Under the first of these overlapping prohibitions, Griffis could grant the Section 404 dredge-and-fill permit only if he determined that the project was overall in the public interest. Second, Section 404 guidelines created a strongly protective three-part hurdle for Westway. If Westway did not need to be built in a "water of the United States" (here the Hudson) because a "practicable" upland alternative existed, then under Section 404 the permit had to be denied. Since Westway was replacing a road that was not in the Hudson and all EIS versions discussed other upland options, including the trade-in option, the alternatives hurdle posed a major challenge. The Corps's Suszkowski thought it the most insurmountable barrier. But he was not the decision maker.

However, other Section 404 barriers also remained. Even if the Corps concluded that Westway was water-dependent and lacked a practicable upland alternative, the dredge-and-fill permit still faced two environment-specific hurdles and a protective mandate in the face of uncertainty. "Special aquatic sites" were protected if they possessed "special ecological characteristics of productivity, habitat, wildlife protection, or other important and easily disrupted ecological values."[68] Even if Westway did not rise to that level of importance, two other protective regulations still applied. The Corps could not grant a Section 404 permit if the dredge or fill would "cause or contribute to significant degradation of the waters of the United States."[69] A harm counted as "significant degradation" if it affected "aquatic system diversity, productivity and stability," including "loss of fish and wildlife habitat." It was this language that tied into the troubling earlier Draft-to-Final SEIS changes and also sank Westway during its first judicial battles. Last, a Section 404 permit could not be granted absent applicant proof, and impliedly Army Corps agreement, that prohibited harms would not occur; uncertainty was itself a potential project killer.

Moreover, science uncertainties were compounded by the truncated one winter of additional striped bass study. Griffis and the Corps had to calibrate their analysis under worst-case scenario regulations. Those regulations were issued under authority of NEPA but were linked to the permit decision due to Griffis's reliance on Final SEIS analysis. In addition, as conceded in internal analyses of United States lawyers, the distinction between NEPA worst-case frameworks and Section 404(b)(1)'s guidelines was in any event somewhat modest; both required use of strongly protective presumptions when confronted with uncertainty, especially about an important aquatic resource.[70] Still, in these permit decisions, rather than under NEPA analysis in an EIS, Griffis principally relied on what he characterized as "the most likely alternatives" of anticipated striped bass impacts.

Even if Griffis concluded that Westway had surmounted these Section 404 hurdles, EPA and other federal natural resource agencies had to undertake their own reviews and could, as had happened earlier, elevate objections and interagency disagreement up the executive branch hierarchy. EPA also, once again, had its own separate Section 404(c) veto authority. And, of course, in this lengthy war over Westway, neither opponents nor supporters were likely to accept regulatory decisions as the final word; whatever transpired at this point, Judge Griesa was likely yet again to scrutinize the decisions.

EXPERT FEDERAL natural resource agencies strongly objected to the Final's revised conclusions, standing by their earlier criticisms and concerns about underplaying of fishery risks. They criticized the Draft-to-Final SEIS language changes as unjustified and recommended permit denial.

EPA, however, stood in a more powerful position, again potentially holding Westway's fate in its hands. First, perhaps its comment letter would persuade Griffis to deny the Section 404 permit. It could also elevate disagreement within the executive branch. Although President Reagan had indicated support for New York's choice to build Westway, perhaps its huge price tag and environmental risks would tip executive branch leadership to side with EPA. This was unlikely but possible. Of even greater importance, EPA also had and still today has its special, unusual power conferred by Congress under Section 404(c). Under this provision, EPA can review, second-guess, and veto a permit already granted by the Army Corps. Vetoes are justified when EPA finds, after opportunity for public comment, that the permitted project would cause "unacceptable adverse effect[s] on . . . fishery areas (including spawning and breeding areas), wildlife, or recreational areas." New data about the Westway site's usage by striped bass made this provision's applicability far more likely than in 1981. Moreover, by 1985, other regions of EPA had vetoed a few other projects permitted by the Corps. Then and now, however, this was a rarely used authority. Due to these EPA roles, especially the veto power, everyone involved in the Westway battles saw the EPA comment letter as of huge importance.

EPA's point person was the newly appointed regional administrator, Chris Daggett. Daggett was only thirty-four when appointed to this position by President Reagan at the recommendation of moderate Republican New Jersey governor Tom Kean and despite New York senator Alphonse D'Amato's championing of another candidate. Daggett had worked on Kean's gubernatorial campaign and had also served as his deputy chief of staff. He also worked on education issues for Kean, drawing on his own doctoral education degree. Daggett describes his philosophy in politics as learned from Governor Kean and an earlier candidate he had helped and admired, Ray Bateman: "Do what you think is right."[71] Despite his appointment to head EPA's regional office for New York, New Jersey, the Virgin Islands, and Puerto Rico, Daggett had little environmental expertise or experience working within the federal government. His main related experience was gained on the job while working for Kean when dioxin was found on the streets of Newark during the summer of 1982. From that experience, he began to develop facility with environmental science and public relations.

When Daggett arrived at EPA's regional office during the summer of 1984, he, like Griffis over at the Corps, could not ease into his job. Westway was already on "the highest burner," as Daggett recalls. That work was made even more challenging when the region's deputy regional administrator, Richard T. Dewling, suddenly left to head New Jersey's Department of Environmental Protection. Daggett viewed his lack of experience as in one respect an asset;

he would be the political point person for EPA decisions, with no choice but to allow his more expert staff to do their jobs as the facts and law required.

Political pressures, however, were great. In Daggett's words, along "came the world of Al D'Amato." Like Senator Moynihan, Senator D'Amato was a vocal supporter of Westway. Early in Daggett's time as regional administrator, during the fall of 1984, Senator D'Amato called and yelled at him for failing to ensure that EPA gave him the usual advance courtesy notice about a grant decision adverse to a constituent county. Daggett and a few of his staff were summoned for a face-to-face meeting with D'Amato. Daggett thought the meeting concerned the grant matter, but D'Amato had another agenda. After brief talk about the grant decision, he bluntly asked, "Are you going to fuck us on Westway?" Daggett would not reveal his hand, responding that he would work with his staff and decide the matter on its merits, and he reviewed the regulatory process for D'Amato.

Daggett buried himself in the Westway files, especially the Final SEIS. In his view, "you did not need a science degree to see" that the Final SEIS "conclusions were not supported by the data that was presented." EPA staff made this point in their technical analysis. Daggett knew about President Reagan's apparent support for Westway, but he wanted to allow his staff to make their recommendations as required by the facts and law. Top EPA leadership in Washington also was part of the process. Edits gradually eliminated much of the strongest language criticizing the Final SEIS. Finally, on the day after President Reagan was sworn in for a second term, January 21, 1985, Daggett signed and released EPA's official letter. Later, internal battles over that letter's editing were revealed and became yet another source of claims of impropriety and political scandal. Nevertheless, toned down or not, the letter itself reiterated earlier concerns, especially placing Westway in the context of overall threats to striped bass populations and plummeting Chesapeake Bay populations. It also pointed out questions left unanswered about striped bass risks, concluding that due to "uncertainty" the "required demonstration [under Section 404] has not been made." EPA therefore recommended permit denial. Daggett also stated EPA's likely intent to elevate objections up the executive branch ladder to the Council on Environmental Quality.

Despite stating a bottom line consistent with earlier criticisms, EPA's letter and attached technical comments packed little power. The final version did not even mention the Draft-to-Final changes. If Colonel Griffis was wavering and awaiting EPA's views, the EPA letter was an ineffective piece of advocacy. It did, however, maintain EPA's bottom-line objection. The Reagan administration became notorious for its many antienvironmental actions, but Reagan appointee Daggett had just sided with the environmentalists in one of the nation's most contentious environmental wars.

Senator D'Amato did not view the letter as innocuous. After Daggett sent D'Amato a copy of EPA's January comment letter by fax, he awaited the senator's call. Much as television advertisements soliciting toll-free responses provoke an immediate flurry of calls, "lighting up a switchboard like a Christmas tree," the call came just minutes later. It lasted only about five minutes, but to Daggett it seemed like a half hour, "like a lifetime." Consistent with his reputation for blunt, profane talk, D'Amato let the language fly. As Daggett recalls, D'Amato berated him: "'What do you know?'" "'You're from New Jersey.'" "'Who do you think you are?'" D'Amato said he would call David Rockefeller, the construction trade unions, the *New York Daily News,* and the *New York Times,* and tell them that Daggett had screwed New York. And Daggett learned that Senator D'Amato did exactly as threatened.

Daggett's letter clearly recommended that the Corps deny the Westway permit, but with little emphasis on the substance of the law's numerous protective requirements. The weak letter seemed to telegraph that, in the end, EPA might fold rather than stand firm in its opposition. But EPA's actual moments of truth had to await the Army Corps's Section 404 permit decision.

Griffis himself was again plagued with indecision, as he had been in waffling over the one-versus-two-winter-study choice. He too wanted to do the right thing, but despite confronting a science-dominated choice, he faced great political pressures. He was subjected to political inquiries from New York and New Jersey senators, press inquiries, and biographical profiles in newspapers.

Griffis also received additional advocacy, including a January 15, 1985, letter from fishery scientist Dovel. His letter was supportive of the Corps's key conclusions, but its actual content should have given Griffis serious pause; Dovel changed his theory yet again, contradicted theories attributed to him and used in the Final, and introduced new assumptions rejected by everyone else. He wrote that the Final SEIS likely overstated striped bass threats, although he praised the "author of the [Final] SEIS" for having an "impressive grasp of details" regarding striped bass science. Since Dovel knew the name of the principal SEIS author (Houston), had regularly spoken with him, and was himself credited by name, this compliment was perhaps tongue-in-cheek. Or maybe he thought it would add clout to his letter. The Final had rejected the overwintering theory, but his letter alluded to "a main overwintering area slightly further upstream."

Dovel also argued that striped bass are "opportunistic," "adaptable," "flexib[le]," and "occurring in a heterogenous distribution pattern." He made these claims although nothing in the Draft or Final SEIS or federal natural resource agency comments supported such a view. In fact, the Final's accompanying responses to comments rejected any such assumption: it would be contrary to required worst-case assumptions and "the alleged hardiness of the species is yet to be established for its immature members under the stress conditions of winter."[72] In language highlighting the changing nature of Dovel's views, he mentioned a new "concept" that had "evolved too late" to be in the Final SEIS. He thought that these "concepts . . . whether called theories or not," might help explain Westway risks. He went on to suggest reasons to think striped bass would continue using other Hudson environments if Westway were built. "It was [his] gut" that estimated impacts were "way too high." He knew of "no data" showing that Westway "will definitely have an adverse impact on a single striped bass." This assertion reversed legal presumptions required under both NEPA and Section 404. But Dovel's letter also revealed that the scientist named in the Draft as the source of the "staging area" theory, then credited in the Final as the source of "migratory" fish theory, now had an even more evolved theory or "gut instinct" for why Westway would not cause harm.

Griffis also had to consider comment letter points made by two scientists from the Corps's own consultant, Martin Marietta Environmental Systems. Tibor Polgar and Douglas Heimbuch had served as technical advisers to the Corps on Westway fisheries analysis. Their comment letter to Griffis was a marked contrast from Dovel's view that the Final SEIS was too pessimistic. They did not mince words: "The conclusion that one quarter to one third of juvenile [striped bass] population could be affected (displaced) by the Westway landfill with no 'critical (over even minor) threat' to the long-term well being of the Hudson River striped bass is totally unsupported by scientific evidence." In this view, a view shared by the federal natural resource agencies, they thought the science simply could not support the Final's optimistic assessment of minimal to no impacts.

Griffis faced the inherent challenge of making a binary yes-or-no decision in the setting of clashing and imperfect scientific knowledge where even the Corps's credited fish expert, Dovel, held views that undoubtedly were a moving target. Even consultants for the Corps viewed the Final's claims as "totally unsupported." Griffis felt that the underlying data probably could support a decision in either direction. Science gaps were exacerbated by the shortened single winter of additional striped bass study, an irksome decision that had overruled Griffis's own contrary judgment. In news stories, transcripts from meetings at the time, and his own and colleagues' recollections, Griffis seriously weighed both denying and granting the permit. He pored over documents spread over the floor of his den at home. He asked his main regulatory affairs expert at the Corps, Suszkowski, to prepare two diametrically opposed Records of Decision with fishery language supporting grants and denials. Suszkowski thought that the permit would ultimately be denied but did as requested.

When Griffis sat down and studied the data, he initially leaned toward denying the permit. The percentage of affected striped bass was "just too much."[73] But after staying up all night and weighing his decision, he reconceived Westway and its effects. The striped bass were "not in a vacuum" but had to be looked at in the context of the whole project; the "aquatic environment was more than just striped bass."[74] In addition, with the benefits of the Clean Water Act and the Hudson's rapid improvement in water quality, he believed fisheries would continue to rebound. Late in this regulatory game, Griffis had shifted his intuitive frame so the denominator of the relevant affected environment changed from the striped bass to the larger Hudson environment. This resulted in a relative reduction in anticipated aquatic harms.

Griffis also saw no troubling changes in the underlying Draft-to-Final SEIS. In communications with Griffis, Corps staffer Houston had explained away the apparent shifts as the result of a mere linguistic clarification. Houston told Griffis that he had in the earlier Draft used language of "significance" not in the sense of large, major, or huge but in the sense of statistically discernible or perceptible. In an internal memorandum, Houston also contested the other fishery scientists' and agencies' criticisms.[75] This was enough for Griffis. There was no indication that Dovel's vacillating views troubled him. His period of indecision was over. He concluded that only a temporary drop in the striped bass stock would result from Westway. With his staff, he started working on a decision granting the permit. He realized that the federal natural resource agency experts would disagree, but they could make their own regulatory choices.

On January 24, 1985, just four days after EPA's weakened objection letter, Griffis announced his decision. He accompanied the lengthy Record of Decision and Section 404(b)(1) Evaluation with a press statement. On the first Section 404 hurdle—whether the Westway project was truly water-dependent and whether there were "practicable alternatives"—Griffis endorsed Westway as one of a kind, unable to be moved out of the Hudson. He called the project a "combined highway, park and development project." He saw this decision as fundamentally one for the FHWA, not the Corps. As worked out during late 1984 in Corps discussions with the FHWA and state, Griffis concluded that Westway was "more than a highway endeavor," but a "bold and innovative plan that includes major revitalization elements." It was an inseparable "replacement highway and revitalization plan." Again and again he alluded to the monetary advantages of the full-blown Westway plan over other options. The city would lose hundreds of millions of dollars if a more modest road were built. No practicable alternative offered Westway's numerous benefits. Similarly, regarding the trade-in alternative, he deferred to the prevailing decision of New York's executive branch leaders: "[T]he Mayor of New York City and the Governor of New York State have determined that Westway, not the trade-in, is the preferred option. I have no basis to disagree with these elected officials." The trade-in was not a practicable alternative that could legally compel Westway to be redesigned and moved out of the Hudson, he concluded. The first and perhaps most legally challenging hurdle had been surmounted. Griffis also concluded that Westway was in the public interest, again deferring to the mayor and governor.

On the much-disputed question of striped bass impacts, the Griffis decision tracked the downplayed impacts evident in the Final SEIS and closely tracked several points made in Dovel's January 15 letter to Griffis. Westway would not cause a "significant degradation of waters of the United States." Although Griffis made some mitigation steps part of the conditions of his permit, they were not a prerequisite for Westway's Section 404 permit. His decision did not predict the fate of the young striped bass often found in the Westway interpier areas. He noted lack of proof that striped bass would perish and thought it "arbitrary to conclude that a displaced fish is likely to be a dead fish."[76] Parroting the Final SEIS theories attributed to Dovel, he concluded that the Westway site was not "unique" for striped bass. He alluded to striped bass not overwintering but making transient use of the Westway area. Despite Chesapeake striped bass population declines, he thought the Westway stock "too small to affect the plight of the coastal stock or significantly influence the existing trend."[77] Although Griffis alluded in places to worst-case data and regulatory requirements, his permit decision repeatedly played down risks and seemed to put the burden of proof on those claiming striped bass harms. The law, however, placed the burden of proof of no harm on the applicant and, effectively, the Corps as the regulatory decision maker. Contradicting the Final SEIS and accompanying responses to comments but echoing Dovel's January 15 letter, Griffis called striped bass an unusually hardy and adaptable fish. The migratory and transient fish use theory attributed in the Final SEIS to Dovel, plus Dovel's belatedly introduced hardiness theory, appeared to have tipped the scales for Griffis.

In his press statement, Griffis stated his findings in less technical terms. It was "time to inject some reason into this process." Chesapeake Bay striped bass populations might be in decline, but he characterized striped bass as a "species with high ecological resilience and a high rate of reproduction." The species had survived hundreds of years of changes to Manhattan's shoreline, from marshy estuary to polluted harbor to site of "derelict and decrepit piers which mark its habitat." He conceded, however, that "[e]xperts have almost unanimously agreed that to determine conclusively the impact on the bass is beyond the state of the art." His conclusion? "I honestly believe that there will be little or no impact to the striped bass population." Even though "no amount of studies could prove beyond a doubt that the landfill would or would not significantly impact the bass," Griffis would grant the permit.

PREDICTABLY, Westway's supporters celebrated, and opponents promised to continue their fight. Governor Cuomo said the permit grant "demonstrates that partnership of governmental, business and labor leaders can work together to the benefit of the entire Family of New York."[78] Mayor Koch declared a "hurrah for the Corps of Engineers" and was "happy" for the city of New York, America, and even striped bass.[79] Carolyn Meinhardt, executive director of the pro-Westway New York Citizens for Balanced Transportation, said the decision "proves that visionary projects can still be built in New York."[80] Benstock criticized the result, saying "something went very wrong."[81]

Beyond the press coverage and sound bite, the regulatory war now turned to EPA. Internal memoranda reveal an EPA that in the region and central office in Washington was intensively analyzing the law and facts about its options. While the strategic choices were debated, EPA's objections to Westway and assessments of risks remained consistent. Its staff saw Westway as harmful and the Corps's decisions as contrary to the law. Analytical memoranda quickly found major inconsistencies and legal errors in the key Corps decision documents. No one from EPA stated in writing the view that Westway should or legally could be built. Partisans weighed in, among them Adrian DeWind, the chairman of NRDC, then and now one of the nation's most respected environmental groups. NRDC had not been active in many of the Westway battles but now called for EPA to commence a Section 404(c) veto hearing to "halt construction of the Westway project."[82]

On February 14, EPA convened a large meeting of EPA scientists, staff, Daggett, and at least one lawyer, plus several outside experts and consultants. They met to discuss options and, in particular, the theories of Dovel relied upon by the Corps. Dovel himself attended and presented his views. A later memorandum reported reactions to those views, none favorable.[83]

First, the consensus was that Dovel was now offering another theory that clashed with the theory attributed to him in the Final SEIS. Second, Dovel explained his results as resting on combining several past sampling efforts. Others at the meeting disagreed with combining these results since "variations in sampling technique" or "longer" work in an area could result in greater catches, "whether or not there were really more fish there." Only with more sampling could Dovel's new theory "be verified." Dovel claimed the greatest numbers of striped bass were in Yonkers, but opponents' past fishery consultant, Ian Fletcher, said studies that were not designed to show "distribution" could not be used to answer such an assertion. The consensus was that Dovel's methodology "had no scientific basis," and "there was no substantive data base to support his current theory." The meeting participants concluded that Dovel's "current theory . . . suffered the same deficiency in data base" as past theories. It "provided no new information that could be used to evaluate the [Westway] project."

Unpersuaded by the Final SEIS, Griffis's decision, or Dovel's explanations, Daggett first wanted to elevate EPA's objection, but the elevation choice was a national EPA decision. A new EPA administrator, Lee Thomas, had just replaced Bill Ruckelshaus. Thomas refused Daggett's entreaty, putting the choice squarely back on Daggett's desk.

The choices for Daggett and the region then were either to veto the permit under Section 404(c), a decision that did reside initially with the regional administrator (subject to later review by EPA leadership), or do nothing. In weighing the 404(c) option, EPA could have started its own legally required notice and public hearing process, both to inform itself and to give partisans an opportunity to make their arguments. But when it came time to start a veto consideration process, the region did nothing. Much as Chuck Warren had failed to assert EPA's veto power to defeat Westway in 1981, Daggett folded. This was a major loss for Westway's foes.

One explanation is that the political pressure was too much. An EPA veto of Westway would have run counter to the views of the president and certainly New York's two vocal senators, as well as state and city leadership. Administrator Thomas did not favor a veto or elevation of the Westway decision. Scientists and staff at involved agencies were well aware of David Rockefeller's pro-Westway advocacy, including his meeting with the secretary of transportation. Later investigations and testimony revealed that Rockefeller and D'Amato themselves visited an EPA lawyer in Washington, arguing that the central office should overrule the "biased" regional EPA.[84] Scientists and agency staff readily acknowledged the "political pressure," describing it as "crushing."[85]

Daggett's own explanation is different, reflecting both pragmatic and legally grounded views and, more important, a misapprehension about the veto decision's effects. Daggett correctly thought that either way Westway would be challenged in court. Contemporaneous internal memos also noted that if EPA were to exercise its permit veto power, the legal and scientific burden would be on it to justify its action.[86] It would have to show that "unacceptable adverse effects" would be likely to occur.[87] As an EPA internal "fact sheet" noted, with a veto, "pressure [would be] immediately transferred from Corps to EPA."[88] Although some critics of regulation portray agencies as rapacious and overreaching, agencies frequently display risk aversion, avoidance of work, and dislike of criticism. These internal Westway documents are far more consistent with these latter theories. EPA was not eager to be in the Westway hot seat.

In addition, EPA scrutinized Section 404(c)'s language and read it to make the veto choice one "committed to the discretion" of the agency and hence unreviewable in the courts. In meetings and letters, plaintiffs tried to persuade EPA that exercise of its veto power would be sound under the law and facts. They also threatened to take EPA to court. But EPA focused on statutory language making that choice "authorized" rather than mandatory, asserting that that language rendered it immune from review in the courts under cases building on Administrative Procedure Act language. In a serendipitous coincidence for an EPA justifying a refusal to commence a 404(c) process, the agency could and did rely on the just-decided Supreme Court case, *Heckler v. Chaney*, which held that agency nonenforcement decisions were generally immune from judicial review.[89]

It is true that EPA would have faced scrutiny and criticism had it utilized the Section 404(c) process, especially if it issued a veto. It would been subject to political pressure and also would have had a burden of scientific proof to satisfy.[90] EPA also had a strong argument that the statute made its Section 404(c) choices judicially unreviewable. But the rest of Daggett's rationale for inaction is far more debatable. The view that a veto or veto proceeding would have made no difference to Westway's likely fate was in error. Judicial review of the Corps's approval was indeed a near certainty, regardless of EPA's action. Nevertheless, had EPA acted on the basis of a record and issued a veto, that judgment would have received some judicial deference. Presumptive outcomes would have flipped. Westway would have been turned down by a federal agency cloaked with the veneer of expertise and explicitly granted statutory authority. Westway's champions would have had to overcome EPA's judgment about aquatic harms, showing that it was arbitrary and capricious. That would have been a tough burden to overcome, especially given the extensive evidence of striped bass risks, Section 404's strongly protective language, the aligned views of the federal natural resource agencies about striped bass risks, and even a Draft SEIS that predicted significant harms.

With no veto, in contrast, Westway's opponents had to make their own case without an unyielding federal agency ally on their side and without the benefit of judicial deference. The burden would fall on them to show that the Corps's judgment granting the permit was arbitrary and capricious or contrary to relevant laws and regulations. Even if the EPA regional office had exercised its veto power and been reversed by senior EPA officials, the record and explanation justifying the region's veto would have become part of the regulatory record. That supplemented record could have changed arguments and possibly outcomes in subsequent judicial challenges. Whether attributable to legal error or political pressure, EPA's complete failure to use its 404(c) authority had the potential to make a crucial difference in the Westway war.

Without an EPA veto standing in his way, and after neither EPA nor the other natural resource agencies even elevated their previously stated objections up the ladder to the Council on Environmental Quality within the Reagan White House, Griffis on February 25, 1985, granted the permit. He expressed pleasure with the resource agencies' decision not to object further: "I thought this old soldier might fade away before we got this permit through."[91] Westway's supporters celebrated. The *New York Times* declared the twelve years of Westway battle a "horrendous, collective failure"[92] but looked forward to Westway's construction.

11

THE TRIAL CRUCIBLE

FTER A SHORT-LIVED EXPECTATION that the Army Corps was going to kill Westway, opponents again found themselves regulatory losers. Despite ongoing objections of the various federal natural resource and environmental agencies, they had folded their cards well before playing their objections up the executive branch ladder. EPA too had disappointed, failing even to seek comments on whether to exercise its Section 404(c) veto power. The new Final SEIS reflected mystifying and so far unexplained changes from the dramatically different Draft's language. Despite the abundant data showing substantial usage of the proposed Westway site by young striped bass, often the highest percentages of all tested sites, the Final SEIS and permit decision dismissed such risks. The regulatory judgments of the Corps were once again vulnerable. In addition, adding pressure for both opponents and New York government leaders, any possible trade-in for Westway had to be completed by a statutory deadline of September 30, 1985. But barring some miraculous conversion of Governor Cuomo and Mayor Koch into Westway opponents, there would be no trade-in if the Corps's actions were upheld. The courts and the United States Congress were therefore now the opponents' focus. On the same day Griffis issued his permit, February 25, 1985, the Westway litigants returned to Judge Griesa's chambers. The project was squeezed from several directions but had won the key regulatory approvals. Once again the critical question was whether Judge Griesa would allow some sort of trial to allow questioning about Westway decision making.

The opponents—now referred to as plaintiffs in front of the court—were now represented by Mitchell Bernard of Butzel & Kass, assisted by Jean McCarroll. They had taken over for Al Butzel after he transitioned away from the full-time practice of law. Up until the time he handed over the legal reins to Bernard and McCarroll, Butzel had been tireless and effective in the lead legal role for opponents for about ten years. Westway was still alive, but through his efforts and the critically important, unfailing efforts of citizen and public interest group opponents, especially Marcy Benstock, Westway was not yet a reality. The opponents were fortunate to turn to Mitchell Bernard as their lead lawyer. Despite legal work on homelessness policies and a recent break from law to pursue his interest in writing for theater, he had been working on Westway for several years and knew the case inside and out. He was not an experienced trial lawyer but quickly proved himself a natural and effective trial advocate.

The Army Corps and state and city agencies asked Judge Griesa to dissolve his injunction. During conferences and in court filings over the next several weeks, the government lawyers once again cloaked their clients' choices in language emphasizing procedural rigor, thorough analysis, and judicial deference to political choices. Benstock's Clean Air Campaign, Friends of the Earth, the Sierra Club, the Hudson River Fishermen's Association, and the other plaintiffs opposing Westway in court took the opposite view. Through Bernard and McCarroll, they painted a picture that emphasized failures of process and explanation. They explicitly aligned their objections with legal and scientific views shared by expert staff and scientists within the nation's environmental and natural resource and fishery agencies. Through this framing and alignment, the plaintiff opponents again hoped to overcome disadvantageous judicial review presumptions and process. Bernard and McCarroll argued that not only should the injunction remain, but contempt sanctions should also be imposed and the permit decisions reversed.

To support their claim that something irregular had occurred, the opponents' main focus now was on the lack of explanation for the many Draft-to-Final SEIS changes regarding striped bass impacts. NEPA's requirement of full, adequate, and honest disclosure and analysis had been violated, opponents argued. They also argued that in granting New York the Section 404 permit, the Corps had violated the law: Section 404 prohibited unnecessary fill in aquatic habitat when there was an upland alternative, prohibited fill that could cause significant degradation of that habitat, and mandated permit denial since neither New York as applicant nor the Army Corps in granting the permit could establish with certainty that habitat harms would not occur. In their view, only with the unexplained and downplayed risks could Westway overcome Section 404's substantive protections. The opponents called for a trial. Once again, Judge Griesa sought a basis for an unexplained government action.

The federal defendants were immediately on the defensive due to a dearth of records reflecting Corps deliberations. Judge Griesa's mandate to maintain records had earlier been challenged but ultimately upheld by the court of appeals. After skirmishing about what issues would be subject to trial inquiry, Griesa indicated that a hearing and perhaps limited trial were needed. Exactly what would be litigated remained a source of contention for several weeks.

WITHIN DAYS, another battlefront opened against Westway. Now that the regulatory process had allowed Westway to proceed, risks to New Jersey's own development plans and concerns about wasteful government spending provoked congressional activity. Although Westway had passed muster with the Army Corps, the Corps's own analysis revealed that Westway's massive filling would make more problematic any water-edge development across the river and harbor, in New Jersey. Several New Jersey federal legislators instigated efforts to cut off federal Westway funds. New York City and State were already unhappy with New Jersey's efforts to entice city businesses over to New Jersey; the heightened opposition to Westway quickly led to recriminations and name-calling.

Although newspapers covered the entertainment provided by this latest New York versus New Jersey border war, the real action in early 1985 was in the United States courthouse, in the chambers of Judge Griesa. Over the next few weeks, as winter turned to spring, opponents and the government tussled first over what exactly the parties and court could address in any hearing or trial. The government pursued three main strategies to limit any third Westway trial before Griesa. First, government lawyers argued in briefs and in court that only the paper record—the actual regulatory documents—should be the focus. Second, the government emphatically opposed turning the trial into a "battle of the experts." It argued that the issue was not whether experts could differ—they surely could. Instead, the only issue was whether the government experts who had been delegated legal authority had exercised their authority in ways that were reasonable. The government argued that the Army Corps had easily surmounted the legal prohibition on "arbitrary and capricious" regulatory actions. Third, the government defendants, especially New York, emphasized in virtually every brief and argument that the decision to proceed with Westway was fundamentally a political choice. Absent evidence of an egregious violation of law, no court had jurisdiction to second-guess that choice; deference to regulatory and inherently political judgments was required by law. Westway had prevailed after intense political and regulatory scrutiny. In court filings and arguments, the government lawyers argued that those political and expert judgments should stand.

For the opponents, Bernard and McCarroll kept hammering at the Draft-to-Final SEIS changes, using those changes to emphasize the need for an actual trial with witnesses, testimony, and latitude to test the Army Corps's claims. How could the basic conclusions be reversed, yet with no new data and no explanatory discussion? They also continued to attack the government's minimal to nonexistent record keeping. Judge Griesa exhibited his own growing curiosity about the SEIS changes and impatience about the lack of records. The government lawyers were decidedly at a disadvantage here. They could not point to any contemporaneous government documents explaining the stark differences between the Draft and Final SEIS.

At a court hearing on April 4, 1985, the U.S. attorney's office made a critical and likely unavoidable concession. Given the problematic changes and explanation gaps, this concession was not a mistake but was likely essential if Westway were to be saved. The government backed down and agreed to a limited trial, thereby opening Westway decision making to another round of scrutiny. This choice was much like the federal government's 1982 agreement to a limited trial. It too had no choice but to defend unexplained and apparently unjustified claims of no fishery risks. The United States assistant attorney taking the 1985 case lead, Howard Wilson, backed off the government's initial firm opposition to discovery and a trial hearing. In open court he stated that he understood that the opponents and judge "will want a hearing" to explain the "change in language" from the Draft to Final EIS. He recited the kinds of questions he anticipated the plaintiffs and judge would want answered: "Was there a change in view? Was there a change in language? What does this all mean on that narrow issue? *On that narrow issue it is appropriate to have discovery and [a] hearing*" (emphasis added). Wilson sought to limit the scope of that concession, opposing "broad based inquiry into everything that the Corps was thinking" or "to have discovery that seeks to redo the whole thing again." That is what the "law says we are not supposed to have."

Wilson, like Nicholas Gimbel and the earlier 1982 trial team, had little choice. Poorly explained government decisions, especially arbitrary and unexplained regulatory changes, are a classic and relatively easy ground for judicial rejection. Their challenge now was somehow to limit the trial's scope, but that was difficult to do. The Draft-to-Final impact statement changes regarding fishery impacts went to the very heart of the opponents' contentions about striped bass risks under both NEPA and the Clean Water Act. Little that the opponents sought to establish could now be excluded. The government defendants would be relegated to emphasizing the need for deference to expert regulators and political judgments. A trial with witnesses, cross-examination, and extensive briefing was unavoidable. The United States would try to fill in explanatory gaps through the trial, but no trial's course is predictable.

ON MAY 20, 1985, the third Westway trial with witnesses commenced in Judge Griesa's courtroom.[1] Griesa emphasized that the trial was not to supersede the administrative proceeding, but he did not preclude the possible presentation of expert witnesses. The judge first allowed the lawyers to offer their basic trial openings, through which they would lay out their anticipated theories and factual showings. Because there was no jury hearing this case, all lawyers knew that they had to win the judge over to their view. Mitchell Bernard went first for the plaintiffs opposing Westway. He emphasized the Army Corps short-circuiting of the planned two winters of striped bass study and that the existence of alternatives to a river-based Westway required permit denial. Bernard spoke in particular detail about the many unexplained changes in the Draft-to-Final Supplemental EIS. His theory and key points were clear and cogent. Assistant United States Attorney Howard Wilson then made his own somewhat more narrow argument for the federal agency defendants, with the focus now on actions by the Corps. The fish impacts had now been thoroughly studied, and the Corps's judgment was that striped bass engaged in migratory movements without dependence on the Westway site habitat. The Corps's conclusion that the bass would therefore experience only "minor" impacts was well justified and certainly not "arbitrary and capricious." In Wilson's view, the Corps had easily surmounted its legal hurdle.

But then Wilson and his team made an unusual choice. If the lawyers for the United States were to maximize their arguments for deference to expert, contemporaneous regulatory judgments, then the main regulatory explanation should have been in referenced decision documents. If witnesses were to be called, they would logically be, and probably only be, the key government decision makers reviewing and explaining the key regulatory decisions. Wilson, however, revealed anticipated, but not certain, reliance on private scientist William Dovel as an expert witness. This was an unusual choice for several reasons. First, Dovel was not a government witness cloaked with the authority and legitimacy of an agency decision maker. Second, he was not really a disinterested expert but someone whose views had been explicitly referenced and relied upon in key Army Corps documents and decisions. He was really a fact witness, although one the government lawyers hoped would be convincing to Judge Griesa. Moreover, the government's team should already have known that Dovel had been paid for much of his work by a foundation linked to the

Rockefeller family; the Rockefellers were widely viewed as ardent Westway supporters. But if Wilson knew of this vulnerability, he did not even mention it. Third, Dovel was an odd expert for the government to rely on at trial because he lacked credentials—namely, a master's or doctoral degree—related to fishery science. Furthermore, and perhaps most worrisome for the United States lawyers, documents already part of the regulatory record revealed that Dovel's views actually had changed several times within the previous year. They had even been considered and rejected as without a scientific basis by EPA and its specially convened group of fishery experts.

It is unclear whether on May 20 the government had an inkling of how Dovel would present as a witness. Regardless, Wilson's opening made clear that Dovel was *the* key fishery expert who provided the underpinning for the key Army Corps conclusions: "[H]e was th[e] person who has most completely articulated the theory that the Corps ultimately accepts for why the fish are in Westway and what's going to happen to them i[f] Westway is built." Dovel's analysis positing migratory movement without site dependence offered the "definitive" work on striped bass in the Hudson. Wilson went on to claim that past attorneys for plaintiffs, including Al Butzel, had recommended that the government work with Dovel. In sum, Wilson's opening established Dovel as the linchpin of the United States' defense of its actions. Judicial review of the Westway decisions would largely rise or fall depending on the reliability of Dovel's work and possibly his testimony. And given the many objections of the federal natural resource agencies, and even objections of private consultants to the Corps, Wilson could not point to other experts or regulators in agreement with the Corps or Dovel. He conceded nothing about significant changes between the Draft and Final SEIS.

For New York State, in his renowned baritone, the lead Kaye, Scholer attorney, Paul Curran, presented an even simpler, basic framework, one that he and co-counsel Bruce Margolius, Lauri Novick, and Kimberly McFadden adhered to throughout the trial. Curran was one of New York City's most renowned litigators, having served as the United States attorney for the Southern District, a state anticorruption prosecutor, and trial counsel on many high-profile cases. He also had served in the state legislature and even run as a Republican candidate for governor against Mario Cuomo. Before Judge Griesa, Curran emphasized yet again the political nature of the Westway judgments and the many leading officials who wanted it built. His message was clear—Westway was the preferred choice of New York and national political leaders. The court should allow it to proceed.

Although the plaintiffs had initiated the trial, the parties went along with the court's suggestion that the government first present key decision-maker witnesses, with plaintiffs then given the opportunity for cross-examination and possible presentation of their own witnesses. The early witnesses presented by the United States left the government defendants in decent although somewhat weakened state. Colonel Griffis and Corps EIS drafter Len Houston reviewed their fishery considerations in depth, including a somewhat impenetrable discussion of probabilities, statistics, worst-case assumptions, and sampling protocols. Judge Griesa occasionally voiced frustration with more technical parts of their testimony, but the government lawyers knew exactly what they were doing. If the Army Corps's actions rested on complex scientific and technical judgments, then the judge would have a harder time rejecting Westway. In addition, these key initial government witnesses appeared credible given their complete rejection of the earlier EIS and trials' "no fish, no impact" story. Still, their testimony was not without hitches. Colonel Griffis conceded early on that few records of deliberations had been kept, provoking plaintiffs' and Griesa's ire. Even on the issue of Draft-to-Final SEIS language changes, both Griffis and Houston spoke of meetings and deliberations but seldom could point to any supporting documentary evidence.

Nevertheless, the government's case was helped by their witnesses' ability to stay on message and tell consistent stories. Griffis and Houston both insisted that there was no intended change in Draft-to-Final SEIS conclusions. Instead, as they explained it, the apparent shifts were actually due to sloppy use of the word "significant." The Draft's apparent identification of significant impacts was, according to Griffis and Houston, actually meant just to identify effects that were in a statistical sense "measurable" or "perceptible." "Significant" was not used in the Draft as a synonym for "major" or to connote harms or risks prohibited by Section 404 of the Clean Water Act. Houston said this with clarity and persistence, withstanding skeptical probing on cross-examination by Bernard and occasional interjected questions by Griesa. Griffis and Houston were consistent in these recollections. Even when Bernard pointed to abundant other Draft language seemingly conceding major harms and risks, Griffis and Houston stuck to their guns, bringing to bear data, protective assumptions, and linguistic clarification.

Judge Griesa remained measured in his comments and questioning but basically warned the assistant U.S. attorneys that the government's ongoing argument that there were no substantive changes of importance in the Draft-to-Final SEIS was unconvincing and contrary to the plain import of the many textual changes. The lack of documents tracking or explaining the changes was a problem. The government's attorneys did not adjust their arguments, needing to work with the facts as their client witnesses presented them; those witnesses were unyielding in the "no changes" tale that in large part rested on different meanings of "significant."

Griffis and Houston also set the stage for the later trial appearance by Dovel. Both stated that Houston had been in frequent communication with Dovel. Houston had even reviewed portions of a paper Dovel was drafting about striped bass use of the Hudson, but he never received his own copy and never read the whole paper. Both praised Dovel as knowledgeable and the source of theories about striped bass use of the Hudson and Westway inter-pier areas reflected in the Final SEIS and Section 404 permit-granting decision. Prompted by thorough questioning by Wilson, Griffis explained that the Corps had rejected several more-optimistic theories and mitigation plans that New York State proposed. The message here was clear—the Army Corps had not cherry-picked the theories most favorable to Westway. Both witnesses explained that their conclusions rested on Dovel's theory that striped bass were not overwintering but migrating passively through the Westway area with no dependence on the physical attributes of the site.

Bernard sought through cross-examination to highlight the irregularity and harmful results of the Army Corps's shortening of the planned two-winter study of striped bass. Since Griffis readily conceded what had happened, Bernard's cross-examination yielded few fireworks or surprises. Griffis also readily admitted that if Westway had been defined as solely a transportation project, then he would have had to deny the permit. He persisted, however, in defining it as a transportation and revitalization project, one that was appropriately regarded as water-dependent in order to achieve its many goals. For his approval not to violate a clear Section 404 requirement, this answer was critical.

Despite Wilson's earlier concession about the need for a hearing with witnesses, he and his allied counsel periodically sought to rein in plaintiffs' questioning and limit the scope of the judge's review. Due to the lack of required maintained records and explanation for changed regulatory conclusions, Judge Griesa generally rejected these government efforts to limit questioning. On the third day of the trial, Wilson again had to concede the record's inadequacy, but virtually every day he and his co-counsel still sought to limit the scope of plaintiffs' questioning. As the third day of testimony wound down on May 23, Griesa warned against undue repetition.

BERNARD DID SCORE some important points. Through his cross-examination, he highlighted tensions between Griffis's decision documents that alluded to striped bass as a hardy and adaptable species and expert federal natural resource agency comments that criticized this Army Corps assumption as inappropriate where the law required worst-case analysis. The documents introduced and questions Bernard raised ensured that Judge Griesa, as the ultimate decision maker, would understand the prevalence of expert agency critical comments aligned with the plaintiffs' claims. Bernard also highlighted Draft-to-Final language changes that had nothing to do with the term "significant," but the witnesses held their ground. Through effective questioning, Bernard also used Griffis and Houston as vehicles to review fishery data. They stated repeatedly that at several intervals during 1984 testing, the planned Westway site was the location of the greatest abundance of striped bass in the Hudson River estuary. Adjusted for effort and size of the testing area, as much as 33 percent of Hudson River young striped bass were at times found in the Westway area. And those numbers were highest early in the belatedly started testing and again during the last two testing intervals. Indeed, the numbers had been rising when testing ended in April. Bernard also punched holes in the migratory-movement theory, forcing Houston to concede that despite the claim that striped bass were moving through the Westway site, no sampling found substantial numbers of fish in the nearby deeper river or Upper Harbor below the tip of Manhattan. Through cross-examination, Houston also conceded that fish tagging and minimal recaptured fish ultimately were not a basis for the migration theory; it was not certain that the tagging efforts were reliable. Despite these problems, it was far from clear that these witnesses' actions and testimony were fatally outlandish. They might have passed the applicable "arbitrary and capricious" action test.

Plaintiffs then presented their only independent witness, architect John Belle. Belle testified about alternative designs that had become part of the politics against Westway. His alternative plan could meet many of Westway's goals, especially a proposal referred to as the River Road alternative. It was not clear if Judge Griesa was warming to the claim that Westway had to be denied because of a viable "upland" alternative, as plaintiffs argued was required by the Clean Water Act. However, a credible Belle could support such a claim. Defendant's counsel Curran and assistant U.S. attorney Marc Rosenbaum effectively highlighted through their questions the many ways Belle's idea was less formed and tested than was the Westway plan. In addition, as Curran's cross-examination highlighted, it was not clear whether this alternative would be fully federally funded or could comply with interstate highway standards. Questions raised doubts about construction disturbances and River Road's suitability for adjacent neighborhoods. Belle referred to the supporters and endorsements of the River Road idea, but Curran confirmed that the Regional Plan Association favored Westway over the River Road. Belle's proposal would also create far less new parkland. Belle handled the questioning well but was largely neutralized by effective cross-examination. At this point, the trial looked like a close call, but close calls go to the government. Plaintiffs had tough work ahead.

Plaintiffs turned to several witnesses for shorter testimony. Remarkably, all the witnesses on which the plaintiffs would rely from this point on were federal employees or agents of the government defendants who had been part of the Westway review process. First was John Bestgen, the regional administrator for the FHWA and hence the official responsible for overseeing the Supplemental EIS discussion of Westway and transportation alternatives. His testimony about the adequacy-of-alternatives analysis and surface road alternatives did little to advance or hurt either side in the trial.

Next plaintiffs turned to Dennis Suszkowski, who had been serving as the chief of the regulatory branch for the region's Army Corps office but had recently moved to work for EPA. Suszkowski had been the key drafter of the alternative denial and grant Section 404 permit documents for Griffis and had been a participant in deliberations over the Draft and Final SEIS. With Griffis, he had sought unsuccessfully to have the Corps's leadership allow two years of fishery study. Suszkowski was also a fishery expert, with a doctorate in marine environmental science. He proved to be an interesting, articulate, and disarmingly frank witness. He, more than the others, explained why the SEIS alternatives analysis was internally inconsistent and inadequate in its failure to analyze other revitalization trends or opportunities. He readily stated his view that there were three practicable alternatives to Westway that did not need to be in the Hudson. Upon cross-examination by federal and state lawyers, however, Suszkowski agreed that Griffis was ultimately the decision maker and he only an adviser; Griffis disagreed on the project definition. Still, if Judge Griesa were to take the bait and see the project's definition and the existence of upland alternatives as grounds for denying the Section 404 permit, Suszkowski had explained the issue with clarity. The plaintiffs were getting back in the game.

Plaintiffs next sought to use several government and government consultant witnesses who had worked on Westway fishery impacts to explain why the SEIS and Section 404 permit lacked a sound basis. The first witness, Douglass Heimbuch of Martin Marietta, had at several stages, starting in 1982, advised the Army Corps on Westway fishery impacts. Heimbuch had advocated the two winters of striped bass study and had tried to resign in protest when the Corps shortened the study to part of one winter. Upon entreaties from the Corps, he continued to serve on its technical steering panel that consulted regarding the winter 1984 study. Heimbuch was a clear and forceful witness for the plaintiffs although actually more of a fact witness whose experience with Westway had been through work for the government. After explaining the sampling logic, Heimbuch criticized Dovel's striped bass migratory-movement theory that Wilson had referenced in his opening. It was "untested," and Heimbuch had earlier recommended that Houston not rely on it. Heimbuch then reviewed high catch-per-unit-effort results in the Westway area, especially during the two last periods as testing drew to a close. He thought that his company's statistical analysis showing that 44 percent of young-of-the-year striped bass used the Westway areas in April could be an underestimate of Westway's importance. Reviewing the actual capture numbers, he confirmed that surrounding capture data were inconsistent with the theory that fish were moving through the Westway sites and into adjacent areas.

Heimbuch refused, however, to make any definitive claim about Westway's impacts. The data and fish movements were too uncertain. In his view, "there is no way to say what the impact would be except that there is a clear and substantial danger to the population." He was firm that no expert could state with confidence that building Westway would result in an insignificant impact on the striped bass stock. Upon Curran's and Wilson's cross-examination, Heimbuch softened this last claim, agreeing that a "reasonable person" could conclude that only a minor impact would result and that his approach could lead to an overestimate of anticipated impacts, as the SEIS stated.

Further questioning and discussion among the judge and lawyers also, however, confirmed that the 1984 study was not designed to explain or confirm fish movement but to provide information on the relative abundance of striped bass in the Westway interpier areas as compared with that in the surrounding waters. This clarification, if understood, could become important. The Corps had relied on theories about fish movement and lack of habitat dependence, as did the United States in its trial opening, but the massive 1984 study had not been designed to test either theory.

After extensive questioning and redirect examination by Bernard, Heimbuch reiterated that a hypothesis of significant adverse impacts was just as plausible as the hypothesis (in the SEIS and permit decision) that there would be little or no adverse impact. Due to Section 404's strongly protective presumptions and prohibitions on fill in a setting of scientific uncertainty about impact, this testimony was important. Upon reconvening for trial the next day, Judge Griesa continued discussions with the lawyers over what it meant. It appeared that the plaintiffs were gaining traction with him.

Several subsequent witnesses proved inconsequential, plus one of plaintiffs' anticipated fishery experts who had been so effective in the earlier Westway trial, Ian Fletcher, fell ill and could not testify. Plaintiffs would have to continue making their case primarily through government employees and consultants. A Fish and Wildlife Service scientist, Frank De Luise, testified briefly, stating his agency's view that even if striped bass used Westway areas in a migratory capacity, destruction of the habitat could and would cause serious harm to the species. Scientist Joseph Mihursky also testified. He was from Malcolm Pirnie, another consulting firm that had worked on Westway for the Corps. He recounted his criticism of Houston's conclusions that there would be no significant impact if 26–33 percent of the striped bass were displaced. He also viewed Dovel's migratory-movement theory as untested and undercut by the data. Like Heimbuch, he simply did not think the data and studies allowed for a "definitive conclusion" about Westway's impacts but saw them as strengthening the conclusion that Westway was a critical habitat. Like De Luise, Mihursky thought that important migratory routes also had to be protected. His testimony was weakened by some effective cross-examination that elicited his agreement that striped bass are tolerant of a wide variety of conditions. He remained firm, however, that during certain life phases striped bass do have more specific environmental requirements.

None of these witnesses was a resounding success for plaintiffs, but in cumulative impact they revealed a consistent rejection of Dovel's assumptions and theories. No one embraced a migratory-movement theory. They were unwilling to state with certainty that major harms would definitely befall striped bass, but they rejected contrary certitude as unfounded. They also did not see such certainty of harms as the relevant legal standard. It was becoming clear that the government would need Dovel himself to establish the credibility of his study and theories underpinning the Final SEIS and Section 404 permit. No one else had spoken in support of those theories.

Plaintiffs then called Jay Benforado of EPA, the witness chosen by the federal government to testify regarding EPA's written objections to Westway. Benforado worked in Washington, coordinating technical review of Section 404 analyses forwarded by the regions. Plaintiffs did not have the monetary resources or time to fly to Washington and take his pretrial sworn testimony. They instead arranged with assistant U.S. attorney Randy Mastro for the plaintiffs' lawyers to interview Benforado the night before his testimony. While Mastro was at that point a relatively inexperienced prosecutor, he subsequently became a renowned prosecutor of organized crime, Mayor Rudolph Giuliani's loyal deputy mayor, and "even by the pugilistic standards of the New York bar, . . . [developed] a reputation as a merciless litigator."[2] As Bernard recalls, the pretrial interview started with witness Benforado's fairly dry recounting of EPA's letter.[3] When Bernard asked Benforado about the changed language in the Final SEIS, Benforado dropped the neutral tone. In Bernard's recollection, Benforado said, "I was shocked. We were bowled over at EPA that the Corps had done this." Bernard explained that this answer was important and that he would ask Benforado about his and EPA's reaction the next day at trial.

The next day's trial testimony started fairly low-key. Benforado offered a straightforward recounting of the Westway issues and reasons EPA thought the project environmentally unsatisfactory and the SEIS analysis lacking, especially regarding alternatives. When Bernard asked him, however, about EPA's reaction to the changed Final SEIS language, Bernard awaited Benforado's statement about EPA's "shock." This time, however, Benforado gave a very different, less incendiary answer. He said the wording "appeared a little different." Far from using language of astonishment, Benforado at the trial merely said that "I think it is also important to say that in the EIS process, documents are rewritten. That is the whole purpose. It is a public exercise where all parties have input and the agency goes back and certainly rewrites the document based on input." This was miles from the answer Bernard had anticipated based on Benforado's interview the night before.

Bernard, a fairly inexperienced trial lawyer, faced a conundrum. In his recollection, he had "no idea how to deal with" this kind of changed, unanticipated testimony. So as he continued to question Benforado in the late afternoon, near the end of the trial day, he also debated internally about what he should do. "Now the choices are obvious. You could either go by it and move on, and give up that piece of evidence. You could turn on him and say, 'Did you meet me in the U.S. attorney's office yesterday? Do you remember my asking you this question? Do you remember what you said? Didn't you tell me you were shocked?' Right? Cross-examine him. But what am I doing then? Undermining the credibility of a witness whose testimony I want! Who has written comments that are favorable to our position in the case. I didn't know what to do."[4] So Bernard went into delay mode: "I just moved on and filled in for twenty minutes and told the judge I wasn't done with him. He would have to come back the following morning. So I would have overnight to think about it."

The trial day ended. A chagrined Bernard saw and confronted Benforado at the elevator, asking him what the changed testimony was all about. Benforado acknowledged that he had conferred with his superiors overnight but told Bernard that "'if you ask me a specific question, I'll answer it honestly." Benforado also alluded to a trove of documents EPA had produced shortly before his testimony and said he would answer questions about them.

That night, Bernard and Jean McCarroll dug through boxes of EPA documents and found blunt, critical notes and memoranda about central office weakening of the EPA objections. Since the two of them were doing all the legal work, they simply had not had a chance to review all the voluminous documents produced by the United States in response to plaintiffs' Freedom of Information Act requests.

Armed with this sequence of progressively weakened drafts and EPA staff memos stating concerns with inappropriate meddling with a scientific judgment, Bernard and the plaintiffs had a far better next day in court. Through these documents and Benforado's more forthcoming testimony, they painted a picture of federal environmental leadership trying to muzzle science-based objections. Political pressure from within the executive branch was confirmed in a January 15, 1985, memo sent to EPA administrator Lee Thomas by his special assistant, Phil Angell. Angell attached a cover note to a January 10, 1985, draft regional administrator letter. Much of the strongest objection language was already gone in this draft, but it still contained pointed criticisms and used language that indicated an EPA Section 404(c) veto was likely. Angell said he was "troubled by both the tone and content of this letter." Then, in a memorable passage that provoked trial questioning and later press coverage, Angell stated, *"It doesn't appear that [EPA regional administrator] Daggett has gotten the message*; nothing will kill this project faster than this letter" (emphasis added). Angell may have thought Daggett had been sent a message, but in later interviews Daggett professed no recollection of pressure from EPA leadership.

However, others within EPA were troubled. Internal critics of the weakened region's letter were concerned that unusual central office involvement in this comment letter would blow into a scandal. EPA was still rebuilding its sullied reputation attributable to actions by President Reagan's first EPA administrator, Ann Gorsuch Burford. Irregular handling of hazardous waste site choices by Gorsuch and a few assistants had come to light and, along with battles over related documents sought by Congress, resulted in congressional investigations and even criminal indictments. In the Westway setting, critics of central office meddling noted that "[m]ajor points in the region's letter have been diluted or omitted and the result is a vague response that the Corps could interpret as a change in EPA's earlier position. Such an interpretation may undermine any potential Corps decision to deny the permit."[5] Internal EPA critics urged clarity in EPA's letter, given its fishery scientists' ongoing objection to the project and their view that it could not be built without violating the Clean Water Act's mandates.

For plaintiffs, Benforado's testimony and the underlying documents were crucial to undercut the government's trial theme that the project's approval was the product of disinterested, expert judgment. And even with the political pressure to approve the project, EPA's region had stuck with its objection. The documents revealed that EPA's direct, initial appraisal of the Final SEIS changes was almost exactly the same as plaintiffs were asserting at the trial. EPA's uncensored (or at least unedited) view was that there were impact statement changes, and those changes were major, played down fishery impacts, and lacked justifying explanation. Benforado and the underlying documents were a boon for the plaintiffs and an embarrassment for the government.

New York Times op-ed columnist Sydney Schanberg was by now closely following the Westway trial. Earlier columns by Schanberg had raised fundamental questions about Westway and had highlighted federal failures to keep records required by Judge Griesa. The EPA documents introduced through Benforado provoked an even more caustic op-ed. Schanberg recounted Draft-to-Final SEIS changes and the lack of accompanying explanation. He also noted the considerable political and private pressure to approve the project, mentioning efforts by David Rockefeller and Senator D'Amato to push the project through. He interpreted the EPA actions and memos as "evidence strongly suggesting that people at the top in Washington were sending out the word" to decision-making agencies that "the project was to be approved—regardless of the evidence against it."[6] His scathing column was a marked contrast to periodic pro-Westway editorials also published by the *Times*.

In the courtroom, the plaintiffs were nearing the end of their witnesses. Their final witness was Mike Ludwig, a fisheries scientist from the habitat conservation branch of the National Marine Fisheries Service. NMFS had drafted the critically important earlier 1980 memo to the Army Corps highlighting fishery risks. That memo in turn had led EPA's regional administrator to highlight fishery impacts in a conversation with Westway's opponents. Those analyses had then set in motion the Westway fishery battles. NMFS was not the final federal decision maker, but it was the federal agency with the greatest fisheries expertise, and Ludwig was the NMFS scientist most involved in reviewing Westway impacts. He thus had the potential to be far more powerful and effective than any independent expert plaintiffs might have found.

Ludwig delivered. He was "amazed" at the Corps's tossing aside of the experts' recommended eighteen-month, two-winter study. To build a project that would displace and threaten 26 to 33 percent of the Hudson striped bass population "goes against all of the . . . basic tenets of good fisheries management." He explained that striped bass were stressed and plummeting in the Chesapeake, while the Hudson was more important and fortunately stable. But Westway was a major threat: "The loss of this 200 acre fill could be that ultimate insult that drives the population in the same direction as the Chesapeake population." He was not saying all would die, but "the level of impacts" would be "excessive and unacceptable [to NMFS], the agency charged with protecting that resource." When the judge read to Ludwig key Final SEIS conclusions downplaying project harms, Ludwig stated that they "d[idn't] make much sense at all." He said special stewardship of the striped bass was needed due to "international and national concern about the resource."

During cross-examination, he conceded having talked about a fish's "happiness" quotient, but he fended off intimations that he was a flake. He also conceded that he would have opposed Westway even without heightened striped bass risks because of his concerns with habitat loss. Ludwig did not emerge unscathed by the cross-examination, but his testimony had pushed the government deeper into a corner.

Witness after witness had criticized the Corps's decision. Of especial importance, Ludwig and the others explained why the migratory striped bass theory credited to Dovel and adopted in the Final SEIS and Section 404 permit decision lacked scientific credibility. Basically, of the fishery experts heard at the trial (other than EIS drafter Len Houston), none agreed with Dovel's theory. The Corps and Dovel had relied on theories that were not even tested by the large 1984 study. Nevertheless, the United States attorneys and Army Corps decision makers had put Dovel and his theories at the heart of their regulatory decision making and trial strategy.

Plaintiffs rested their case. Remarkably, despite battling for the right to present experts, they ended up making their case almost entirely through the federal government's own documents, regulators, and government contractors. Only their one architect witness was not a government witness or agent. Perfunctory motions to dismiss their challenge were quickly rejected by Judge Griesa.

THE GOVERNMENT ATTORNEYS had to decide how to proceed. They could have relied on deference principles and the solid testimony of Corps officials Griffis and Houston, but the parade of subsequent witnesses had left many of their claims in tatters. And the attorneys also had been repeatedly confronted by Judge Griesa's questions about the basis for the many Draft-to-Final SEIS changes. Griesa had not revealed his hand, but a victory for Westway was surely in doubt.

The U.S. attorneys decided that they had to present Dovel himself. They did so, calling him as an expert on striped bass impacts. On June 25, 1985, Dovel took the oath. The junior member of the U.S. attorney team, Randy Mastro, was responsible for Dovel and proceeded to introduce him. Dovel was introduced more as an expert than as a fact witness. Mastro had Dovel recount his considerable fisheries experience, including thirty years' work as a fisheries biologist, with eight years of striped bass experience in the Hudson. He had published a dozen articles and received environmentalist awards, and he had also been involved in meetings convened by the Corps to decide how much study was needed to assess Westway impacts. He had also met repeatedly with the drafter of the fishery language for the Final SEIS, Len Houston.

The government needed Dovel to explain the theory underpinning the Final SEIS conclusions and the Corps permit grant.

Dovel's initial testimony was clear, direct, and definite. He did not think Westway would harm striped bass, and he had never thought it would. He also did not think striped bass overwintered in the Westway interpier area. By the period of May to November of 1984, "there was no thought in [his] mind that [striped bass] could be overwintering in Westway," and he had told Len Houston of that view. He recounted his extensive contacts with Houston, which included sharing drafts of Dovel's Hudson striped bass report. In his testimony, he explained the migratory-movement theory in considerable depth and with great clarity. He was an unusually clear and confident witness, emphatic in the solidity of his conclusions. He displayed none of the scientific doubts and wariness about drawing definitive conclusions exhibited by the earlier fishery scientists and regulators. Whether Dovel's certitude would be a strength or weakness remained to be seen.

Late in that first day of his testimony, conflict ensued when he alluded to his own striped bass report, which he had worked on "day and night" during September and October 1984 and ultimately typed up in April 1985. Dovel said he had never given the report to the Corps. As a postdecision document, this report therefore appeared legally and factually irrelevant to the Corps's actions. But as argued by the U.S. attorneys and explained by Dovel, it did contain his key theory and conclusions, information that he had shared with Houston in personal conversations and in preliminary written forms. Nevertheless, even though this 135-page report dated to April 1985 was not part of the government's actual decision-making record and, at the time of typing, postdated the permit and NEPA decisions, the assistant U.S. attorneys sought at trial to have it admitted as Exhibit MMM. No one other than Dovel and the government lawyers had yet read it.

The judge was dubious, but the lead U.S. trial counsel, Howard Wilson, was emphatic, as he had been at the start of the trial: the report "*was the definitive work by the witness that the Corps relied on. He is an expert*" (emphasis added). Bernard objected, mainly on the grounds that Houston had never had the actual report and it postdated the challenged regulatory actions. Whether it was appropriately viewed as an expert's report was a different issue. The trial day ended, with Dovel to return the next morning. The admissibility of the report remained unresolved.

THE GOVERNMENT LAWYERS were already struggling, but the next trial day, June 26, the tide decisively turned. Few if any federal trials with the United States as a defendant explaining a regulatory action have ever taken such a disastrous shift. As the day started, Judge Griesa recounted that he had spent the night reading this "definitive" document that had been represented as providing the "expert" conclusions that provided the intellectual basis for the Corps's key actions. Dovel was asked to leave the courtroom so the judge and lawyers could talk. The discussion that ensued, however, was in open court.

Incredulous, Judge Griesa asked Wilson and Mastro if they had read the Dovel report, known now as Exhibit MMM, before they introduced it. Yes, they had. The judge then proceeded to express amazement and befuddlement. The report was "an astonishing document." "It presents nothing of any conclusory nature. It's just one hypothesis after the other." Griesa found even more puzzling that, contrary to Dovel's previous testimony, the report didn't reject overwintering. He gave the U.S. attorneys another chance to change course: "I want to know do you still offer it?" But the U.S. attorney's office was at this point so locked into the importance of Dovel and his reliability that they had little choice but to plunge ahead. Wilson had touted Dovel's expertise at the beginning of the trial and had further vouched for him and his report late the day before. Houston and Griffis had further explained that the Corps's decision documents rested on Dovel's work. Furthermore, both the Draft and Final SEIS alluded to his views and influence. Randy Mastro, arguing for the Corps and United States, said they still wanted to offer it as a *"synthesis of analysis of all the data* that has been available" (emphasis added), and he again emphasized Dovel's immersion in the science regarding Hudson River striped bass. And although the U.S. lawyers could not concede that they were embattled, they surely also were aware that they needed a credible witness who agreed with the analysis and permit grant by the Corps; other than Houston and Griffis, no trial witness or federal agency fish expert in the record or at trial had provided this much-needed support.

In light of the government's insistence on introducing Exhibit MMM, Judge Griesa continued reviewing it out loud in open court, highlighting particular pages' conclusions that flat out contradicted the Final SEIS and other passages that criticized the Corps's Final SEIS. Most troubling for the government, Griesa caught a glaring problem. Despite Dovel's direct examination testimony of no physical dependence on the Westway interpier areas and no overwintering, Exhibit MMM actually said that "protected enclosures characterized by water depth more than about 20 feet and low water currents *may be uniquely beneficial to overwintering striped bass but may not be a prerequisite for species survival. Overwintering areas are probably best defined as areas where fish concentrate but not necessarily characterized by lack of fish activity"* (emphasis added). This seemed to intimate, if not directly state, both that striped bass found in concentrations in the Westway site should be defined as "overwintering" and that the interpier Westway environment could be "uniquely beneficial." And although Dovel's direct testimony had emphasized the migratory-movement theory, the report itself seemed to undercut this theory, actually stating that "the dynamics of fish movement . . . cannot be developed without a substantial mark and recapture effort." The EIS and underlying study involved fairly limited mark and recapture efforts. Where Dovel's report alluded to fish "movement patterns," the document qualified its language by referring to that view as something Dovel "would speculate." On and on, quoting page after page, Judge Griesa pointed out ways the report revealed waffling and uncertainty. It also contradicted both Dovel's testimony and the Corps's decision documents. And the judge could not find the word "conclusions" anywhere. In a bit of likely inadvertent humor, Randy Mastro helpfully pointed out four pages where the word did appear. The judge admitted the exhibit into evidence. Dovel was let back into the courtroom, and Mastro's direct examination continued.

Dovel emphatically rejected that any further studies were necessary or even of value. In this view, he was contradicting every other fishery expert heard in court and the conclusions of several panels of scientists who had sought additional study of Westway fishery impacts. All had thought that more study would help but had compromised in agreeing to a two-winter study. And that study had been shortened to less than one winter. But in Dovel's view, additional study was "not at all" needed. Gently led by Mastro's questioning, Dovel recounted all the data and studies he had reviewed. He provided the key, declarative statement that Corps and U.S. attorneys sought to buttress references in the Final SEIS and Section 404 permit decision: "[T]hrough this intensive effort to analyze the whole system I have developed the basic pattern of movement." And that "movement in the lower Hudson is migratory. The animals are constantly in motion. Therefore, their momentary occurrence is not dependency and if there is no dependency on that particular habitat being substrate, there can be no impact." Clear, direct, and confident, Dovel confirmed what Houston and Griffis had said about his views.

Mastro then had to pursue areas of potential trouble for Dovel. No witness arrives without flaws, but a smart attorney will address those problems head-on so they do not appear overlooked or intentionally buried. Such questioning seeks to "declaw" the sources of potential trouble during cross-examination. Mastro therefore asked about Dovel's use of "hypothesis" language in the report. Dovel explained that the report reflected "the first cut" of "the evolution from a theory or hypothesis to conclusion." He stated that "I have not been able, frankly, to make the editorial changes and have the document put in a final form." But it was still "essentially as it will occur in final form." Judge Griesa had to clear this up. Did the report contain conclusions?

Dovel reassured the judge that references to "hypotheses" would be changed in a finalized version to "say certain activities occur."

Then, guided by Mastro, Dovel began to clarify several of these problem points. Where it said that "overwintering may be a misnomer," he said it would be changed to "[o]verwintering is a definite misnomer" and "inappropriate for the Hudson because fish, young striped bass in this case, do not stay any place for any duration." Further seeking to declaw report language, Mastro drew Dovel's attention to another place where his report still alluded to striped bass overwintering farther up the river, near Yonkers. For a scientist who had just claimed definitively that overwintering was an inappropriate concept for young striped bass in winter, this was a problem. Dovel explained that he had used the phrase as a "typical fishery biologist," meaning only "the broad area in which fish can be found in the winter." Strengthening his current disavowal of the "overwintering concept" (despite his report's use of the term), he emphasized that "[o]verwintering is really an exceptionally bad term to use. It is very deceiving." Mastro also sought to diminish harm that might be caused by questions about who had funded Dovel's work. Dovel readily confirmed that George Lamb, who "handles environmental matters for Laurence Rockefeller" (David Rockefeller's brother), had funded his salary for three months of work on the report. Dovel also confirmed that, during the trial, he was a "paid expert witness for the government."

Mastro drew his direct examination to a close by eliciting clear, declarative statements. After recounting efforts to tag striped bass, Dovel concluded that the tiny number of tagged bass caught again in Westway interpier areas meant that "the fish being tagged left the area." This was presented as confirmation of the migratory movement theory underlying the Corps's decision documents. He again definitively stated that Westway was not "critical habitat" for striped bass. "There is no dependency by striped bass in the Westway or other similar areas in the lower Hudson." He again stated that he did not think "further study" would "help on the question of Westway impacts," although it could help understand the "migratory pattern." He then backed away from even this slight interest in more study. He "kn[e]w why fish concentrate" upriver near Yonkers and he now knew the "basic pattern of movement"; further study would "only corroborate" what he already knew. He definitively rejected others' contrary conclusions and other scientists' hedging in light of scientific uncertainty. For Dovel, there was simply no doubt: "We can establish exactly why fish are in various areas." Westway would not have "any impact." Mastro and the government turned the witness over to Bernard for cross-examination.

12

THE CROSS-EXAMINATION

LAWYERS CAN WAIT their whole lives for a moment where their skills can make or break a case. Far more rare are multibillion-dollar cases involving all levels of government and the future shape of the world's leading city. Bernard's cross-examination of Dovel had become the critical moment for Westway. Despite the ongoing political opposition advocacy by Benstock and many others, as well as increasing scrutiny and criticism in news columns in New York City and other national papers, New York City and State remained firm in their support for Westway. Congressional action guaranteeing or killing the project appeared unlikely, although congressional interest was growing. The trial was the focus of Westway partisans, and Dovel had become the most important witness. His testimony had offered some glimpses of weakness, perhaps most obviously with his possible overconfidence when all other scientists conceded uncertainty. But Dovel had also helped by offering the only expert validation, outside the Army Corps, for the conclusion that Westway posed no significant risks to striped bass. The question now was whether his views and certitude could hold up under Bernard's questioning.

Dovel's belatedly produced report, however, had changed everything. As Judge Griesa's questions had revealed, report statements seemed to conflict both with Dovel's testimony and with Corps analysis. As Bernard recalls, once he read the report, he "could not wait to show up in court the next morning." Now was his chance. The courtroom was packed, including his clients,

Figure 12.1. Mitchell Bernard, as shown here in a mid-1980s photograph, took over as the opponents' lead lawyer in 1984. His 1985 trial work, especially his lengthy cross-examinations of witness William Dovel and Corps decision makers, revealed the questionable assumptions underlying the Army Corps of Engineers 1984 approvals of Westway. *(Source: Natural Resources Defense Council; photographer Daniel Gelbwaks.)*

especially Marcy Benstock and Bunny Gabel, who were there virtually every day. At this point, *New York Times* op-ed columnist Sydney Schanberg was also often in court. Even in Bernard's eagerness to cross-examine Dovel, he could not have anticipated all that was about to transpire. He was about to commence one of the law's epic high-stakes cross-examinations, occurring over most of four trial days. Many billions of dollars were at stake, as was the shape of the world's leading city and a hugely valuable fishery. This was a make-or-break moment.

Bernard started with the basics. Was Dovel really an expert? It turned out he had taken only two graduate-level fisheries biology courses. His only work for the previous two years had been as an "independent consultant," with intermittent compensated fisheries work. Bernard began to use Dovel's own past statements to undercut the unusually firm scientific claims in his direct examination testimony. Dovel dodged a bit but then began to backtrack and waffle. Years later, lead U.S. trial counsel Wilson recalled that it was "painful to watch [Bernard] take my witness apart."[1] Dovel conceded that he had earlier advised the Corps that expert judgments could not be expected until "all reasonable efforts had been made to obtain baseline data." That statement had accompanied the expert fishery panel's recommendation of two winters of new study, as well as collection of information about habitat characteristics and food availability. Dovel conceded that most of that recommendation had been disregarded, with 1984 Westway testing including only one winter of sampling and no food and habitat study. Bernard was highlighting that Dovel claimed definitive knowledge despite lacking information that he and a consensus of other experts had previously agreed was essential.

Bernard also sought to cast doubts on Dovel's neutrality, focusing on his successful efforts to obtain funding from George Lamb, who in turn was linked to the Rockefeller family and the Jackson Hole Preserve foundation. The Rockefellers were active, vocal Westway supporters. They had been instrumental in creating and leading pro-Westway business groups. Dovel conceded that he "may well have said" that his work on Westway fishery impacts could "'be most beneficial for the Westway concern." He claimed, however, not to know what results Lamb favored on the proposed Westway project. Dovel did recall saying something like "Westway could use" his study.

As Bernard's questioning clarified, Dovel's "definitive" report actually remained in the drafting stage in early 1985, when Colonel Griffis had made his Section 404 permit decision. Yet the Draft SEIS, the Final SEIS, and the United States government's lawyers had attributed key fish impact conclusions to views of Dovel. How could the Corps have relied on an unfinished report for such a high-stakes decision?

Bernard began to bear down. Dovel had shown great confidence about the lack of Westway impacts during his direct testimony. But confronted by Bernard with actual 1984 data, he admitted fish might collect in large numbers in the Westway site for "several weeks," or even a couple of months. Dovel admitted that it was "impossible to tell what would happen to those fish and what the level of occurrence would be in the area" since testing had stopped as striped bass abundance hit its peak in April 1984. Dovel tried to return to his migration theory, stating that the last two sampling periods would be "looking at different fish," but then admitted that the data collected could not confirm that claim. Dovel also admitted that the comprehensive (but shortened) 1984 testing often revealed virtually no striped bass in areas where he had claimed they were abundant.

Bernard finally asked a key question. How could Dovel "know if a fish spends 4 weeks in a lower river habitat that the fish doesn't need the habitat?" In contrast to his definitive initial direct testimony statements, Dovel's answer revealed a far more tentative theory: "I don't know that it doesn't, except that my basic pattern of movement has created the profile of movement which suggests to me not only where they are moving but why they are moving." With his "I don't know," and "suggests to me" language, Dovel was suddenly hedging his claims. He did not know about water depths in other nearby Hudson habitats but agreed that striped bass would not use shallow areas during cold periods. He did not know about relative habitat diversity and richness on the Manhattan or New Jersey side of the Hudson. In addition, questions and answers reaffirmed that the large 1984 study of striped bass was designed to reveal "relative abundance," not to "show movement." This admission was important; Dovel's theory of migratory striped bass movement without dependence on any particular habitat was built on sampling designs and data that could not support such a hypothesis.

Dovel did not back down, however. He claimed support for his migratory-movement theory from the almost complete lack of recaptured tagged fish. But tagging had not started until halfway through the study, initially killing many tagged fish in the process. Army Corps and consultant documents questioned whether the tagging technique had worked and called for caution in using tag return data. Dovel was still "quite satisfied that not a single tag came off"; he would "guarantee you the tags didn't come off." His certitude was becoming a liability.

When Dovel nevertheless insisted that fish were moving into other adjacent Hudson River areas, Bernard drew his attention to actual data, methodically showing minimal capture in those surrounding areas. Dovel resisted. "Frankly, I think you are putting too much emphasis on the numbers you are looking at." Bernard and opponents, however, were going to make sure that Dovel grappled with problematic data and the abundant evidence about the protocols and goals of those studies. None were designed to test and prove Dovel's theory.

Bernard asked Dovel about the recent mid-February 1985 meeting at EPA where his theory was presented. The federal and state government attorneys leapt in, unsuccessfully seeking to keep minutes of that meeting out of the trial. The document could not help them. At that meeting, Dovel had defended the sufficiency of the sampling and his own conclusions relied upon by the Corps, but the minutes once again revealed that Dovel stood alone in his views: the minutes stated that "[a]ll but Dovel said . . . under-pier sampling was unsuccessful . . . , since sampling was sporadic and not performed in a manner that would yield useable data." Even worse, the minutes concluded that "'the consensus of the meeting's participants was that *the methodology used by Mr. Dovel to combine the studies had no scientific basis and that there was no substantive data base to support his current theory*'" (emphasis added). Dovel did not remember such a conclusion. He did, however, recall that EPA's focus was on "numerical quantification and that was not at all my presentation." This rejection of Dovel's approach by a collection of fishery and environmental methods experts convened by EPA was yet another blow to his credibility.

If this trial were akin to the formalized battling of a boxing match, then Bernard had Dovel cornered and on the ropes, with his testimony already severely undercut. But when Bernard turned to Dovel's report to start a new line of questioning, the judge broke in and called it a day. Dovel had an evening to rest, consult with his lawyers, and collect his thoughts.

A BIT PAST 10:00 A.M. on June 27 the trial resumed, and Dovel returned to the stand. Bernard turned to Exhibit MMM, Dovel's April 18, 1985, typed Hudson striped bass report offering the rationales relied on by federal government decision makers and called "definitive" in court by Westway's federal lawyers. Assistant U.S. attorney Mastro's direct examination had highlighted the key supportive conclusions in that report, but Dovel had yet to face skeptical and adversarial questioning. Bernard got to work.

Bernard first established that the report was substantially based on an earlier handwritten draft written during September and October 1984. Dovel had reviewed the earlier draft with Army Corps EIS drafter Len Houston. He also readily conceded that the typed trial Exhibit MMM was itself still a draft—actually a "first draft"—to be shortened and revised for submission for publication. If "the evidence is there" to "support[] what you might call hypothes[e]s in other sections," then in a final version report language "will be changed from hypothesis to conclusions." Dovel emphasized again that he had already "reached conclusions, positive conclusions with respect to how this document relates to impacts of Westway." The changes he anticipated were characterized as "minor," "fine-tuning, subtle changes" to "an inappropriate word here or there." Dovel said he had reviewed the whole report in recent weeks.

Bernard established through Dovel's ready concessions that the Army Corps had never actually seen the typed report and that Dovel had not yet submitted it for peer or scientific review. These were problematic concessions. Billions of dollars and the shape of Manhattan, as well as the fate of many of the Hudson's young striped bass, rode on this unreviewed report lacking any outward signs that it was sound. It had substantial weight to carry, especially since fishery experts outside the Corps had either reached contrary conclusions or, at a minimum, thought Dovel's views lacked a basis.

Just a few minutes into Dovel's second day of testimony, Bernard's cross-examination began to elicit a strange, almost surreal series of exchanges. The shift in tone started when Dovel emphatically disagreed with Bernard's intimation that his report was based on "fragmentary data"; he would not "classify" it that way "at all." It was not fragmentary "in any way," although Dovel said some biologists might consider some of the data basis fragmentary. But it turned out that Bernard was not inquiring based on speculative insinuations. He directed Dovel to only the second page of the report, which stated that "[u]nfortunately, only fragmentary data exists for some important aspects" of understanding striped bass use of the area. Dovel was asked to explain. Now his answer changed. The data were "not equal in completeness," but now his view was that the new 1984 data collected for Westway were "not . . . fragmentary in any way." And what would he do with that language? "That will be changed," and the "fragmentary data" language would come out. Now Bernard was puzzled. Didn't Dovel have all of New Jersey Consortium data when he handwrote the document in September or October of 1984? Yes, Dovel conceded.

Now the judge got into the game, also puzzled. He read more of the "fragmentary data" language to Dovel and asked him if he "believe[d] that was the situation as you set it down?" Dovel gave an elliptical, largely unresponsive answer but finally said yes. Bernard then asked when and why Dovel had decided to change the language. "I would make some change as a result of our discussion," Dovel answered. The judge interjected—the discussion in court? Dovel said yes, "the discussion in court is helping me focus on the words, would help me focus on the words I use so that I would not confuse anybody with respect to whatever value they may gain from the document." Judge Griesa ended this exchange with an acerbic comment: "It's nice to know that court sessions have some value."

Bernard turned to Dovel's methodology. Hadn't his report combined data from survey designs that were not comparable or compatible with one another? Dovel resisted until Bernard drew his attention to his own report language: the report "thus attempts to combine the results from several investigations in a composite graphic [that] are complicated by the incompatibility of some key data arrays." This language, too, would be adjusted, Dovel explained. A report reference to a high abundance of striped bass above the George Washington Bridge was, as Dovel had to admit, from studies that included no adjustment for "probability of capture." Even more remarkably, courtroom exchanges established that Dovel's report relied on studies that did no sampling at all in Westway interpier areas, were from different years, generally stopped in December, or stopped well north of the city, up the Hudson near Yonkers. Dovel agreed that this part of his approach was "discouraged or rejected" by the Corps, yet in court his views had been called definitive to explain the Corps's regulatory choices. Bernard's cross-examination was highlighting the same methodological flaw EPA and other fishery scientists had found. Dovel was using these varied and incompatible data sets to draw conclusions about the relative importance of the Westway area and derive a theory about striped bass movement. A strange fog of confusion was descending on the court.

Judge Griesa turned Dovel to an important passage in the report. The report stated (in the judge's paraphrase) that "for the winter of 1983–84, the greatest concentration of young bass in the Hudson estuary was located north of the metro area and predominantly in the Yonkers zone." The next passage, however, backtracked by stating that other investigations, including the Army Corps 1984 investigation, "do not contradict this conclusion but may not support it fully due to variations and inadequacies in sampling design." Dovel admitted that the "Army Corps 1984" data language was an allusion to the recent 1984 New Jersey Consortium testing for Westway analysis. The judge wanted to know the basis for this key claim. Did the reference to "all data" include data above and beyond the Westway-oriented studies? Griesa was seeking quite basic information—what was the basis for Dovel's claim that "the greatest concentration" of striped bass during 1983–84 was by Yonkers?

After a break, Dovel more forthrightly said the "all data" included investigations that had not even sampled south of Yonkers (which is about fourteen miles away from the Westway site), did not sample past mid-December, and did not examine areas north and south of the George Washington Bridge. Dovel agreed that these data could not support claims about comparative abundance above and below the George Washington Bridge. Bernard closed in for the kill on this "the greatest concentration" claim. He reviewed study after study, showing few actual capture results that allowed for comparative claims and similarly few showing many striped bass north of the bridge or near Yonkers. In fact, most data sets showed the striped bass numbers highest south of the George Washington Bridge, many in the Westway area. Dovel did not seem to grasp that his key claim was in the midst of demolition. He stated, "I must say you are spending a lot of time on data that I didn't consider most important in my analysis." The judge instructed the witness just to take it "step by step."

Finally, after more questions, concessions, and some banter among the lawyers, Judge Griesa revealed that by now he too was at a loss to understand. How could Dovel's Exhibit MMM report conclude "that the bulk of the fish in winter are up around Yonkers, because we [have] been through the . . . data and it doesn't support it." Dovel explained that he "used all of the data" to develop a "pattern of movement for the whole river." Bernard sought to turn to overwintering language, but the judge still wanted to nail down the basis for this important Dovel claim that the "greatest concentration" of striped bass was near Yonkers. Bernard sought to move on; he did not think he should have to "show what the reasoning is and why it's valid." So the judge asked Dovel himself—what was his basis? Dovel then said it was "primarily" the 1984 data collected by the

New Jersey Consortium for Westway. Now Bernard knew Dovel was in trouble. He stuck with the "greatest concentration" claim.

Bernard proceeded to look at each interval for the 1984 study, in the various sampling locations. When he sought to look at separate charts and data, Dovel resisted—he found them valuable "in composite." He also emphasized that the changing numbers revealed that striped bass were "constantly moving," with the data creating a "profile of movement through the whole area." But Bernard wanted to see which data supported Dovel's quite specific conclusion. Chart after chart and data sets contradicted it, although a few testing intervals did show high striped bass captures near Yonkers. During the same and other intervals, however, substantial numbers were found elsewhere, often near or in the proposed Westway site. Dovel claimed the data established striped bass "beginning to form a concentration in the Yonkers area." The actual data, however, showed rising and falling numbers in Yonkers, but also by and in the proposed Westway site. Dovel never identified data that supported this key report claim. Still, he was "positive" about conclusions he could draw about bass movements revealed by these data.

Bernard and the judge tried to tease out what conclusions in Dovel's report were based on data or his own creation of "catch per unit effort" numbers derived from "a measure of density" simply multiplied out by acreage. What about unsamplable areas, like those under the Westway site's twenty-one piers? Dovel did not "believe" that these areas contributed to fish in the wintertime. Bernard asked, "your personal belief?" Dovel demurred—"that is my conclusion." Bernard echoed him, "That is your conclusion?," to which Dovel confusingly replied, "or belief." To put it mildly, Dovel was not doing well. When he revealed that he had not subjected his own analysis to assessment for statistical validity or assessment of the standard error, Bernard asked how he then could know what the numbers really revealed. Again, Dovel returned to broad language, saying he was not as concerned with "subtle changes in numbers" as he was with "the broad changes in a pattern" or "basic movement pattern."

Several questions elicited that Dovel had averaged striped bass capture numbers from the river's-edge Westway interpier areas (where numbers were often quite high or even highest) and adjacent deep areas (where numbers were low to zero). Bernard's questions confirmed that this averaging made Westway look relatively unimportant. Judge Griesa alluded to the earlier trial, where similar averaging had been used to downplay the importance of the Westway site. He asked Dovel, if we drew "a separate bar for Westway," wouldn't his chart be "quite different?" When Dovel said "it would change the pattern," the judge quickly replied, "Certainly it would." The judge then looked at how Dovel's averaging of low- and high-capture areas changed his "pattern of movement" data. With only one modest exception, Westway's importance would have skyrocketed. Forced to work with the actual data, Dovel alluded to "the big peak" of striped bass in late testing period data, conceding it was "an enormous peak." But his averaging had obscured that peak. With only one exception, eliminating the averaging caused the Westway numbers to increase, often by 50 percent and sometimes by doubling.

Dovel again referred to changes he would be making to his report. He would edit it both to describe the averaging and to change his zones to geographical areas. He would also change several references to "hypothesis" to something more "solid," perhaps "conclusion" or "established pattern" or "interpretation."

Bernard switched his focus. Dovel's report stated that "it seems logical that the longer the duration of fish occurrence in a habitat the more we can assume occurrence is synonymous with some degree of dependence." With the many Westway area samples confirming substantial striped bass presence, this language seemed like a crucial concession. In fact, it appeared to align Dovel with all the other fish experts who had commented to the Corps and testified at trial, but all in opposition to the Corps's permit grant. But Dovel "no longer agree[d] with the comments as stated here. They will come out." Did Dovel stand by the report statement that "duration of occurrence can only be determined through mark and recapture studies," a technique that the report stated "has not been adequately employed in the lower Hudson"? Dovel had believed these statements when he wrote them in September 1984, but he now thought they were "no longer appropriate because I know what the movement is and, therefore, can determine whether or not there is dependence."

Bernard tried to put this exchange into coherent form. "Are you saying that as of the end of October [1984]," when Dovel was finishing the handwritten form of the report, "this sentence we have been talking about just wasn't true in your view anymore?" Dovel's answer? "Yes." The judge asked for the exchange to be read back to him. Dovel had just said that the draft he had handwritten was, when written, not true in his mind anymore. Bernard did not want to risk letting Dovel clean up this exchange. It was devastating to the credibility of both Dovel and this so-called definitive report, so he sought to move on. Showing his usual inquisitorial style, however, the judge elicited from Dovel confirmation that his answer was not the result of confusion.

AFTER A BREAK, the judge returned to this exchange. He asked Bernard to read Dovel the preceding passage: discerning the importance of "other wintering areas in the upper harbor is complicated by the knowledge that young striped bass may in reality constantly be on the move through that region and *there does not appear to be means of separating dependence on a habitat from chance occurrence there*" (emphasis added). This passage conflicted with both Dovel's current certitude and the Corps's SEIS and Section 404 decision conclusions that there was no striped bass dependence on the Westway habitat. Did Dovel "agree with it when [he] wrote it?" Yes, Dovel agreed with it then. Today? No, he did not agree with it, and "perhaps in October" had reached that contrary conclusion. But this statement had evidently been in Dovel's handwritten report and in the typed version from months later. These inconsistencies posed a major problem for the government and Westway's future.

When Bernard pressed Dovel on a related sentence stating that "the longer the duration of occurrence, the more we can assume occurrence is synonymous with some degree of dependence, " Dovel stated that "it is a general statement I would agree with now, *but not with respect to Westway*" (emphasis added). Dovel insisted that although "Westway is a fish habitat," Westway and the "general areas around the lower Hudson" "would be an exception to this general statement" linking the duration of occurrence and habitat dependence. When handwriting his report, he had concluded Westway was an exception. However, neither the handwritten draft nor the typed version reflected that changed conclusion, a conclusion of absolutely crucial importance to Westway's fate. What about his report's statement about the need for "mark and recapture" to determine duration of occurrence? This was a fine general statement, but it too "did not apply to the Westway situation."

This was a disastrous exchange for the government, Westway supporters, trial lawyers, and Dovel. Dovel was disavowing his own report and asserting that he handwrote language with science claims he had already rejected. His testimony added qualifying exception language not present in his report and, without any explanation, he claimed that although a general statement was true, it did not hold true for Westway.

Reflecting upon Dovel's courtroom performance roughly twenty years later, Randy Mastro would only shake his head and talk about learning experiences.[2] The main lawyer for New York State, Paul Curran, remained chagrined and critical that Dovel had not been adequately prepared.[3] At the time, all the government's lawyers were surely suffering as their crucial witness and the definitive synthesis report proved to be a lethal combination. Dovel's testimony was not yet finished, but it was clearly awful for Westway and a boon for the opponents. Bernard was not about to let him go.

Nevertheless, Dovel inexplicably became even more bold and confident in his conclusions, digging himself deeper into a hole. When Bernard asked about tagging efforts and their reliability, Dovel said he no longer even needed that data: he "didn't think additional mark and recapture studies [were] necessary to answer the question of Westway."

Bernard shifted gears, drawing scrutiny to a major problem for the Corps and Westway's supporters. If the report's actual language contradicted the Corps's conclusions, how could the Corps explain itself with reliance on Dovel? Dovel confirmed he had reviewed report graphics and "the substance of the entire report" with EIS drafter Houston. But couldn't a reader like Houston "get the impression that you meant the opposite of what you say you mean? You think that is fair?" Dovel's reply: "I think so." Dovel could not, however, recall disclaiming report language aligned with what Westway's opponents and natural resource agencies had long been claiming. Bernard's cross-examination was establishing that Dovel's written report in reality did not support the Army Corps's conclusions.

As the day wound down, Dovel was asked to step off the witness stand. The lawyers and judge started battling over what exactly this report was and why it had been introduced. Bernard had just had a field day but quickly questioned whether it was an expert report at all, especially since "it turns out it is not his views at all." The head of U.S. attorney team, Howard Wilson, stepped into the fray instead of the less experienced Mastro, even though Dovel was Mastro's witness. Wilson stated that "a key witness" had "written 150 pages of material." It "shows a lot of work." To not introduce it would have, in the government's view, been "simply a mistake." Wilson also asserted that accusations of wrongdoing would have been made had the report not been introduced.

Judge Griesa, however, referred back to and quoted the government lawyers' claims about the value of the report as a "synthesis of all the data" and a "statement of [Dovel's] conclusions." The judge stated the obvious: Dovel had disclaimed many of his written conclusions. He mused out loud that "I will have to figure out what to do about this," where a witness "does not incorporate what he says were his conclusions" but "types it up with things that were not his conclusions." These report and testimony problems were not "even hinted at in the direct examination." The judge characterized the day's events as "this very bizarre situation."

The trial would not resume until after the weekend, on Monday, July 1. Judge Griesa suggested that the government have someone, perhaps FBI agents, go and pick up the September-October handwritten draft. Dovel and government attorneys had a respite to regroup and strategize on how to salvage Dovel's disastrous first two days on the stand.

ON MONDAY DOVEL returned to the stand. The handwritten draft remained missing, but the attorneys had unexpectedly turned up an earlier intervening draft that Dovel had apparently forgotten. Attorney representations and witness testimony soon clarified that it had been typed in December 1984, with edits in the form of deletions and handwritten additions made between December 1984 and April of 1985, when Exhibit MMM had been typed. This new version of the report was accepted as Exhibit NNN. Dovel had to start his new day of testimony with backpedaling and an admission that his earlier confident chronological presentation "was not accurate." And the assistant U.S. attorneys had to fall on their own swords too, taking responsibility for the confusion, error, and failure to find the additional document earlier.

The judge asked Dovel to leave the courtroom. He reviewed the testimony problems, the attorney's vouching for Dovel and his report, and the problems with the report's content. He addressed the lawyers with "some admonishment": they had "an obligation to get with [their] witnesses, and if something doesn't wash, tell them this story doesn't wash, and I want the truth. You are not doing that. You ought to start doing it." Judge Griesa also returned to the Draft-to-Final changes, reiterating that testimony so far did "not wash" as an explanation of the changes.

Bernard had not yet had a chance to review Exhibit NNN and could have sought a break to review it in detail, but this would have given Dovel and the government attorneys more time to regroup. He decided to proceed as best he could, depending on co-counsel's McCarroll's ability to review this new document and help him with questioning. The previous trial day's pattern resumed when Dovel again began rejecting language in his own April report (Exhibit MMM). The report stated that "protected enclosures characterized by water depth more than about 20 feet and low water currents may be uniquely beneficial to overwintering bass but may not be a prerequisite for species survival." Dovel agreed that the Westway interpier areas were "one of the protected enclosures" alluded to in the report. But now he would "change the whole sentence" to a near opposite statement, something like "Because the fish adapt to open natural areas, protected man-made enclosures could not be unique or especially beneficial to the species." Dovel agreed that this would be a "pretty substantial change." Although he claimed plans to make the change since "before late October," it had remained in all written drafts, including the "definitive" April report.

Bernard stuck with the supposedly definitive April 1985 report, turning to language stating that "I have the feeling that such areas of the lower Hudson may represent optimal overwintering sites within a much larger natural habitat." Dovel did not hem and haw about the sites referenced: he admitted that they were references to the Westway interpier basins. But this too was now rejected. His trial testimony and own documents continued to clash: the report elements backed Westway's opponents, but his testimony stuck with the "no impact" conclusion due to the passive migratory-movement hypothesis (which he now often called a conclusion). Bernard could not resist tweaking Dovel. What about the report's "feeling" language? Was it still "a feeling or have you transcended feeling on this point?" Dovel said he now had "conclusions," "confident conclusions."

Bernard started on a new line of attack, to powerful effect. Were there any new data to explain the changed conclusions? No new data, Dovel responded, just "a lot of additional work." And, in fact, Bernard asked, there weren't any new data of any kind collected between September and the trial, correct? Dovel agreed. And when Dovel sought to explain his own new, different theories and why they did not require more "mark and recapture" efforts, he also had to concede that that explanation was not yet anywhere in his typed reports.

Midmorning, after extensive rejection by Dovel of key language in both of his own typed drafts, the judge resumed an inquisitorial role, returning to Dovel's basic theory, restating it at length and with clarity. But where was this theory in his report, the judge asked? Dovel had to admit that it was "was spread throughout" the report. So the judge then sought to find the elements of the theory, even if they were scattered throughout the typed drafts. With the help of Dovel's attorneys, some supporting language was found, but other elements remained missing. It was apparent now that neither of the "definitive" report drafts contained a direct and cohesive statement of Dovel's views stated in his direct trial testimony or referenced in the Army Corps Final SEIS and Section 404 permit decision.

Bernard's questions became more direct but the exchanges more befuddling. Bernard started simply asking, "Did you believe this when you wrote it?" Dovel, in turn, would answer no or explain the ways in which he didn't, when writing it, agree with his own report's language. A few similar points during the first two days had provoked the judge to ask for a rereading of the trial transcript; at this point, it was becoming the new normal. Just as the relationship between Exhibits MMM and NNN began to become clear, Dovel revealed that he had given a full clean, typed version in December to George Lamb, the Rockefeller contact and Westway supporter who had paid Dovel for much of this work. It was clear that yet another version might soon be before the court.

Dovel started to claim that the report was "written without reference to the impacts of Westway," insisting he was only trying to create a "life history information for striped bass in the Hudson River." He stuck with this line even as Bernard traced Dovel's contacts with Lamb and many contemporaneous meetings with Houston concerning the Westway SEIS and Section 404 permit decision. Dovel professed no Westway-related rationale for edits seemingly linked to Westway construction risks. Language that "interpier basins" "probably constitute uniquely beneficial overwintering habitats for young bass" that are "unnaturally beneficial" had been in the handwritten draft and the December typed draft but had been crossed out by the April typing. Bernard's intimation drawn from Dovel's own documents was clear: Dovel's post-December edits downplayed the Westway site's significance. Things were only getting worse for Dovel and the government as the trial day drew to a close.

DOVEL'S LAST DAY on the stand, July 2, started with two pieces of unfortunate news for Westway. First, the *New York Times* op-ed columnist Sydney Schanberg had written a scathing column on the trial's strange turns. He did a particularly effective job in reviewing political and business pressures exerted on Westway decision makers, especially the efforts to convince Chris Daggett, the EPA regional administrator, to back down from his objections. In Schanberg's view, based on a close paraphrase of the EPA comment memo by Phil Angell, "people at the top were sending out the word . . . that the project was to be approved—regardless of the evidence against it."[4] Even though the *Times* editorial board continued to support the project, and its reporters had only episodically reported on the trial, Schanberg and the *Times* wielded clout both in New York City and in Washington. His piece could not help.

In the courtroom on July 2, the trial started with the second piece of bad news that caused yet more confusion and backpedaling injurious to the Corps and Westway's future. Dovel and lawyers for the United States attorneys had secured more documents undercutting Dovel's testimony. They arrived with a copy of the typed December 1984 draft Dovel had provided to George Lamb. So now the court, lawyers, and witness had to keep track of claims and testimony about three different, partial drafts of a still incomplete report. The chronology hence was the following: December typed draft to Lamb (Exhibit OOO); markup edit of December to April (NNN), and the so-called definitive April report that had first been introduced in court by lawyers for the United States (Exhibit MMM). And by this point Dovel had rejected much of his own language as unsound and in need of dozens of major changes. The U.S. attorneys also produced new documents that were communications from Dovel to Lamb about work on the report. These confirmed that Dovel was pitching his report work by linking it to Westway, contradicting his previous day's trial testimony, as he quickly conceded.

The government's hoped-for clean, definitive scientific expert was an unmitigated disaster, leaving their scientific claims in shambles. And this was in part because the government clients and witnesses had not shared these drafts in advance with their own lawyers and the opposition. Why that did not happen has never been made clear. But most of the disaster was due to their content; in critical passages these reports failed to support or even flat-out contradicted Dovel's testimony, Corps claims about fishery impacts, and the United States lawyers' trial claims. And in many places, what the reports said helped the project opponents.

And Dovel did not stand by much of the December Lamb draft either. It conceded "lack of knowledge of what constitutes primary overwintering characteristics or stimulates fish movement." Yet Dovel had repeatedly testified that by October he had rejected both overwintering theories and the idea that there was any striped bass dependence on particular habitat. And this statement was in the typed December draft provided to Lamb, not some internal working document. This statement and his testimony could not be reconciled. At a minimum, it was another passage casting major doubt on Dovel's memory, expertise, or veracity. He testified that that passage also did not apply to Westway and that by the next edits he had deleted it.

What about the Lamb version passage that it was "impossible to determine duration of movements purely from the nature of available data"? Dovel yet again adopted the now-familiar odd circumlocution: he said "it was not" "true at the time [he] wrote it" in December 1984. He similarly rejected his own passage stating it was a "good possibility" that fish passed through the metro area in one direction; this contradicted a two-directional movement theory propounded in court. And he did not agree with his own written claim that "the definition of the essential characteristics of overwintering habits for immature striped bass in the Lower Hudson is difficult and must at this point be somewhat speculative." Dovel testified that he had rejected that passage several months before it appeared in his own typed December report. Did "young bass . . . seek out comfortable habitats," as written in the December typed version? No, that did not reflect Dovel's current view.

Bernard was finished with four days of cross-examination. Dovel's testimony was left in a confusing mess but not due to complex scientific questions beyond judicial aptitude. Far from establishing authorship of a definitive report confirming that Westway posed no fishery risks, Dovel as a witness and his several report drafts were quite clearly unreliable. It is hard to imagine that any judge in America would have found him and his testimony worthy of credence. Bernard, by contrast, had succeeded beyond any Westway opponents' wildest expectations. The linchpin of the Army Corps's Final SEIS and Section 404 permit conclusions, the source of the claimed definitive report that was a synthesis of the key data, had turned out to be a disastrous witness. The much-touted report clashed with his trial testimony. Even worse for Westway's supporters, that report and earlier drafts often supported the

Westway opponents' views. His views were clearly a rapidly moving target. He had repeatedly stated that a scientific claim was true generally but not for Westway. By the end of his four days of trial testimony, he had repeatedly testified that he did not agree with his own words when written or typed, and did not stand by them in court. Of greatest importance, if Dovel and the reports were discredited, the crucial and essential underpinnings of the Army Corps's SEIS and Section 404 decisions were weakened, if not destroyed. How could the Corps's analysis and conclusions be upheld?

New York State's attorneys and Randy Mastro for the United States had to try to rehabilitate Dovel. They asked him a small number of questions, but this time Mastro tried to show that none of these inconsistent, changing drafts had been shown to the Army Corps. Dovel now said he had only showed graphics to Houston, although earlier he had alluded to sharing parts of the substance of the report with Houston. The new questioning revealed an unavoidable, essential new ploy for the United States attorneys: they had to run from dependence on Dovel. This was a difficult change in tack due to the SEIS language relying on Dovel, as well as the attorneys' and earlier witnesses' many references to reliance on Dovel and his theories. The government defendants were now in a perilous hole. It was questionable whether they could dig themselves out.

On the basis of Dovel's testimony, Schanberg wrote another blast against Westway.[5] Calling it "flimflam," he reported on Dovel's vacillations and revisions. He also called and reached George Lamb, further illuminating what Lamb had sought from Dovel. Dovel had said that neither he nor Lamb had said anything about the report's reaching a conclusion favorable to Westway. Lamb, who never testified during the trial, readily admitted that he wanted Westway built and had told Dovel of that preference. "'Of course I did.'" Lamb said Dovel emphasized he wanted to complete the fish study and that Dovel had stated that it "'[m]ade no difference to Dovel whether Westway [was] built,'" but Lamb told Schanberg that "'I told him that if you can show that this project [Westway] would not hurt the fish population, I would like to see Westway go forward.'" As correctly traced by Schanberg, it was after these conversations that Dovel's report and theory started to change to the "migratory" theory and claims of no adverse impacts on young striped bass.

The government's lawyers were still not going to give up. On July 3, the same day that the plaintiffs filed a lengthy court document detailing changes between the Draft and Final SEIS, the United States put Len Houston, the Army Corps SEIS fisheries drafter, back on the stand. This time he dropped his earlier insistence that Draft-to-Final SEIS changes were minor and not substantive. He still emphasized that most of those changes related to unfortunate different meanings of the term "significant." He now conceded, however, that between the Draft and Final the Corps adjusted language by abandoning the "overwintering" and "staging" concepts to capture how and why striped bass used the proposed Westway area. This testimony made a bit better sense of the changes, but it also drew attention yet again to Dovel's erratic theories and testimony. After all, he was credited in the SEIS for this shift in theories. Furthermore, Dovel's influence on Griffis's Section 404 decision was also now conceded at trial and apparent in the decision documents themselves.

Mastro, however, did a better job during this round of Houston's testimony in eliciting testimony about Draft-to-Final changes that increased predicted impacts. This testimony was helpful for Westway's prospects, partially countering the theory that Houston and the Corps had without justification downplayed threatened harms. It was hard to imagine, however, that anything Houston said would be enough to rescue the project from its disastrous trial revelations.

Houston also had to explain several newly discovered interim SEIS drafts reflecting Draft-to-Final SEIS changes. His answers, mostly during Bernard's cross-examination, revealed that long after Houston had dated his rejection of the staging and overwintering theories, he had nevertheless drafted or retained SEIS language that quite directly anticipated major, substantial harms from Westway. Some of this language actually was even more pessimistic than the Draft in reviewing risks to striped bass. This was especially true in a September 25 interim impact statement draft. If Houston's earlier abandonment of the overwintering and staging area theories meant Westway's harms would be reduced, then the interim drafts should have reflected such a change. They did not. Instead, especially in the September 25 draft, they said that the Westway project could cause a "major decline" and push striped bass "a major step closer to permanent endangerment of the Hudson River stock." Other passages said the striped bass "commercial fishery would likely be severely impacted and even lost." The Westway site interpier areas were still characterized as providing a "sheltering aspect" that could "play a greater role in the young fish's ability to survive the trip." These passages, like many in the original public Draft SEIS, simply could not be explained as hinging on the meaning of the word "significant."

As Bernard's questioning drew to a close, Houston finally conceded what was now fairly obvious: although two earlier interim drafts generally anticipated greater impacts, changes in later drafts leading up to the Final SEIS generally went in the direction of reducing anticipated impacts. Predictions of harms were watered down and language was changed to avoid hot-button Section 404 significant harm language. Houston concluded by admitting that reliance on Dovel's migratory-movement theory was part of the reason for these increasingly downplayed changes.

New York State's attorney, Paul Curran, asked Houston a simple but direct question. Was Houston for or against Westway? Houston readily stated that he was against it. It was not clear if Curran was setting himself up to argue that Houston was biased against Westway or just trying to send a message that Houston as a Westway opponent would not be skewing analysis to help the project. The latter was far more likely.

Desperate for some scientific witness who could support the Army Corps's conclusions, the United States introduced one last witness, Charles Henry Wahtola. He was a scientist who had been the program manager for Westway's sampling program and ultimately responsible for overseeing the 1984 New Jersey Marine Sciences Consortium striped bass relative-abundance study. Through Wahtola, the lawyers for the United States tried to revive reasons to believe that lack of recaptured tagged fish meant that they had moved out of the proposed Westway area. Wahtola also stated clearly that he thought Westway would have "little or no" impact on striped bass. He, like Dovel (but without reliance on Dovel), did not believe the fish were dependent on the habitat. He also thought additional studies were not needed. Bernard's cross-examination illuminated Wahtola's ongoing dependence on the Corps for work and also highlighted the many parts of the Westway process where Wahtola played no role. Bernard finished quickly. Since Wahtola had not been mentioned before, he was solely an expert. His views could not have formed part of the basis for the regulatory actions now challenged. But maybe the federal government's attorneys hoped Wahtola would be credited as an expert and get Westway over the "arbitrary and capricious" hurdle. His brief testimony seemed unlikely to rescue the federal government's case. New York State's attorney, this time Kimberly McFadden instead of Paul Curran, did little more than try to show that work from the Army Corps was a small part of Wahtola's firm's business.

The trial with witnesses was over. The lawyers now had to parse the record from the thirty-day-long trial and many exhibits, also weaving in relevant laws, regulations, and case precedents, to fashion persuasive posttrial briefs.

13

JUDGMENT DAYS

WESTWAY STILL had its legal approvals, but in mid-July of 1985 it faced several pressing threats. Westway's partisans awaited judicial rulings from Judge Griesa and faced the trade-in deadline of September 30, 1985. If they fought too long over Westway, they all could lose, jeopardizing a trade of close to two billion Westway dollars for mass transit improvements and a more modest road. Congress could still intervene and give Westway more time or exempt the project from ordinary prohibitions, but instead a growing congressional coalition advocated banning federal funding of the Westway landfill. New Jersey legislators were active in these efforts to unfund the project, but they were allied with other states' representatives, as well as with environmentalists, New York City Westway opponents, and fiscally conservative legislators opposed to pork-barrel spending on what many called a boondoggle. Regardless of what Judge Griesa ruled after an expedited posttrial briefing schedule, appeals to the Second Circuit Court of Appeals were a certainty. And that appellate court, in turn, would assess not only the federal defendants' compliance with Section 404 of the Clean Water Act and NEPA but also whether Judge Griesa had overstepped his authority. Had he unduly turned a political and regulatory choice into a judicial battle? Had he shown sufficient deference to agency and legislative judgments? The substantive law and scientific data were mostly on the opponents' side, while administrative law deference doctrine decidedly favored Westway's supporters.

The Westway trial before Judge Griesa had undoubtedly highlighted the project's legal vulnerabilities. Federal fishery, environment and natural resource agencies and experts, as well as private fishery consultants working for the Army Corps, virtually all disagreed with the Corps's conclusions regarding fishery impacts. The key witnesses for the Army Corps on fishery impacts, Len Houston and William Dovel, had not helped. Their testimony, cross-examination, and belatedly revealed draft documents left little firm basis for the Army Corps's conclusions. This was not a case involving a lone citizen objector or a close scientific call. The overwhelming judgment of experts, most of whom were regulators and scientists within federal natural resource agencies or consultants for the Corps, was that Westway's environmental risks meant it could not be built under the law's protective assumptions and mandates. If sound science supported the claims of no significant risks to striped bass, a major question was why neither the Corps, New York, nor any other powerful Westway supporters could identify scientific support or aligned, credible experts. In the regulatory process and at trial, no one constrained Westway's champions from assembling more powerful support. The logical conclusion was that Dovel provided the best scientific support Westway's champions could find, yet the trial had left his claims in tatters.

But because the Army Corps had granted the Westway permit and the federal natural resource agencies had not played their objections up the executive branch hierarchy, the opponents still faced an uphill battle. Perhaps a concession that a few experts clashed would be enough for Westway to squeak by. Close calls usually go to regulators; that is the essential effect of judicial deference. However, that norm was complicated here by numerous environmentally protective statutory and regulatory provisions that required worst-case assumptions, permit denials when faced with uncertainty, and prohibitions against avoidable or harmful fill in rivers like the Hudson. How would courts sort out these countervailing scale-tippers? Lawyers' advocacy skills would matter.

THE TOUGHEST STRATEGIC judgment for the federal government's lawyers was how to pitch their posttrial briefs. The government had to work with the decision documents, data, the regulatory record, and trial evidence to justify the Army Corps NEPA analysis and grant of the Section 404 permit. In any contested case, a good argument will usually anticipate criticism and opposing data and views, explaining why victory is nevertheless appropriate. How should the government handle the calamity of the Corps's and lawyers' heavy reliance on Dovel and problematic draft reports and interim Final SEIS drafts? And the lawyers faced the double challenge of explaining the Corps's persistent and unconvincing denial of any substantive changes between the Draft SEIS and the Final, as well as Len Houston's belated trial concession that the Final SEIS did actually contain changes. On both issues, Judge Griesa had telegraphed that the United States faced a skeptical judge. No one could think that Dovel had carried the odd and heavy burden placed on him by the United States, New York, and other Westway supporters. So how would the federal and New York State lawyers thread the needle, maintaining calls for deference yet addressing weaknesses?

The massive initial United States brief, filed on July 19, 1985, a mere week after the trial's close, was perplexing.[1] The brief barely addressed the government's vulnerabilities. About a quarter of it reviewed the underlying regulatory process and applicable legal requirements. It never addressed the problems created by Dovel's testimony, only describing him as one of many supportive players in the Westway process. It did address some of the Draft-to-Final changes but basically emphasized commonalities in Draft and Final conclusions. Hewing to the early trial testimony of Houston, the United States lawyers argued that "significant" merely meant statistically discernible. Nothing in the brief laid out for Judge Griesa how he could construct an opinion ruling for their side despite the many weaknesses highlighted at trial. The United States attorney's office instead emphasized case law calling for judicial deference, called Westway a case involving clashing expert judgments, and kept saying the case was ultimately about the misuse of the term "significant" in the Draft SEIS.

In an implicit concession that the Final SEIS and Record of Decision lacked key explanation, the United States brief cited to trial testimony far more than to the contemporaneous decision documents. Supreme Court cases have long established that contemporaneous decision documents and records are the key documents upon judicial review of an agency's action, and the United States would therefore ordinarily have made them the centerpiece of its brief. But the lawyers' briefing choice was not necessarily a bizarre mistake; the underlying documents had so many gaps and the record was so problematic that the lawyers may have decided they could win only by combining the decision materials with their best trial support. And it was far from clear that the Army Corps itself could have done better in constructing a basis for granting the Section 404 permit; at its core, the problem for Westway was the abundant striped bass science data that under the law's protective mandates logically pointed toward findings of harm, or at least risk, and thus a permit denial.

The United States lawyers emphasized the opposition witnesses' unwillingness to state with certitude that disastrous harms would befall the striped bass. This lack of certitude, they argued, indicated that Dovel's and Houston's views, as well as the Griffis decisions, were reasonable. But these witnesses opposing Westway had in reality linked scientific uncertainties and protective legal requirements to conclude that the project should not be built. Perhaps, however, the United States might have scored some points by excerpting their tentativeness.

If there was a clever new play in the United States brief, it was to try to raise the legal burden faced by the plaintiff opponents. Under the law, opponents actually had to show only that the regulatory judgments were arbitrary and capricious or contrary to the law's requirements. The United States lawyers, however, implied that opponents had to establish that government decision makers and witnesses had "motives to lie." But for this claim, they could cite only to snippets of attorney arguments and claims earlier in the case. No case precedents required proof of wrongful motive or dishonesty. Overall, the posttrial brief for the United States was a puzzler. It basically failed to grapple with either of the Westway decision's two greatest vulnerabilities: the Draft-to-Final changes that were not linked to the word "significant" and the implications of reliance on William Dovel now that he and his reports were likely to be discredited by the court.

New York's brief, filed by Kaye Scholer and signed by Paul Curran, stayed out of the federal law thicket and sidestepped most of the trial debacles, not even mentioning Dovel's role or problematic trial testimony.[2] It downplayed the Draft-to-Final SEIS changes. The brief had an overarching simple, direct message woven throughout, the very same theme introduced in the state's trial opening: the Westway project had been exhaustively analyzed and represented the preferred outcome of leaders from all levels of government. Furthermore, in an echo of the United States' wrongful motive argument, the brief asserted that the plaintiff opponents had failed to establish any "sinister scheme" to grant the permit. The Westway project was a logical, superb package. As had the United States, New York argued that there was no viable alternative to the project's combination of transportation, park, and revitalization goals. The Army Corps's analysis of alternatives was more than adequate under the law.

Despite the small legal team of only two lawyers and the incessant demands of the lengthy trial, Mitchell Bernard and Jean McCarroll filed a massive and effective brief two days later, on July 19, 1985.[3] Benefited by great trial testimony and the project proponents' weak regulatory record, but challenged by case law that mostly emphasized the need for judicial deference to regulatory judgments, their 156-page brief spent only about 25 pages on legal argument, with the rest focused on the facts. Their legal argument emphasized that, under both Supreme Court and lower court precedents, lack of adequate contemporaneous explanation and forthright disclosure of risks justified the trial and searching judicial review. Because they had presented no experts but relied on government and government fact witnesses who also had expertise, they were able to sidestep further argument about expert roles. Although the trial had focused little on the issue of "alternatives" analysis, which was relevant to both Section 404 and NEPA claims, plaintiffs laid out their arguments again. The United States FSEIS had done a poor job in providing apples-to-apples comparisons of Westway alternatives, especially on alternatives' development potential. Under Section 404 of the Clean Water Act, a viable alternative that did not inherently demand filling required a permit denial. The trial had given plaintiffs little reason to think they would win on this point. Still, perhaps this clean legal argument might succeed before Judge Griesa or on appeal.

Plaintiffs also made effective use of the Army Corps's failure to keep contemporaneous notes, as required by Judge Griesa and in 1982 upheld by the court of appeals. In their brief, the plaintiff opponents renewed their request for a finding of contempt but also, in a deft piece of advocacy, used the lack of written evidence of deliberations over changing Army Corps conclusions as critical evidence of arbitrariness. The lack of supportive records also provided grounds for lesser deference to the Army Corps, plaintiffs argued. And in a somewhat paradoxical twist, they spent more time than the government defendants in tracing the regulatory actions and original decision documents. Their brief offered a logical narrative, including review of how the Army Corps, at Governor Cuomo's request, had short-circuited the planned two-winter study of striped bass impacts. They argued that this truncated analysis and the data it revealed were central to the Corps's many speculative calls and should in turn have triggered protective worst-case assumptions under NEPA and virtually compelled denial of the Section 404 permit. As the plaintiffs wove their tale, that choice set in motion the missteps on the part of the Corps that followed.

The plaintiff opponents' most pointed advocacy hammered on fishery impacts. They first focused on Draft SEIS language that did not use the word "significant" alone but in varied linguistic formulations predicted major harms to young striped bass.[4] They showed how the weight of federal expert fisheries judgment was on the opponents' side. They closely parsed Houston's testimony and his belatedly produced interim drafts of the Final SEIS, explaining how these drafts undercut the claimed reasons for the reversed conclusions in the Final SEIS. The Army Corps's belated explanations for changes were "false," "not credible" and "not worthy of belief."[5] Subsequent drafts began "the process of washing away, without analysis or basis, the straightforward [Draft and earlier interim Final drafts'] language that would have compelled the Corps to deny the landfill permit for Westway."[6] And, accurately, plaintiffs pointed out that these changes were "utterly unexplained in the documents themselves."[7] By revealing tensions between these drafts, Houston's testimony, and Army Corps conclusions, plaintiffs constructed a powerful story. But their strongest salvos were yet to come.

The United States and New York may have avoided the role of Dovel in their briefs, but the plaintiff opponents made him a centerpiece. Who had developed the original "staging area" Draft SEIS theory? Dovel. The same held true for the different, new migratory-movement theory that appeared in the Final SEIS and was relied upon by the Corps in the regulatory actions and at trial. Houston explained his changing views as linked to conversations with Dovel. Dovel's January 1985 letter to Army Corps decision maker Griffis was echoed in the Griffis Record of Decision issued a few days later. And since the Army Corps and United States lawyers had repeatedly identified Dovel as *the* source of the fishery impact theories underlying the Draft SEIS, the Final SEIS, and the Section 404 permit decision, as well as the author of the definitive supportive report, the opponents' focus made sense. Dovel was no bit player.

The unexpected gift to the opponents was Dovel's trial testimony. Had he never been called at trial, the project would still have been in major trouble, but the outcome would have been hard to predict. Dovel, however, was the government's witness, allegedly their key expert, called upon to firm up the government's claims. That trial call had backfired. On the stand, he had proved too confident in opening claims, forgetful about his changing views, and most inexplicably, in frequent vehement disagreement with his own written fishery report drafts. Worse yet, those drafts contained language that supported the conclusions of the federal fishery experts and the plaintiff opponents.

Because the law contained strong prohibitions on fill in the setting of uncertainty and required worst-case assumptions, vacillating and contradictory views from Dovel were a disaster for Westway.[8] The Army Corps and United States lawyers had "relied on the untested hypothesis of an unqualified, unreliable biologist to arrive at conclusions that were unsupported by the available data" and contrary to the law's protective requirements.[9] When Dovel testified, "the roof caved in on the government's" case.[10] Plaintiffs asserted that that Dovel was "not an expert at all" but the author of report drafts that were "pure speculation."[11] They contrasted the Corps's great reliance on Dovel with its failure to heed the views of the federal fishery experts in other agencies, as required by its own regulations, or even to consult with them in the late, key stages of deliberations. The plaintiffs' striped bass discussion was a tour de force of compelling, clear advocacy.

In closing, plaintiffs made an unusual request. Agencies frequently err, but the ordinary relief is for courts to remand to the agency to try again.

Plaintiffs, however, argued for a permanent injunction, citing a bit of supportive case law but mainly emphasizing similarities in Corps missteps revealed in both the 1982 and 1985 trials.

Judge Griesa welcomed oral arguments on July 22, a few days prior to any reply briefs. Standard wisdom is that little in law is won or lost in oral arguments, and most of the arguments were indeed predictable. One lengthy exchange between Mitchell Bernard for the opponents and Judge Griesa, however, revealed an analytical shift. Griesa initially revealed uncertainty as to whether he could even look at the inadequate-alternatives issue in light of his own earlier case rulings. After Bernard clarified his position, however, the judge's skepticism was replaced by comments indicating possible agreement on the issue.[12] Bernard also did well in emphasizing a fact that had become a bit buried: the final statistical analysis done for the Corps showed that 44 percent of young-of-the-year striped bass in April used the Westway area, meaning that the government's own experts were reporting actual usage levels that were higher than the Corps's reasonable worst-case analysis. The judge discouraged plaintiffs from pursuing claims that the federal defendants had wrongful states of mind or had wielded or been subjected to improper influence.[13] They did not have this heightened, more difficult proof burden. For reasons that were not clear, Bernard nevertheless periodically used language suggesting a "fix" or sought to connect the dots to establish improper influence.

Wilson, arguing for the United States, smartly picked up on plaintiffs' insistence in briefs and in court on using language of wrongful intent and conspiracy, saying that they had proved no such thing.[14] However, despite Judge Griesa's encouragement and entreaties for Wilson to assume, for the sake of argument, that Draft-to-Final changes were substantial and then explain whether the United States choices could still be upheld as having a "rational basis," Wilson resisted. He even tried to explain key troubling language changes as attributable to Houston, who "doesn't write or speak that well."[15] That line did not persuade. Griesa responded that Houston wrote "beautifully" and that his writing "is not difficult to follow if you just read the plain words."[16] Wilson did better in showing the many Corps actions inconsistent with any predetermined effort to grant the permit and hide impacts. Reviewing Army Corps biologist Dennis Suszkowski's testimony, Wilson was particularly good in showing how Suszkowski had forthrightly testified that he believed the Corps's alternatives analysis was legally inadequate. Why would Suskowski have made that admission, then lied about what Houston meant in his use of the term "significant"?[17] Wilson steadfastly avoided any admissions or concessions, apart from agreeing on the difficult issues he faced in the case.

Paul Curran, for New York, was brief and direct. He had two main points. First, the analysis of Westway had been thorough and voluminous. Any major process with extensive documentation will end up with confusion and documentary inconsistencies, especially upon cross-examination; such gaps and confusion do not establish wrongdoing. He closed with his usual refrain: Westway was the political choice of New York's leaders and should be allowed to proceed.

As Judge Griesa had welcomed, the parties filed reply briefs a few days later. The plaintiffs' reply, filed a day before the United States reply, plowed little new ground. The attorneys had, however, adjusted in light of the oral argument. They now refuted the defendants' intimation that they had to show corruption or improper pressure as behind the questionable Westway actions. They merely had to show arbitrariness and a lack of reasoned basis for the actions. In perhaps a somewhat risky choice, however, they went on to discuss "circumstantial evidence" that showed pressure and might provide a "persuasive explanation for the Corps's conduct."[18] They also called the Corps's FSEIS analysis a "fabrication," rather than simply unsupported and arbitrary. And once again they laid out their key alternatives-analysis claim.

In its reply, filed the next day, the United States no longer ran from Dovel's testimony. Nevertheless, even after the plaintiffs' powerful briefs and oral argument a few days earlier that had confirmed Judge Griesa's skepticism about the testimony, the United States attorneys did not completely abandon reliance on Dovel. Perhaps they simply could not do so given all that had happened. Instead, they worked with supportive testimony and reiterated their claim that Dovel was an expert. But they also started to distance themselves, arguing that the Corps had conducted its own "independent evaluation and analysis." They conceded that at times Dovel was "confusing" and his testimony "conflicting."[19] And "the fact remains that no one from the Corps ever read or received any of [Dovel's draft reports] during the remand process."[20] He was now only "one of several experts" relied on by the Corps, and the Corps had not accepted all of Dovel's views.[21] In a twist, they argued that the earlier draft report Dovel had shared with George Lamb, a draft that predicted harms from Westway and had led to extensive trial examination, "serve[d] to demonstrate that Mr. Dovel is honest and his testimony credible." If he had been trying to write a pro-Westway piece, "it surely would not have looked like this."[22] Predictably, they did not focus upon how Westway impacts were progressively downplayed in drafts after Dovel met with Lamb.

AS ALL AWAITED the trial court's decision, Sydney Schanberg offered his own verdict in an infamous *New York Times* column on July 27.[23] Entitled

"Cajun Flies and Westway," Schanberg's op-ed blasted the project and New York's newspapers, impliedly including his own employer. He analogized inspectors' discovery of a fly infestation and food violations in a New Orleans celebrity chef's New York kitchen to the unseemly Westway process and trial. He saw Westway as a major story, a tale of "wheeling and stealing on a grand scale," that "oozed out" during the trial showing that "the political fix" was in. Yet New York's newspapers had paid little attention to "the chicanery" surrounding this "mega-boondoggle." The *Times* had published articles about the project and lengthy 1985 trial but only intermittently. Only the *Newark Star-Ledger* had paid regular ongoing attention to the Westway battles, with detailed reporting by Arthur K. Lenehan.

Westway had left many casualties during its fourteen-year voyage, and now Schanberg was added to the list. Shortly after the "Cajun Flies" piece, the *New York Times* abruptly took away his coveted New York City op-ed column, asking him to take on a new beat. He declined that opportunity and left the *Times* shortly afterward. There was no public explanation, let alone a conceded linkage to Westway columns, but the clash between the *New York Times* editorial board, which continued to champion Westway, and Schanberg had become increasingly stark.[24] Schanberg's fame and Pulitzer Prize from his Cambodia "killing fields" coverage was inadequate to save his column. Schanberg's losing his column itself became national news. CBS News did not mince words about what had happened. In a CBS *Sunday Morning* story, reporter Ron Powers said the *Times* had "silenced one of its reporters."[25] He reported that the *Times* would not comment on the reason for the decision, but Powers drew the connection between Schanberg's hard-hitting Westway criticisms and the clash with the *New York Times* editorial board. Schanberg would "hang on after the trendiness had worn off and all that was left was the passion, the outrage, the hunger to see justice done." Powers saw the *Times* as losing "a voice of conscience regarding its own city."

TWO WEEKS LATER, Judge Griesa issued his Westway ruling.[26] Like everything associated with Westway, it, too, was massive, totaling 132 typed pages. His language was far less colorful than Schanberg's columns, but Griesa's lengthy opus was another resounding loss for Westway. His opinion fastidiously laid out the grounds for his conclusions, interspersed with occasionally scathing language. Unexpectedly, he even ruled for the plaintiffs on their argument that the Final SEIS failed to provide required symmetrical alternatives analysis. The project was not a mere highway, but the Final SEIS alternatives analysis failed to discuss alternative development paths and potential, with and without Westway. Instead it avoided the issue. The opponents' briefs had been a bit perfunctory on this issue, but perhaps because of oral argument clarification had struck home.

The heart of the opinion focused on the striped bass impact claims. His ruling accepted much of the logic in the opponents' brief, but he also wove in with greater emphasis where the weight of fishery impact analysis stood. In data, comments during the regulatory process, testimony, and even many of the government's and Dovel's documents and drafts, the Westway site's substantial use by young striped bass was incontrovertible. And federal fishery agencies and their experts hewed to the view that that substantial use required habitat protection, views that should have been given (under slightly changing wording in the same regulations) either "great weight" or (under the revised regulations) "full consideration" by the Army Corps.[27] Judge Griesa's opinion relied on the legal requirements, protective presumptions, and prohibitions of the Clean Water Act, not just NEPA, to explain why "adverse impact of this kind mandates denial of a landfill permit." The project was vulnerable not just because of failures to disclose or analyze under NEPA but because of substantive mandates under Section 404 of the Clean Water Act and its extensive implementing regulations. The defendants' skirting of frank discussion of Westway's fishery threats linked to avoidance of a near-mandatory Section 404 permit denial. After all, Section 404's binding regulations put the onus on the permit applicant to "demonstrate[] that such a discharge will not have an unacceptable adverse impact" on an aquatic ecosystem. That ecosystem focus was on avoiding "significant degradation" of habitat that could adversely affect "ecosystem diversity, productivity, and stability," including "loss of fish and wildlife habitat."[28] And Section 404's statutory language, cross references, and implementing regulations made clear that a permit could not be granted if "insufficient information exists on any proposed discharge to make a reasonable judgment" regarding legally prohibited impacts.[29]

Like the opponents' brief, Judge Griesa's opinion traced the truncated studies and government deliberations after his earlier remand order and then reviewed what the various rounds of habitat testing revealed. He also included attention to EPA's involvement, especially trial exhibits indicating pressures on EPA's regional office to downplay impacts.

Judge Griesa devoted substantial attention to Dovel's importance, conflicting reports, and erratic testimony. He highlighted how decision documents revealed reliance on Dovel. Of all the outside experts, Dovel was the "only one who supported the Corps's analysis of impact."[30] His testimony, however, was found to be "wholly irresponsible" and "remarkable in the annals of courtroom testimony."[31] Dovel provided "astonishing answers" and testimony that was a "collection of assertions so irresponsible that it is shocking that the Government ever tendered him as a witness."[32] After parsing relevant documents and the testimony of Len Houston and Dovel, the judge concluded that the "migratory theory" ultimately embraced by the Corps was "arbitrary and without a reasonable basis." Rather than using required "worst case analysis," the Corps had "arbitar[ily] reject[ed] . . . over-wintering and accept[ed] the migratory theory."[33] The judge did not buy into the United States' argument converting fishery experts' tentativeness into reasons for deference to the views of Dovel and Houston. Griesa noted that these federal fishery experts saw the Army Corps's "conclusion regarding minor impact as without basis in existing scientific data and unsupport-able." And these experts were not mere "partisan opponents" but experts within agencies whose views were to be given serious consideration. More-over, "their track record in the Westway matter is one of being right."[34] Throughout the opinion, Griesa noted the lack of explanation for changing conclusions in the various decision documents and Dovel reports, whether draft or final.

Judge Griesa completely rejected the Corps's arguments that there was no change in conclusions between the Draft and Final EIS. That claim was "sheer fiction." The changes were "so stark, so fundamental, and so plainly stated that it [was] utterly impossible" to credit contrary claims and testimony.[35] The absence of contemporaneous explanation for these many changes, especially with the special record keeping requirement, was evidence of the lack of "rea-soned basis" for the changes and conclusions.[36]

Likely anticipating the Second Circuit's review, Judge Griesa closed by defending his holding of a trial. In one possibly important omission, he failed to cite the United States' acceptance of a limited trial, nor did he point out that it was only the government that in the end sought testimony of witnesses presented as experts. That government concession about the need for a trial provided an additional legal justification for holding one, although it would not have insulated Griesa from criticisms that the actual trial was too intru-sive. He paraphrased and cited the foundational administrative law Supreme Court case, *Citizens to Preserve Overton Park*,[37] which, as discussed earlier, after a disputed regulatory action allows trials that "go outside the record where it is incomplete and where substantial questions arise which cannot be resolved by the administrative record."[38] He rejected the plaintiffs' claim of "improper influence," but still found the Corps's action legally wanting.[39]

In a closing paragraph, presented almost as an afterthought, Judge Griesa addressed the question of remedy. Granting the opponents' request, he did not just reject the government actions and remand the matter but stated that "two failures to justify the Westway landfill and federal funding . . . should bring the matter to an end." He issued a permanent injunction against additional federal consideration of the Westway project: "There is simply no legitimate purpose to be served by further proceedings." That unusual permanent injunctive remedy was sure to be vulnerable on appeal.

WITH THAT RESOUNDING CONCLUSION, Westway was knocked down, perhaps never to rise again. But maybe it was not "dead yet"; truly final outcomes are a rarity in regulatory wars.[40] A permanent injunction may have been Judge Griesa's answer, but two venues could reach contrary conclusions. Most obviously, the court of appeals might reverse. But only seven weeks were left until the trade-in deadline. Moreover, Griesa's extraordinarily thorough opinion, especially in light of the underlying record, was no easy target for reversal. And even an unlikely victory for Westway before the Second Circuit would probably not be conclusive; appellate courts typically will note a lower court's error and then send the matter back to that court, perhaps for a further remand to the agency for action under a corrected understanding of the law. Thus, even an appellate court victory for Westway's supporters might come too late to be of use.

Both supporters and opponents now had to fight a multifront battle, preparing for the court of appeals, leaning on New York regarding trade-in options, and working the halls of Congress to cement the project's defeat or perhaps win a legislative rescue. The trial court ruling, however, left opponents in a greatly strengthened position. In addition to their long-standing arguments against Westway rooted in the law's environmental protections, against pork-barrel spending, and for mass transit, they could add appeals to the rule of law, respect for the judiciary, and even deference to a trial court's on-the-spot credibility determinations. And a federal judge had agreed that their environmental concerns were meritorious. Judge Griesa's ruling was not the final word on Westway, but it changed arguments and likely outcomes.

With limited time to figure out all of the trade-in logistics, city and state officials started with contingency planning, uncertain whether they would win on appeal or even get a timely ruling. Only if Congress provided a trade-in extension could New York avoid risking billions by awaiting uncertain judicial and political outcomes. Knowing, however, that legislators in Washington and even judges read the papers, New York City and State leaders and other Westway supporters in public refused to concede anything. They quickly developed a near mantra about the trade-in option: trade-in dollars, especially for mass transit, were an unreliable prospect. New York could never know if those dollars would materialize. Future regulators or legislators could change their minds. Benstock and her allies challenged this claim, preparing fact sheets about past trade-in successes. And on this issue several top federal officials had, at different points, reassured state and city officials that a trade-in would be real and reliable. Still, Westway's champions persisted with this claim that trade-ins were an unreliable option.

In Washington, the anti-Westway alliance of New Jersey legislators, environmentalists, mass transit advocates, and opponents of wasteful pork-barrel spending was gaining momentum. New York continued pushing for a legislative rider that would extend New York's trade-in deadline, but nothing moved. New Jersey senator Frank Lautenberg sought to encourage a trade-in. Seeking to preclude Westway but address deadline risks, alleviate concerns that Westway could eliminate New Jersey's future waterfront development, and also cap federal spending, Lautenberg proposed a bill that would provide eight years of $220 million in funding to New York from the Highway Trust Fund for substitute roads or mass transit projects, as long as no landfilling occurred.[41] Two committees were considering amendments that would, with slightly varying language, remove most federal funding for Westway. And Pennsylvania representative Lawrence Coughlin even championed an appropriations rider that would prohibit spending on Westway landfilling for a year. Judge Griesa's ruling became part of Westway's congressional politics, adding a new reason to kill the project. Lobbyists for New York State and City were quickly fighting a rearguard action, trying just to maintain the legal status quo.

WHILE POLITICAL MANEUVERING continued in New York and Washington, appellate briefs were filed. It was becoming clear that Westway's best, and perhaps last, chance was a complete win before the Court of Appeals for the Second Circuit.

The United States trial court briefs, on their own, had been a bit mystifying in their failure to address case infirmities. The appellate brief for the United States, filed on August 17, 1985, as part of an expedited appeal process, was far more powerful.[42] It also perhaps revealed a strategy behind the unconvincing trial court briefs. Those briefs had conceded virtually nothing, other than the reply's brief's belated attempt to address criticisms of Dovel and downplay reliance on him. In their brief written for the Second Circuit, the lack of concessions below allowed them to have a singular focus. And that focus now was a blistering attack on Judge Griesa for "judicial overreaching of the highest order." The United States brief accused him of having ignored the regulatory record and of having conducted an improper de novo review of the questions addressed by the Army Corps and Federal Highway Administration. De novo judicial review is generally prohibited since it involves a judge undertaking an altogether new assessment of a question delegated to and first heard before an agency.

Their brief argued that Judge Griesa had "substituted his judgments" without a basis. With lengthy citations to cases calling for judicial deference to expert regulators, they made basic administrative law concepts central. And because Wilson's team had conceded almost nothing before Griesa (apart from agreement on the need for a limited trial, which at this point went unmentioned), it was able on appeal to attack all aspects of the judge's ruling and trial behavior. Perhaps they had thought they were likely to lose before him so had not even attempted limited concessions to regain credibility and perhaps fashion a winning trial-level argument. Such a strategy contained a kernel of logic, albeit risk as well since appellate courts rarely will revisit all of a trial court's findings.

The appellate brief focused almost exclusively on the different uses of the word "significant" in the Draft and Final SEIS, only elliptically referring to the many other Draft passages that quite clearly were discussing major impacts. This made for a powerful read but raised risks too; the opponents were sure to highlight the many other Draft passages without the word "significant" but that anticipated major impacts. And, as with its trial briefs, the assistant United States attorney team could not avoid buttressing its arguments with citations both to regulatory documents and to many trial passages and exhibits. Apart from an opening summary of the Clean Water Act's requirements, the focus was almost entirely on NEPA's requirements of forthright disclosure and reasoned analysis. The brief provided almost no argument about how Westway had overcome the Clean Water Act's protective assumptions and prohibitions. It basically sidestepped the most problematic legal provisions. Nevertheless, the brief was far more effective and powerful than arguments at the trial level. If the court of appeals judges did not delve deeply into the record and opinion below and instead saw complicated science and difficult regulatory judgment calls, the deference and overreaching themes might work.

New York's brief tracked many of the United States points and strategies, especially in targeting Judge Griesa. He had "turned environmental law and its rule of reason upside down," conducted a "school masterish review," and then "arbitrarily flunked a $2 billion project for perceived deficiencies in English Composition."[43] They attacked the judge for rejecting the federal actions "without a scintilla of evidence to show that construction of Westway will harm the Hudson River striped bass fishery."[44] This argument flipped the actual legal burdens under the Clean Water Act and surely stretched if not ignored what the evidence actually indicated, but it was nevertheless an effective flourish. Despite record-keeping violations, which New York conceded, the brief argued that "the citizens of New York State and City should not be penalized for the Corps'[s] transgressions."[45] Like the United States,

New York's lawyers argued that the trial court had committed "clear error" in misunderstanding the Draft SEIS language to virtually compel a Section 404 permit denial. The problem here, however, was that all of the commenting federal natural resource agencies, and apparently even Colonel Griffis himself, had read the Draft the same way. And Curran's team for New York further made the argument that the federal natural resource agencies' views should have been given little weight because they were "bias[ed] against Westway."[46]

But the opponents (formally identified on appeal as the plaintiff-appellees), had their own tale to tell. Their brief, filed nine days later, on August 26, 1985, was an effective and thorough rejoinder. It started by reviewing the regulatory history, including how the trial became necessary. The opponents then addressed a forceful United States argument that Judge Griesa had erred in asserting that Dovel alone, among the experts, supported the Army Corps conclusions. The United States brief had only obliquely addressed the substance of what the federal fishery expert agencies had said in repeatedly objecting to Westway. The opponents left little doubt about the regulatory and trial record. They wove together official agency comments at multiple stages to show how the weight of federal and federal contractor expert comments was arrayed against the Corps's conclusions.

As with their trial brief, the opponents showed how much of the government's actions traced back to views espoused by Dovel, whom they presented as unreliable and vacillating. They reviewed many of the key Draft SEIS passages lacking the word "significant" but anticipating major impacts. They showed how the Final SEIS had changed in ways that always downplayed harms, yet without explanation. For over thirty pages, they put before the court Draft SEIS language that the United States had skirted. The attempt to sidestep these many other passages had made an initially powerful impression but left the United States vulnerable; this briefing choice did not give the appellate judges a road map for a response that explained away these many other passages.

The opponents agreed with the government defendants that NEPA analysis was subjected to review under a "rule of reason" but emphasized cases concerned with failures to confront relevant data. And ultimately the question was whether the actions were arbitrary and capricious. Predictably, they emphasized Supreme Court language calling for "thorough, probing, in-depth review,"[47] rather than cases and passages emphasizing deference. Unlike the United States brief, however, the brief filed by Bernard and McCarroll also included several pages about the deference courts of appeals are to show to trial judges, especially judges making rulings that include credibility determinations.

All could be lost if the appellate court found Judge Griesa overreached in his trial. If the judge had engaged in improper de novo review, his actions were indeed vulnerable. The opponents disputed this claim, reviewing Supreme Court and lower court precedents, including numerous cases that were binding law within the Second Circuit, to argue that the judge's actions were well justified and nothing like de novo review. Trials following regulatory actions are not common but had happened earlier in the Westway battles and in other cases, yet without any subsequent finding of legal infirmity. As the plaintiff opponents pitched their argument, when faced with inadequate explanation and an incomplete record, as well as questions about whether the usual "presumption of regularity" had been overcome, Griesa had legal support for a trial "directed at finding out how and why the agencies arrived at the decisions under review."[48] Quoting the United States Supreme Court, they explained that he could "'obtain from the agency . . . such additional explanations of the reasons for the agency decision as may prove necessary.'"[49] Illuminating the unexplained was appropriate and, in their view, the judge had done just that with his trial. And plaintiffs had strong support in Griesa's conclusions; despite the defendants' claims that he had "substituted his own judgment," the judge had not decided what an SEIS had to say or whether a permit could be granted. He had simply found the government's actions arbitrary and capricious and lacking a reasoned basis. All that trial questioning examined was the reasonableness of the government's choices. That was not de novo review, they asserted.

The ruling was difficult to predict, especially after oral argument on August 29 revealed an apparently divided court. Two of the judges, Richard Cardamone and George C. Pratt, had recently been appointed to court of appeals seats by Republican presidents, likely indicating that they had the support of New York senator Alphonse D'Amato, whose pro-Westway views were well known. Walter Mansfield was the third judge on the panel. He had been appointed to the federal bench by a Democratic president but then appointed to the court of appeals by Republican Richard Nixon. Questioning seemed to indicate that the government defendants had an ally in Judge Cardamone, while Judge Mansfield's queries reflected questions and doubts emphasized by the opponents. Judge Pratt was harder to read.[50]

AS THE COURT of appeals decision was awaited, maneuvering continued in Washington. New York's best ally on the extension efforts was New Jersey representative James Howard. Howard opposed Westway but also voiced concern with putting New York into a tight time squeeze while the city and state resolved legal battles and assessed their options. Other opponents, however, welcomed the pressure. A proposed extension for Westway ran into a wall when staffers for Senators William Proxmire and Gordon Humphrey indicated that their senators might filibuster such a measure and prevent a vote until after the trade-in deadline had passed.[51]

At this point, Benstock was in Washington and working closely with Jill Lancelot of the National Taxpayers Union, an opponent of Westway focused on tax policy and wasteful spending. Brent Blackwelder, who now headed Friends of the Earth and was a well-known environmentalist on the Hill, joined Lancelot and Benstock in their efforts to stop Westway and secure a trade-in. Lancelot opposed the extension, calling for everyone to "play by the rules."[52] Benstock argued that granting an extension would be "an open invitation to corruption that has affected the process before." She said the project was "fundamentally illegal and wrong" and an extension would only send it through yet more judicial and regulatory review.[53]

During the first few week and a half of September, Benstock, Lancelot, Blackwelder, and other Westway opponents continued making the congressional rounds, ultimately coalescing around Representative Lawrence Coughlin's appropriations rider. This rider would have prohibited federal spending on Westway landfill for a year. It had been defeated in committee votes, but Coughlin pushed it to the House floor for consideration as an appropriations rider. It was fiercely debated on September 11, 1985, as a prelude to a vote. Most opponents supported the amendment, although Representative Howard thought it poorly drafted and favored the House's deferring to an upcoming committee vote on a bill to end the project. A few legislators opposed the measure because it was a rider and hence would circumvent the ordinary process of committee deliberations and votes. Judge Griesa's ruling was cited in support of the measure, although New York representative Bill Green argued against the rider and intimated that Griesa was biased and his rulings unsound. Other representatives argued for the measure as a vote against profligate pork-barrel spending on a boondoggle and hence a vote for fiscal responsibility, but Green disagreed. He stated that one way or the other, New York would have Westway or trade-in funds. Coughlin and others, including New York's Ted Weiss, strongly disputed Green's point. They emphasized that a trade-in would provide New York a capped amount of roughly $1.75 billion; a full Westway project, in contrast, would be a "blank check" from the National Highway Trust Fund that was likely to quickly rise from $2 billion to somewhere between $4 and $10 billion.

As debate was winding down and potentially nearing a vote, legislators reported that the Second Circuit had just minutes earlier issued its opinion, unanimously upholding key parts of Judge Griesa's ruling and rejecting others. Howard and a few others argued for delaying a vote so the opinion could be studied. They and all Westway's partisans wanted to know what the court had ruled.

DESPITE PREDICTIONS of a divided court based on the judges' oral argument questions, the Second Circuit's ruling was clear and decisive.[54] On the central issue of fisheries impact analysis and the requirements of NEPA and Section 404 of the Clean Water Act, all three judges agreed with Judge Griesa. Judge Cardamone started his opinion by stating the problem at the heart of the case: "A change in something from yesterday to today creates doubt. When the anticipated explanation is not given, doubt turns to disbelief. This case is capsulized in that solitary simile." After tracing the project's history, the court quoted Draft SEIS language that anticipated major impacts but mostly without use of the term "significant." The government defendants' near-exclusive focus on the term had failed. The court noted that despite major changes in the Final, "no new data [had been] collected."[55] In the court's view, "the central issue on which this case hinges is the Corps' denial of the change that clearly emerged from its draft report to its final report."

In reviewing the relevant requirements of NEPA and the Clean Water Act, the Second Circuit Court pointed out with statutory and regulatory quotes that the Clean Water Act, unlike NEPA, contains strong, substantive protections. It provides for "a more substantive power of review," and "prohibits agency action whenever certain environmental impact thresholds ha[ve] been met." It "prohibits an agency from sanctioning a project that it finds will have a significant adverse impact on the marine environment." And if an agency grants a Section 404 permit despite significant adverse impacts on marine wildlife, "the agency determination must be reversed."[56] The court undoubtedly saw the critical link between the changing impact conclusions and Section 404's protections.

But what about claims that Judge Griesa had overreached in his trial and conclusions? The court was troubled by the federal defendants' claim that the trial court had conducted an improper de novo review on the merits. More than had the parties or Griesa, the Second Circuit closely reviewed law regarding judicial review of agency action. It emphasized the appropriateness of tough "hard look" review of high-stakes regulatory judgments. It said that de novo review was rarely allowable but that "plenary review," where a court seeks through a trial to supplement a "record [that] is so sparse as to make judicial review ineffectual," was allowed. Such plenary review could include "testimony and additional explanation."[57] So which sort of review had Griesa provided? The court concluded that he had engaged in inappropriate de novo review. Its discussion reflected confusion on what actually had happened at trial, where only the United States had introduced a witness identified as an expert, but it echoed the defendants' strident "judicial overreach" arguments and the claim that any witness other than the decision makers should be viewed as an expert. In reality, all witnesses but Dovel had focused on what happened during the regulatory process. They had been part of the underlying regulatory process. Nevertheless, the court stated that Griesa had erred by allowing plaintiffs "to call their own expert witnesses, and by substituting those witnesses' interpretation of the data for the views of experts that the Corps relied upon."

Any glimmer of hope this language provided for Westway's lawyers and supporters was short-lived. The court stated that Judge Griesa's unduly rigorous trial was "not reversible error." The same flaws that the opponents and Griesa had identified were found by the court of appeals. The Corps's violation of the record-keeping order had justified more intrusive review. Because the Draft SEIS conclusions would have required denial of the Section 404 permit, the "absen[ce of] explanation" of changed conclusions from the Draft to the Final was fatal. The court was unpersuaded by the "significant equals 'measurable but minor'" argument. "No court should allow the use of semantics to succeed in an attempt at glossing over an environmental violation. Neither Judge Griesa nor we are required to defer to the Corps' Orwellian-like 'doublespeak.'"[58] An explanation for changes was needed, and "that explanation should have been in the final report."[59] Judge Griesa could have held a hearing with testimony, but he went too far. Nevertheless, the "FSEIS did not satisfy the requirements of either NEPA or the Clean Water Act."[60] The Section 404 permit was invalidated.

But the plaintiffs' victory was not complete. The court disagreed that the Corps had failed to give adequate consideration to the contrary views of the federal natural resource agencies. In a surprisingly brief discussion, it also rejected Judge Griesa's conclusion that the Corps's alternatives analysis was legally infirm. Picking up an argument in the defendants' briefs, the court said that with all the publicity and debate, the idea that alternatives were not known and the public was uninformed was "far-fetched." In this point, the court of appeals made its own mistake, neglecting to discuss Section 404 and its substantive prohibitions linked to alternatives; the opinion here seemed focused only on NEPA.

The plaintiff-appellees—Westway's opponents—had clearly carried the day, but the question of relief remained. As was predictable, even without the court's disagreements with parts of Judge Griesa's ruling, the permanent injunction was rejected. A remand directly back to the federal defendants was necessary. Only the agencies charged with implementing the law could decide, under a correct view of law, on the merits of Westway. The court did not mandate new investigation: "Perhaps a fresh look at the collected data could produce a clear, logical, and good faith explanation for the change."

The court conceded that its ruling might condemn Westway "to oblivion." It noted that some would cheer and others cry. Adopting a posture of judicial restraint, the court stated that its role had to be shaped by congressional priorities. "Congress has decreed that a project may not proceed without an acceptable environmental impact statement." And the court reiterated the Clean Water Act's priorities and that building Westway might have caused an "even greater loss," "gambling on the loss of this major east coast fishery resource."[61] The decision to issue the permit was therefore arbitrary and capricious.

Judge Mansfield added his own opinion, concurring and dissenting in part. He was more supportive of Judge Griesa's 1985 trial and disagreed that it had been de novo. He also dug more deeply into flaws in the defendants' actions and the underlying data, faulting the Corps's "failure to get essential facts" about fishery risks and doubting that, on the evidence adduced, the Corps could ever approve Westway. The remedy, if one was to be had, "lies with Congress, not the courts."[62]

BUT NO CONGRESSIONAL rescue of Westway looked likely. The trade-in option would expire in nineteen days, on September 30. The legislative momentum was to place another nail in Westway's coffin. As Westway's supporters and opponents read the court of appeals decision, congressional debate on the very same day continued. Representative Coughlin's funding cutoff rider remained the proposal on the table. Several legislators expressed no particular fondness for Westway, yet they feared creating a precedent for congressional second-guessing of locally supported but federally funded highway projects.[63] New York was far from alone in enjoying the federal Highway Trust Fund gravy train. Final speakers, including upstate New York Representative Gerald Solomon, joined others in characterizing the project as a wasteful pork-barrel project that violated the intent of the Interstate Highway Act. He, like Ted Weiss, argued the project would "fill the pockets of a very few multimillionaire[] real estate interests in New York City."[64] Others focused on the environmental risks. Representative Sylvio Conte stated that Westway was still the "environmental and financial fiasco" that former congressman Ed Koch Koch had denigrated as a mayoral candidate, before adjusting his views as the new mayor.

The time for voting arrived, still on September 11, 1985. When the votes were tallied, Westway had suffered yet another drubbing, losing 287 to 132 in the House. Although the House vote to cut off Westway landfill funding did not conclude the legislative process, it made abundantly clear that regardless of Senate actions, the House opposed Westway. And since any law, be it substantive or a rider or a date extension, requires the House and Senate to agree before sending a bill for the president's signature, the House vote meant Congress would never vote to save the project; even an extension looked unlikely. When Benstock was not speaking with legislators and their staff, she watched the debate from the Capitol's viewing gallery. She described the vote as the "highlight of her working life."[65]

WITH THAT CONGRESSIONAL vote and the court of appeals ruling, the supposed juggernaut of Westway was running out of what little momentum it retained. But opponents in Congress might also never pass a new law killing Westway. Mayor Koch therefore did not surrender immediately, characterizing the court ruling and congressional vote as a "blow," but "it is not a body blow and doesn't endanger Westway at the present moment."[66]

The court of appeals remand meant that the federal defendants could try again, but the court's ruling also made clear that both NEPA and the substantive protections of Section 404 had to be weighed. The Army Corps could never complete another striped bass analysis and new permit ruling within three weeks. The Corps would have to consider extensive sworn trial testimony, the earlier Draft and Final SEIS, and the federal natural resource agency comments and objections. And, presumably, new opportunities for comments would be required, and new Draft and Final SEIS analysis. New court challenges would surely follow. Most significantly, the data and law posed huge hurdles. Without a sound basis to explain away fishery risks, it was doubtful that Westway could ever be permitted, even if it had more time.

So the choices were narrowed: either seek a trade-in now or push for an essential but long-shot legislative extension on the trade-in option to allow time for Army Corps reconsideration. Supporters could even give up on the trade-in, going for broke on Westway as long planned and hoping for the best on remand. That option risked $1.75 billion. An even longer-shot option was to seek Supreme Court review. That also would take too long in the absence of an extension. But the votes for a congressional extension simply were not there.

Within a few days of Westway's own disastrous September 11, New York State and City officials abandoned Mayor Koch's guardedly optimistic assessment. They suddenly were overtly considering and championing a trade-in option. Earlier arguments that a trade-in would not generate reliable federal commitments started to disappear.[67] And, in reality, as Benstock and many other citizen and elected opponents of Westway had long argued and documented, New York's leaders had received numerous earlier assurances from federal leaders in the executive branch and Congress that trade-in dollars would actually be delivered. No one in New York City and State leadership was going to play a game of chicken that could risk that much money.

Discussion turned to the structure of a trade-in. What percentage should go to a replacement road and how much to mass transit? How reduce the risk that a future Congress would not provide anticipated mass transit support out of the federal general fund? Once again, a federal legislative fix was proposed, this time by New Jersey congressman and Westway opponent Frank Guarini. He introduced a bill in the House that would guarantee both road and mass transit funds from such a trade-in.[68] After that proposal gained little momentum and time extension efforts hit yet more legislative opposition, Public Works Committee chair Representative Howard gave up, declaring "Westway is dead. Congress won't let them build Westway."[69] Now Mayor Koch changed his public tune, admitting that you could hear the project's "death rattle." Senator Moynihan concurred.[70]

A few days later, Mayor Koch and Governor Cuomo went public with their surrender and call for acceptance of a trade-in. Anything else would be a "reckless gamble" that would be unlikely to overcome legal impediments. To avoid the risk that federal mass transit support in a trade-in would prove unreliable, the governor and mayor came up with a federal-state monetary shuffle. They would seek trade-in funds with 80 percent for highways and only 20 percent for mass transit, but the state in turn would reallocate already secured transportation funds for city mass transit use. Through this shuffle, described in joint public statements and confirmatory letters to United States Secretary of the Department of Transportation, Elizabeth Dole, and to the head of New York's Mass Transit Authority, the federal government would hand over $1.725 billion to New York State to be paid over about six years. With the state funding reallocation, the deal would result in a final highway-mass transit mix of at least $1.035 billion for public transit and up to $690 million for a West Side Highway replacement. This worked out to a planned 60 percent split for transit and 40 percent for roadwork.

On September 26, four days before the trade-in deadline, this deal was officially announced and submitted to Secretary Dole. At a press conference, Mayor Koch called the deal a way to "make the best of a bad situation" while also characterizing the monetary shuffle as an "extraordinarily ingenious" solution.[71] He also indicated that if the replacement road did not cost the anticipated $800 million, "any savings go to [Mass Transit Authority head] deep-pockets Kiley."[72] Senators D'Amato and Moynihan voiced their support, but with regrets.

Westway's opponents were not quite ready to celebrate. Benstock was worried that the transit money would not materialize.[73] She also said, however, that she was "elated" and it was a "wonderful historic day" when mass transit gets "at least $1 billion if the Mayor and Governor live up to their commitment."[74] She was happy but was not about to let down her guard. City Council president Carol Bellamy, who had opposed Westway and was also at the time a candidate for mayor, was hostile. She characterized the deal as a "shell game" that would "rob mass transit."[75] *New York Times* columnist John Oakes similarly questioned whether the commitment to mass transit could be trusted.[76] Koch did not deny that the agreement lacked enforceability and would not bind successors, but he said that voters should throw him out of office if he was not good to his word.

Days later, on the legal trade-in deadline date of September 30, Secretary Dole signed an agreement to the deal. Her signature sealed Westway's demise and victory for its opponents. After she offered signing pens to city and state representatives in attendance, Senator Moynihan huffed that he didn't "know why they thought this was an occasion for giving out pens."[77] Showing himself a gracious loser, Governor Cuomo wrote Marcy Benstock a short congratulatory note, commending her "commitment, [her] courage, and [her] competence." He expressed hope that next time they would be "on the same side."[78]

After devoting over a decade of her life to the Westway war, Marcy Benstock had no regrets. In a lengthy *New York Times* profile of this "dedicated foe," she declared, "It was worth it. Absolutely, it was worth it."[79] Westway was truly, finally, dead.

14

ASSESSING WESTWAY'S OUTCOME

A LATE 1985 *NEW YORKER* cartoon shows an eager young man at a
bar, addressing a woman to his left: "I beg your pardon. Would you
care to either celebrate or mourn the demise of Westway with me?"[1]
Famed *New York Times* columnist Russell Baker likened Westway's defeat
to one of those "Frank Capra fables . . . in which innocent small-town boys
with a civics book faith in democracy challenged the big shots and won."[2]
And those big shots "had big money, heavy political muscle and immense
lobbying know-how." Governor Cuomo's take was not far different: "They
just stopped Westway in in its tracks, [a] project that the whole establish-
ment wanted."[3] He bemoaned the result but applauded the process and the
power of citizens. Architecture critic and urbanist Paul Goldberger mused
that perhaps Westway was brought down by hubris that led New York to seek
too much.[4]

Westway's defeat was indeed a remarkable accomplishment. Opponents prevailed against incredible odds and powerful interests. This chapter
assesses that defeat, starting with an examination of the consequences, then
looking at the outcome both under the law and facts relevant to the Westway
proposal and as a lens to critique the law's attributes in modern regulatory
wars, especially over environmental stakes. While commentators include
many who bemoan Westway's defeat, others praise the result and the process
that allowed citizens, politicians, and agency scientists to oppose and defeat
a project supported by many powerful interests. Hence part of this clash of

Figure 14.1. Most Westway trade-in dollars supported mass transit, but they also funded a replacement surface road and a new bike and running trail along the Hudson River. Hudson River Park was also created, leading to public spaces on some piers and ongoing debates over the public-private mix of area land usage, as well as concerns from some Westway opponents about possible future in-water development. *(Source: Paul Sutton of PCN Photography.)*

views hinges on whether Westway's defeat reveals legal or political dysfunction, even if it was a sound result under the law. Westway's lengthy war and defeat also offer lessons about the law, especially in complicated regulatory wars involving all branches and layers of government, citizen activists, and clashes over environmental risks and urban priorities.

The consequences of Westway's defeat. Part of the Westway-as-tragedy perspective is rooted in anticipated negative consequences for New York City. Senator Moynihan, David Rockefeller, and other Westway supporters often presented the project as a bellwether that would tell America whether New York, or perhaps Americans, could still do great things, could build splendid edifices. Moynihan saw Westway as the "century's Central Park," defeated by civic leaders who now specialized in trying to "prevent[] things from happening." He dismissed striped bass concerns.[5] In another interview, Moynihan asserted that a "kind of stasis . . . is beginning to settle into our public life. We cannot reach decisions."[6] However, contrary to supporters' claims that Westway was a linchpin of Manhattan's revitalization, Westway's demise did not doom Manhattan, choke off new development of the Lower West Side, or even prevent the development of a new park along the West Side abutting the Hudson. Choices were made and the area prospered.

Even before the Westway battles ended, New York City's revival and a sustained real estate boom were under way. Redevelopment did not depend on Westway. Westway opponent Bunny Gabel made this argument during a 1984 hearing in front of the Army Corps, months before the Corps nonetheless pointed to revitalization goals in approving the project: it was "ludicrous" to see Westway as needed. What was needed was to "remove the threat of Westway" so the area would fully flourish.[7] About a year later, Donald Trump similarly opined that the West Side would boom once the risks of Westway disruptions were gone.[8] They were right.

Even Jane Jacobs would likely have applauded the many-faceted, incremental changes that followed Westway's defeat. She saw the project as a "death sentence[]" for the surrounding neighborhoods.[9] She might have disliked New York City's growing glitz and skyrocketing real estate prices, but adjacent neighborhoods thrived in Westway's wake. As Deputy Mayor Wagner had predicted, without Westway, the Lower West Side's renaissance continued but through a more organic and gradual process.[10] Abandoned piers were converted to new uses and bits of river-edge path were built and connected, substantially funded by Westway trade-in dollars. Nearby decrepit buildings and commercial areas became coveted lofts, restaurants, and sites of new construction. The Gansevoort meatpacking district at the northwestern corner of Greenwich Village, which would have been partly demolished by an interchange link to Westway, became among the city's most vital nightspots, with top restaurants and crowded bars.

The surface road–Route 9A–that was once under the former elevated West Side Highway now handles the area's traffic. It is not beautiful, but it works. Contrary to fears of Westway opponents that it would become an overblown, vastly expensive road and eat away trade-in transit funds, the replacement road was scaled back in cost. Of course, whittling the project down from initial grand and expensive visions required another round of battles, leading Marcy Benstock to characterize Westway, even after its apparent defeat, as like a "vampire [that] refuses to be killed."[11] The modest road built with Westway trade-in dollars now provides bike paths, river vistas, and easier access from residential neighborhoods to the Hudson River's edge.

Westway was also not the only way to provide citizens with access to a river-edge park and views. Through state legislation and federal, state, and private support and investment, a new park, Hudson River Park, is partly built between the road and the Hudson and on adjacent piers. Its mapped footprint (some of which includes flowing Hudson River waters), covers much of the same acreage slated for Westway and extends further north. Through that park and related work on the replacement road, as well as other city transit improvements, a continuous bike and pedestrian path now extends most of the length of Manhattan's western edge, running along the Hudson. Some Westway opponents love the park, especially attorney Al Butzel. He was actually among Hudson River Park's legal architects and early stewards, provoking a clash with his former client, Marcy Benstock, who saw such work as a raising a legal conflict.[12] Benstock calls the new park "Son of Westway" and remains wary of what she sees as creeping commercialization in the park and threats to the Hudson.[13] The park and linked development remain a work in progress, including periodic pushes to allow more commercial development on piers and resulting clashes over the appropriate public and private mix of Hudson River pier and waterfront uses.[14] Benstock also fears in-water development. The park continues to experience financial ups and downs, slowing efforts to complete some of its planned public areas.[15] Most pro-Westway partisans and their attorneys denigrate the new road and park as nothing compared with the promise of Westway.

What exists now works, is a vast improvement on conditions prevailing throughout the Westway wars, and has provided both public spaces and newfound private wealth. Furthermore, neither the new road, bike path, nor park construction has caused the sorts of long-term disturbances and disruptions that Westway construction and linked new real estate development would have caused. The views of Manhattan from Hudson River Park's publicly accessible piers, surrounded by the Hudson's flowing waters, are stunning. The nearby High Line Park, built in the bed of an adjacent former elevated rail line a few blocks to the east of the Hudson, also attracts foot traffic and has provided an additional economic boost to now-thriving Lower West Side neighborhoods.

Westway's trade-in dollars—the rallying cry for many of Westway's opponents—did in fact arrive and provide the hoped-for direct federal funding for the surface roadway work, as well as much-needed mass transit improvements. These trade-in dollars did not compare with the vast amounts Westway would likely have generated, since trade-in amounts were fixed rather than subject to a highway's "costs to completion" usual cost escalations. That was a known reality. Claims that trade-in funds would never materialize, however, proved unfounded, as Benstock and opponents had long claimed. Senator D'Amato was even able to start the trade-in dollars flowing a year ahead of time.[16] Trade-in-deal money slated for transit under the "ingenious" shuffle of state and city funds did actually go there, and there was more when the replacement road came in at far less than its estimated $690 to $800 million.[17] Both of these successes followed yet more citizen monitoring and advocacy at local, state, and federal levels. Between Westway dollars, new bond revenues, and more sophisticated management, critically needed subway upgrades started to be made. Since the mid-1980s, the reliability and condition of New York City's subways have vastly improved.

Much of the Westway war hinged on the mass transit-versus-highway choice, as well as on competing views of what makes for a thriving and great city. Was a singular grand project essential for Manhattan's revival, as Westway's supporters argued? That claim was proved wrong. And no period of "stasis" followed, as evidenced by the new Hudson River Park, bike paths, High Line Park, improved mass transit, and large but not giant buildings by "starchitects" along 9A and Hudson River Park.[18] If there is a problem today, it is economic vitality that is crowding out mixed uses and an economically heterogeneous population.

And the striped bass? As discussed in greater depth below, as a result of special protective federal striped bass legislation, the Westway decision and similar protection of all waters of the United States from fill and development through Section 404, improved fishery management, and improved water quality flowing from the Clean Water Act's protections, striped bass are among the nation's and oceans' few fishery success stories. They rebounded from their perilous 1970s and early 1980s numbers and, despite occasional population drops, are generally flourishing. In contrast, many other fisheries that have lacked such focused political and legal attention and commercial forbearance have crashed.[19]

So a consequentialist perspective does not confirm Westway's defeat as a disaster but as a shift that produced many benefits for New York City and protected the environment as well. Of course, Westway would have generated benefits as well—most of all, many years of federally paid construction costs, a park, and the creation of new developable land. But New York City and the environment without Westway did well too, perhaps better.

Was the outcome of the Westway war legally sound? Perhaps the most persistent claim of Westway supporters and others who offer Westway as a warning parable or evidence of environmental law overreach is that Westway's defeat was a huge legal and political error based on outlandish, opportunistic arguments by opponents and resulting misjudgments by Judge Griesa. A *New York Times* editorial captured that talking point in August of 1985 when it asserted that "[i]t is hard to imagine what so exercised the judge."[20] Author Phillip Lopate provides a brief review of Westway's history in his book *Waterfront: A Journey around Manhattan*. He similarly concludes that Westway was "decided in court by some picayune inconsistencies of presentation and self-protective maneuvers typical of bureaucracy, some value judgments about what constitutes a significant adverse impact, which might have gone either way, and the judge's dislike of a witness."[21] Governor Carey similarly claimed that Westway's first defeats turned on procedural irregularities. Randy Mastro, a former member of the 1985 United

States attorney team and now a prominent private-sector lawyer, characterizes Westway's defeat as turning on a "procedural flaw" that "set back the city twenty years in the development of the West Side of Manhattan."[22] Under these views, Westway's travails and defeat involved mere procedural niceties that were missed, a few citizen fomenters, and a trial judge who overreacted. Such denigrations of Westway's defeat reveal several fairly persistent components: the antidemocratic claim, usually rooted in a focus on a single judge or the claim of a single opponent; inattention to the priorities and requirements reflected in applicable law; omission of the mass transit trade-in as a constant opposition motivator; and neglect of Westway's defeats in Congress.

Some of these criticisms may, however, reflect a broader indictment of how the law and linked political sphere work. Responsive analysis hence requires consideration of both what happened under the law and broader criticisms of the law. But at both levels, Westway's defeat was sound.

Why do these erroneous claims about the Westway war and defeat persist? Perhaps some of these characterizations that portray the defeat as an antidemocratic tale about makeweight concerns are a weapon in larger battles to marginalize or undo the law's powerful empowerment of citizens, to weaken environmental law's protections, or (through a more parochial lens) to set the stage for new development in or near New York City's adjacent waters. Regardless of the roots of these claims, they are inaccurate. Westway's defeat was not inevitable, but the results in the courts were correct; any other outcome would have required the courts to turn a blind eye to the law's protective dictates, to what the science showed, and to government actions that fell squarely within prohibitions on arbitrary and capricious conduct. And political unwillingness to rescue Westway was similarly a sound choice, although far from an inevitability.

First, the antidemocratic claim is specious. In reality, Westway died because of sound, fact-based rejections in judicial and political venues and a slow-building but ultimately formidable coalition of environmental, transit, and anti-pork-barrel advocates. And while there were notable individual heroes—most of all Benstock, allies like Bunny Gabel and John Mylod, and lawyers Mitchell Bernard and Al Butzel—they were not tiny in number or alone in their views. Most opponents were linked to organizations, some of which were substantial. The opponents included many politicians at all levels of government, especially most local legislators, and, of crucial importance, federal agency scientists and staff.[23] Those scientists did their jobs and reported what the science revealed. Their objections and analyses were framed by what the law required, not by mere personal predilections.

And when tested in the political crucible of majoritarian politics, Westway repeatedly came up short. The 1985 majority vote of the House of Representatives to defund Westway indicated a readiness to shelve the whole project. Supporters could not even garner sufficient votes to buy time. The earlier 1983 appropriations rider gambit to give Westway a congressional green light also failed. As Benstock quips in response to the lone-opponent hypothesis, "We couldn't have won in Congress if it was [just] one lone West Side woman."[24] Polls indicated citizens preferred a trade-in for mass transit to Westway.[25] Opponents constituted the majority of commentators during public hearings. Top White House staff bluntly told President Carter of the divide between the pro-Westway governor and mayor and anti-Westway local legislators.[26] Mayor Koch's own deputy mayor, Robert Wagner, concluded the trade-in made better sense for New York. Governor Cuomo's appointed Westway investigator, Thomas Puccio, reached the same conclusion. And those political judgments included only passing consideration of the values and concerns underlying environmental laws. New York State's legislature twice passed bills refusing to commit state dollars if federal funding did not come through, but both bills were vetoed by the governor.[27] Even Koch and Carey saw vehement opposition to Westway as smart electoral politics, at least in their initial campaigns for mayor and governor, respectively. Naysayers were not few in number, nor were they lacking in democratic provenance.

Opponents' motives were substantial. They preferred mass transit over highways and sought to limit federal spending on an extraordinarily high-cost project that might have crowded out other states' anticipated highway projects and possibly even New York City's future capital projects. They advocated compliance with the law, especially environmental laws requiring protection of the habitat of a commercially valuable but embattled fishery. None of these goals reflected irrational kookiness or marginal priorities. Project supporters' goals also were sane, even if often motivated by short-term gain and profit, as well as by Westway's touted public benefits. In reality, Westway had both substantial supportive and opposing constituencies. Arguments mocking or marginalizing opposition forces—whether the people, the law, or the environmental and urban stakes—are rooted in error.

The lone-judge hypothesis also falls short. Federal law and regulations, not the judge, dictated the nation's priorities. Judge Griesa withstood huge pressure and a barrage of political and press criticism to rule as he thought the law and facts required. Critics of Westway's defeat tend to forget or omit that on the most disputed and central issues regarding fishery impacts and the law's protective mandates, he was found right in both 1982 and 1985 by appellate courts. He did overreach in his injunctive orders, but all judges were in agreement that the regulatory judgments approving Westway were arbitrary and capricious. Furthermore, investigations after the 1982 trials found even greater improprieties than had Griesa and questioned the wisdom of building the project.

It is true that citizens' ability to participate in political, regulatory, and judicial venues proved essential to Westway's defeat. That empowerment of citizens, however, is due to priorities set forth in the United States Constitution, the enduring Administrative Procedure Act, and environmental laws that explicitly authorize citizens to challenge illegality. Even Westway supporters like Governor Cuomo refused to criticize this legal empowerment of citizens.

Spinners of the "procedural error" line err in their recounting of the actual legal infirmities of the Westway proposal. It is indisputable that Westway faced a major, substantive legal hurdle due to the Clean Water Act's strong protections and, earlier, the Clean Air Act's protections. The legal battles were not just over inadequate analysis under NEPA, a law that is now only procedural in its mandates. The "briar patch" cure dodged Air Act barriers. Water impacts proved far more problematic. Ever-growing fishery data and analysis by consultants to the Corps kept making Westway's future more and more tenuous.

It is worth emphasizing that in all the battles over Westway and fishery impacts, no witness, lawyer, or brief filed by pro-Westway lawyers ever questioned the data showing remarkably high percentages of young striped bass in the proposed Westway interpier areas. Arguments instead focused on deference and the reasonableness of the "no significant harm" conclusions. It is doubtful that with full and forthright analysis of the data regarding fishery impacts, especially under worst-case assumptions and required protective presumptions and prohibitions, Westway ever could have surmounted Section 404's hurdles. Plaintiffs had the burden to establish flaws in the government's actions. Nevertheless, scientific realities and Section 404's legal presumptions put a heavy burden on New York State as the applicant and on the Army Corps's regulators and attorneys, who had to defend any permit grant.

Maybe Westway could have squeaked through if reviewing judges had turned a blind eye under some extreme form of deference; a cascade of deferential reviewing judgments perhaps would not have caught Westway's risks and analytical infirmities. But when regulatory judgments were probed—as Supreme Court precedents require under "hard look review" of high-stakes regulatory judgments—their shortcomings were hard to ignore. No smoking gun ever proved intentional government malfeasance during the 1982–85 regulatory process, but the law required no such thing. Rationality and legal compliance were required. The earlier 1970s regulatory claims tested in court in during the 1982 trials did involve more overt deceptions and willful wrongdoing.[28]

The Westway wars were pervaded by political strong-arming, shoddy or short-circuited studies, regulatory shirking, and flimsy scientific claims, especially in the Army Corps's fishery analyses underpinning both the 1981 and 1985 permit grants. The 1985 judicial verdicts were also sound, and close to required, because Army Corps decision makers reversed key conclusions with virtually no explanation.[29] The Corps also relied on a biological theory that rested on shaky foundations, was undercut by actual scientific data, and had been derived by a disastrous consultant and later trial expert. If politics were to trump these legal constraints and scientific barriers, then either an amendment to the Clean Water Act was required or, as was tried without success, a project-specific law was needed to allow Westway's construction. But no legislative rescue arrived. Instead, Congress voted to defund the Westway landfill.

A permit denial hence would have had abundant, sound grounds and been virtually untouchable in the courts given the law's mandates, the data, and the weight of expert opinion finding significant fishery risks. In contrast, the regulatory judgment actually made by the Corps was vulnerable. The Hudson River Estuary is huge, and the Hudson is one of the world's great and magnificent rivers. The Westway interpier areas, however, represented a minuscule fraction of the estuary's waters, yet data again and again showed that this relatively tiny site contained a substantial percentage of young-of-the-year and yearling striped bass. Martin Marietta—one of the consultants relied upon by the Corps—provided a final best statistical estimate of 44 percent actual peak 1984 young-of-the-year usage in the Westway interpier area. These numbers posed a formidable challenge for anyone trying to justify a Section 404 grant. Dennis Suszkowski of the Corps (and later EPA) recalled anticipating that perhaps 0.01 percent of striped bass would use this two hundred-acre portion of the vast New York Harbor estuary. He was shocked when early estimates based on data floated a 10 percent number, then 26 percent and 33 percent, and finally that 44 percent figure. In his words, "If this didn't satisfy an unacceptable adverse impact, what would it take to deny?" The studies "confirmed the risk."[30]

Perhaps as a result of this tsunami of fisheries analysis criticism or maybe this combination of data and the law, the Corps found few scientific allies other than Dovel. The United States' dependence on Dovel and his theories was stated and reaffirmed so many times in regulatory materials and during the trial that by the time he started to testify at the 1985 trial, there was no going back. When Dovel's theory and supposedly definitive report turned out to be flimsy and filled with contradictory language, Westway was in major trouble. Despite legally required worst-case assumptions and applicant burdens to establish no risks and even no uncertainty about substantial risks prohibited by Section 404, the Corps nevertheless adopted an outlier, speculative theory about striped bass risks that had been rejected by federal fishery experts. The weak science and weak witness that proved fatal to Westway were not a fluke or aberration but reflective of tensions between the actual data, the law's requirements, and questionable regulatory and scientific claims of Westway's supporters and the Army Corps. If the United States, New York, and Westway's powerful allies could have relied on stronger science or a better witness, they surely would have done so.

Looking back, Dovel still stands by his migratory-movement theory that the fish move without dependence on any particular habitat, but he believes that it was "premature" for him to have testified about a report in progress. It was a year too early, in his view.[31] Upon a recent review of the Final Supplemental EIS, he thinks it reflects a "total lack of understanding [of] all participants" of "what the data could mean."[32] He still disagrees with a focus on numbers and statistics, instead advocating attention to why fish use particular habitats. Other fishery experts remain convinced that, due to the fishery data from the 1980s that "buried [Westway's supporters] in evidence of the importance" of the Westway site, the habitat had to be protected.[33]

In the end, only a last-second expert trial witness offered conclusions that might have saved the Army Corps's and attorneys' claims. But because of Dovel's much touted importance and disastrous testimony, an end-of-trial expert could not bootstrap the government's case to victory. An agency's actions rise or fall on the basis of their contemporaneous explanation.[34] Judge Griesa's rejection of the FSEIS and Section 404 permit grant and the Second Circuit's affirmance on the key fisheries issues were sound, correct decisions. And the Second Circuit's 1985 affirmance of Griesa's rejection of the Corps's fishery analysis was unanimous, even with an appellate panel that included two judges generally viewed as on the court due to support of Republican and Westway champion Senator Alphonse D'Amato.

Thus these legal and scientific realities, combined with egregious government missteps and particularly effective Westway opponents, were the cause of Westway's defeat, not mere procedural missteps or the existence of numerous opportunities for public scrutiny and objection. When tested in the courts and in Congress, Westway met with defeat, and for sound reasons.

That Westway's defeat was a legally sound, correct outcome does not mean it was inevitable; in law, as in any setting of clashing interests, long shots sometimes prevail. Neither the law nor the political realm provides such certainty. Getting Westway to its endgame 1983–85 period of jeopardy was dependent on many actors' strategic and sometimes imprudent actions over numerous years. With different political leadership, lawyers, opponents, and judges, Westway might have survived. The seemingly inexhaustible Marcy Benstock and attorneys Al Butzel and Mitchell Bernard were able to adjust, learn, and reveal Westway's vulnerable foundations in courts, political venues, and the press. Similarly, agency staff and scientists played an essential role by applying the law and considering actual data when their leadership and even presidents were ready to approve Westway. Their regulatory comments and, in a few instances, subsequent trial testimony, provided the credible scientific counter to Corps conclusions and Dovel's reports and testimony.

It is true that with less government blundering, Westway might have faced less endgame political and legal scrutiny. And few judges would have displayed Judge Griesa's immunity to political pressure and fastidious attention to the law and facts revealed before him. Some judges might have shown greater deference at every stage and never let plaintiffs establish the need for three lengthy federal trials. But in the Westway federal court battles, the federal defendants conceded the need for the trials that confirmed Westway's legal infirmities; one trial was requested by the FHWA and the other two followed federal concessions that inadequate regulatory records made limited trials appropriate.

Claims that Westway did not deserve defeat under the law and facts are hence in error. Its history shows that defeat of huge, high-stakes projects is possible and offers insights into how litigants and public-project stakeholders should play the game. The outcome of a regulatory war, however, is highly dependent on the particular legal artillery provided by applicable law, the stakes, and the facts. Section 404's strong protections and the unusual facts revealed about striped bass usage of the Westway site were a necessary element in the confluence of factors causing its defeat in the courts. Westway's defeat was a sound outcome under the law.

Does Westway's war reveal a sound legal and political system? Even if the outcome was sound under the law, the second-level question remains. Does the lengthy Westway war reveal a broken or imprudent body of law and politics? Westway's battle lines reflect common clashing perspectives regarding legal protection of the environment, but the laws and motivations at play in the Westway war, while subject to debate, reflected sound policy and logical motives.

Westway's champions seemed to believe that the usual rigid and rigorous legal constraints should have been modified for a project offering so many claimed public and private benefits. And the law was unyielding and Westway's path long and difficult. Congressional rescues came up short. And the courts did not grant Westway a break just because many powerful politicians, unions, and business leaders supported it. Political scientist David Vogel posits that the creation of "multiple veto points" makes any change in the legal status quo difficult, especially where the threat is to the environment.[35] Urbanist professors Altshuler and Luberoff also look at urban megaprojects as particularly imperiled by the veto points they face; they trace changed federal, state, and local megaproject choices as efforts to avoid such barriers.[36] Westway's placement in the water represented a strategy to avoid locally motivated opposition, while also creating land for development and a park. So if part of the veto point hypothesis is that environmental laws may create an enduring status quo, then this thesis is partly confirmed by the Westway tale. Enduring and strong environmental laws were indeed critical to Westway's defeat. Moreover, it was not just Westway that failed to trigger a loosening of environmental laws' strictures; while environmental laws are under almost constant assault, most have remained strong and sometimes even strengthened since they were enacted in their modern, protective form starting in the 1970s.[37]

However, are enduring environmental laws that are protected in Congress and the courts a problem or a virtue? Commentary about Westway states or at least implies that the laws were overly protective in the Westway battles, killing the project for little gain or over inconsequential stakes. Westway's actual history reveals that the project posed genuine environmental risks. Irregularities and questionable judgments pervaded the regulatory process. The project was exorbitantly expensive, provoking fiscal concerns at all levels of politics. And applicable laws, as amended during the Westway war, offered New York City and its citizens a legitimate highway-versus-mass transit choice, as well as means to further a preference for gradual, small-scale urban change over the abrupt and massive disruptions and changes that Westway would have entailed.

The law's many points of scrutiny and veto-gates can indeed create a cumulative drag on any project, even one that might provide spectacular benefits. As discussed earlier in reviewing the art of regulatory war, both project proponents and opponents can use delay and complexity to their benefit. Urbanist Jane Jacobs gave great weight to the power of delay. She once suggested that the way to defeat Westway was to hold on to "the powers-that-be," using time as an ally. She said that expressways will never be defeated in a single stroke but need to be "nibbled to death by ducks."[38] But delay did not defeat Westway. Delays were certainly part of the battles, but despite them, again and again Westway won crucial victories before agencies and in court. Wherever the law left wiggle room, political pressures trumped enforcement of the law's environmental protections and other punishments for regulatory irregularities. Public scrutiny and opportunities for public objection, along with attendant delay, were not enough to defeat Westway. So multiple points of regulatory scrutiny and attendant delay, in themselves, were not fatal. Delay did allow opposition coalitions to build, especially in Congress. However, it took a strong, unyielding law in Section 404 of the Clean Water Act, environmental facts that linked to protective legal requirements and presumptions, citizen enforcement rights, and a major defeat in Congress to kill Westway. Delay can be strategically wielded, and persistence is essential—which is another way of understanding Jacob's comment—but a strong law enforced in court, especially with strong congressional allies, is and was far more decisive.

And not all legally created hurdles, delays, and veto points reflect imprudence. Laws like the Clean Water Act and its protective Section 404 are, at their essence, intended to do just what they did: require decision makers to pause and consider risks and enforce congressional priorities, often with the goal of preventing slow or piece-by-piece cumulative destruction of crucial environmental assets like wetlands and estuarine habitats. And NEPA, too, was designed to confront decision makers with the longer-term costs of environmentally harmful actions. These laws fundamentally changed the rules of the game, especially for large-scale water-linked development. Such laws counteract strong private and political incentives to sacrifice the environment for short-term private and political benefits. Unowned waters and land at the edge of water, like many public lands and parks, are a beautiful and tempting place to build because they are of great value yet may not require anyone's displacement. Development of waterfront sites certainly can generate private wealth and governmental benefits like jobs and, if not subject to prodevelopment tax-break inducements, even tax revenues. And, as provided in Westway's plan, land at the water's edge or created from new government-created fill will create opportunities for government giveaways to political or business allies on favorable terms. Such giveaways can generate both political and private benefits, even if not necessarily in the public's interest. Moreover, especially in urban environments, pockets of nature and waterfronts often are not seen as a part of nature worthy of protection.[39]

Imagine, however, if every waterfront and water-based project desired by a city could escape regulation and be built as a result of passionate local support, or perhaps willingness of the federal government to pay for a project. Few wetlands and rivers would escape building. The cumulative impact could be disastrous, even if some projects were worthy of support from a more local perspective.[40] Changing the law to weaken its substance or reduce points of scrutiny or provide some project-specific trump would imperil resources, such as aquatic habitats, that are most valuable in their cumulative, aggregate functioning. Services and functions provided by nature are easy to overlook and difficult to replicate.[41] Habitat destruction often cannot be repaired or mitigated. Furthermore, a project like Westway would have irreversibly modified part of one of the world's most significant estuaries. Delay and legal scrutiny wisely rise with the level of threatened risk, even to an environment that may not intuitively seem environmentally important.

Furthermore, even if one adopts a more neutral view about the law's substantive wisdom, there is value and virtue in legal battles that reaffirm that the United States respects the rule of law. Congress, the Corps, and EPA, through long-standing laws and regulations, had created a body of law that required protection of Westway's environment. Making that law real showed respect for a democratically determined social priority. Mitchell Bernard believes passionately that the Westway outcome was a vindication of the rule of law, where the law empowered citizens to catch slipshod government conclusions and rely on the independent federal judiciary to enforce the law. In Bernard's words, the case was about "the sanctity of the legal process, that no matter how powerful you are, you are accountable to the law. And that courts have the authority to vindicate, in this case, statutory rights that belong to politically powerless people, this group of nonprofit organizations, to check the arbitrary exercise of government power."[42] Bernard in particular values the law's ability to check legal abuse, where people "play fast and loose with the rules, and manipulate facts, science, numbers, interpretation of analyses. . . . The legal system is there to make that right. That is what happened [with Westway]. And that is a vindication of a fundamental strength in our system of laws."[43] "Sometimes the rule of law triumphs over enormous power."[44] Fisheries advocate and Westway opponent John Mylod agrees, seeing citizens' ability to illuminate legal irregularities in court, coupled with the effective, steadfast work of Marcy Benstock, as crucial to Westway's defeat and a remarkable attribute of America's legal and political system.[45] Bunny Gabel remarked "how really thrilling it was to be part of the American democratic experience."[46]

Governor Cuomo, an ardent Westway supporter, regretted the outcome but also refused to condemn the law and process. He too saw Westway as an important affirmation of the rule of law: "[I]t reaffirms a truth basic to our government: the importance and the power of citizen-based organizations, the ability of the people to have the final word—not just in the voting booth but in the intricate processes of government we've established." In his view, "no individual, no branch of government, no private corporation can assume the power that rightly belongs to all of us, as people." Westway's battles were a "trophy to citizen activism, to advocates like Marcy Benstock."[47]

Westway and environmental law's frames. Westway's battles and competing perspectives on its fate also reflect several competing frames or worldviews about man, the environment, and progress.[48] Westway's partisans, who largely could be divided into camps of environmentalists and environmental skeptics, viewed the Westway battles, like many other clashes over the environment and risk regulation, in fundamentally different ways.

Supporters and Corps regulators generally revealed environmental skepticism, viewing nature and the environment as resilient, fungible and appropriately subject to man's use and dominion. Hence the environment was a low priority. Many of Westway's major players and supporters—ranging from Craig Whitaker to Mayor Koch to Governor Cuomo to William Dovel to Army Corps decision makers—fundamentally doubted that there was any environmental issue worthy of concern. Under this view, striped bass were a garbage fish, resilient, hardy, and able to adjust to change.[49] And noting Manhattan's dynamic physical transformations and periodic expansions into the Hudson over several hundred years, Westway supporters surmised that striped bass would weather yet more change. When Mayor Koch suggested moving striped bass to a motel in Poughkeepsie, he was displaying his usual wit but also questioning whether the Westway environment mattered. A related strain was that one just should not expect major cities to be places for natural resource protection. Or, as Dovel theorized, maybe striped bass were not dependent on any particular habitat or environmental substrate but just passively moved through and around the proposed Westway area. Regardless of the law's highly protective thresholds, regulators in the Corps and Westway's supporters minimized the environmental stakes, thought urban progress should continue, and repeatedly sought to put the burden of proof on opponents.

Opponents tended to adopt a more environmentalist perspective, seeing the environment as vulnerable and in need of protective, precautionary presumptions. This view was reflected in the actions of fishery and environmental scientists in the federal natural resource agencies and in state government, as well as in actions of citizen opponents like Marcy Benstock, John Mylod, Bunny Gabel, and aligned environmentalists. They first focused on the air and urban quality-of-life issues and fought for investment in mass transit over a highway. Then they focused upon fishery impacts. Their view was that fish population dynamics were difficult to understand; habitat protection was essential to the long-term health of fishery resources. They saw striped bass populations plummeting in the Chesapeake and Delaware due to pollution and habitat loss and sought to protect the Hudson's important habitats from similar harm.

In addition, while project supporters seemed reflexively to see all parts of the Hudson as equally suitable for the striped bass, fishery experts and Westway opponents saw the aquatic environment as varied and the Westway interpier sites as of special value. No opponent or scientist claimed to know exactly why young striped bass were so often found in the interpier areas proposed for Westway; they saw heavy use and therefore thought the law and sound science called for precautionary protection of the habitat. Opponents' emphasis on protecting this particular much-used aquatic environment pre- saged more recent efforts to protect fisheries by rigorously protecting habitats used during critical fish population phases.[50] In addition, the environmental- ist opponents tended to frame the battle within a broader geographic frame and on a longer timeline. The battle was not just about Westway acreage in isolation or at that time but about the broader effects of its destruction. For Westway's opponents, the preference for mass transit over highways and fish- ery concerns were linked motivators; they opposed unnecessarily despoiling any environment.

This divide in perspectives persists, but Westway's fate was not balanced on a scale where these competing concerns could legally be given equal weight; federal environmental laws decidedly favored the river-preserving outcome. Applicable laws insisted on analysis of direct and indirect effects, cumulative impacts, and alternatives. And if fill was unnecessary, signifi- cantly harmful, or of uncertain impact on fishery resources, Westway could not be approved. Those legally required protective assumptions were essen- tial to the project's demise.

A related divide reflected in the Westway wars concerns the ubiquity of uncertainty in assessing environmental risks and a growing divide between precautionary responses and demands for quantification of risks and sound science before regulators can impose regulatory constraints. The Clean Water Act and NEPA were both enacted with history and provisions reflecting acknowledgment of scientific uncertainty and the need for environmental precaution. Both reflect statutory strategies designed to compel the gathering and analysis of data about environmental harms; the permit approval process served as an "adjudicatory trigger" for enhanced information about the envi- ronment.[51] And both laws did just that, provoking substantial, intense analy- sis of Hudson River fisheries and threatened impacts. However, despite the intensive efforts, little could be conclusively claimed about the harms West- way would cause. To Colonel Griffis's credit, he conceded uncertainty on the critical question of what harms would occur due to Westway. Nevertheless, he granted the permit, while the law's answer, especially in Section 404 of the Clean Water Act, reflected a societal commitment to environmental protec- tion with decidedly protective mandates and presumptions.[52]

Westway's history reveals a clash between the veneer of data and science- driven decision making and actual decision making that jettisoned most reli- ance on data in favor of changing, speculative claims to overcome Section

404's protections. Supporters and Corps decision makers both called for data gathering and quantification, especially to establish striped bass risks. They could not fathom blocking Westway on the basis of harms that could not be firmly established, regardless of what the law actually required. The 1977 EIS claims and subsequent regulatory actions were completely indefensible and reflected virtually no concern with the law or the environment. But even Colonel Griffis, who showed much greater rigor and neutrality in many of his actions, in his 1985 decision repeatedly reversed legally mandated presumptions, faulting opponents for not establishing that harms would befall striped bass. He also repeatedly stepped away from having to say no to the project: first, he opted for two winters of study because he thought he would otherwise have to deny the permit; then he looked at the Draft's predictions of substantial harms and talked about the need for mitigation; then, when mitigation proved not to be a viable option and despite huge percentages of striped bass in the Westway site, Griffis shifted his analytical frames and relied on the no-dependence and migratory-movement theories, as well as a last-second changed conception of the imperiled habitat that reduced the relative importance of Westway. Similarly, Len Houston and William Dovel reached their conclusions on the basis of unsupported theories about fish movement, lack of habitat dependence, and young striped bass adaptability. Maybe their theories could eventually have been proved right, but none of the Hudson River striped bass studies were designed to test those theories.

Thus, these Corps decision makers and their chief consultant defaulted to environmental skeptic frames or worldviews, letting assumptions of resilience and unimportant habitat trump what the relative-abundance numbers seemed to indicate, as well as what fishery experts at the federal natural resource agencies officially stated in their critical Westway comments. Despite all the talk of percentages, statistics, and testing protocols, the Army Corps's decision makers and their most important consultant actually relied in the end on broad-brush theories that basically said the remarkably high percentages of young bass found in the slated Westway site did not matter; the Corps' decision makers simplified the world, gave virtually no weight to the data, but nevertheless wrapped up their conclusions in talk of quantifiable science and data. To use law professor Wendy Wagner's apt phrase, it was a "science charade."[53] Precautionary approaches, despite being the law, were rejected for what on the surface appeared to be a quantifying, data-driven review. In reality, the actual decisions adopted an antiprecautionary perspective that lacked actual data-based support, drew conclusions unsupportable by the survey designs and goals, and clashed with the law's required protective presumptions.[54] The Corps's decision relied heavily on the only scientist who claimed to know what would happen, yet far more trained scientists uniformly questioned such certitude. The regulatory decisions were inconsistent with sound science and the law's required protective frames.

Similarly, since the early 1980s, advocates of regulatory reform and opponents of precautionary modes of regulation and "command and control" environmental strategies have sought to raise hurdles to regulation and allow for greater private adjustment in achieving regulatory goals. This has often been accomplished through imposition of cost-benefit and risk-risk analysis, calls for sound science, and greater reliance on economic analysis and market-based regulatory tools.[55] Confronted by congressional refusal to mandate such quantified regulatory methods, their supporters have made a quintessential regulatory-war move, shifting their efforts to a more favorable venue. Few laws mandate their use, but more quantified and market-oriented modes of analysis have become increasingly prevalent tools in the executive branch. The urge to quantify risks and move away from precaution-based laws remains powerful. Today, however, as in the Westway battles, judgment calls and assumptions not driven by science or numbers can make massive differences in what quantified analysis supposedly indicates about a policy choice. Talk of math and quantification may mask assumptions, politicized decision making, and intuitive leaps that lack any sound foundation.[56]

Consistent with ongoing divides regarding such quantified analytical methods, Westway's proponents and opponents differed in how they balanced environmental concerns against economic benefits. Supporters touted the multibillion-dollar price tag and promises of federally reimbursed cost escalations as a source of immediate jobs and wealth for New York City. Even if the project might be shifting sites of spending more than generating new wealth, Westway was presented as a quick and certain source of money and employment. Political credit would (it was hoped) be quickly available. The traditional open spigot of 90 percent federal financing for interstate highway projects like Westway provided essential support and motivation for this project. Other people's money–that 90 percent funding paid by taxpayers across the country—would fund New York metropolitan-area jobs, a buried highway, a park, and development. And vast wealth, as well as political gain, stood to be generated since many neighboring real estate owners would be enriched when a surface highway became a park, as well as when New York State chose contractors and gave away or leased newly created acreage for development. Opponents sought to offer their own countervailing monetary quantification, affixing monetary values to striped bass and longer-term investment in mass transit upgrades. Striped bass benefits were at least a hundred million dollars a year along the East Coast, but the magnitude of Westway's threat to striped bass remained unclear. Trade-in proceeds for mass transit undoubtedly were less than any interstate highway reimbursement.

However, far more New York City and metro area residents used mass transit than used cars and roads; rescuing mass transit provided value beyond the amount of the trade-in dollars and resulting construction. Westway's champions focused on immediate new wealth and jobs, downplaying the economic benefits of status quo fishing interests, incremental improvements for subway riders, and the gradual wealth creation and more organic Lower West Side development that followed after Westway's demise.

But these cost-benefit calculations ultimately did not decide Westway's fate. Scientific realities, coupled with the law's long-established protections, were more than Westway could overcome. In the Westway story, nature provided a consistent tale that ultimately could not be avoided. After extensive data-gathering efforts, one verity remained: young striped bass were found in high, sometimes highest numbers, right where Westway was proposed to be built. And once Congress changed the law to allow a trade-in for mass transit, two competing uses motivated Westway's supporters and detractors.

The Westway battle thus involved several common divides in battles over the environment, especially when progress or wealth-generating activity collides with a protected environment. Those divides persist today, especially in battles over the law's protection of rivers and wetlands, as well as in persistent disagreements about climate and the necessity of a regulatory response. Opponents of regulation are often skeptical about the capacity of humans to destroy nature's functioning, whether involving a river or the world's climate. Religious beliefs in the appropriateness of man's dominion over nature and near-religious beliefs in the miracles of markets can lead to environmental skepticism. One side fundamentally doubts that particular environments matter. Nature is viewed as either insignificant, endlessly resilient, or appropriate for despoiling for human beings' current benefit. If allegedly vulnerable species have survived previous environmental assaults, then why not allow yet more progress? On the other side, environmental advocates see the environment as vulnerable and in need of constant vigilant protection. Cumulative harms can tip the scales and cause permanent change. Precaution is the order of the day.[57] Westway's competing analytical frames remain prevalent today.

The fishery impacts that became the make-or-break issue for Westway provide both cautionary and optimistic lessons about these clashing analytical frames and the potential promise of environmental regulation. Broader fishery trends provide strong affirmation that attention must be paid to preserve fisheries. Many of the world's major fish stocks have since the 1980s fallen into precipitous decline, often due to overfishing and habitat harm.[58] Many are imperiled or, for now, commercially extinct. As recounted earlier, in the 1970s and 1980s, striped bass were plummeting along the East Coast and in other major river estuaries, while the Hudson had held its own and hence was becoming relatively more important. Those striped bass population drops led to the unusual step of fish-specific federal legislation that created special striped bass protections. And the Westway battle itself created a strong precedent, heeded by regulators, courts, and potential waterfront developers, about the strength of Section 404's protections. Westway was not built, and it remains true today that development in America's waters is legally disfavored. With these special protections, and surely other factors that remain a mystery, striped bass have rebounded. As a recent report stated, the recovery of East Coast striped bass since the mid-1980s is viewed as among the great success stories of environmental protection.[59]

But such extraordinary fishery efforts and similar successes are not the norm. The endless-resilience angle has been repeatedly challenged, if not disproved, by the devastation of the world's fisheries during recent decades. On a national and international scale, battles over climate change and greenhouse gas emissions reflect similar divides over science, economic risks and progress, and the need for regulatory intervention. Effective regulation on both fronts—to protect fisheries and to address the causes and risks of climate change—remains elusive but with occasional progress.

Lessons for lawyers, regulators, and policy design. Lawyers, officials, and policymakers working in regulatory, legislative, and litigation settings can learn much from Westway. Several of the more egregious Westway mistakes would, or at least should, be unlikely today, especially willful government blindness to scientific realities. Government lawyers should have learned from Westway's demise. Former FHWA lawyer Edward Kussy commented that he and other government lawyers use the Westway experience to persuade government clients to work honestly with information and not ignore problematic facts.[60] Walter Mugdan at EPA regularly shares his own Westway history and its lessons. Government lawyers today would likely work more actively with regulators on impact statements and permit decisions, especially where a project is in the political spotlight, is of huge economic importance, and has engendered debate, political scrutiny, and litigation. It is remarkable that Colonel Griffis sent out the Draft SEIS despite his staff's objections and, as far as we can tell, with minimal legal vetting. Regulators need to identify strong data and supportive experts supporting their regulatory actions when judicial review awaits. That the federal government, New York, and even the Rockefellers relied on such weak science remains a puzzler, unless it reflects a possible reality that they could find no other supportive expert.

But maybe Westway is less of an exception than we assume. Litigation and news stories regularly reveal agencies that have done shoddy work or capitulated to political or economic pressures but been caught in their imprudence. Postmortem analyses of the 2010 BP oil spill found abundant similar evidence of regulatory laziness and failure.[61] Earlier investigations of the Minerals Management Agency revealed an agency that had surrendered its watchdog role. Agencies monitoring public lands and resource extraction industries are frequently found by courts to have slipped on the job. Investigative journalism in winter 2011 revealed a politicized EPA that had repeatedly failed to act to address growing risks of natural gas extraction.[62] After Vice President Cheney's political initiative to encourage energy production in the United States and reduce regulatory burdens, EPA during the Bush administration sought to push through remarkably broad air pollution regulatory breaks that were of dubious legality. EPA surely knew of the risk of judicial rejection but proceeded nonetheless. And several were subsequently found illegal and unjustified.[63] Politics can trump legality and science-based decision making but will sometimes be caught if the courthouse doors are open to challenges.

As confirmed in Westway regulatory and trial mishaps, lawyers are often unable to anticipate unpredictable witness and client behavior. They also will often have to make the best case they can, especially within government, where politics frequently creates pressures upon agencies to stretch the tether of the law, if not ignore it. Still, one wonders if the federal defendants' attorneys in 1985 could have done something to avoid their clients' and witnesses' belated production, during trial, of new reports and draft impact statements. The revelation during trial of Dovel's earlier drafts, especially with their problematic language, virtually ensured that his testimony would not be credited. Former assistant United States attorney Mastro doubts that the United States would have presented Dovel as a witness had it known in advance about these additional drafts.[64] It is important to recall that Dovel was called to the stand by the United States and offered as an expert witness; he was not dragged up to the witness stand by opponents over government objections.

Westway's fate serves as a reminder that lawyers cannot just accept their clients' or witnesses' first story; they need to be tough on their own clients and witnesses to avoid debacles in court. Had lawyers and regulators for the United States really pushed and probed Dovel's reliability and challenged Corps regulators' choices before trial, perhaps they would have avoided the implosion in court. Perhaps the Army Corps would have denied Westway its essential Section 404 dredge-and-fill permit. Such a result would have infuriated supporters, but would have been far easier to defend than the actual 1985 permit grant. Maybe the Corps overestimated the latitude for judgment provided by deference doctrines. In contrast, Fritz Schwarz successfully guided the city and state through the air permit process by resisting his client's efforts to short-circuit the process.

Westway also offers lessons for what makes a good lawyer. Al Butzel's persistence, quick learning, and superb advocacy skills both kept Westway at bay and, in the case of investigator Thomas Puccio, persuaded Puccio to adopt Butzel's logic and even language and recommend abandonment of Westway. Mitchell Bernard's trial-setting attention to witnesses' answers and well-crafted but improvised questions made him, even as a novice trial lawyer, into a powerhouse cross-examiner. He was not stuck on some script but listened and adjusted when the unexpected arose. That he remained oriented during the confusing Dovel testimony is itself a wonder. The Bernard and McCarroll briefs similarly showed clear, forceful logic and argument. On the government side, Paul Curran never let the judges forget the political element of the choice to build Westway.

Another lesson for lawyers is the importance of anticipating opponents' arguments. Perhaps the United States attorney's office lawyers working on their 1985 Westway posttrial briefs thought they were sunk before Judge Griesa so just kept playing the predictable deference game, without hope of winning at the trial level. They were dealt an exceedingly difficult hand by politicians and regulators, as well as seriously problematic scientific facts. But their only real chance rested on their ability to deal with the disastrous trial turns and the problematic Draft-to-Final SEIS changes. They also had to deal with the unfortunate political end run instigated by Governor Cuomo that resulted in shortened data collection. Instead, they just kept making the same arguments, even relying on Dovel in their posttrial briefs. It was extraordinarily unlikely that the court of appeals could have credited Dovel's testimony after Judge Griesa's firsthand observations of Dovel as a trial witness. The federal government's lawyers might have done better to concede the problematic twists and try to construct an argument for why they nevertheless deserved to win. On the other hand, perhaps they hoped that the appellate judges would not really delve into the trial testimony. That was a long-shot strategy that did not work either. Beyond broad appeals to deference and political choice— which are undoubtedly often an effective and powerful combination— Westway's federal lawyers held no obvious winning hand.

Westway's battles affirm how important it is for lawyers and government regulators to maintain a judge's confidence. Judges will give lawyers and their government clients little credence if they see analytical gaps or regulatory evasion within agencies or evidence of overargument, evasive and unresponsive briefs, or shoddy preparation of witnesses. Much of the legal work for the state, city, and federal government showed great skill, even when it involved dealing with difficult facts and law. Nevertheless, at points during the 1982 and 1985 battles, attorneys for the state and federal government parties lost the judge because of one or more of these mistakes attributable to them or their government clients. The United States' final brief to the Second Circuit Court of Appeals, in contrast, was a remarkably effective effort despite the challenging underlying facts, but earlier choices they and regulators made left them in a tough place.

Westway's opponents played a smarter game, both maintaining their focus and adjusting their strategy when a witness like Dovel gave them so many gifts. They were careful not to overargue or alienate Judge Griesa. They did, however, risk much when they kept using language of intentional wrongdoing and bad faith; they did not need to make such a showing and ultimately wisely backed away from it. Lawyers need to argue in forms that lend themselves to incorporation into a regulator's action or judge's opinion. The opponents did so, convincingly weaving facts and law together.

Nevertheless, despite their lawyers' great skill, the opponents' ultimate victory cannot be credited to their being better legal gladiators, although perhaps they were. Such a view would excessively elevate the role of lawyers and implicitly downplay the law, scientific data, and substantial political groundwork that allowed them to win in court and hold on to that victory. Most crucial for the opponents, their citizen and not-for-profit clients pursued a multifront battle, not just in the courts but by building political coalitions that changed the law (through the trade-in option) and twice in Congress rejected Westway. In the regulatory and judicial venues, the crucial assets for the opponents were the laws and enduring regulations that made protection of aquatic habitat a national priority. Fish data about the Westway site gave them better facts and stronger law on their side, although they still had to overcome presumptions favoring deference to expert regulatory judgments. By maintaining their poise and not overclaiming, as well as by emphasizing the importance of the rule of law before a rule-of-law judge, they played the facts and the law well. They never fell into judicial disfavor.

Westway warnings and federalism games. Westway serves as a strong warning about the risks of excessive deference to agencies, especially where high-stakes scientific judgments are involved or where political appointees or elected officials become involved in regulatory judgment calls. Lawyers for the United States and New York played the deference card repeatedly. However, as a result of the sequence of irregular and illegal actions, as well as press, political, and public attention, the regulatory process was progressively made more open to scrutiny and probing. Despite advance warning that the world was watching and litigation probable if not certain, imprudent and questionable scientific and regulatory judgments once again pervaded the 1982–85 decision making. Even after initial 1982 judicial rejections and three political confirmations of those rejections, the later 1985 trial revealed scientific conclusions and decisions that once again, viewed charitably, lacked a sound basis. Recent scholars have documented the many ways science can be "bent" or misused;[65] Westway is yet more evidence of the risks of scientific abuse and bogus conclusions.

The Westway battles also, however, reaffirm the value of science-based agencies like the federal natural resource agencies while also highlighting risks posed by political involvement. The agencies kept looking at Westway data and risks, as well as the law's protective mandates, and calling for the project's rejection. Professional agency scientists, benefitted by civil servant job protection, did not yield. A divide over Westway arose during the Reagan administration between political leaders, who largely capitulated in the face of political pressure or themselves created the pressure, and staff scientists and career regulators who let the facts and law drive their conclusions.

Westway teaches that judicial readiness to defer to an agency's choice merely because scientific judgments are involved or to heighten deference because of the involvement and support of political leaders, can leave illegal and illegitimate actions unchecked.[66] Despite recent scholarship advocating heightened deference when there is greater involvement of democratically accountable leadership, political pressures can lead to illegality. Deference to executive branch regulatory policymaking made through public notice and comment procedures makes sense due to the democratic accountability inherent in such an open, quasi-legislative and participatory process that sets national policy. High-stakes adjudicatory judgments like Westway's requested Section 404 permit, in contrast, often implicate vast resources and billions of dollars for small numbers of partisans who may seek great personal or political advantage through those judgments. Risks of lawless capitulation in the face of political and private pressure are considerable, as shown in Westway's history. Meaningful judicial review remains important and perhaps should be more rigorous for regulatory actions involving high-stakes adjudicatory decision making.

We will never know exactly why Westway decision makers apparently blundered in so many crucial ways, but the project's history suggests some explanations and offers several lessons. One possibly counterintuitive explanation is that Westway's political and private champions may actually not have blundered at all. Even if they knew that they had to win a legal long shot, they could have felt that the effort was worthwhile given Westway's anticipated benefits.

Why regulators erred or reacted imprudently is the tougher question. The most obvious answer is that they faced extreme political pressure. They also had to adjust in light of political efforts to circumvent regulatory constraints. Stealth appropriations riders sought to sidestep environmental laws, and agency and department heads, governors, mayors, senators, and leading business leaders leaned on and castigated regulatory decision makers. President Reagan himself spoke in favor of Westway and criticized regulatory roadblocks; President Carter's top staff remained more neutral but also communicated directly with the regulators. Perhaps in response, scientists, consultants, and regulators either made egregious mistakes, capitulated, avoided criticism, or ignored or skewed their application of data.

Westway's tale reaffirms how important it is for courts to assess agency science claims with care, looking for indicia of work by sound, independent experts. Perfect information and certainty cannot become a prerequisite for either regulatory protection or project approvals, since science will seldom offer certainty. A sound second-best strategy was evident in regulations calling for the Army Corps to give substantial weight to expert natural resource agency views. Laws requiring consultation are a logical antidote to tunnel vision or capitulation to pressure and hence might have helped check scientific error. But the Army Corps never seemed to give those views more than passing attention.[67]

Another option to encourage sound, rigorous science is to provide meaningful opportunities to test important agency science claims. This unusual attribute of the Westway battles deserves note.[68] Partly because of prudent concessions by government lawyers in 1982 and 1985 and even the FHWA's request, Westway's regulatory actions were subjected to three district court trials. And, especially in 1985, the cross-examination of the influential consultant for the Corps, William Dovel, was crucial to reveal the flimsy underpinnings of the Corps's regulatory conclusions. Such hearings and expert cross-examination remain a legal possibility but are a rarity and disfavored under the law. Court-created legal doctrine, statutes, and regulatory process seldom create opportunities to test critical science claims. The Supreme Court's *Vermont Yankee* case generally limits the ability of courts to tell agencies to open up their process; in addition, deference principles applicable to courts limit their ability to provide a judicial venue for testing agency claims that may be unsound.[69] For agencies or private actors happy with a regulatory judgment, this typical avoidance of scrutiny and cross-examination is surely welcome. But high-stakes regulatory judgments can, as in the Westway case, truly present substantial risks, whether to the environment, health, or a project or product wrongly subjected to regulatory rejection.

Whether through legislative amendments, regulatory process changes by agencies themselves, or shifts in Supreme Court doctrine, increasing meaningful opportunities to probe and check agency science claims would help prevent future regulatory science errors or imprudence. Such opportunities to challenge science claims are especially important where, as with Westway, agencies are making an adjudicatory decision with vast money and resources at stake. Legislators would still need to decide on the critically important presumptions to be applied to such agency science. Those presumptions—whether protective and precautionary or leaning in an antiregulatory direction—would shape the nature of later probing in agency or judicial settings. If regulators knew such scrutiny was ahead, that would create incentives for agencies to be rigorous in the first place. Such scrutiny, and anticipation of it, would concededly slow agency process that is already often slow. But such an adjustment to provide room for testing science, if fairly applied in light of legal presumptions about such science, would create an equal opportunity benefit; it would help both those seeking regulatory protections and those seeking to avoid it. Westway illuminates the value of this rarity—cross-examination of agency scientific claims.

The Westway saga is consistent with several prevalent views about federalism while also calling into question the emerging judicial tendency to try to divide the world into distinct and separate federal, state, and local spheres.[70] Federal environmental agencies are generally reputed to be the most protective, zealous regulators; this view was corroborated repeatedly, although leaders at the federal natural resource agencies twice buckled under political pressure and failed to press their environmental objections. Nevertheless, on the scientific merits, the expertise and professionalism of the agencies proved crucial. The plaintiffs' case in 1985 was made primarily by federal government scientists and their consultants who put agency views into the regulatory record. And when asked, these witnesses provided direct and sustained explanations for why Westway violated the law and deserved defeat. State environmental regulators were less vocal at times, but even they at several points criticized and even rejected Westway for its environmental impacts.

Debates over federal, state, and local roles often include an antifederal strain, with associated claims that state and local governments are closest to and hence most accountable to their citizens. Under this perspective, these governments should be the presumptive arbiters of choices with primarily local impacts. But the natural environment virtually never matches political boundaries; the effects of political and regulatory choices can far exceed political boundaries and the terms of decision makers.[71] Thinking about environmental and political stakes thus often presents uncertainty about what governments are most implicated. Moreover, even if some New York City constituencies stood to be the main beneficiaries of Westway, it was not a New York City project. The intermingling of federal, state, and local roles in funding, planning, and battling over Westway precluded any simplistic federalism-based line drawing. If built, Westway would have affected more than just New York's environment and natural resources. Westway's defeat reflected a federal veto not of a city and state project but of an overwhelmingly federally financed project where federal law allowed for two end uses of highway dollars. Federal, state, and local choices and laws were intertwined and their actions interdependent.

Whether state and local politicians were sensitive to their constituents' priorities leads to a mixed answer. More groups opposed than supported Westway, and polling data at a few points indicated that numerically more citizens preferred a trade-in to Westway. Most state, local, and federal legislators took positions that they thought were aligned with their constituents and hence opposed the project. It was executive branch leaders at the city, state, and federal level who were Westway's most persistent and ardent champions, although New York's senators also remained supporters. Mayors, governors, and presidents may have viewed the hunt for jobs and a thriving economy as their predominant task, leading them to favor the influx of dollars and jobs Westway promised. Or perhaps they sought the support of business leaders who would benefit from Westway work and doling out of newly created acreage for development. Mayor Koch explained his shift from strident Westway opponent to mayoral supporter as linked to his mayoral goal of supporting New York City's great industry, "development."[72] These proclivities are consistent with a strain in federalism study that predicts local governments will see economic vitality and growth as among their highest priorities.[73] Apart from Mayor Koch's periodic threats to drop Westway if the state failed to support mass transit, there is scant evidence in the Westway tale of executive leaders showing sensitivity to opponents' views, let alone to environmental concerns. Simplistic federalism tales do not easily fit Westway's more complicated array of laws, actors, actions, jurisdictional and temporal lines, and resulting incentives.

The critical role of citizen enforcers of the law and an independent judiciary. Westway affirms the importance of citizens' powerful roles in the regulatory process, in the courts, and in the political realm as well. Westway really did turn out to pose a major risk to young striped bass. Earlier air pollution risks were revealed, illuminated, and battled by citizen opponents. Those challenges led to delays and modest redesign to address the risks; with those changes, the Clean Air Act hurdles proved surmountable. Furthermore, citizens' ongoing efforts to prompt a trade of Westway funds for mass transit involved a fundamental political choice between highways and mass transit. Citizens' ability to battle on despite contrary regulatory conclusions or regulatory capitulation twice was a necessary precondition for questionable fishery claims to be revealed in court. Political and economic pressures twice led federal and state regulators to surrender without fighting in final possible political venues, although they never withdrew or reneged on their agencies' environmental objections. Both in 1982 and in 1985, citizens' statutory right to challenge the Army Corps decisions was essential to reveal the questionable government conclusions. In those legal venues, they succeeded, however, only because under the facts and law they had sound claims.

And without a judge protected by life tenure, as all federal judges are under our Constitution, political pressures would likely have been too much. Judge Griesa, however, maintained a tough, starchy, no-nonsense, rule-of-law attitude. He did not view citizen and environmentalist opponents and their lawyers with disfavor but as legitimate players in the legal system. He expected compliance with the law and honest testimony. It did not matter who was before him. That he was a former corporate lawyer, appointed by a Republican president after nomination by a Republican senator, never appeared to color his judgment against the environmentalists and transit advocates who kept fighting Westway.

Groups like Benstock's Clean Air Campaign and her allies pursued their arguments in every possible setting, including courts, agencies, and formal and informal political venues. Without their ability to keep pursuing their contentions in court, their political clout would have been greatly weakened. But opponents' political successes also kept pressure on the project.

The possibility that citizen litigants' lawyers could receive an attorneys' fee and cost award if pursuing a sound case, as Congress provided in the environmental laws at issue during the Westway war, was crucial to facilitate citizen litigation. Few citizens and their lawyers can or will engage in multi-year battles without at least the possibility of a fees and cost award. In post-trial motions, both in 1982 and in early 1986, the Butzel-Bernard-McCarroll opposition litigation team was awarded attorney's fees.[74] Those amounts did not add up to a full market-level award, but between compensation paid by opponents through fund-raising during the battles and the fee awards, the legislative design worked. A successful judicial challenge to address illegality did not lead to lawyer poverty but to a decent level of compensation. However, the far more numerous hours that Westway's opponents themselves devoted to the project's defeat in political and regulatory venues was subject to no similar cost shifting.

WESTWAY'S DEFEAT was thus neither a fluke nor an unsound result. Federal laws and dollars made Westway attractive, but other federal legislative amendments opened up the trade-in option, thereby incentivizing opponents. Federal law also created durable and powerful protections for the environment. Judicial rejections were legally and factually sound but did not alone defeat Westway. Political choices, priorities, and Westway-specific actions were crucial as well. The laws and political systems that led to these outcomes reflected rational, defensible policy.

EPILOGUE

If Westway Were Proposed Today?

WOULD A MODERN Westway-like project today suffer the same fate? In a literal sense, no. Most important, the particular federal interstate highway funding regime that made Westway so attractive to New York City is mostly gone. Westway as a proposal existed only because it would bring billions of federal highway dollars into the city and state. And the trade-in option that motivated many Westway opponents was replaced with federal laws providing local governments with somewhat increased ability to choose between highways and mass transit. A mega-interstate highway project could not today be designed in a gold-plated fashion, then be traded for transit funding. The particular federal inducements that drove supporters and opponents are now gone.

But most elements of regulatory war illuminated by Westway's battles remain the same. Federal monetary munificence still drives projects, whether for work on roads, for other subsidized infrastructure, or through legislatively earmarked projects. Development-oriented interests, because of either patronage or mere desire for profit, remain powerful political forces at all levels of government. And battles never end that seek to unskew federal and state funding that often still favors highways over other transit projects and other infrastructure not dependent on cars. Much of American urban sprawl results from the funding of highway construction over other transit alternatives.[1]

And battles over environmental harms from large public and private projects remain ubiquitous. Regulatory policymaking that creates the basic rules and policies guiding permit reviews, product approvals, and safe levels of emissions or exposures predictably provoke battles before agencies and subsequent judicial challenges. Both project-specific actions and broader policymaking still today provoke battles that track moves and countermoves evident in the Westway war. The basic components of such regulatory wars remain substantially unchanged. As a single case study, Westway's tale cannot prove anything about the outcome of the next major regulatory battle, but it can and does provide valuable illumination for why the law cannot be understood through a mere focus on judicial conclusions. The law shapes political actions, and political choices shape legal battles before agencies and courts. The Westway war sheds light on the venues and strategies at play in complex regulatory wars. Westway's particular legal protections, presumptions, participation rights, scientific data, case-based doctrine, and degrees of deference—the varying sorts of legal artillery implicated by most regulatory actions—were strategically manipulated and used in dozens of venues by all Westway partisans. Some laws remained durable foundations for the Westway battles, but other laws and regulations changed and, as a result, fundamentally changed the Westway battle lines.

Regulatory wars are today still fought in numerous interdependent political and legal venues. Both supporters and opponents will seek victories before regulators, before courts, and also in Congress. In such high-stakes regulatory battles, sophisticated legal work involves adept strategic maneuvering in many legal venues, sometimes concurrent, sometimes in a long sequence over years. Neither supporters nor opponents can ever rest or confine their attention to one legal or political realm.

The cast of characters would also be similar. Private actors would generally support projects and activities generating profits, while politicians at all levels of government would assess proposals with attention to jurisdictional benefits and credit-claiming opportunities. Politicians would assess monetary benefits for their jurisdictions, job creation, and other means to please powerful supporters, as well as provide services and amenities citizens demand. Not-for-profits and citizens would have their own interests and goals and typically would line up on both sides of a major regulatory battle. Where a project or proposed activity would create risk or threaten the environment, agencies would again be centrally involved in assessing and regulating those risks. But agencies would not work in a vacuum; as in the case of Westway, they would hear from and themselves reach out to politicians, the private sector, citizens, and organizations favoring and opposing the agency action. Citizens affected and not-for-profits dedicated to protecting a threatened amenity will inevitably play a role. Most partisans would work with legal counsel and focus on their preferred issues, pushing conflicts into venues that might advantage them. Invariably, environmental harms and other risks would bring science into play. As in the Westway battles, scientific data and, especially, legal presumptions and burdens about that data will always be a crucial determinant of outcomes.

Skewed resources would still generally advantage the proponents of a major regulatory action—whether supportive private actors or government agencies—especially an action promising both private and political gain. This is especially so where the gains would be concentrated on a small number of people and the resulting harms or risks would be dispersed and suffered in small ways by many, or even just by the environment. The smaller group of beneficiaries would usually more easily coordinate than would larger numbers of people whose health or environmental resources would be affected or threatened.[2] The Westway battles are somewhat consistent with this standard political economic prediction, but the leadership of Westway's opponents actually ended up more coordinated than did project supporters. Marcy Benstock's Clean Air Campaign and a small number of opposition allies, as well the opponents' attorneys, remained diligent in monitoring and participating in local, state, and federal political venues, whether their advocacy involved legislatures, agencies, or courts. For a time, Lowell Bridwell tried to serve in a similarly coordinating role for Westway. Once he left, however, Westway's supporters lacked anyone taking a long-term strategic perspective. As one of the lead federal Westway lawyers, Nicholas Gimbel, commented, after 1982 the Westway project was a "headless horse" with "no one who could take a longer lens and say 'this is how we should do it.' . . . No one was in charge."[3] Fritz Schwarz, former Cravath Swaine & Moore lawyer and Westway attorney for New York, observed the same problem; once Lowell Bridwell left, Westway drifted.[4] Local, state, and federal officials, whether politicians or regulators, as well as private proponents of Westway, simply lacked a counterpart to the small number of persistent citizen and attorney opponents, as well as persistent agency scientist and staff critics and political opponents like Congressman Ted Weiss. This lack of coordination and politically pressured actions hurt Westway's prospects.

A question worthy of future analysis concerns this Westway revelation: how often will citizens or lawyers facing a battle with skewed stakes and resources nonetheless gain some advantage due to their leadership's own small numbers, coordination, and knowledge? Perhaps a variable hurting large regulatory actions and projects, especially where they unavoidably involve all layers of government and face multiple approval hurdles, is that only rarely can any one person really be in charge. With greater intertwining of federal, state, and local roles under contemporary federalism regimes, coordination will always be a challenge. Maybe opposition coordination and dispersed or absent coordination on the pro-project side is not the exception.

In contrast, Robert Moses, who reigned mostly before the advent of modern environmental laws and such intermingled government roles, could and did use his own power and development authorities to seize firm control of projects and often ram them through. Moses-style concentrated power, which was more "authoritarian" and subject to few legal constraints, may be a thing of the past.[5]

One part of future regulatory wars would be unchanged. Politicians and agencies would still play the deference card, seeking to insulate their decisions from citizen, attorney, and judicial second-guessing, but citizens and the courts would still play a crucial role participating in and subsequently scrutinizing those regulatory actions. At most, deferential review frameworks would favor the initial government action, not guarantee victory. As in the Westway battles, much would hinge on where burdens and presumptions legally rest and whether opportunities exist to test disputed claims raised during the regulatory process. And multiple agencies with different regulatory turfs will often have to focus on different democratically set policies, data, or science and hence may clash on a proposed action, thereby creating a record for all stakeholders to use.

Most important, the particular issues and laws triggered, as well as the nature of the government action, will always influence outcomes in regulatory wars. Environmental and risk-regulation laws are remarkably diverse in their goals, strategies, strength, and rigidity. Merely informational laws would only inform the process. Many laws protecting the environment or reducing risk act only to alleviate harms or reduce pollution; few laws would stop an underlying project or prohibit an action. Other laws, however, can act like Section 404 of the Clean Water Act and pose a far more rigid obstacle. Section 404, however, is unusually powerful. Because the environment itself is dynamic and because changing laws also can generate environmental improvements or eliminate protections, a new Westway-like proposal's fate would largely depend on its particular design and risks, as well as the state of the changing legal and natural environment.

Turning to the particular physical environment involved in the Westway battles, a major question is whether a substantially more healthy East Coast striped bass fish population would now change fish scientists' perspective on the importance of the Westway interpier areas. With more fish and a cleaner Hudson, the percentage threat might today be diminished. On the other hand, Section 404's protective language and regulations, including the broad prohibition on unnecessary filling, remain largely unchanged today from the time of the Westway wars. If threatened habitat remained heavily utilized by young, vulnerable striped bass, it would likely still be protected from "significant degradation." And if other surrounding development eliminated other sheltering habitat, then the site could be of even greater importance. Changing scientific views might also modify the scientific consensus about the value of the Westway site. The striped bass and aquatic habitat factor, if replayed today, is thus hard to predict. Despite the still-strong protections of Section 404, the calculations and analysis would surely be different.

A modern battle against a project like Westway would encounter several legal changes, some regulatory, but most due to Supreme Court decisions from the last two decades. Westway teaches that in high-stakes regulatory wars, partisans will opportunistically shift their focus to promising legal venues. On the regulatory front, the NEPA worst-case regulation was substantially weakened during the Reagan administration and remains weakened today. Westway started to founder due to early failures to heed the mandates of the worst-case regulation. On the other hand, opponents of environmental protection and, especially, Section 404 have sought legal relief in Congress but met with little success. Similarly, agencies have provided only modest relief, at least under the Clean Water Act. Proponents of regulatory relief have therefore turned to the courts.

A similar new project would encounter several potentially important changes due to court decisions. While few environmental or risk-regulation laws have been weakened by Congress, an increasingly conservative Supreme Court has actively recast much administrative and constitutional law doctrine since 1990. These changes would raise new hurdles for citizen opponents.

Most important, the Supreme Court has raised new "citizen standing" barriers for citizen litigants.[6] As a constitutional matter, this body of law asks what kinds of litigants can "stand" before and be heard in federal court. At the time of the Westway battles, standing doctrine posed little or no problem for citizens seeking to enforce the nation's environmental laws, especially where Congress had welcomed citizen lawsuits with provisions creating a cause of action and rights to awards of fees and costs. In contrast, a modern Westway-like battle, and especially a challenge to any broad national regulatory action, would be near-certain to start today with challenges to the constitutional suitability of the plaintiffs seeking to be heard in court. Could plaintiffs show real "injury-in-fact?" What injury would they experience? And if a court intervened, could it trace harms from the challenged conduct to the particular plaintiff's interests? Would a court victory really redress the harms?

Many of these sorts of questions used to be drawn from the courts' interpretations of statutory provisions, but since 1993 they have been constitutionalized. And this means that the courts play an unavoidable role in deciding who and what they will hear. In cases involving regulatory decisions where citizens have sought to protect environmental amenities, especially actions involving threats to species or broad health impacts, the Supreme Court has created a challenging new terrain. The Court itself is fundamentally divided on the basics of standing doctrine, meaning that access to the courts is far from certain. For example, a Hudson River fisherman like John Mylod today would likely easily satisfy standing tests if a project like Westway were at stake, but others with a less direct monetary or physical connection to the Hudson could face tougher hurdles. Still, if Court language holds sway, then mere aesthetic and environmental concerns should suffice.

Any plaintiff, however, might be found unsuitable to challenge a national regulatory change in water policy. Citizens face especially high standing hurdles where the impact of the challenged action and judicial relief are uncertain, where the action is of broad scope, and where risks created are probabilistic in nature.[7] The Supreme Court in the 1990s directly and explicitly created standing doctrine that ensures that targets of regulation, such as industry, can get into court to challenge government action, while beneficiaries seeking protection from the laws will face a substantially harder time.[8] For a frequent narrow majority of today's Supreme Court justices, it does not matter that Congress may have enacted a law reflecting congressional desire for citizen monitoring and enforcement. Other decisions rooted in statutory analysis have limited citizen access to the courts under the Clean Water Act.[9] Although Congress has retained fee-shifting provisions in environmental laws, in other areas of regulation the Supreme Court has limited the power of courts to award fees to litigants, reducing incentives for citizens and their lawyers to challenge private or government illegality.[10]

The courthouse doors thus are less open for citizen suits and other litigation challenging government and private illegality, but they are far from closed. Litigation by citizens, not-for-profits, and state attorneys general is regularly initiated and has checked government and private illegality regarding emissions of greenhouse gases, power plant toxics, water pollution, and many other areas of safety, health, environmental, and risk regulation.[11] Periodically, however, citizens are denied access to the courts on standing grounds, regardless of the merits of their challenge.

Risks to the environment, health, and safety often arise because of government failures to act. Late in the Westway war, the Supreme Court decided the *Heckler v. Chaney* case.[12] That decision strengthened EPA's resolve not to battle further against Westway. EPA internally assessed *Heckler* as rendering a choice not to act unreviewable in the courts. Since that time, further case developments have made agency inaction even more difficult to challenge in court. Unless a law sets a deadline for agency action, or in firm language mandates a particular, discrete action, an agency that refuses to act will often be immune from citizen litigation and judicial oversight.[13]

And although critics of the Clean Water Act have been unable to weaken that law in Congress or through changes in implementing protective regulations so important to the defeat of Westway, the Supreme Court has issued decisions shrinking the reach of waters subject to federal protection. Since 2001, the Court has issued two major decisions, in the *SWANCC* and *Rapanos* cases, that weakened what kinds of "navigable waters" under the Clean Water Act are protected "waters of the United States."[14] The Hudson would remain subject to federal jurisdiction, but more attenuated sorts of waters, especially sporadically flooded areas in drought-prone areas and wetlands distant from waters plied by commercial traffic, will often no longer be protected. The implications of these cases continue to be worked out before agencies, courts, and maybe in Congress, but the extent of waters subject to federal protection is now substantially smaller than it was in 1985.

In addition, a growing body of legal and political science data suggests that judges today are often influenced by their political backgrounds. Judges have always been influenced by their experience and worldviews, so it is unclear whether this is a new or worsening problem. Regardless, the view is broadly held today that the judiciary is politicized. Increasingly divisive federal politics may more often today be reflected in judicial appointees who are themselves inclined to rule in accordance with their political backgrounds. Especially in regulatory cases involving the environment, the ideal of judges who will enforce the law regardless of their personal political views may be elusive.[15] It is hard to gauge whether deference to agency scientific judgments is growing, since improved agency science and deliberations would rightly result in more judicial affirmations of agency judgments. It is, however, undoubtedly challenging to persuade judges to dig into the science underlying a high-stakes regulatory judgment, as Al Butzel observed about contemporary environmental litigation.[16] The latitude for agency judgment calls provided by deference doctrines and constrained access to the courts can leave error or inappropriate political interventions undiscovered and unchecked.[17] Judges like Griesa, as well as the rigor and care with which he reviewed Westway's regulatory judgments due to citizens' challenges to Westway decisions, may be more of a rarity today.

The basic moves and artillery in a regulatory war like the Westway battles thus will remain much the same. Nevertheless, the law is itself dynamic. Different laws create different sorts of entitlements, roadblocks, and procedures. Laws range from the symbolic to the rigid and powerful. Citizens remain major players in all venues in regulatory wars, but their roles and power will vary from law to law. And in the face of legislative resistance (or a partisan logjam), advocates for weakened risk-regulation and environmental laws have succeeded in changing the law through the courts. Judicial doctrine today will keep more citizens out of court. The environment is often still despoiled and risks still substantial because the law's protections can be porous or nonexistent. Regulators may at times be indifferent or subservient to the forces that they are supposed to regulate. Nothing guarantees that citizens and aligned lawyers will have the time, money, skills, and commitment to take on powerful adversaries.

But at times a high-stakes regulatory action will present genuine difficult trade-offs and motivations for going to regulatory war. And sometimes protective laws will give those citizens a fighting chance. Marcy Benstock's Clean Air Campaign was a remarkably formidable adversary, as were the opponents' lawyers and many environmental, transit, and government allies, especially agency scientists who provided essential expertise and comments. Motivated by the Westway transit trade-in option, opposition to boondoggles, and environmental concerns, and empowered by environmental law, especially Section 404's strong protections of America's waters, Westway's opponents fought a tenacious, successful fourteen-year battle.

Westway's history provides insights into how such regulatory wars can be fought, but nothing in its tale confirms heroic expectations that citizens can alone always be there to protect the environment and check illegality. The law's content is a critical determinant of citizens' power. Few laws have the unyielding strength of Section 404 of the Clean Water Act. And while citizen opposition was essential to Westway's defeat, so were diligent natural resource regulators who provided the essential scientific insights that shaped those battles. Westway's history does not support claims that environmental laws are misguided in their strength or that grand projects are undeservedly doomed to defeat. Challenged regulatory actions will at times involve important environments and imperiled species, and sometimes the law will empower citizens and their lawyers to make the law's protections real. Advocates championing boondoggles can seek too much and, as Robert Moses predicted in 1974, stir up broad congressional opposition. And sometimes the defeat of grand projects will set in motion other auspicious developments. New York City's Lower West Side of Manhattan flourished after Westway's defeat, although environmental concerns and clashes over water-edge or in-water development continue. The law did prevail in the Westway war, thereby strengthening our nation's legal fabric. Westway's lessons endure.

ACKNOWLEDGMENTS

D URING MY EARLY years of work as a public-interest and then private-sector environmental and land use lawyer and litigator in New York City during the mid-1980s to early 1990s, many colleagues, clients, friends, lawyers, regulators, and acquaintances mentioned the 1971–85 Westway battles, both alluding to the lessons of Westway and also at times drawing on their own experiences linked to Westway. I, however, never did any Westway-related work as a lawyer. As a professor, I again encountered Westway-related decisions in textbooks I used for teaching. Those many comments and references piqued my interest in understanding how a project championed by so many powerful interests could meet with defeat. After initial naive hopes that I could find those answers quickly, I periodically began to travel to New York City from my job as a professor of law at Emory Law School in Atlanta to search for illuminating archival materials and speak with the many partisans who actually participated in Westway planning, politics, and its 1971–85 regulatory war. It soon became clear that a significant contribution of this book would be to shed light on the many ways in which law and legal and political advocacy, often outside the courts, shaped the Westway war and shapes many other similar high-stakes regulatory battles. Missing documents and transcripts threatened to derail the project, but eventually most critically important materials were found.

I owe a debt of gratitude to the many Westway partisans who shared their recollections and, in some cases, their files. Many are mentioned or quoted in the book's text and endnotes, but for putting up with my on-site review of voluminous documents or for tracking down and sending me archival materials, I must provide special thanks to Marcy Benstock, Mitchell Bernard, Al Butzel, the late Paul Curran (and his law firm, Kaye Scholer), Margaret (Bunny) Gabel, Michael Gerrard, Jay Hakes, Jean McCarroll, Walter Mugdan, Frederick A. O. (Fritz) Schwarz, and Craig Whitaker. Institutional assistance, access, and permissions were provided by the clerk's office of the United States Courthouse for the Southern District of New York, Jesse Cowell, United States District Court Judge Thomas P. Griesa, the National Archives and Records Administration, Connie Fishman and the Hudson River Park Trust, the Jimmy Carter Presidential Library and Museum, the Ronald Reagan Presidential Library and Museum, the Edward I. Koch Collection within the La Guardia and Wagner Archives at LaGuardia Community College/ CUNY, the Bella Abzug Papers within the Columbia University Library, the United States Army Corps of Engineers, the New York State Department of Transportation, the Federal Highway Administration, and the United States Environmental Protection Agency.

Emory Law School and summer research grants and occasional leaves were essential to my work on this book. I earlier published two conference-linked law review articles that helped advance my thinking about Westway and this book. Those articles were "The Regulatory Fragmentation Continuum, Westway and the Challenges of Regional Growth," 21 *Journal of Law & Politics* 323 (2005), and "Adjudicatory Triggers of Enhanced Ambient Environment Information," 83 *Indiana Law Journal* 583 (2008). I also benefited from presentations of portions of the book or these two earlier articles at law school colloquia or conferences at Emory Law School, Cornell Law School, Georgetown University Law Center, Indiana University Maurer School of Law, University of Michigan Law School, and University of Virginia School of Law. My friends and political scientists Richard Doner and Randy Strahan provided sound suggestions for my research and framing of this project. In addition, innumerable conversations with Tom McGarity, Rob Glicksman, Rena Steinzor, Wendy Wagner, and others involved with the work of the Center for Progressive Reform about environmental law, risk regulation, and the intersection of law and politics influenced my work on this book.

Emory Law School librarian Terry Gordon repeatedly helped me track down obscure sources and provided invaluable assistance. Corky Gallo of Emory Law School helped with images, and the superb photographer Paul Sutton of PCN Photography supplied wonderful images of the current state of the Hudson, adjacent Hudson River Park, and waters and old piers originally slated for elimination as part of Westway's plan. Current and past administrative assistants Radine Robinson, Brenda Huffman, and Daniel Kim provided critical aid when my technical limitations were too much. Many researchers worked on parts of the above-referenced articles and this book. Particularly substantive and valuable assistance was provided (in alphabetical order) by current or former law student research assistants Sarah Keith Bolden, Julie Pedigo Bowling, Jeremy Corcoran, Michael Eber, Madeline Gwyn, Phillip Kaczor, Thomas Jefferson (Jeff) Kerr, Michelle Lacko, Mandy Schmitt Mahoney, David Mashburn, Chandani Patel, Ashley Pecora, Abigail Rives, Gina von Sternberg, and Vivek Upadhya. Professor colleagues who offered valuable commentary and support during presentations of parts of my Westway research are many, but I especially owe thanks to friend, sometimes coauthor, and Emory Law School dean Robert Schapiro, as well as professors Robert Ahdieh, Hope Babcock, David Barron, Peter Byrne, Lisa Heinzerling, Marc Miller, Tanina Rostain, Peter Strauss, and Jonathan Z. Cannon. I also thank anonymous readers A, B, and C for providing excellent suggestions to me and Cornell University Press for ways to improve this book. I also thank Cornell University Press, its editors, and copyeditor Jamie Fuller for their suggestions and this publication opportunity.

I would particularly like to thank my wife, Lisa Ellen Chang, and daughters, Tian Lee Buzbee and Seana Ellen Buzbee, for their support and tolerance during my work on this book. Lisa in particular made invaluable editing suggestions and put up with many disrupted days and nights, as well as my periodic travel for archival work or interviews. I also thank my father, John Buzbee, and late mother, Ellen Wade Buzbee, for all the wonderful experiences, education, love, and adventures they provided. (I should note that my late mother, as a new lawyer, was among the many, many people who did some work related to Westway.) Betsy Wade Boylan and James Boylan both provided encouragement and excellent suggestions about this project. My late step-grandmother, Helen Wade, gets credit for being the first person to recognize and encourage my interest in environmental science and politics. Finally, I thank a few teachers and professors who at critical points in my education helped me learn to think on my own, frame questions, and (I hope) write effectively. Those great teachers were public school teachers Neil J. Maloney and Michael Sidoroff and Amherst College professors Richard Foglesong (now at Rollins College), visiting professor and novelist Mary Gordon, and William Pritchard.

NOTES

INTRODUCTION

1. Author interview with Edward Koch (April 23, 2002).

2. Author interview with Dennis Suszkowski (May 26, 2005).

3. Letter from David Rockefeller to William Ruckelshaus, Administrator, Environmental Protection Agency, copying Michael Deaver, Deputy Chief of Staff to President Ronald Reagan, White House Office (July 27, 1984).

4. Marcy Benstock, *For a Westway Trade-In,* N.Y. TIMES, Nov. 8, 1980, at A23.

5. Comment of Morton Getman of Coalition Favoring the Construction of Westway, quoted from a television interview transcript in Helen Wanderstock, *Westway, in* CONTROVERSY: POLITICS OF TECHNICAL DECISIONS 83 (Dorothy Nelkin ed., 2nd ed. 1984).

6. Koch interview.

7. Letter from Mario Cuomo, Governor, State of New York, to Marcy Benstock, Executive Director, NYC Clean Air Campaign Inc. (Sept. 30, 1985) (on file with author).

8. Koch interview.

9. Thousands of articles discuss Westway. For publications providing more substantial and analytical perspectives on Westway and its battles, although often with claims that this book questions, see generally *Westway Project: A Study of Abuses in Federal/State Relations: Hearings before a Subcomm. of the H. Comm. on Gov't Operations,* 98th Cong. (Comm. Print 1984) (providing compilation of materials regarding Westway); COMM. ON GOV'T OPERATIONS, THE WESTWAY PROJECT: A STUDY OF FAILURE IN FEDERAL/STATE RELATIONS, H.R. REP. NO. 98-1166 (Comm. Print 1984) (discussing results of twenty-month investigation of Westway and related federal decision making and federal and state interactions); STATE OF N.Y. COMM'N OF INVESTIGATION, THE WESTWAY ENVIRONMENTAL APPROVAL PROCESS: THE DILUTION OF STATE AUTHORITY (June 1984) (discussing results of investigation into improper actions by state agencies during push for Westway); ALAN ALTSHULER & DAVID LUBEROFF, MEGA-PROJECTS: THE CHANGING POLITICS OF URBAN PUBLIC INVESTMENT 89–90, 102–04, 229–34 (2003) (weaving Westway into a discussion of regulatory issues faced by megaprojects); JOHN CRONIN & ROBERT F. KENNEDY, JR., THE RIVERKEEPERS: TWO ACTIVISTS FIGHT TO RECLAIM OUR ENVIRONMENT AS A BASIC HUMAN RIGHT 159–63 (1997) (recounting in brief form the litigation surrounding Westway); ROBERTA BRANDES GRATZ, THE BATTLE FOR GOTHAM: NEW YORK IN THE SHADOW OF ROBERT MOSES AND JANE JACOBS 211–26 (2010) (excerpting a discussion between the author and Jane Jacobs

on the perils of Westway); PHILLIP LOPATE, WATERFRONT: A JOURNEY AROUND MANHATTAN 78–113 (2004) (discussing the Westway saga and expressing disappointment that the highway was never built); DICK RUSSELL, STRIPER WARS: AN AMERICAN FISH STORY 91–99, 106–07, 152–53, 155, 167–70 (2005) (focusing on the role of striped bass in stopping Westway); JOHN WALDMAN, HEARTBEATS IN THE MUCK: A DRAMATIC LOOK AT THE HISTORY, SEA LIFE, AND ENVIRONMENT OF NEW YORK HARBOR 131–43, 148–49 (1999) (recounting the author's work as a young scientist, including work on striped bass surveys in the Hudson for Westway); Albert K. Butzel, *Recapturing New York City's Waterfront Part I: The Demise of Westway and the Birth of the Hudson River Park*, 13 ENVTL. L. N.Y. 217, 217–22 (2002) (reviewing the the Westway project and battles and the creation of the Hudson River Park); William W. Buzbee, *Adjudicatory Triggers of Enhanced Ambient Environment Information*, 83 IND. L.J. 583, 583–607 (2008) (using Westway as a case study to discuss examples of legal adjudicatory triggers that elicit environmental information); William W. Buzbee, *The Regulatory Fragmentation Continuum, Westway and the Challenges of Regional Growth*, 21 J.L. & POL. 324, 324–63 (2005) (discussing types and implications of regulatory fragmentation as exemplified by Westway); Regina Herzlinger, *Costs, Benefits, and the West Side Highway*, 55 THE PUBLIC INTEREST 77 (1979) (analyzing the early Westway process and managerial choices and strategies); Wanderstock, *supra* note 5, at 73 (focusing on the sources of opposition to Westway and the political pressures bearing on the decision-making process); Daniel Ackman, Comment, *Highway to Nowhere: NEPA, Environmental Review and the* Westway *Case*, 21 COLUM. J.L. & SOC. PROBS. 325, 325–84 (1988) (discussing how the interplay between the courts, administrative agencies, and the political arena contributed to the demise of Westway); Albert Amateau, *Why Westway Sleeps with the Fishes*, THE VILLAGER, June 16–22, 2004, *available at* http://www. thevillager.com/villager_59/whywestwaysleepswith.html (discussing history of Westway and Hudson River Park); Adam Nagourney, *A Ghost of Westway Rises along the Hudson: An Old Idea for the Waterfront Pared Down, Still Provokes Passions*, N.Y. TIMES, March 3, 2002, at 33 (discussing the history of Westway and the Hudson River Park); William Tucker, *Westway Story*, AM. SPECTATOR, Jan. 1986, at 27 (discussing role of environmentalists in the defeat of plans to build Westway and redevelop the lower Manhattan waterfront); Lawrence Elliot Levitz, Westway: The Blocking of an Interstate (Aug. 1982) (unpublished M.P.A. thesis, University of Texas at Austin) (on file with the University of Texas Libraries) (providing an overview of the anti-Westway coalition and various methods of opposition as of the time); Paul Ramon Pescatello, Westway: The Road from New Deal to New Politics (1986) (unpublished Ph.D. dissertation, Cornell University) (UMI Dissertation Services) (discussing history of highway policy and politics with primary emphasis on Westway); Haisook Song, Politics and Roads: The Implementation Process and the Obstruction of the Federal-Aid Highway Program (June 1998) (unpublished Ph.D. dissertation, Fordham University) (on file with author) (looking at case studies of failures to complete federal-aid highways, including the Westway project); *West Side (Joe DiMaggio) Highway: Historic Overview*, NYC ROADS, http://www.nycroads.com/roads/west-side/ (discussing the history of Westway and the current West Side [Joe DiMaggio] Highway).

10. For a study of the many challenges Boston faces in addressing its own urban challenges, including comparative discussion of other cities but with more of a state-law focus, see GERALD E. FRUG & DAVID J. BARRON, CITY BOUND: HOW STATES STIFLE URBAN INNOVATION (2008).

11. Suszkowski interview.

1. THE WESTWAY PLAN

1. For a thorough review of the growing federal role in financing interstate highways, see OWEN D. GUTFREUND, 20TH-CENTURY SPRAWL: HIGHWAYS AND THE RESHAPING OF THE AMERICAN LANDSCAPE 55–59 (2004).

2. Albert Butzel, *Recapturing New York City's Waterfront, Part I: The Demise of Westway and the Birth of the Hudson River Park*, 13 ENVTL. L. N.Y. 217, 218 (2002).

3. Edward N. Costikyan, *The Value of Westway*, N.Y. TIMES, Jan. 28, 1978, at 21.

4. VINCENT J. CANNATO, THE UNGOVERNABLE CITY: JOHN LINDSAY AND HIS STRUGGLE TO SAVE NEW YORK 443–91 (2001).

5. JONATHAN SOFFER, ED KOCH AND THE REBUILDING OF NEW YORK CITY 105–20 (2010).

6. LYNN A. SAGALYN, TIME SQUARE ROULETTE: REMAKING THE CITY ICON (2001).

7. ROGER P. ROESS & GENE SANSONE, THE WHEELS THAT DROVE NEW YORK: A HISTORY OF THE NEW YORK CITY TRANSIT SYSTEM 333–51 (2013).

8. *Ford to City: Drop Dead*, N.Y. DAILY NEWS, Oct. 30, 1975, at 1.

9. SOFFER, *supra* note 5, at 129–31.

10. Washington Irving, *A History of New York*, excerpted in WRITING NEW YORK: A LITERARY ANTHOLOGY 2 (Philip Lopate ed., 1998).

11. ERIC W. SANDERSON, MANNAHATTA (2009); THE GREATEST GRID: THE MASTER PLAN OF MANHATTAN 1811–2011 (Hilary Ballon ed., 2012).

12. Author interview with Craig Whitaker and Peter Kiernan (Mar. 15, 2005); author interview with Craig Whitaker (May 23, 2012); PHILLIP LOPATE, WATERFRONT: A JOURNEY AROUND MANHATTAN 84–85 (2004).

13. Whitaker interview.

14. *Id.*

15. LOPATE, *supra* note 12, at 105.

16. Richard Witkin, *Long-Range Plans Could Transform West Side Highway into U.S. Road*, N.Y. TIMES, Jan. 25, 1974, at 65.

17. *Hole Shuts Some Lanes of West Side Highway*, N.Y. TIMES, July 15, 1974, at 48.

18. Tri-State Transportation Commission, *Transportation 1985: A Regional Plan* (1966), excerpted at http://www.nycroads.com/roads/west-side (site visited Mar. 12, 2013).

19. Regina Herzlinger, *Costs, Benefits, and the West Side Highway*, 55 THE PUBLIC INTEREST 80 (1979).

20. *Id.*

21. Bunny Gabel, *Fighting the Highway, in* THE NEW ENVIRONMENTAL HANDBOOK 261 (Garrett De Bell ed., 1980).

22. *See generally* ROBERT A. CARO, THE POWER BROKER: ROBERT MOSES AND THE FALL OF NEW YORK (1974). For more recent analyses, many more favorable about Moses and his legacy, see ROBERT MOSES AND THE MODERN CITY: THE TRANSFORMATION OF NEW YORK (Hilary Ballon & Kenneth T. Jackson eds., 2007).

23. Whitaker interview; West Side Highway Project, Final Environmental Impact Statement (FEIS) (1977); West Side Highway Project, Final Supplemental Environmental Impact Statement (FSEIS), Vol. I, Non-Fisheries Portion (Nov. 1984), at III-1 to III-13.

24. Edward C. Burks, *West Side Rail Line Urged Instead of a New Highway*, N.Y. TIMES, Aug. 27, 1973, at 33.

25. Late 1974 documents refer to the selection of the "modified outboard" plan, although later permit approvals date actual Federal Highway Administration approval of the plan to 1977. Modest road interchange modifications followed and were detailed in the November 1984 FSEIS, at III-1 to III-13.

26. Memorandum of Rebecca Hanmer, Director, Office of Federal Activities to the Administrator [of the Environmental Protection Agency], Subject: Westway Highway Project in New York City; Briefing Memorandum (undated but appears to be from 1978).

27. The Westside Highway North of 42nd Street: A Proposal for Discussion (August 1974).

28. Paul Ramon Pescatello, Westway: The Road from New Deal to New Politics (1986) (unpublished Ph.D. dissertation, Cornell University) (UMI Dissertation Services), at 232–36.

29. Bunny Gabel, draft of Westway battle history, likely for the Friends of the Earth Newsletter, undated but probably from 1976; Gabel correspondence to author, May 27, 2010; Pescatello, *supra* note 28, at 232–36.

30. U.S. Army Corps of Engineers, Record of Decision with attached Section 404(b)(1) Evaluation (Jan. 24, 1985) [hereinafter 1985 ROD]. All environmental impact statements included similar park descriptions.

31. Early documents into the early 1980s claimed 110 acres, but with a number of project adjustments, the final project design by 1984 was claimed to create 97 acres of developable land for real estate development. 1985 ROD, at 3.

32. Westway Memoranda of Understanding (July 31, 1981), at 5.

33. Westside Highway Project, Draft Environmental Impact Statement (DEIS) (April 25, 1974); Whitaker interview.

34. Memorandum from Robert Wagner Jr. to Mayor Ed Koch re Westway (Dec. 13, 1980), at 7.

35. ALAN ALTSHULER & DAVID LUBEROFF, MEGA-PROJECTS: THE CHANGING POLITICS OF URBAN PUBLIC INVESTMENT 230 (2003).

36. Herzlinger, *supra* note 19, at 77.

37. Memorandum from Craig Whitaker to Lowell K. Bridwell (1977).

38. Westway accordian pamphlet from Westway Management Group. Undated, but cover diagram references FEIS and includes reference to all permits having been granted, likely indicating a 1981 publication.

39. Butzel, *supra* note 2.

40. Boston's Big Dig project experienced even more egregious cost overruns, so far costing more than three times its original estimated costs, but with the federal government footing most of the bill. *See* ALTSHULER & LUBEROFF, *supra* note 35, at 116–20 (2003). Federal Highway Administration attorney Edward Kussy believes Westway could easily have cost at least $7 billion. Edward Kussy, Attorney, Federal Highway Administration, comments at Georgetown University Law Center (Nov. 6, 2003).

41. *See* Seth Stern, *$14.6 Billion Later, Boston's Big Dig Wraps Up*, CHRISTIAN SCIENCE MONITOR, Dec. 19, 2003, *available at* http://www.csmonitor.com/2003/1219/p02s01-ussc.html. Subsequent final work and ongoing repairs are estimated to push the Big Dig over $15 billion.

42. Whitaker interview.

43. Herzlinger, *supra* note 19, at 96.

44. *Id.*

45. Koch interview.

46. Mario M. Cuomo, Governor, State of New York, Statement before the U.S. Army Corps of Engineers regarding the Draft Environmental Impact Statement on Westway (July 12, 1984), at 2.

47. New York City Transit, *Subway Ridership Reporting*, Mar. 22, 2012 (reporting through graph mid- to late 1970s "subway ridership" hovering between 3.5 million and 3.7 million riders a day).

48. Frank J. Prial, *City Proposes a New West Side Highway*, N.Y. TIMES, April 4, 1971, at 63.

49. See chapter 4 (discussing 1980 city and Mayor Koch vacillation over trading in Westway and demands for state protection of the city if costs were not paid).

50. Robert Moses, Westway leaflet, original in Bella Abzug Archives, Columbia University. Surrounding documents and contemporaneous news stories indicate it was published in 1974.

51. *Id.*; see also Emanuel Perlmutter, *Moses Has West Side Highway Plan*, N.Y. TIMES, Nov. 25, 1974, at 60 (reporting on the opposition of Moses and quoting leaflet).

52. Moses, Westway leaflet, *supra* note 50.

53. Robert Alden, *New West Side Highway above River Proposed*, N.Y. TIMES, Aug. 29, 1971, at R1.

2. HIGHWAYS, SUBWAYS, AND THE SEEDS OF DISSENT

1. *See* Mary Russell, *Highway Trust Busters Rebuffed*, WASH. POST, April 4, 1973, at A8 (reporting on "trust busters'" efforts and a 1973 defeat).

2. For excellent discussions of the overall political dynamics of the Highway Trust Fund, see TOM LEWIS, DIVIDED HIGHWAYS: BUILDING THE INTERSTATE HIGHWAYS, TRANSFORMING AMERICAN LIFE 211–37 (1997); GEORGE M. SMERK, URBAN MASS TRANSPORTATION: A DOZEN YEARS OF FEDERAL POLICY (1974) [hereinafter SMERK, URBAN MASS TRANSPORTATION]; George M. Smerk, *How Now, Highway Trust Fund?*, BUS. HORIZONS, April 1974, at 32 [hereinafter Smerk, *Trust Fund*]. See also ALAN ALTSHULER & DAVID LUBEROFF, MEGA-PROJECTS: THE CHANGING POLITICS OF URBAN PUBLIC INVESTMENT (2003) 87–88, 176–206 (2003) (reviewing growing federal support for rail transit after the long highway focus, as well as the trade-in provision's history).

3. *See* SMERK, URBAN MASS TRANSPORTATION, *supra* note 2, at 82; Smerk, *Trust Fund*, *supra* note 2, at 34.

4. *See* John B. Anderson, *Providing for Consideration of H.R. 16656, Federal-Aid Highway Act of 1972*, 118 CONG. REC. 34065–67 (daily ed. Oct. 5, 1972) (citing 30–01 ratio as a reason for busting the Highway Trust Fund). John Anderson also referenced a letter from President Nixon supporting mass transit proponents. *See id.*

5. *Id.*

6. For recollections of Abzug's work for cities and against Westway, *see* SUZANNE BRAUN LEVINE & MARY THOM, BELLA ABZUG 161–64 (2007) (an oral history).

7. *See* Congressional Quarterly, Inc., *Lack of Quorum Kills Highway Aid Compromise*, 28 CONG. Q. ALMANAC 879, 891 (1972) [hereinafter CQ, *Lack of Quorum*] (quoting statement by Abzug from a House hearing on March 23, 1972); *see also* Bella Abzug, *Providing for Consideration of H.R. 16656, Federal-Aid Highway Act of 1972*, 118 CONG. REC. 34069 (Oct. 5, 1972) ("I think mass transit is just as important to people as is police protection. It is just as important to working people as is food and clothing.").

8. *See* Charles A. Vanik, *Providing for Consideration of H.R. 16656, Federal-Aid Highway Act of 1972*, 118 CONG. REC. 34106 (Oct. 5, 1972).

9. *See* Edward I. Koch, *Providing for Consideration of H.R. 16656, Federal-Aid Highway Act of 1972*, 118 CONG. REC. 34106–07 (Oct. 5, 1972).

10. LEWIS, *supra* note 2, at 230.

11. *See infra* notes 12–22 and accompanying text.

12. *See* ALAN ALTSHULER, THE URBAN TRANSPORTATION SYSTEM: POLITICS AND POLICY INNOVATION 38 (1979) ("By specifying that the transit aid would be financed from the general fund, [transit advocates] ingeniously managed to reconcile urban demands for flexibility with the insistence of pro-highway groups that the Highway Trust Fund continue to be reserved for highway uses.").

13. *See* HOUSE REPORT NO. 93-118, *reprinted in* 1973 U.S.C.C.A.N 1859, at 1925 (statement of Gerry Studds); Congressional Quarterly Inc., *Highway Act: Compromise on Mass Transit Funds*, 29 CONG. Q. ALMANAC 435 (1973) [hereinafter CQ, *Highway Act Compromise*] at 447. Abzug was heavily involved with the 1973 Act, but she did not personally create the transfer provision. As Professor Altshuler recounts, he, on behalf of Massachusetts governor Sargent, lobbied extensively for creation of an interstate transfer provision. *See* ALTSHULER, *supra* note 12, at 38 & n.4; Alan Altshuler, *Massachusetts Gov. Sargent: Sarge in Charge*, J. ST. GOV'T, July–Aug. 1989, at 153, 156–58.

14. For a succinct history of this highway project, see http://www.kurumi.com/roads/3di/i695.html (visited on July 20, 2012); *see also* ALTSHULER & LUBEROFF, *supra* note 2, at 187–88.

15. This use of general Treasury funds parallels the compromise approach of the Wright-Clausen amendment. The risk of impoundment led Studds (joined by Abzug) to try to revive their stronger interstate transfer proposal.

16. *See* LEWIS, *supra* note 2, at 225 (describing the mass transit coalition); CQ, *Highway Act Compromise, supra* note 13, at 448.

17. *See* CQ, *Highway Act Compromise, supra* note 13, at 447. For details on this procedural debate, see *id.* at 447–48.

18. *See id.* at 448; *see also* Congressional Quarterly, Inc., *Lobbies, 1973, in* 4 CONGRESS AND THE NATION 1973–1976 (1977), *available at* http://library.cqpress.com/congress/catn73–0009170050.

19. *See* CQ, *Highway Act Compromise, supra* note 13, at 452; *Conferees Designate Part of Road Fund for Transit*, N.Y. TIMES, July 21, 1973, at 57.

20. The interstate transfer provision was codified at 23 U.S.C. § 103(e)(4) (1973). Only "route[s] or portion[s] thereof on the Interstate System" were eligible for withdrawal.

21. President Richard Nixon, Statement on Signing a Highway and Mass Transit Bill (Aug. 13, 1973), *available at* http://www.presidency.ucsb.edu/ws/index.php?pid=3933. For more on Nixon's support for breaking the Highway Trust Fund, see LEWIS, *supra* note 2, at 232.

22. *See What the Highway Act Will Do for Mass Transit*, RAILWAY AGE, Oct. 8, 1973, at 34 (quoting a transit industry leader as saying that the 1973 Act "represents an opening wedge" which holds "considerable symbolic importance").

23. Author interview with Craig Whitaker and Peter Kiernan (Mar. 15, 2005). Quoted language from Kiernan that follows is from this interview unless otherwise specified.

24. Edward C. Burks, *West Side Rail Line Urged instead of a New Highway*, N.Y. TIMES, Aug. 27, 1973, at 33.

25. Paul Shinoff, *Watching New York City's War over Westway*, WASH. POST, July 2, 1978, at A1.

26. *Id.*

27. *Id.*

28. Steven R. Weisman, *City Plans a Tunnel for West Side Road South of 42d Street*, N.Y. TIMES, Nov. 27, 1974, at 1, 49.

29. Transcript of Combined Public Hearing on the Proposed Design of the Modified Outboard Alignment, Also Known as Westway, Developed for the Construction of the West Side Highway between the Brooklyn Battery Tunnel and the Lincoln Tunnel in the Borough of Manhattan (May 23, 1977), at 58.

30. The Federal Aid Highway Act of 1978 later changed the federal contribution to 85 percent for trade-in projects, making the federal-state-local funding 85–10–5 percent, respectively. West Side Highway Project, Final SEIS, Vol. 1, Non-Fisheries Portion (Nov. 1984), at IX-4.

31. Pub. L. No. 93–503, 49 U.S.C. § 1604 (1974). *See* Congressional Quarterly, Inc., *$11.9-Billion Mass Transit Bill Signed*, 30 CONG. Q. ALMANAC 688, 688 (1974).

32. *See* Congressional Quarterly, *supra*, at 693 (quoting Bill Frenzel, R-MN, that the bill was a "big-city boondoggle"); *id.* (quoting Del Clawson, R-CA, that "This is not a big-city bill . . . in the plural. . . . It is a one-city bill" in reference to New York) (first ellipses in original).

33. *See, e.g.*, Michael J. Malbin, *Mass Transit Bills Slowed by Jurisdictional Dispute*, NAT'L J. REP., Apr. 20, 1974, at 571, 577 ("More than any other House Public Works Committee member, Rep. Abzug was trying to make a case for a bill . . . to provide federal operating subsidies for transit companies.").

34. *See House OKs Mass Transit Aid Plan*, L.A. TIMES, Aug. 21, 1974, at A1; Michael J. Malbin, *Defeat of Transit Bill Clears Way for Long Range Measure*, NAT'L J. REP., Aug. 10, 1974, at 1205, 1206; Mary Russell, *Mass Transit Funds Halved in House Vote*, WASH. POST, Aug. 21, 1974, at A27.

35. *See* Federal-Aid Highway Amendments of 1974, P.L. 93–643 § 125 (1975).

36. *See* Congressional Quarterly, Inc., *Highway Act Extension Sent to Conference*, 31 CONG. Q. ALMANAC 735, 735 (1975) [hereinafter CQ, *Highway Act Extension*] (noting pressure to open up or even kill the present form of the "historically sacrosanct" Highway Trust Fund).

37. *See id.* at 735.

38. Excellent discussions of the 1976 provisions are contained within the House Conference Report. *See* H.R. REP. NO. 94–716 (1975), *reprinted in* 1976 U.S.C.C.A.N. 798, 799, 806 (describing new transfer provisions); *id.* at 828–31 (minority views of Reps. Harsha and Cleveland) (criticizing Abzug amendments). *See also* CQ, *Highway Act Extension*, *supra* note 36, at 737, 740–41.

39. Trade-in funds were eventually used "for the complete range of eligible projects—from rail transit and freeway construction, to bus fleet and bridge replacement, to transit station and local street rehabilitation." U.S. DEP'T. OF TRANSP., THE INTERSTATE HIGHWAY TRADE-IN PROCESS, VOLUME 1: ASSESSMENT, at I.2 (1982).

40. *See* CQ, *Highway Act Extension*, *supra* note 36, at 742 (ellipses in original). Harsha's floor amendment to roll back Abzug's changes failed.

41. *See* James C. Cleveland, *Westway and the "Dirty Dozen,"* N.Y. TIMES, Mar. 7, 1977, at 25.

42. P.L. 94–280, 1976 U.S.C.C.A.N. 798, 90 Stat. 425 (1976) (codified at various portions of 23 U.S.C.).

43. *See Ford Signs $17.5 Billion Bill Extending Highway Aid*, N.Y. TIMES, May 6, 1976, at 58.

44. Whitaker and Kiernan interview.

3. THE ART OF REGULATORY WAR

1. SUN TZU, THE ART OF WAR 25 (Zhiye Luo ed., 2007).

2. *Id.*

3. Heckler v. Chaney, 470 U.S. 821, 847–48 (1985) (Marshall, J., concurring) ("Entitlements to receive these benefits or to be free of these injuries often run to specific classes of individuals whom Congress has singled out as statutory beneficiaries.").

4. Author interview with Craig Whitaker and Peter Kiernan (Mar. 15, 2005).

5. National Environmental Policy Act of 1969, 42 U.S.C. §§ 4321–4347 (2006).

6. Clean Air Act, 42 U.S.C. §§ 7401–7671q (2006).

7. Clean Water Act, 33 U.S.C. §§ 1251–1376 (2006).

8. Rapanos v. United States, 547 U.S. 715 (2006); Solid Waste Agency of N. Cook County v. U.S. Army Corps of Eng'rs, 531 U.S. 159 (2001); United States v. Riverside Bayview Homes, 474 U.S. 121 (1985).

9. *See* United States v. Nixon, 418 U.S. 683, 696 (1974) ("So long as this regulation remains in force the Executive Branch is bound by it, and indeed the United States as the sovereign composed of the three branches is bound to respect and to enforce it.") (citing United States *ex rel.* Accardi v. Shaughnessy, 347 U.S. 260 (1954)).

10. Administrative Procedure Act, 5 U.S.C. §§ 551–559, 701–706, 3105, 7521 (2006).

11. *See* PETER L. STRAUSS ET AL., GELLHORN AND BYSE'S ADMINISTRATIVE LAW ch. 8, § 4 (10th ed. 2003).

12. *See* Henry P. Monaghan, Marbury *and the Administrative State*, 83 COLUM. L. REV. 1 (1983).

13. For discussion of riders and their effects, see Jack M. Beermann, *Congressional Administration*, 43 SAN DIEGO L. REV. 61, 84–90 (2006); Richard J. Lazarus, *Congressional Descent: The Demise of Deliberative Democracy in Environmental Law*, 94 GEO. L.J. 619, 635–37 (2006).

14. 437 U.S. 153 (1978).

15. *Id.*; Holly Doremus, *The Story of* TVA v. Hill: *A Narrow Escape for a Broad New Law, in* ENVIRONMENTAL LAW STORIES 110 (Richard J. Lazarus & Oliver A. Houck eds., 2005); Elizabeth

Garrett, *The Story of TVA v. Hill: Congress Has the Last Word, in* STATUTORY INTERPRETATION STO-RIES 58 (William N. Eskridge, Philip P. Frickey, and Elizabeth Garrett eds., 2010).

16. Robertson v. Seattle Audubon Soc'y, 503 U.S. 429 (1992); Sandra Beth Zellmer, *Sacrificing Legislative Integrity at the Altar of Appropriations Riders: A Constitutional Crisis*, 21 HARV. ENVTL. L. REV. 457 (1997).

17. *See* ROBERT L. GLICKSMAN ET AL., ENVIRONMENTAL PROTECTION: LAW AND POLICY ch. 2 (6th ed. 2011).

18. For a judicial recounting of this saga, see Cobell v. Kempthorne, 532 F. Supp. 2d 37 (D.D.C. 2008).

19. GLICKSMAN ET AL., *supra* note 17, at ch. 3.

20. *See* William A. Fletcher, *The Structure of Standing*, 98 YALE L.J. 221 (1988); William W. Buzbee, *The Story of* Laidlaw: *Standing and Citizen Enforcement, in* ENVIRONMENTAL LAW STORIES 201 (Richard J. Lazarus & Oliver A. Houck eds., 2005).

21. ZYGMUNT J.B. PLATER ET AL., ENVIRONMENTAL LAW AND POLICY: NATURE, LAW, AND SOCIETY ch. 10 (4th ed. 2010) (discussing "roadblock" statutes).

22. ALEXIS DE TOCQUEVILLE, DEMOCRACY IN AMERICA 270 (J. P. Mayer ed., George Lawrence trans., Anchor Books 1969) (1848).

23. 5 U.S.C. § 706(2)(A); Citizens to Preserve Overton Park v. Volpe, 401 U.S. 402 (1971).

24. *See* Cynthia R. Farina, *Statutory Interpretation and the Balance of Power in the Administrative State*, 89 COLUM. L. REV. 452 (1989).

25. SEC v. Chenery Corp., 322 U.S. 194 (1947); Kevin M. Stack, *The Constitutional Foundations of* Chenery, 116 YALE L.J. 952 (2007).

26. *Chenery*, 322 U.S. 194.

27. *Overton Park*, 401 U.S. at 420.

28. *See* Michael Herz, United States v. United States: *When Can the Federal Government Sue Itself?*, 32 WM. & MARY L. REV. 893 (1991).

29. U.S. CONST. art II, § 3.

30. *See* William W. Buzbee, *Asymmetrical Regulation: Risk, Preemption, and the Floor/Ceiling Distinction*, 82 N.Y.U.L. REV. 1547 (2007).

31. *Id.*

32. McNollgast, *The Political Origins of the Administrative Procedure Act*, 15 J.L. ECON. & ORG. 180 (1999); George B. Shepherd, *Fierce Compromise: The Administrative Procedure Act Emerges from New Deal Politics*, 90 Nw. U.L. REV. 1557 (1996).

33. *See* ANTHONY FLINT, WRESTLING WITH MOSES: HOW JANE JACOBS TOOK ON NEW YORK'S MASTER BUILDER AND TRANSFORMED THE AMERICAN CITY (2009); ROBERTA BRANDES GRATZ, THE BATTLE FOR GOTHAM: NEW YORK IN THE SHADOW OF ROBERT MOSES AND JANE JACOBS (2010). *See also* note 45 and accompanying text.

34. Comments of Edward Kussy, Attorney, Federal Highway Administration, Georgetown University Law Center (Nov. 6, 2003).

35. Buzbee, *The Story of* Laidlaw, *supra* note 20; Cass R. Sunstein, *What's Standing after* Lujan? *Of Citizen Suits, "Injuries," and Article III*, 91 MICH. L. REV. 163 (1992).

36. *See* Thomas O. McGarity, *Some Thoughts on "Deossifying" the Rulemaking Process*, 41 DUKE L.J. 1385 (1992) (discussing "hard look review" and its effects).

37. *See* STRAUSS ET AL., *supra* note 11, ch. 8, § 4 (introducing concept of polycentric regulatory battles).

38. Such provisions, contained in most environmental laws but with somewhat varied language and resulting case law, authorize judicial award of fees and costs to a plaintiff who has been substantially successful. *See* Harvard Law Review Association, *Awards of Attorney's Fees to Unsuccessful Environmental Litigants*, 96 HARV. L. REV. 677 (1983).

39. Author interview with Mitchell Bernard ((May 24, 2005). Clean Air Campaign and Butzel & Kass files reveal fund-raising by Benstock and Butzel, as well as fund-raising for Westway opposition efforts by the Open Space Institute (a not-for-profit headed by John Adams, who at the time was also executive director of the Natural Resources Defense Council; Butzel was counsel to the Open Space Institute), Gabel and her husband, Dan Gabel, as well as fund-raisers on the Hudson River sloop *Clearwater*. Bunny Gabel also recalls fund-raising by Bill Bowser and the West Village Committee; John McNally, Steve Max, and Lynn Bender of Upper West Side Westway opposition groups; Tom Stokes, Mary Ann Rothman, and Mel Stevens. Foundation support to opposition groups or attorneys fighting against Westway was provided by the New York Foundation, the Friends of the Earth

Foundation, the J. M. Kaplan Fund (with the help of Joan Davidson, who then headed the fund), and through the efforts of Patricia Hewitt at Joint Foundation Support. Roberta Gratz assisted with some of the grant-related writing. E-mail from Marcy Benstock (Jan. 3, 2013); e-mail from Margaret (Bunny) Gabel (Jan. 4, 2013); e-mail from Isabel Rivera at the New York Foundation(Jan. 25, 2013); telephone interview with Marcy Benstock (Oct. 17, 2005).

40. E-mail from Margaret (Bunny) Gabel (Jan. 4, 2013). Brower had been executive director of the Sierra Club and during most of the Westway battle years headed the Friends of the Earth.

41. Author interview with Dennis Suszkowski (May 26, 2005).

42. Author interview with Marc Rosenbaum (Mar. 12, 2003).

43. Ada Louise Huxtable, *Will Westway Turn into the Opportunity of the Century*, N.Y. TIMES, Jan. 23, 1977, at 79.

44. *The Road Not Taken* (Thirteen WNET, New York Public Media), *available at* http://www.thirteen.org/nyvoices/highlights/road_not_taken.html (comments of Craig Whitaker).

45. *Id.*; FLINT, *supra* note 33, at ch. 5; GRATZ, *supra* note 33, at 215–17; Owen Gutfreund, *Rebuilding New York in the Auto Age, in* ROBERT MOSES AND THE MODERN CITY: THE TRANSFORMATION OF NEW YORK 92–93 (Hilary Ballon & Kenneth T. Jackson eds., 2007); Paul Ramon Pescatello, Westway: The Road from New Deal to New Politics (1986) (unpublished Ph.D. dissertation, Cornell University) (UMI Dissertation Services), at 123–30.

46. For a history focusing on Jacobs's role, see FLINT, *supra* note 33, at ch. 5.

47. Sam Roberts, *Battle of the Westway: Bitter 10-Year Saga of a Vision on Hold*, N.Y. TIMES, June 4, 1984, at B1.

48. DANIEL A. MAZMANIAN & JEANNE NIENABER, CAN ORGANIZATIONS CHANGE? ENVIRONMENTAL PROTECTION, CITIZEN PARTICIPATION, AND THE CORPS OF ENGINEERS (1979).

49. *Id.*

50. *See* STRAUSS ET AL., *supra* note 11, at 484–93.

51. For discussion of how different legal settings generate different sorts of "records," in a setting criticizing recent Supreme Court federalism jurisprudence, see William W. Buzbee & Robert A. Schapiro, *Legislative Record Review*, 54 STAN. L. REV. 87 (2001).

52. BENJAMIN N. CARDOZO, THE NATURE OF THE JUDICIAL PROCESS 16–24, 103–04, 108, 113–15 (1960).

53. Rosenbaum interview.

54. *See* William W. Buzbee, *Recognizing the Regulatory Commons: A Theory of Regulatory Gaps*, 89 IOWA L. REV. 1 (2003).

55. *See* Hope M. Babcock, *Grotius, Ocean Fish Ranching, and the Public Trust Doctrine: Ride 'Em Charlie Tuna*, 26 STAN. ENVTL. L.J. 3 (2007).

56. *See* ALAN ALTSHULER & DAVID LUBEROFF, MEGA-PROJECTS: THE CHANGING POLITICS OF URBAN PUBLIC INVESTMENT (2003).

57. CHRIS MOONEY, THE REPUBLICAN WAR ON SCIENCE 66–69 (2005).

58. Motor Vehicle Mfrs. Ass'n v. State Farm Mut. Auto. Ins. Co., 463 U.S. 29 (1983).

59. THOMAS O. MCGARITY, THE PREEMPTION WAR: WHEN FEDERAL BUREAUCRACIES TRUMP LOCAL JURIES (2008).

60. For discussion of Exxon's funded studies, see Thomas O. McGarity, *A Movement, A Lawsuit, and the Integrity of Sponsored Law and Economics Research*, 21 STAN. L. & POL'Y REV. 51 (2010); Alan Zarembo, *Funding Studies to Suit Need*, LOS ANGELES TIMES, Dec. 3, 2003, "The Nation," at col. 1 (discussing Exxon's funding of research used to fight punitive damages claims); *see also* Exxon Shipping Co. v. Baker, 554 U.S. 471, 501 n.17 (2008) ("Because this research was funded in part by Exxon, we decline to rely on it.").

61. PHILLIP LOPATE, WATERFRONT: A JOURNEY AROUND MANHATTAN (2004).

62. Author interview with Walter Mugdan (Feb. 10, 2011).

63. Sam Roberts, *For Stalled Westway, a Time of Decision*, N.Y. TIMES, June 5, 1984, at B1.

64. *Id.*

65. Jenniefer Steinhauer, *Another Big Idea Brought Down by Politics*, N.Y. TIMES, June 7, 2005, at A1.

66. *Id.*

67. Author interview with Michael Gerrard (Oct. 2000).

68. *Id.*

69. Ketcham's link to Citizens for Clean Air is discussed in Bunny Gabel, Draft History of Westway Battles (undated edited manuscript, but content indicates from 1970s, likely 1976), at 22A.

70. William Tucker, *Get Out of Town*, Am. Spectator, July 1996 (recounting battles over a Manhattan sports stadium and likening it to Westway).

4. THE ROAD WARRIORS AND THE NEW ENVIRONMENT

1. Mancur Olson, The Logic of Collective Action: Public Goods and the Theory of Groups (2d prtg. 1971).

2. For analogous explorations of how leadership in congressional settings can arise and be effective despite often contrary assumptions derived from political economic models, see David R. Mayhew, America's Congress: Actions in the Public Sphere, James Madison Through Newt Gingrich (2000); Randall Strahan, Leading Representatives: The Agency of Leaders in the Politics of the U.S. House (2007).

3. Author interview with Marcy Benstock (June 15, 2007). Except where citing to other authority, quotes of Benstock are derived from this author interview of Benstock. Other Benstock interview dates and correspondence are separately cited.

4. See *infra* notes 27–46 and accompanying text.

5. Author interview with Edward Koch (April 23, 2002).

6. Jack Newfield, The Education of Jack Newfield 170 (1984).

7. *Id.* at 172.

8. Benstock interview.

9. Newfield, *supra* note 6, at 175.

10. *Id.* at 173.

11. Clearwater Navigator, Nov.–Dec. 1986, at 13.

12. Author interview with Marcy Benstock, Bunny Gabel, and John Mylod (May 27, 2010).

13. Newfield, *supra* note 6, at 179.

14. Telephone interview with Sydney Schanberg (Oct. 3, 2000).

15. Action for Rational Transit, *Statement of Purpose*, Mar. 1975, including listing of all affiliated organizations.

16. Walter H. Waggoner, *Business Lobby Group for City Is Organized by David Rockefeller*, N.Y. Times, June 11, 1980, at B10.

17. Paul Shinoff, *Watching New York City's War over Westway*, Wash. Post, July 2, 1978, at A1; *see also* Peter Freiberg, *New Yorkers Do Battle over a Billion-Dollar Highway*, Planning, Oct. 1978, at 14–17 (discussing groups battling over Westway).

18. Bunny Gabel, Draft History of Westway Battles (undated edited manuscript, but content indicates from 1970s, likely 1976) [hereinafter *Gabel 1976 History*].

19. Those opponents appearing as plaintiffs alongside the NYC Clean Air Campaign were Sierra Club, Committee for Better Transit, West 12th Street Block Association, Citizens Committee of Hudson County, NJ, and a few individuals. The City Club of New York, Business for Mass Transit, Friends of the Earth, and the Hudson River Sloop Clearwater had joined as plaintiffs by 1985, and the Citizens Committee of Hudson County, NJ, had been dropped.

20. Butzel's role and the Storm King Case are recounted in Allan R. Talbot, Power Along the Hudson: The Storm King Case and the Birth of Environmentalism (1972).

21. *See, e.g.,* Michael Gerrard, Butzel & Kass, Point-by-Point Response to Tri-State Report on Westway (Dec. 21, 1978) [hereinafter *Gerrard Point-by-Point Response*]; Michael Gerrard, *How Public Works Projects Affect Employment: A Case Study of Westway and Its Transit Alternatives*, with cover language indicating published by or on behalf of Sierra Club (Atlantic Chapter) & Open Space Institute (Nov. 1977).

22. Author interview with Jean McCarroll (Mar. 14, 2005).

23. Author interview with Marcy Benstock (Mar. 25, 2010).

24. *Gabel 1976 History, supra* note 18.

25. Cary Coglianese, *Social Movements, Law, and Society: The Institutionalization of the Environmental Movement*, 150 U. Penn. L. Rev. 85 (2001–02).

26. Benstock, Gabel, and Mylod interview (May 27, 2010).

27. Memorandum for the President from Stuart Eizenstat and Orin Kramer, Subject: Westway Project in New York City, Aug. 20, 1980, at 1.

28. In a 1976 poll conducted by CBS, respondents were evenly split as for or against Westway. However, when asked specifically about the trade-in option, 67 percent preferred the option

to the Westway project. Shinoff, *supra* note 17, at E2; ROBERTA BRANDES GRATZ, THE BATTLE FOR GOTHAM: NEW YORK IN THE SHADOW OF ROBERT MOSES AND JANE JACOBS 229 (2010); Emily Plishner, Letter to the Editor, *A Question Questioned*, N. Y. TIMES, Nov. 6, 1982, § 1, at 26. *See also Gerrard Point-by-Point Response, supra* note 21, at 6–7 (critiquing small Tri-State survey of twenty-one respondents and claim of popular support and reporting that a "half dozen" polls found 2–1 votes against Westway and for a trade-in).

29. Combo Critique, West Side Highway Project (January 1975) (critique published by combination of adjacent community boards identifying themselves collectively as "Combo").

30. See U.S. Army Corps of Engineers, Record of Decision (Jan. 24, 1985), at 16–18; Final Supplemental Environmental Impact Statement, Westside Highway Project, Vol. III, Parts 1 and 2, Comments and Responses (Nov. 1984).

31. Dena Kleiman, *Board of Estimate Votes against the Westway Plan,* N.Y. TIMES, Dec. 22, 1978, at B1.

32. *Cuomo Vetoes Westway Limits*, N.Y. TIMES, Apr. 19, 1985, at B5; Josh Barbanel, *Legislature Adopts Restriction on Westway Funds,* N.Y. TIMES, April 1, 1982, at B8; Josh Barbanel, *Governor Vetoes Spending Limit on the Westway,* N.Y. TIMES, April 13, 1982, at B3.

33. Steven R. Weisman, *Koch Calls Westway a "Disaster" and Vows It "Will Never Be Built,"* N.Y. TIMES, Nov. 28, 1977, at A1.

34. Sidney H. Schanberg, *Time to Put Westway Away*, N. Y. TIMES, June 6, 1981, at A23 (quoting Carey in 1974).

35. Michael Gerrard, *The Saga of Westway*, 2 AMICUS J. 10, 11 (1980).

36. Koch interview.

37. A fourth president, President Nixon, could also be counted as a supporter in light of his department's actions approving addition of the project to the interstate highway network, but since he also supported the trade-in provision and anti-Westway groups coalesced after his 1974 resignation, he did not have to take sides during the Westway war.

38. Koch interview.

39. PAUL E. PETERSON, CITY LIMITS (1981); see also GERALD E. FRUG & DAVID J. BARRON, CITY BOUND: HOW STATES STIFLE URBAN INNOVATION 23–26 (2008).

40. Koch interview.

41. Memorandum to File 2121—Transportation Plan Evaluation, from George Haikalis, Re: Is Westway the Best Way (July 28, 1978).

42. See *Gerrard Point-by-Point Response, supra* note 21; Report by the Comptroller General of the United States, United States General Accounting Office, *Tri-State Regional Planning Commission's Approval of the Westway Highway Project in New York City,* June 1, 1982, at iii–iv, 10, 17–18 (confirming Commission's pro-Westway stance but noting lack of supportive analyses assessing the main Westway-related conflicts in generating that stance).

43. EDWARD I. KOCH & WILLIAM RAUCH, MAYOR 112–14 (1984).

44. Koch interview.

45. Memorandum from Robert F. Wagner, Jr. to Edward I Koch "Re: Westway" (Dec. 13, 1980), at 22–23.

46. *Id.* at 20.

47. The state legislature twice sought to preclude the state's covering Westway funding shortfalls. *See supra* note 32. It was doubtful that the legislature would have provided the funding supposedly promised by this agreement.

5. SEARCHING FOR WESTWAY'S ACHILLES' HEEL: AIR POLLUTION?

1. Regina Herzlinger, *Costs, Benefits, and the West Side Highway*, 55 THE PUBLIC INTEREST 77, 83 (1979).

2. Talk of the Town: Notes and Comment, NEW YORKER, June 6, 1977, at 27.

3. Combo Critique, West Side Highway Project (January 1975), at 6 (quoting from Robert Caro, *Annals of Politics: The Power Broker; IV—Point of No Return*, NEW YORKER, Aug. 19, 1974, at 56–57).

4. *See* Ralph Blumenthal, *U.S. Cuts $327 Million from Estimated Cost of Westway Project,* N.Y. TIMES, July 12, 1977, at 12; *see also* Leslie Maitland, *Westway's Fate Is Still Uncertain after Eight Years of Controversy*, N.Y. TIMES, Oct. 15, 1979, at A1, B10 (tracing controversies over Westway and difficulty in determining who was winning).

5. *See* Paul Shinoff, *Watching New York City's War over Westway,* Wash. Post, July 2, 1978; for discussion of *TVA v. Hill, see* chapter 3, notes 14 and 15 and accompanying text.

6. Two rulings review these claims' history. *See* Council of Commuter Orgs. v. Metropolitan Trans. Auth., 524 F. Supp. 90 (S.D.N.Y. 1981), and Action for Rational Transit v. Westside Hwy. Proj., 536 F. Supp. 1225, 1232–34 (S.D.N.Y. 1982) (subsequent history of both cases omitted).

7. Author interview with Frederick A. O. (Fritz) Schwarz, Jr. (May 31, 2007).

8. Author interview with Walter Mugdan (Feb. 10, 2011); author interview with Albert K. Butzel (May 2, 2001).

9. Butzel 2001 interview; author interview with Michael Gerrard (Oct. 2000).

10. Paul Ramon Pescatello, *Westway: The Road from New Deal to New Politics* (1986) (unpublished Ph.D. dissertation, Cornell University) (UMI Dissertation Services), at 267–68.

11. Steven R. Weisman, *Westway Project Seems Stalemated,* N.Y. Times, Dec. 6, 1978, at A1.

12. Butzel 2001 interview.

13. Report to the Commission from Albert J. Rosenthal, hearing officer, Sept. 15, 1977, at 2–3.

14. Editorial, *Spreading Smog over Westway,* N.Y. Times, Sept. 30, 1977, at 21.

15. Richard J. Meislin, *Carey Doubts Need for Pollution Study on Westway Plan,* N.Y. Times, Nov. 19, 1977, at 14.

16. Steven R. Weisman, *Delays on Westway Assailed by Adams in Call for Action,* N.Y. Times, Dec. 14, 1978, at A1.

17. *Text of Adams Letters on Westway Project Delays,* N.Y. Times, Dec. 14, 1978, at B9.

18. Letter of state assemblyman Jerrold Nadler and eleven other state assemblymen to the president (Dec. 14, 1978); letter of representatives Ted Weiss, Jonathan Bingham, Hamilton Fish, Andrew Maguire, Charles Rangel, and Fred Richmond to the president (Dec. 8, 1978).

19. Letter of Ruth Messinger and thirteen other city council members to the president (Dec. 18, 1978).

20. John B. Oakes, *Westway Panic Button,* N.Y. Times, Dec. 19, 1978, at A21.

21. Schwarz interview.

22. Richard J. Meislin, *Westway Builders, Citing Data Error, Win a Delay on Key Hearings,* N.Y. Times, July 6, 1978, at D16.

23. Author telephone interview with Judge Thomas P. Griesa (Oct. 21, 2005).

24. Comments of Walter Mugdan and Frederick A. O. (Fritz) Schwarz, Jr. at program, *The Rise and Fall of Westway,* held at the Association of the Bar of the City of New York (Oct. 18, 2005).

25. David A. Andelman, *New Effort Begun to End Deadlock over Westway,* N.Y. Times, July 26, 1980, at 21. These amendments were inserted in section 110(c)(5)(b)(i) of the Clean Air Act in the Moynihan-Holtzman amendment as part of a deal to allow New York City to reduce reliance on East River bridge tolls. For discussion of this amendment, *see* Region 2 of EPA, *Evaluation of the State Implementation Plan Revision Submitted by New York in Fulfillment of the Moynihan-Holtzman Amendment* (Sept. 1979).

26. Memorandum for the President from Stu Eizenstat and Orin Kramer, Subject: Westway Project in New York City (Aug. 20, 1980), at 2.

27. David A. Andelman, *Federal Formula Expected to Help Westway Project,* N.Y. Times (Sept. 10, 1980), at B1.

28. Administratively confidential memorandum for Jack Watson, Stu Eisenstat, and Gene Eidenberg, from Bruce Kirschenbaum and Myles Link, Subject: New York State: Westway and State Clean Air Plan (Aug. 27, 1980), at 3. Watson was the White House chief of staff and Eisenstat the chief domestic policy adviser to the president.

29. October 13, 1980, hand notation by "Stu" on memorandum from Myles Lynk to Stu Eizenstat, Subject: EPA and New York's Clean Air-Transportation Plan (Oct. 10, 1980).

6. WESTWAY'S FILL AND AMERICA'S PROTECTED WATERS

1. Section 10 of the Rivers and Harbors Act also required a permit, but because it provided the Corps with greater discretion in its less rigid protections, as well as a Supreme Court decision construed to deny citizen enforcement of Section 10, it became a nonissue for Westway. Although Section 10 was periodically part of Westway advocacy until its dismissal, this book generally omits this advocacy element.

2. Author interview with Marcy Benstock (May 6, 2001).

3. *Id.*

4. 42 U.S.C. §§ 4331 and 4332.

5. *Id.*

6. 40 C.F.R. § 1502.22(b) (as in effect during this portion of the Westway battles).

7. *See* ROBERT L. GLICKSMAN ET AL., ENVIRONMENTAL PROTECTION: LAW AND POLICY (6th ed. 2011) at 286–97, 317–25 (presenting cases and discussing NEPA's procedural mandates).

8. 33 U.S.C. § 1251(a).

9. 40 C.F.R. § 230.10(a).

10. *Id.* § 230.10(c).

11. *Id.* § 230.12(a)(3)(iv).

12. Memorandum of Dennis Suszkowski for Record, Westway—Changes to the Section 404(b) (1) Guidelines (undated but dated during a later trial to January of 1983).

13. East and Hudson Rivers, New York, Pub. L. No. 90–483, § 113, 82 Stat. 736 (1968) (codified as 33 U.S.C. § 59c-1) (stating through geographic descriptions and mentioning its applicability "only to portions of the above-described area which are bulkheaded and filled," that the waters that became the Battery Park City landfill "are hereby declared to be nonnavigable waters of the United States").

7. THE PUBLIC FISH STORY

1. West Side Highway Project, Draft Environmental Impact Statement (April 25, 1974) (DEIS), at 94, 100–101.

2. Letter of James T. B. Tripp of the Environmental Defense Fund to Colonel Clark Benn, district engineer of the Army Corps (July 13, 1978).

3. Technical Report on Water Quality, Part 2, prepared by Alpine Geophysical Associates, May 1974, at 98 (cited and quoted in Sierra Club v. United States Army Corps of Eng'rs, 536 F. Supp. 1225, 1240 (S.D.N.Y. 1982) (subsequent case history omitted)).

4. *See* Steven R. Weisman, *Delays on Westway Assailed by Adams in Call for Action*, N.Y. TIMES, Dec. 14, 1978, at B8. For a book-length recounting of the Storm King battles, see ALLEN R. TALBOT, POWER ON THE HUDSON (1972).

5. Those investigations are discussed in chapter 9. Internal memoranda and deliberations of federal agencies cited in the paragraphs that follow are, unless otherwise specified, from COMM. ON GOV'T OPERATIONS, THE WESTWAY PROJECT: A STUDY OF FAILURE IN FEDERAL/STATE RELATIONS TOGETHER WITH DISSENTING VIEWS, H.R. REP. No. 98–1166 (Comm. Print 1984) [hereinafter 1984 H. Rep.]. That report, in turn, cites extensively to an appendix with documents and hearing testimony entitled *Westway Project: A Study of Abuses in Federal/State Relations: Hearings before a Subcomm. of the H. Comm. on Gov't Operations*, 98th Cong. (1984) [hereinafter 1984 H. Rep. App.].

6. This history and quotations that follow continue to be drawn primarily from 1984 H. Rep. and 1984 H. Rep. App., *supra* note 5.

7. These internal deliberative activities and quotes continue to be drawn from the subsequent congressional report and appendix. *See supra* note 5.

8. *Id.*

9. Author interview with Charles (Chuck) Warren (May 6, 2001).

10. *Id.*

11. *Three US Agencies Said to Drop Their Objections to Westway Plan*, N.Y. TIMES, Mar. 11, 1981, at B7.

12. *Id.*

13. *See* chapter 4, notes 27–47 and accompanying text.

8. ENTER THE INDEPENDENT FEDERAL JUDICIARY AND THE POWER OF LAW

1. Author interview with Charles (Chuck) Warren (May 6, 2001).

2. Author interview with Albert K. Butzel (May 2, 2001).

3. Author interview with Michael Gerrard.

4. *See* JOHN CRONIN & ROBERT F. KENNEDY, JR., THE RIVERKEEPERS: TWO ACTIVISTS FIGHT TO RECLAIM OUR ENVIRONMENT AS A BASIC HUMAN RIGHT 160 (1997); DICK RUSSELL, STRIPER WARS: AN AMERICAN FISH STORY 93 (2005).

5. 401 U.S. 402 (1971).

6. Author interview of Frederick A. O. (Fritz) Schwarz, Jr. (May 31, 2007).

7. Comments of Nicholas Gimbel, at program, *The Rise and Fall of Westway*, held at the Association of the Bar of the City of New York (Oct. 18, 2005).

8. Author interview with Fletcher Griffis (Mar. 24, 2005).

9. Action for Rational Transit v. West Side Highway Project, 517 F. Supp. 1342 (S.D.N.Y. 1981) (subsequent history omitted).

10. Silva v. Lynn, 482 F.2d 1282, 1285 (1st Cir. 1973). The *Silva* case was later cited and used for this proposition by the court of appeals in a later Westway ruling. *See infra* note 19 and accompanying text.

11. Author interview with Albert Butzel (Mar. 6, 2013).

12. Action for Rational Transit v. West Side Highway Project and Sierra Club v. United States Army Corps of Eng'rs, 536 F. Supp. 1225 (S.D.N.Y. 1982).

13. He also found the grant of the Rivers and Harbor Act Section 10 permit legally invalid.

14. Butzel (2013) and Gerrard interviews.

15. Sierra Club v. United States Army Corps of Eng'rs, 541 F. Supp. 1367 (S.D.N.Y. 1982).

16. This meeting was mentioned earlier, in chapter 7.

17. Vermont Yankee Nuclear Power Corp. V. NRDC, Inc. 435 U.S. 519 (1978).

18. Sierra Club v. Hennessy, 695 F.2d 643 (2d Cir. 1982).

19. Sierra Club v. United States Army Corps of Eng'rs, 701 F.2d 1011 (2d Cir. 1983).

9. REEXAMINING THE 1971–1982 DEBACLES

1. Memorandum of Albert K. Butzel to Tom Puccio (Mar. 9, 1983).

2. The *Sierra Atlantic* journal republished the report in its entirety. Copies do not reflect the date, but it appears to be the spring 1983 issue, at pages 5–8.

3. Sydney H. Schanberg, *The Same Old Scandal*, N.Y. TIMES, May 10, 1983, at A25.

4. Edward C. Burks, *President Holds the Line on Westway as Congressman Makes Plea*, N.Y. TIMES, Feb. 13, 1977, at 45.

5. The content of many of the documents revealing Westway-related meetings and internal agency debates are discussed in chapter 7 at notes 5–8 and accompanying text. Many of them were not revealed until the federal investigation.

6. Many of these analyses were quoted in the previous two chapters.

10. WESTWAY'S SECOND CHANCE

1. The study provision was codified at 16 U.S.C. § 757g, enacted from S. 838, Pub. L. No. 96-118, 93 Stat. 859 (1979). Fishing limitations were in the Atlantic Striped Bass Conservation Act, Pub. L. No. 98-613, 98 Stat. 3187 (1984).

2. Author interview with Marcy Benstock (Feb. 24, 2006).

3. Rider description handout entitled "Westway Project—Amendment for Protection of Striped Bass," reported as distributed by supporters during October and November 1983. For the rider's text, see "Amendment to H.J. Res. 403, Offered by Mr. Addabbo and Mr. Green," attached to letter of Ted Weiss to Claude Pepper (Nov. 3, 1983).

4. Joe Conasan, *Undermining the Law: Cuomo's Cynical Westway Strategy*, VILLAGE VOICE, Nov. 15, 1983, at 7.

5. *Senators May Seek Westway Action*, N.Y. TIMES, Oct. 26, 1983, at B28; Jane Perlez, *White House Won't Aid Move to Spur Westway*, N.Y. TIMES, Nov. 12, 1983, at A27.

6. Topics Editorial, *Good Moves: Bassway*, N.Y. TIMES, Nov. 7, 1983, at A22.

7. Conasan, *supra* note 4, at 7.

8. Benstock 2006 interview; author interview with Marcy Benstock, Bunny Gabel, and John Mylod (May 27, 2010).

9. Conasan, *supra* note 4, at 7.

10. *Id.* at 96.

11. Letter from Friends of the Earth and environmental groups to Appropriations Committee members (Nov. 2, 1983).

12. Perlez, *White House Won't Aid Move, supra* note 5.

13. Jane Perlez, *US Supports Westway but Is Holding Up Funds*, N.Y. TIMES, Nov. 17, 1983, at B3.

14. Telegram from Robert Abrams to members of the Senate and House from New York State (Nov. 18, 1983).

15. John B. Oakes, *Way beyond Westway*, N.Y. TIMES, Nov. 30, 1983, at A31.

16. Author interview with Fletcher Griffis (Mar. 24, 2005).

17. *Id.*

18. Maureen Dowd, *The Westway's Man in the Middle (Fletcher Hughes Griffis, Jr.)*, N.Y. TIMES, June 27, 1984, at B4.

19. *Id.*

20. Butzel disputes the nature of opponents' recommendation, recalling that Dovel was mentioned as someone with sampling experience, not as a high-powered scientist. Author interview with Albert K. Butzel (Mar. 6, 2013).

21. Griffis interview.

22. *Id.*

23. *Id.*

24. *Id.*

25. *Id.*

26. Author interview with Dennis Suszkowski (May 26, 2005).

27. Transcript of briefing at Pentagon (Oct. 4, 1983), as transcribed by Butzel & Kass from a tape produced by the Army Corps of Engineers, at 30–31.

28. *Id.* at 25.

29. Westway files of Craig Fuller, Assistant to the President for Cabinet Affairs, Office of Cabinet Affairs (on file at Ronald Reagan Library).

30. Griffis interview.

31. Suszkowski interview.

32. *Id.*; Trial Transcript at 1913, Sierra Club v. United States Army Corps of Eng'rs, 614 F. Supp. 1475 (S.D.N.Y. 1985) [hereinafter 1985 Trial Transcript].

33. 1985 Trial Transcript at 924–26, 3396–98.

34. Butzel 2013 interview; author interview with Mitchell Bernard (May 24, 2005); comments of Mitchell Bernard at program, *The Rise and Fall of Westway*, held at the Association of the Bar of the City of New York (Oct. 18, 2005).

35. Suszkowski interview.

36. *Sierra Club*, 614 F. Supp. at 1495 (quoting the press release).

37. West Side Highway Project, Draft Supplemental Environmental Impact Statement (DSEIS), Vol. II, Fisheries Portion (May 1984) at 42.

38. *Id.* at 18.

39. *Id.* at 22.

40. *Id.* at 23.

41. *Id.* at 43.

42. *Id.* at 28, 30.

43. *Id.* at 30.

44. *Id.* at 31.

45. *Id.* at 31.

46. *Id.* at 32.

47. *Id.* at 33.

48. *Id.* at 43.

49. All such letters are included in the FSEIS Comments and Responses (Nov. 1984).

50. Sam Roberts, *Hearings Open on Whether Westway Is "Imperative" or Is a "White Elephant,"* N.Y. TIMES, June 27, 1984, at B1.

51. Letter from David Rockefeller to William Ruckelshaus, Adm'r, Environmental Protection Agency, copying Michael Deaver, Deputy Chief of Staff to President Ronald Reagan, White House Office (July 27, 1984) (on file with author).

52. Sierra Club v. United States Army Corps of Eng'rs, 614 F. Supp. 1475, 1501–02 (S.D.N.Y. 1985); testimony of Douglas Heimbuch of Martin Marietta, 1985 Trial Transcript at 1961, 1967–94.

53. Suszkowski interview.

54. West Side Highway Project, Final Supplemental Environmental Impact Statement (FSEIS), Vol. II, Fisheries Portion (Nov. 1984), at 40.

55. *Id.* at 59.

56. DSEIS, Vol. II at 43 and 32.

57. FSEIS, Vol. II at 51 (emphasis added).

58. *Id.* at 66.

59. *Id.* at 60.

60. DSEIS, Vol. II at 31–32.

61. FSEIS, Vol. II at 50.

62. DSEIS, Vol. II at 31.

63. FSEIS, Vol. II at 50.

64. *Id.* at 45–46.

65. *Id.* at 43.

66. Late in the 1985 trial, a limited concession of changes was made. See chapter 11.

67. Reagan library files of top staff contain numerous analyses prepared by Rockefeller's pro-Westway groups, as well as notations indicating the supportive views of Labor Secretary Donovan.

68. 40 C.F.R. § 230.3(q–l).

69. 40 C.F.R. § 230.10(c).

70. Internal legal memoranda from the U.S. attorney team that would soon be defending the Westway decisions in court saw this overlap and developed arguments for why the mere recourse to worst-case analysis under NEPA did not automatically mandate permit denial under Section 404. Memorandum from Marc Rosenbaum to Howard Wilson re "Interplay between CEQ Regulation concerning Worst Case Analysis and the EPA's 404(b)(1)(c) Guidelines" (Mar. 6, 1985).

71. Author interview with Christopher Daggett (May 26, 2005). Except as separately indicated below, the succeeding paragraphs with quotes of Daggett and recounting of conversations involving Daggett are from this interview.

72. FSEIS, Vol. III, Comments and Responses, Part 1, II-30 (Nov. 1984).

73. Griffis interview.

74. *Id.*

75. Len Houston, review of Westway FSEIS comment letters (Jan. 22, 1985).

76. U.S. Army Corps of Engineers, Record of Decision (Jan. 24, 1985), at 53.

77. *Id.* at 20.

78. Public Papers of Governor Mario Cuomo, Governor Comments on Decision (Jan. 24, 1985), at 1156.

79. Daniel Lazare, *Army Official Backs Permit for Westway*, Record (N.J.), Jan. 25, 1985; Sam Roberts, *Westway Landfill Wins the Support of Army Engineer*, N.Y. Times, Jan. 25, 1985, at A1.

80. Lazare, *supra* note 79.

81. Roberts, *supra* note 79.

82. Letter from Adrian DeWind on NRDC letterhead to Lee Thomas and Christopher Daggett (Feb. 8, 1985).

83. Memorandum to files from Kirk Stark, Program Operations Branch (Mar. 8, 1985) (recounting Feb. 14, 1985 meeting and including attendance sheet).

84. Arthur K. Lenehan, *Rockefeller Pressured EPA to Back Westway: Financier and D'Amato Attacked Regional Chief as 'Pro-Jersey,'* Star-Ledger, June 25, 1985 (reporting on trial testimony and documents confirming the visit).

85. Memorandum to files of Michael Ludwig, Fish and Wildlife Service (Jan. 9, 1985) (recounting meeting of scientists and staff from most involved federal agencies; only Army Corps is reported as invited but not in attendance due to fear of "legal reprisals and gas").

86. Memorandum analyzing Section 404(c) issues from Catherine A. Winer to Doug Blazey, Regional Counsel (Mar. 22, 1985).

87. EPA briefing paper to Region II, Application of Section 404(c) "Veto" to Westway (Nov. 29, 1984).

88. *Id.*

89. 470 U.S. 821 (1985).

90. EPA Nov. 29 briefing paper, *supra* note 87, attached question and answer about EPA decision not to initiate veto proceedings.

91. Daniel Lazare, *Road Is Cleared for Westway: Major Obstacle to Project Falls*, Record (N.J.), Feb. 26, 1985, at A3.

92. Editorial, *Westway's Endless Last Mile*, N.Y. Times, Jan. 26, 1985, at A20.

11. THE TRIAL CRUCIBLE

1. All trial-linked quotations that follow in this and the next chapter are drawn from the actual 1985 trial transcript. Trial Transcript, Sierra Club v. United States Army Corps of Eng'rs, 614 F. Supp. 1475 (S.D.N.Y. 1985). Other sources are, as necessary, separately cited.

2. Patrick Radden Keefe, *Reversal of Fortune,* NEW YORKER, Jan. 9, 2012, at 42.

3. Author interview with Mitchell Bernard (May 24, 2005).

4. *Id.*

5. Sydney H. Schanberg, *Getting 'the Message,'* N.Y. TIMES, July 2, 1985, at A19.

6. *Id.*

12. THE CROSS-EXAMINATION

1. Comments of Howard Wilson, at program, *The Rise and Fall of Westway*, held at the Association of the Bar of the City of New York (Oct. 18, 2005).

2. Author interview with Randy Mastro (May 24, 2005).

3. Author interview with Paul Curran (May 25, 2005).

4. Sydney H. Schanberg, *Getting 'the Message,'* N.Y. TIMES, July 2, 1985, at A19.

5. Sydney H. Schanberg, *The Testimony Doesn't Wash*, N.Y. TIMES, July 6, 1985, at A21.

13. JUDGMENT DAYS

1. Federal Defendants' Post-trial Memorandum (July 19, 1985).

2. New York State Department of Transportation's Post-trial Memorandum (July 17, 1985).

3. Plaintiffs' Post-trial Memorandum (July 19, 1985).

4. For review of these many passages, see chapter 10, notes 37–48 and 54–65 and accompanying text.

5. Plaintiff's Post-trial Memorandum, at 66–67.

6. *Id.* at 71.

7. *Id.* at 79.

8. See *id.* at 30 (citing and discussing 40 C.F.R. § 230.1(c)).

9. *Id.* at 34.

10. *Id.* at 89.

11. *Id.* at 97–98.

12. Trial Transcript at 4931–55, Sierra Club v. United States Army Corps of Eng'rs, 614 F. Supp. (S.D.N.Y. 1985).

13. *Id.* at 4926–27.

14. *Id.* at 4958–59.

15. *Id.* at 4972.

16. *Id.* at 4972.

17. *Id.* at 4961–63.

18. *Id.* at 14–18.

19. Federal Defendants' Post-trial Reply Memorandum (July 25, 1985), at 3.

20. *Id.* at 27.

21. *Id.* at 30.

22. *Id.* at 8.

23. Sydney H. Schanberg, *Cajun Flies and Westway*, N.Y. TIMES, July 27, 1985, at 23.

24. Author interview with Sydney Schanberg (Oct. 3, 2000); ERIC ALTERMAN, SOUND AND FURY: THE MAKING OF THE PUNDITOCRACY 142 (2000); JOSEPH C. GOULDEN, FIT TO PRINT 243–48 (1988); http://atlanticyardsreport.blogspot.com/2012/03/Sydney-schanberg-back-story-citys.html.

25. *Sunday Morning* (transcript of CBS television broadcast Sept. 1, 1985).

26. Sierra Club v. United States Army Corps of Eng'rs, 614 F. Supp. 1475 (S.D.N.Y. 1985).

27. *Id.* at 1484 (citing 33 C.F.R. § 320.4(c) and changed language set forth in 49 Fed. Reg. 39478 (Oct. 5, 1984), including the observation that "Comments on the amendment indicate that no substantive change was intended").

28. *Id.* at 1483–84 (citing and quoting 40 C.F.R. §§ 230.1, 230.10(c)).

29. 33 U.S.C. § 1343(c)(2), cross-referenced in 404(b), 33 U.S.C. § 1344(b); 40 C.F.R. 230.12(a)(3) (stating that a proposed discharge must be specified as "failing to comply with the guidelines" where "(iv) There does not exist sufficient information to make a reasonable judgment" regarding compliance).

30. *Sierra Club*, 614 F. Supp. at 1509.

31. *Id.* at 1480, 1510.

32. *Id.* at 1511.

33. *Id.* at 1512.

34. *Id.*

35. *Id.* at 1501.

36. *Id.* at 1507, 1511–12.

37. Citizens to Preserve Overton Park v. Volpe, 401 U.S. 402, 420 (1971).

38. *Sierra Club*, 614 F. Supp. at 1516 (also citing Environmental Defense Fund v. Costle, 657 F.2d 275 (D.C. Cir. 1981)).

39. *Id.* at 1507.

40. The full language, drawn from Monty Python's apparently deceased old man in *Monty Python and the Holy Grail* (1975) is "I'm not dead yet."

41. Frank R. Lautenberg, *A Westway Plea*, N.Y. TIMES, Aug. 20, 1985, at A27.

42. Brief of Defendants-Appellants United States Army Corps of Engineers and Federal Highway Administration (Aug. 17, 1985), Sierra Club v. United States Army Corps of Eng'rs, 772 F.2d 1043 (1985).

43. Brief of Defendant-Appellant New York State Department of Transportation at 5 (Aug. 16, 1985), Sierra Club v. United States Army Corps of Eng'rs, 772 F.2d 1043 (1985).

44. *Id.* at 13.

45. *Id.* at 23.

46. *Id.* at 56.

47. *Id.* at 38 (citing *Overton Park,* 401 U.S. at 415).

48. *Id.* at 44.

49. *Id.* (quoting Camp v. Pitts, 411 U.S. 138, 142–43 (1973)).

50. Arthur K. Lenehan, *Judges Appear Split on Westway as They Question Supporters and Foes*, NEWARK STAR-LEDGER, Aug. 30, 1985, at 19.

51. Arthur K. Lenehan, *Senate Threat Looms on Westway Trade-In*, NEWARK STAR-LEDGER, Sept. 1, 1985, at 1, 25.

52. *Id.*

53. *Id.*

54. Sierra Club v. United States Army Corps of Eng'rs, 772 F.2d 1043 (1985).

55. *Id.* at 1048.

56. *Id.* at 1051.

57. *Id.* at 1052.

58. *Id.* at 1053.

59. *Id.* at 1053.

60. *Id.*

61. *Id.* at 1055.

62. *Id.* at 1060 (Mansfield, J., concurring and dissenting in part).

63. 131 CONG. REC. 7351–55 (daily ed. Sept. 11, 1985) (reporting introduction of Rep. Coughlin amendment to H.R. 3244).

64. *Id.* at 7358.

65. Author interview with Marcy Benstock (June 15, 2007).

66. Michael Oreskes, *House Votes by Big Margin to Bar Funds for Westway*, N.Y. TIMES, Sept. 12, 1985, at B8.

67. Sam Roberts, *Cuomo Is Urged to Give Up on Westway Alternative*, N.Y. TIMES, Sept. 15, 1985, at 48 (reporting union opposition to a trade-in but Cuomo's initiation of contingency trading planning).

68. 131 CONG. REC. H7520-03 (daily ed. Sept. 17, 1985) (reporting introduction of H.R. 3316); 131 CONG. REC. E4069-01 (daily ed. Sept. 17, 1985).

69. Michael Oreskes, *Moynihan Sees No Way to Win a Westway Vote*, N.Y. TIMES, Sept. 19, 1985, at B9.

70. *Id.*

71. AP, *N.Y. Arrives at a Plan for Westway Trade-in*, Newark Star-Ledger, Sept. 27, 1985, at 1.

72. Sam Roberts, *Koch and Cuomo Slice Westway Pie in Plan for Federal Funds Trade-In*, N.Y. Times, Sept. 27, 1985, at B1.

73. AP, *supra* note 71, at 1.

74. Roberts, *supra* note 72, at B1.

75. *Id.*

76. John B. Oakes, *Post-Westway Political Games*, N.Y. Times, Oct. 18, 1985.

77. Michael Oreskes, *Westway Funds Trade-In Wins Federal Approval*, N.Y. Times, Oct. 1, 1985, at B3.

78. Letter from Mario Cuomo, Governor, State of New York, to Marcy Benstock, Executive Director, NYC Clean Air Campaign Inc. (Sept. 30, 1985).

79. Joyce Purnick, *Dedicated Foe Resumes a Life without Westway*, N.Y. Times, Sept. 29, 1985, at 56.

14. ASSESSING WESTWAY'S OUTCOME

1. Cartoon by Dana Fradon, New Yorker, Oct. 14, 1985, at 136.

2. Russell Baker, *Big One Gets Away*, N.Y. Times, Oct. 9, 1985, at A23.

3. Joe Conason, *Westway Sleeps with the Fishes*, Village Voice, Oct. 1, 1985, at 13.

4. Paul Goldberger, *Westway Options: Sense of Restraint*, N.Y. Times, Aug. 26, 1986, at B2.

5. *Interview with Pat Moynihan*, American Enterprise Online, http://www.taemag.com/issues/articleid.17286/article_detail.asp (site visited Sept. 2, 2005).

6. Cited in Alan Altshuler and David Luberoff, Mega-Projects: The Changing Politics of Urban Public Investment vii (2003) (citing to Alan Finder, *Westway: A Road That Was Paved with Mixed Intentions, Losing Confidence and Opportunities*, N.Y. Times, Sept. 22, 1985, sec. 4 at 6).

7. Bunny Gabel, Remarks at the New York Branch of Friends of Earth, Public Hearing on Westway, Felt Forum, New York, N.Y. (June 26–27, 1984).

8. Conason, *supra* note 3.

9. Jane Jacobs, quoted in Roberta Brandes Gratz, *How Westway Will Destroy New York: An Interview with Jane Jacobs*, New York, Feb. 6, 1978, at 30–34.

10. *See* Memorandum from Robert Wagner Jr. to Mayor Ed Koch re Westway (Dec. 13, 1980); Roberta Brandes Gratz, The Battle for Gotham: New York in the Shadow of Robert Moses and Jane Jacobs 227–43 (2010).

11. Mark Singer, *Miracle with Vampire*, New Yorker, Dec. 16, 1985, at 32–35.

12. Stephen L. Kass and Jean M. McCarroll, *Westway Redux?*, N.Y. Law Journal, June 23, 2000, at 3 (comparing Westway and Hudson River Park and grounds for opposition to each).

13. *See* Michael A. Rivlin, *A Splendid Park, but at What Price?*, 2 Estuarine (Winter/Spring 1999) (reporting on Hudson River Park battles, including Benstock's opposition).

14. Lisa A. Foderaro, *A Community Battles for the Soul of a Park*, N.Y. Times, March 1, 2013, at 30; Joseph De Avila, *Struggling Trust Seeks Funds for Hudson Shore*, Wall St. J., April 19, 2012, at A15.

15. Charles V. Bagli and Lisa W. Foderaro, *Times and Tides Weigh on Hudson River Park*, N.Y. Times, Jan. 28, 2012, at A16.

16. Susan Milligan, *Congress Agrees on Road Funds*, Newsday, Nov. 14, 1985, at 20; Michael Oreskes, *D'Amato Offers Plan to Speed Westway Trade-In*, N.Y. Times, Oct. 3, 1985, at A1.

17. Case Studies of Urban Freeways for the I-81 Challenge, Syracuse Metropolitan Transportation Council (Feb. 2010); Gratz, *supra* note 10, at 231–33; Tom Robbins, *Westway, the Highway That Tried to Eat New York, Defeated 25 Years Ago This Week*, Village Voice Blogs, Oct. 10, 2010 (quoting mass transit advocate Gene Russianoff that 1.4 billion of Westway dollars ultimately went to mass transit).

18. Gratz, *supra* note 10.

19. Andrew Rosenberg et al., *Rebuilding US Fisheries: Progress and Problems*, 4 Frontiers in Ecology 303 (2006).

20. Editorial, *Parks, Piers, Pollution and Westway*, N.Y. Times, Aug. 9, 1985, at A26.

21. Philip Lopate, Waterfront: A Journey around Manhattan 105 (2004).

22. Author interview with Randy Mastro (May 24, 2005).

23. Additional analysis focused on supporters and opponents at the city and state level is provided in chapter 4, notes 27–47 and accompanying text.

24. Author telephone interview with Marcy Benstock (May 18, 2004).

25. *See* chapter 4, notes 27–47 and accompanying text.

26. Memorandum for the president from Stuart Eizenstat and Orin Kramer, Subject: Westway Project in New York City, Aug. 20, 1980, at 1.

27. *Cuomo Vetoes Westway Limits*, N.Y. TIMES, Apr. 19, 1985, at B5; Josh Barbanel, *Legislature Adopts Restriction on Westway Funds*, N.Y. TIMES, April 1, 1982, at B8; Josh Barbanel, *Governor Vetoes Spending Limit on the Westway*, N.Y. TIMES, April 13, 1982, at B3.

28. *See* chapter 9 (recounting political investigation findings); Comments of Howard Wilson, at program, *The Rise and Fall of Westway*, held at the Association of the Bar of the City of New York (Oct. 18, 2005).

29. *See, e.g.*, Motor Vehicle Mfrs. Ass'n of United States v. State Farm Mut. Auto. Ins. Co., 463 U.S. 29, 43 (1983) (rejecting agency reversal of policy lacking any explanation); Friends of the River v. F.E.R.C., 720 F.2d 93, 106 (D.C. Cir. 1983) ("[T]he EIS makes it possible for the public and reviewing courts to consider conveniently how and why the agency made its final choices. . . . [T]he EIS requirement inhibits post hoc rationalizations of inadequate environmental decision-making."); Natural Res. Def. Council, Inc. v. Callaway, 524 F.2d 79, 94 (2d Cir. 1975) (faulting a final EIS for failing in its "vital task of exposing the reasoning and data of the agency"); Greater Bos. Television Corp. v. F.C.C., 444 F.2d 841, 852 (D.C. Cir. 1970) ("An agency's view of what is in the public interest may change, either with or without a change in circumstances. But an agency changing its course must supply a reasoned analysis. . . .") *cert. denied*, 403 U.S. 923 (1971).

30. Author interview with Dennis Suszkowski (May 26, 2005).

31. Author telephone interview with William Dovel (Jan. 28, 2010).

32. E-mail from William Dovel to author (Feb. 15, 2010) (on file with author).

33. E-mails from F. Michael Ludwig to author (July 14, 2012) (on file with author); e-mails from John Waldman to author (July 26, 2010) (on file with author).

34. SEC v. Chenery, 318 U.S. 80, 88–90 (1943).

35. ALTSHULER & LUBEROFF, *supra* note 6 at 74–75 (citing David Vogel, *Representing Diffuse Interests in Environmental Policymaking, in* DO INSTITUTIONS MATTER? GOVERNMENT CAPABILITIES IN THE UNITED STATES AND ABROAD 267 (R. Kent Weaver & Bert A. Rockman eds., 1993)).

36. *Id.* at 72–75, 86, 227–32, 254–56.

37. *See* RICHARD J. LAZARUS, THE MAKING OF ENVIRONMENTAL LAW, ch. 7 & 8 (2004).

38. Gratz, *supra* note 9, at 35.

39. Dave Owen, *Urbanization, Water Quality, and the Regulated Landscape*, 82 U. COLO. L. REV. 431, 488–89, 495–98 (2011).

40. *See* William W. Buzbee, *The Regulatory Fragmentation Continuum, Westway and the Challenges of Regional Growth*, 21 J.L. & POL. 324, 358–63 (Spring–Summer 2005) (analyzing the idea of project-specific "trumps" of regulatory protections).

41. James Salzman & J. B. Ruhl, *Currencies and the Commodification of Environmental Law*, 53 STAN. L. REV. 607, 612 (2000).

42. Author interview with Mitchell Bernard (May 24, 2005).

43. *Id.*

44. Letter from Mitchell Bernard to Phillip Lopate (Mar. 16, 2004).

45. Author interview with Marcy Benstock, Bunny Gabel, and John Mylod (May 27, 2010).

46. *Id.*

47. Governor Mario M. Cuomo, Remarks to the Environmental Planning Lobby Conference (Silver Bay, Lake George), Public Papers of Governor Mario M. Cuomo 1985 (Albany 1989), at 729.

48. For discussion of frames and different perceptions of risk, see Dan M. Kahan, *Cultural Cognition as a Conception of the Cultural Theory of Risk, in* HANDBOOK OF RISK THEORY: EPISTEMOLOGY, DECISION THEORY, ETHICS AND SOCIAL IMPLICATIONS OF RISK 725–60 (R. Hillerbrand, P. Sandin, S. Roeser, & M. Peterson eds., 2012). *See also* William Boyd, *Genealogies of Risk: Searching for Safety, 1930s–1970s*, 39 ECOLOGY L.Q. (2012) (discussing changing and clashing "risk thinking," and risk versus precaution divides).

49. Author interview of Craig Whitaker (May 23, 2012).

50. Alec Wilkinson, *The Lobsterman: How Ted Ames Turned Oral History into Science*, NEW YORKER, July 31, 2006 (reporting on fisherman and MacArthur "genius" award winner Ted Ames and new efforts to save struggling fisheries by protecting intensively used habitats). Federal fisheries

law now reflects a newfound mandate to protect habitat. The Sustainable Fisheries Act, Pub. L. No. 104–297, 110 Stat. 3559 (enacted Oct. 11, 1996).

51. William W. Buzbee, *Adjudicatory Triggers of Enhanced Ambient Environment Information*, 83 IND. L.J. 583, 583–94 (Spring 2008) (using Westway as a case study to assess the efficacy of adjudicatory trigger strategies to elicit environmental information).

52. For a recent exploration of the divergence between precautionary approaches and quantified approaches such as cost-benefit analysis, risk-risk analysis, and shifts to market-enhancing modes of regulation, *see* DOUGLAS A. KYSAR, REGULATING FROM NOWHERE: ENVIRONMENTAL LAW AND THE SEARCH FOR OBJECTIVITY 2–16, 180–81 (2010).

53. Wendy Wagner, *The Science Charade in Toxic Risk Regulation*, 95 COLUM. L. REV. 1613 (1995).

54. For a recent analysis of regulatory science and the judicial role, *see* Emily Hammond Meazell, *Super Deference, the Science Obsession, and Judicial Review as a Translation of Agency Science*, 109 MICH. L. REV. 733 (2011).

55. *Id.*; *see also* William Boyd, *Ways of Seeing in Environmental Law: How Deforestation Became an Object of Climate Governance*, 37 ECOLOGY L.Q. 843, 910–13 (2010) (analyzing implications of the push for "objectification" and "equivalence" in environmental policy and how they may create "false precision" and diminish the primacy of protective choices made by political and social institutions).

56. Thomas O. McGarity, *Professor Sunstein's Fuzzy Math*, 90 GEO. L.J. 2341 (2002) (critiquing arsenic regulation cost-benefit analysis, with emphasis on the indeterminacy of such analyses due to the many required judgment calls).

57. For exploration of the limitations of cost-benefit analysis, the clash with democratically determined priorities, and ways to protect the environment and regulate risk without false precision of quantification efforts, see FRANK ACKERMAN & LISA HEINZERLING, PRICELESS: ON KNOWING THE PRICE OF EVERYTHING AND THE VALUE OF NOTHING (2004).

58. *See* Elizabeth Kolbert, *The Scales Fall*, NEW YORKER, Aug. 2, 2010, at 70–73 (discussing fisheries struggles and books on the subject); Sam Sifton, *Catch of the Day*, N.Y. TIMES BOOK REVIEW, Aug. 1, 2010 (discussing fisheries struggles and reviewing PAUL GREENBERG, FOUR FISH: THE FUTURE OF THE LAST WILD FOOD (2010)).

59. *See* Atlantic State Marine Fisheries Commission, 2011 and 2010 Striped Bass Fishery Management Plan Reviews (reporting striped bass are not overfished, although down from a 2004 peak, and overall showing Atlantic stock at levels fifteen to twenty times 1985 levels). The Hudson stock is even healthier. Hudson River Fisheries Unit of the N.Y. Department of Environmental Conservation, 2011 Stock Survey. *But see* Christopher Joyce, *Morning Edition: Atlantic Weather May Be Key Culprit in Fish Decline* (National Public Radio broadcast Jan. 25, 2011) (reporting recent population drops and new science linking weather patterns and striped bass population).

60. Edward Kussy, Comments at Georgetown University Law Center (Nov. 6, 2003).

61. *See* National Commission on the BP Deepwater Horizon Oil Spill and Offshore Drilling, *Report to the President: Deep Water: The Gulf Oil Disaster and the Future of Offshore Drilling* (Jan. 2011).

62. Ian Urbina, *Regulation Lax as Gas Wells' Tainted Water Hits Rivers*, N.Y. TIMES, Feb. 27, 2011, at A1.

63. Many of these battles involved Clean Air Act New Source Review regulatory revisions. *See, e.g.*, New York v. EPA, 443 F.3d 880 (D.C. Cir. 2006); New York v. EPA, 413 F.3d 3 (D.C. Cir. 2003).

64. Mastro interview.

65. *See* THOMAS O. MCGARITY & WENDY E. WAGNER, BENDING SCIENCE (2008); RESCUING SCIENCE FROM POLITICS (Wendy Wagner & Rena Steinzor eds., 2006).

66. *See* Meazell, *supra* note 54 (discussing "super deference" to agency science assessments and changing judicial approaches). For the argument that presidential involvement should heighten deference, see Elena Kagan, *Presidential Administration*, 114 HARV. L. REV. 2245 (2001). For analysis of risks of enhanced deference due to involvement of politically accountable leadership, see Thomas O. Sargentich, *The Emphasis on the Presidency in U.S. Public Law: An Essay Critiquing Presidential Administration*, 59 ADMIN. L. REV. 1 (2007) (challenging Kagan's thesis and suggesting it would lead to a reduction in pluralistic debate that is a valuable contribution to government decision making); Peter L. Strauss, *Legislation That Isn't—Attending to Rulemaking's "Democracy Deficit,"* 98 CAL. L. REV. 1351 (2010) (discussing the tension between the "democracy deficit" in rulemaking and potential problems of political and presidential influence).

67. *See* ROBERT A. SCHAPIRO, POLYPHONIC FEDERALISM: TOWARD THE PROTECTION OF FUNDAMENTAL RIGHTS ch. 3 (2009). *See also* PREEMPTION CHOICE: THE THEORY, LAW, AND REALITY OF FEDERALISM'S CORE QUESTION (William W. Buzbee ed., 2009) at chs.1, 2, & 6.

68. I credit Professor Lisa Heinzerling for suggesting I grapple more with this issue of testing agency science.

69. *See* chapter 3, notes 11–12 and 23–27 and accompanying text (discussing deference doctrine).

70. *See* SCHAPIRO, *supra* note 67, at ch. 3; PREEMPTION CHOICE, *supra* note 67.

71. William W. Buzbee, *Recognizing the Regulatory Commons: A Theory of Regulatory Gaps*, 89 IOWA L. REV. 1, 4–28 (2003) (exploring how environmental harms and commensurate regulatory turfs often do not exist, contributing to regulatory gaps and failures).

72. Author interview with Edward Koch (April 23, 2002).

73. *See generally* ALTSHULER & LUBEROFF, *supra* note 6; GERALD E. FRUG & DAVID J. BARRON, CITY BOUND: HOW STATES STIFLE URBAN INNOVATION (2008); PAUL E. PETERSON, CITY LIMITS (1981).

74. Stipulation and Order of Settlement of Application for Costs and Attorney's Fees, Sierra Club v. United States Army Corps of Engineers, et al. (S.D.N.Y. June 20, 1986) (awarding $187,115.00, with $60,000 paid by the Army Corps and the rest by New York State). A request for fees by Action for Rational Transit plaintiffs, represented by William Hoppen, was denied. Action for Rational Transit v. West Side Highway Project, 1987 WL 16363 (S.D.N.Y. Aug. 26, 1987).

EPILOGUE

1. *See* OWEN D. GUTFREUND, 20TH-CENTURY SPRAWL: HIGHWAYS AND THE RESHAPING OF THE AMERICAN LANDSCAPE ch. 1 (2004). *See also* William W. Buzbee, *Urban Sprawl, Federalism, and the Problem of Institutional Complexity*, 68 FORDHAM L. REV. 57, 63–64, 77–91 (1999) (analyzing political and economic factors contributing to sprawl and making it difficult to combat).

2. *See* chapter 4, notes 1–2 and accompanying text, discussing Mancur Olson's work and others developing this theory.

3. Comments of Nicholas Gimbel, at program, *The Rise and Fall of Westway*, held at the Association of the Bar of the City of New York (Oct. 18, 2005).

4. Author interview with Frederick A. O. (Fritz) Schwarz, Jr. (May 31, 2007)).

5. Author interview with Craig Whitaker and Peter Kiernan (May 15, 2005).

6. For a chapter tracing changes in this body of law and divides on the Supreme Court, see William W. Buzbee, *The Story of Laidlaw: Standing and Citizen Enforcement, in* ENVIRONMENTAL LAW STORIES (Richard J. Lazarus & Oliver A. Houck eds., 2005). For debate on standing law after the Court's major ruling in Massachusetts v. EPA, 127 S. Ct. 1438 (2007), see *Access to the Courts after* Massachusetts v. EPA: *Who Has Been Left Standing*, 37 ENVTL. L. RPTR. 10692 (Sept. 2007).

7. *See* F. Andrew Hessick, *Probabilistic Standing*, 106 NW. U.L. REV. 1 (2012); Bradford C. Mank, *Summers v. Earth Island Institute Rejects Probabilistic Standing, but a "Realistic Threat" of Harm Is a Better Standing Test*, 40 ENVTL. L. (2010); Jonathan Nash, *Standing's Expected Value*, 111 MICH. L. REV. 1283 (2013).

8. Lujan v. Defenders of Wildlife, 504 U.S. 555 (1992).

9. Gwaltney of Smithfield, LTD v. Chesapeake Bay Found., Inc., 484 U.S. 49 (1987).

10. *See* ROBERT L. GLICKSMAN ET AL., ENVIRONMENTAL PROTECTION: LAW AND POLICY 183–85 (6th ed. 2011) (discussing citizen litigation and fee-shifting developments).

11. *See* PREEMPTION CHOICE: THE THEORY, LAW, AND REALITY OF FEDERALISM'S CORE QUESTION (William W. Buzbee ed., 2009); THOMAS O. MCGARITY, THE PREEMPTION WAR (2008).

12. *See* chapter 10, notes 89 and 90 and accompanying text.

13. Norton v. Southern Utah Wilderness Alliance, 542 U.S. 55 (2004).

14. Rapanos v. United States, 547 U.S. 715 (2006); Solid Waste Agency of N. Cook County v. U.S. Army Corps of Eng'rs, 531 U.S. 159 (2001).

15. Richard L. Revesz, *Ideology, Collegiality, and the D.C. Circuit: A Reply to Chief Judge Harry Edwards*, 85 VA. L. REV. 805 (1999).

16. Author interview with Albert K. Butzel (Mar. 6, 2013).

17. *See* Emily Hammond Meazell, *Super Deference, the Science Obsession, and Judicial Review as a Translation of Agency Science*, 109 MICH. L. REV. 733 (2011). For a case where the Sierra Club unsuccessfully sought to put sounder science before a resistant United States Forest Service, see Sierra Club v. Marita, 46 F.3d 606 (7th Cir. 1995) (allowing the Forest Service to "use its own methodology, unless it is irrational").

INDEX

Page numbers followed by letter *f* refer to figures.

fishery impacts of Westway: Army Corps on, 12, 88–89, 90, 91, 92, 93, 102, 127–28, 223; data on, 222, 223; discussion at 1982 trial, 104–5; discussion at 1985 trial, 160–91; Dovel's views regarding, 136–37, 140, 141, 146–47, 163, 170, 172, 173, 189, 190, 197, 224; Draft EIS on, 84–86; Draft SEIS on, 132–38; Federal Highway Administration on, 88, 89, 90, 91–92; Final EIS on, 88–89; Final SEIS on, 139–42, 154; Fletcher on, 99, 104; initial disregard for, 19; Judge Griesa's 1985 ruling on, 201–2; judicial appeal based on, 100, 102–3; LMS study of, 90–92, 94, 109, 110, 111, 118, 119; and mitigation plans, 91, 93; natural resource agencies on, 88–89, 93–94, 95; NMFS memorandum on, 93–94, 98, 106, 107; opposition's focus on, 98–99, 229; posttrial (1985) brief on, 196–97; State Commission of Investigation on, 118–19; supporters' dismissal of, 3, 85–86; two-winter study of, curtailing of, 130–31, 161, 163, 196; two-winter study of, decision to undertake, 127–29; worst-case scenario for, 134, 135, 139–40
Flacke, Robert, 75, 77
Fletcher, Ian, 99; exhibit created by, 105f; at February 14 EPA meeting, 151; inability to testify at 1985 trial, 164; testimony at 1982 trial, 104, 105, 106
Ford, Gerald, 28–29, 30
Friends of the Earth, 12, 124, 126, 155, 208, 264n40
FWS. See Fish and Wildlife Service

Gabel, Bunny, 53f, 54, 228, 263n39; at 1985 trial, 175; on Abzug, 29; on Benstock, 56; on citizen participation, 58; continuity of efforts of, 50, 220; environmentalist perspective of, 229; on New York City's revitalization, 217; on public hearings, 12; Westway air permit proceedings and, 69
Gabel, Dan, 53f, 263n39
Garrison, Lloyd, 57

Gerrard, Michael, 50, 57, 99, 103
Gianelli, William, 130
Gimbel, Nicholas, 101, 103, 157, 246
Giuliani, Rudolph, 165
Goldberger, Paul, 215
Gorsuch Burford, Ann, 167
Green, Bill, 124, 126, 208
Greenwich Village, 60, 217
Griesa, Thomas P., 100–101, 101f; 1982 ruling by, 108, 112–13; in 1982 trials, 103–12; 1985 ruling by, 200–203, 208, 224; in 1985 trial, 156–91, 198–99; appellate courts on rulings by, 112–14, 221–22; on ART case, 102, 106; attacks on, Westway supporters and, 115, 204–5, 219, 220, 221; contempt-of-court trial and, 130–31; de novo review accusations against, 204–5, 207, 209–10, 211; on Dovel's "definitive" report, 171, 172, 174, 179–84; immunity to political pressure, 5, 221, 225, 242, 250; injunction ordered by, 108, 112–13, 203; investigations following 1982 ruling by, 115–20; opposition's return to, 154–56; record-keeping order of, 131–32, 156, 157, 160, 196, 210; on Schwarz, 76
Griffis, Fletcher "Bud": Dovel's letter to, 146–47, 149, 190, 197; and Draft SEIS, 132, 133, 206, 234; and Final SEIS, 139, 142, 143; indecisiveness of, 145, 146; Record of Decision and Section 404(b)(1) Evaluation, 142, 147–50, 153, 231; and two-winter study decision, 127–30; uncertainty conceded by, 230; as witness at 1985 trial, 160–62
Guarini, Frank, 213
Gutman, Dan, 69

Haikalis, George, 61
Hall, John R., III, 94
hard look review, 209, 222
Harsha, William H., 29
Heckler v. Chaney, 152, 249
Heiberg, E. R., III, 94
Heimbuch, Douglas, 163–64
Hennessy, William C., 76, 89–90, 120

regulatory commons, 46–47

regulatory wars, 31, 33, 52–53; agencies' role in, 37, 39, 46, 245; citizens' role in, 40–42, 43–44, 46, 53, 241–42, 250–51; courts' role in, 38–39; delaying tactics used in, 49–50, 226; elements of, Westway tale illuminating, 4–5, 244–51; federal vs. state agencies in, 40; focal points in, 58; judges' role in, 45–46; judicial deference doctrine in, 44, 45, 193, 195, 222, 247; key characteristics of, 37; laws as empowerment and artillery in, 5, 6, 22, 30, 33–36, 38, 41, 42, 51, 75, 81, 211, 220–22, 227–28, 247, 251; leadership continuity and, 47–48; long-term vs. short-term perspectives on, 42; military wars compared to, 33–36; outcome of, factors influencing, 225; politics and, 5, 33, 34, 36–37, 38, 47, 51, 53, 239; science component in, 47, 49, 246; sources of uncertainty and complexity in, 39–40; strategic use of disparate resources in, 48–49; today, 245–48; variety of, 37–38; venues for, strategic choice of, 44; wealthy interests and, 48. *See also* opponents; supporters; Westway war

River Road alternative, 162

Rivers and Harbors Act, 114, 267n1

Riverside Park, 13

Rockefeller, David: and Dovel's funding, 159, 173, 176, 186; pro-Westway advocacy by, 1, 56, 59, 61, 77, 125, 137, 141, 151, 168; on Westway's defeat, 216

Rockefeller, Laurence, 173

Rogers, Edward L., 93

Rosenbaum, Marc, 43, 46, 162

Rosenthal, Albert J., 70, 71–73

Rothman, Mary Ann, 13, 53f

Route 9A, 217, 219

Ruckelshaus, William, 125, 137–38, 151

Sargent, Francis, 24, 261n13

Save Riverside Park, 13

Scenic Hudson case, 57

Schanberg, Sydney, 56, 117, 118, 168, 175, 187, 189, 199–200

Schumer, Charles, 50

Schwarz, Frederick "Fritz," 11, 68, 75–76, 101, 235, 246

science: misuse of, 238; and regulatory decisions, 230–32; role in regulatory war, 47, 49, 246; sound, encouraging, 239–40; uncertainties in, 230–31

Second Circuit Court of Appeals: review of Judge Griesa's 1985 ruling, 202, 203, 204–7; Westway opinion of 1983, 112–14, 123; Westway opinion of 1985, 208–11, 224

Section 404, Clean Water Act, 35–36, 81–83, 247, 251; appropriations rider aiming to override, 125; Army Corps obligations under, 81, 88; Army Corps violation of, judicial challenge of, 155; EPA's veto power under, 95–96, 143, 144, 151; Judge Griesa's reliance on, 106, 201; mitigation requirements under, 91; and Westway battles, 82–83, 88, 227

Section 404 permit for Westway: Army Corps 1981 decision on, 92–95, 96, 97, 235; Army Corps 1985 (Griffis) decision on, 142, 147–50, 153, 231; barriers to, 129, 142–43; EPA's failure to assert veto power over, 151–53; EPA's veto authority and, 95–96, 143, 144, 151; injunction on, 108, 112–13, 203; invalidation of, 210; Judge Griesa on, 107, 108, 123; Second Circuit Court of Appeals on, 112–14, 123; vulnerabilities in, 193, 195

Seeger, Pete, 42, 79

SEIS. *See* Supplemental Environmental Impact Statement

September 11, 2001, 10

Sidamon-Eristoff, Constantine, 18

Sierra Club, 56, 100, 106, 112, 126, 155

Silverstein, Peter, 99

SIP. *See* State Implementation Plan

Smith, Walter, 127–28, 130

Solomon, Gerald, 211

Stafford, Robert, 126

staging area theory, 136–37, 197

standing doctrine, 248, 249